During the afternoon of M—— auburn-haired woman whose —— tually an American household word went for a swim in the Pacific. She was not seen to come out of the water. Thousands of Californians who had thronged to hear the dynamic Aimee Semple McPherson preach at her floodlit Angelus Temple were stunned at the news of her disappearance. Two people died in the attempt to find her body. Services were held for her at the Temple and a memorial fund was collected.

Meanwhile, however, letters had begun to come in, demanding $500,000 ransom for the return of Sister Aimee. And five weeks after she vanished, Aimee turned up in a Mexican border town with a circumstantial story of having been kidnaped and then imprisoned in a desert shack, and of having escaped on foot across miles of sandy wastes.

The missing shepherd was welcomed back to life with great rejoicing by the Temple flock. But certain skeptics — among them the Los Angeles district attorney — had doubts about her story. Why was no shack to be found that would fit her description? Why was she neither sunburned nor thirsty when she returned? And who was the mysterious "Miss X," so remarkably like the evangelist, who had occupied, with a "Mr. McIntyre," a rented honeymoon cottage at Carmel-by-the-Sea while Aimee was gone?

These questions led to a grand-jury investigation with sensational surprises of its own, and eventually brought the evangelist and certain others into court, where the disclosures made were as startling — and as hilarious — as anything that had preceded. The Los Angeles District Court was turned into a three-ring circus; newspapers fought pitched battles for witnesses. A judge was eventually impeached as a result of the furor, and half a dozen public figures were ruined. But Aimee's story was never shaken.

"Hence, horrible shadow!
Unreal mockery, hence!"
            —*Macbeth*

THE
VANISHING EVANGELIST

[The Aimee Semple McPherson Kidnaping Affair]

By LATELY THOMAS, *pseud.*

1959

THE VIKING PRESS · NEW YORK

First published in 1959 by
The Viking Press, Inc.
625 Madison Avenue, New York 22, N.Y.

Published in Canada by
The Macmillan Company of Canada Limited

Library of Congress catalogue card number: 59-8351

Printed in U.S.A. by Vail-Ballou Press, Inc.

To Folly

Acknowledgment

The most important and comprehensive source of information regarding Aimee Semple McPherson and her career is the newspaper press. Few persons have ever been so consistently or extensively publicized over so long a period; no actress, for example, ever accumulated as long a "string" of press notices as the pastor of Angelus Temple. Among the many newspapers, magazines, pamphlets, and fugitive publications that have been culled, principal acknowledgment must be made to the Los Angeles *Times,* the Los Angeles *Examiner,* the San Francisco *Chronicle,* and the New York *Times.*

Basic sources for the events of the kidnaping episode of 1926 are the legal transcripts of Mrs. McPherson's preliminary hearing (3600 pages, nearly 900,000 words) and of the Hardy impeachment trial in 1929 (1400 pages, 350,000 words).

Books consulted include: two autobiographies by Aimee Semple McPherson—*This Is That* (Los Angeles: Bridal Call Publishing House, 1923) and *In the Service of the King* (New York: Boni & Liveright, 1927); a pastiche of autobiographical writings by Mrs. McPherson, compiled posthumously, *The Story of My Life* (Hollywood: International Correspondents, 1951); and *Sister Aimee* by Nancy Barr Mavity (New York: Doubleday, Doran, 1931)—an especially valuable source for both actual and suggested material, to which a heavy debt is owed.

Extremely helpful have been the verbal recollections of contemporaries of the evangelist, newspaper reporters, former associates, and others possessing special knowledge of the period and the personalities involved. For the generous imparting of this information, in many conversations over a long period of time, gratitude is expressed.

Responsibility for any errors of detail, impossible to avoid completely in the telling of a story so complex and so controversial, lies wholly with the author.

1926

	S	M	T	W	T	F	S		S	M	T	W	T	F	S	
Jan						1	2						1	2	3	**Jul**
	3	4	5	6	7	8	9		4	5	6	7	8	9	10	
	10	11	12	13	14	15	16		11	12	13	14	15	16	17	
	17	18	19	20	21	22	23		18	19	20	21	22	23	24	
	24/31	25	26	27	28	29	30		25	26	27	28	29	30	31	
Feb		1	2	3	4	5	6		1	2	3	4	5	6	7	**Aug**
	7	8	9	10	11	12	13		8	9	10	11	12	13	14	
	14	15	16	17	18	19	20		15	16	17	18	19	20	21	
	21	22	23	24	25	26	27		22	23	24	25	26	27	28	
	28								29	30	31					
Mar		1	2	3	4	5	6				1	2	3	4		**Sept**
	7	8	9	10	11	12	13		5	6	7	8	9	10	11	
	14	15	16	17	18	19	20		12	13	14	15	16	17	18	
	21	22	23	24	25	26	27		19	20	21	22	23	24	25	
	28	29	30	31					26	27	28	29	30			
Apr					1	2	3							1	2	**Oct**
	4	5	6	7	8	9	10		3	4	5	6	7	8	9	
	11	12	13	14	15	16	17		10	11	12	13	14	15	16	
	18	19	20	21	22	23	24		17	18	19	20	21	22	23	
	25	26	27	28	29	30			24/31	25	26	27	28	29	30	
May							1		1	2	3	4	5	6		**Nov**
	2	3	4	5	6	7	8		7	8	9	10	11	12	13	
	9	10	11	12	13	14	15		14	15	16	17	18	19	20	
	16	17	18	19	20	21	22		21	22	23	24	25	26	27	
	23/30	24/31	25	26	27	28	29		28	29	30					
Jun			1	2	3	4	5				1	2	3	4		**Dec**
	6	7	8	9	10	11	12		5	6	7	8	9	10	11	
	13	14	15	16	17	18	19		12	13	14	15	16	17	18	
	20	21	22	23	24	25	26		19	20	21	22	23	24	25	
	27	28	29	30					26	27	28	29	30	31		

Contents

Illustrations

   Acknowledgment for the use of photographs is made as follows:
   Los Angeles Times, nos. 4, 5, 6, 10, 13, 20, 24, 26–32, 40, 41;
   Pacific and Atlantic Photos, Inc., nos. 7, 9, 14, 18; United Press
   International, nos. 11, 12

Prelude

On the evening of May 18, 1926, the wealth, wit, and fashion of Hollywood and Los Angeles crowded to an event of the first magnitude, the gala dedication of the newest temple of cinematic art, the Carthay Circle Theater, far out on what was then the western fringe of the city. The selected film, acknowledged in advance to be a masterpiece, in fact the latest of Cecil B. De Mille masterpieces, was *The Volga Boatman*. William Boyd played the romantic lead, a way station on his arduous ascent to Hopalong beatitude. The audience was as brilliant and soigné as the theater's appointments. No detail, no adjunct purchasable by publicity, was overlooked that might enhance the éclat of this premiere in an age when the Hollywood premiere was hitting its super-colossal stride.

What, then, the shock, the chagrin, the sorrow of the film élite when, the next morning, they expectantly picked up the newspapers and found their extravaganza relegated to inside pages! The front pages were virtually pre-empted by a lady who had not even been present—who, moreover, was the most vocal enemy of the moving picture.

That was the point of the headlines. A lady was missing, a lady whose name was as familiar to every person in Los Angeles as that of the brightest screen star—the premiere female evangelist of the age, Aimee Semple McPherson. Had a dozen eminent divines disappeared under similar circumstances, the furor could not have been greater.

Born on a Canadian farm, the child of a onetime Salvation Army lassie and a Methodist farmer, Aimee Elizabeth Kennedy McPherson had led an adventurous and dramatic life for every one of her thirty-five years. When a few weeks old she was dedicated to the Lord's service in a Salvation Army barracks. In school she was a tomboy, gifted with a talent for theatricals and elocution and an instinct for leadership. After a period of youthful religious skepticism, into which she threw herself with self-dramatizing intensity, she was converted at seventeen to an extreme form of "Holy Roller" Pentecostalism by a roving preacher, Robert Semple. They married and went as missionaries to China, where Semple soon died, leaving her friendless, penniless, and with a month-old daughter, whom she christened Roberta.

Aimee straggled back to the United States, and after an unfortunate second marriage to Harold S. McPherson, a wholesale grocery clerk (the offspring of which was a son and which eventually culminated in divorce), she set out, without training, to preach an uninhibited kind of revivalism to the Ontario rustics. Her sincerity and her dynamic personality, coupled with an inborn ability to sway crowds, brought rapid recognition. With her first collection she bought a tattered, moth-eaten tent and took off as an itinerant evangelist, sponsored by no church, carrying a message of joy and spiritual excitement to the poor, the backward, and the contemned. Living from hand to mouth, she followed the call from Maine to Florida. Often hungry; sleeping in tents, in automobiles, in barns and wayside shelters; struggling to save her canvas from hurricane and slashing rain; swinging a maul like a circus roustabout; jeered by unbelievers and despised by decorous churchmen; anathematized by co-religionists for preaching in contravention of Paul's injunction that women should keep silent in the churches, she persisted, and in a few years advanced, by dint of grit, incredible labor, and incomparable platform gifts, to the front rank of evangelists.

In this role she preached in many cities, notably St. Louis, Denver, Washington, Dallas, San Francisco, and Montreal, addressing audiences of ten to sixteen thousand frantically applauding persons jammed into the largest auditoriums existing. She traveled to Australia and later to England, where she filled the Royal Albert Hall, London's largest indoor meeting place. Her warmth, her womanly charm, and her magnetic power of persuasion were irresistible.

In 1923—five years after she was joined by her mother, Minnie Kennedy, as business manager—Aimee dedicated Angelus Temple, an arena-like hall seating more than five thousand persons, designed by herself, with furnishings estimated to represent an investment of a million and a half dollars. This huge edifice she reared on Echo Park in Los Angeles (where she had arrived in December 1918 with ten dollars and a tambourine) from the proceeds of evangelistic campaigns in other cities. Her duties as its director absorbed her tremendous energies, and soon its membership was advertised as totaling more than ten thousand, the largest single church congregation in the world; and there were branches. At the outset of radio broadcasting she acquired her own radio station and through it spread her voice and message all over the West. Sister, as her fanatically devoted followers called her, was a power in Los Angeles, financially, politically, and religiously.

Her contributions to her community were many and ingenious; they were of the kind that get talked about. They ranged from the practical welfare of the Temple commissary, which distributed food, clothing, rent money, and medical assistance to any needy caller, day or night, investigating afterward, to pioneering the correct-time service: the public was cordially invited to call Angelus Temple, around the clock, and be told the exact time cheerfully.

At first Sister was warmly endorsed by other Los Angeles churches and pastors; but gradually these turned against her, repelled both by the lurid sensationalism which kept her ampitheater filled week after week, and by her supposed financial practices. Complaint also was made (with or without justification) that Aimee's Temple members were, in the main, lured away from less boisterously shepherded flocks.

Unlike most Protestant churches, which vest their property in boards of trustees, Angelus Temple and its offshoots were owned outright by its pastor and her mother, in a fifty-fifty partnership. No accounting of monies was rendered; and Minnie Kennedy, a hard-fisted, shrewd businesswoman, was as autocratic as her daughter in controlling the affairs of the sprawling, emotional organization. Sister's delight in hard work, her bubbling confidence, her flair for attracting a large, uncritical audience enabled her to override opposition and flourish. Her methods, she proudly conceded, were spectacular beyond anything seen in churches. One technique she developed with consummate skill was the staging of "illustrations" of her sermons—tableaux and pantomimes, acted on a fully equipped stage behind the speaking platform, dramatizing the story and presenting the moral in cartoon terms.

In everything that touched self-advertising, Aimee was an admitted genius. That many of her publicity-getting stunts lacked dignity did not bother her; her tastes, sentimental, garish, heartily and healthily vulgar, matched those of the multitude. Thus by 1926 Aimee McPherson, her flamboyancy, her copperish-auburn hair, her expensive clothes, and her imposing home beside the Temple had become a stock topic of controversy in Los Angeles. "Aimee stories," scurrilous and admiring, were a staple of gossip. Yet neither covert sneers nor open antagonism diminished her enormous zest.

Her enemies pilloried the vaudevillism of her Temple spectacles and her asserted worldliness, yet thousands loved her. Her charm was proverbial. Her frank enjoyment of such outward feminine indulgences as beautiful garments and the arts of the beauty parlor was unaffected and engaging; having started with nothing, she had no illusions about the sordid meannesses imposed by poverty. She enjoyed being a success and she was never ashamed of her origins. Athletic and physically inexhaustible, she was a splendid horsewoman and a strong swimmer, and she delighted to exhibit her prowess. Her Temple collections were rumored to range into the millions of dollars, but in default of figures nobody knew; undoubtedly rumor exaggerated. Yet for money, except as the accepted symbol of power, Aimee cared little; indeed, without her mother to manage the finances there would never have been an Angelus Temple; Sister took lavishly and gave lavishly, and that was one potent element in her appeal.

To many Los Angelenos a vague mist of scandal hovered over the domed sanctuary on Echo Park. To her rapt followers, the Temple was the embodiment of earthly and heavenly glamour, the emotionally satisfying, exciting hub and inspiration of their otherwise drab lives. In the triumphs of Sister they triumphed; with her they trod a primrose path to Heaven.

In 1926 Aimee stood at her apogee. That January she left on a trip to the Holy Land (a loving present from her church); it was her first extended absence from the city since the Temple was built. In April she was welcomed home by hymn-singing thousands who pelted her with flowers. She resumed her pulpit and her numberless administrative tasks. On May 18 she went for a routine afternoon outing at a Los Angeles city beach. She entered the water and was not seen to come out.

That simple action detonated the uproar that was to continue for eight months; a decade later the echoes were still reverberating. This book is the chronicle of that extravagant epic. It is not a study of motivations or hidden beliefs; it is a narration of what people at the time saw and heard from day to day, of what secret moves were made behind what closed doors during the months of suspense—the whole cat's-cradle of unlikely suppositions leading to impossible conclusions.

Is the tale true? The actions unfolded as they are told here. There are no fictitious characters. No names are disguised. Every word of direct quotation is taken from records, much of it uttered under oath. The tale is as true as sworn testimony.

THEME I

Threnody

"Children dear, was it yesterday
(Call but once) that she went away?"
—MATTHEW ARNOLD,
"The Forsaken Merman"

Genesis

Mother Kennedy received the news sitting down. She was looking over an account book in her combined home and office beside the Temple when the door opened and Brother Arthur entered. Brother J. W. Arthur was chairman of the board of elders of the church. He walked to Mother Kennedy, placed both hands on her shoulders, and said, "God bless you. . . . I don't know how to tell you. Sister went swimming this afternoon at twenty minutes to three and she hasn't come back yet."

For an instant Minnie Kennedy did not grasp the sense of his emotion-muffled words. In the doorway hovered Blanche Rice, a devoted assistant and sometime secretary; her hand pressed against her half-opened mouth, her eyes swam with dismay. Mrs. Kennedy's glance quickly shifted back to Brother Arthur. "What?" she snapped.

"They have looked everywhere. Sister cannot be found," repeated the elder. Emma Schaffer, Sister McPherson's secretary, had just telephoned him from Ocean Park beach. Emma was sobbing so much that she was incoherent, but a man had taken the phone and explained that Sister had been missing more than an hour. Lifeguards were searching, but there was no trace.

A spasm transformed Minnie Kennedy's naturally placid, firm features; she groaned and slowly bowed her head on her hand. "Drowned!" she moaned.

Impulsively Blanche Rice ran and flung her arms around the older woman. She sobbed.

Minnie Kennedy shook her head. "I think our little Sister is gone," she repeated several times. Her own tears flowed. Brother Arthur, lips compressed into deep lines of suffering, stood beside the women clinging to each other.

The telephone rang in the outer office. Blanche Rice went to answer it. A call from the beach, for Mother Kennedy.

Wiping her eyes, Minnie walked heavily to the telephone. Frank Langan was speaking; he was the manager of the Ocean View Hotel,

3

where Sister changed into her bathing costume. Emma was hysterical; Langan was telephoning for her.

"It is now nearly five o'clock and we have not been able to find Mrs. McPherson," he said. "She has not returned to the hotel."

Langan paused.

"She is drowned," said Mother Kennedy.

"No, Mother Kennedy, no!" exclaimed the horrified manager. "She is not drowned as far as we know, but up to this time we have not been able to find her. You had better come down."

"Well," said Mother, "do all you can. I don't think it would do me any good to come down. Where is her car?"

Sister's expensive Kissel automobile was parked in front of the hotel.

"Well, have it sent in and get her belongings," Mother Kennedy advised. Then she hung up. Briefly she told Brother Arthur to drive out to the beach and pick up Emma, who did not know how to drive.

Gaunt, ashen-faced Emma Schaffer, weeping continuously, reached the Temple home in the car driven by Brother Arthur at about 6 o'clock. She brought the yellow and white sports dress Sister McPherson had worn to the beach, her shoes and stockings, her Bible, and her purse with its contents of $200 in a neat roll of bills and a handful of change. Sister's Kissel followed, driven by E. M. Sterns, a St. Paul salesman who was staying at the Ocean View Hotel and had volunteered to help.

Mother Kennedy led Emma Schaffer upstairs and into her own bedroom. Then she closed the door on the other members of the frightened Temple household, huddled on the stair landing, and ministered to the inarticulate, trembling secretary alone. When she emerged she told Blanche Rice there was no doubt Sister was drowned. The only thing they could do for Sister's sake was to carry on. Already the crowd was assembling in the Temple next door for the scheduled evening showing of Sister's "Journeylog" account of her recent tour of the Holy Land. Mother Kennedy told Blanche she would give the talk herself.

By this time the news was public. The story broke too late for the final editions of the evening newspapers, but the morning extras were tumbling into the streets. "Evangelist McPherson believed drowned!" newsboys yelled in downtown Los Angeles. Yet before the extras appeared, the word had spread throughout the city; police and newspaper offices were besieged with telephone calls, some coming from as far away as Baltimore and Canada. By 6 o'clock, although the extras were just coming out, two hundred members of Angelus Temple converged on Ocean Park. At 7 p.m. Roderick Morrison, a student preacher in the Temple

Bible School, announced over the Temple's radio station KFSG (Kall Four Square Gospel): "We have very sad news. We believe Sister McPherson has been drowned. Tonight we feel that she is asleep in the ocean. We ask prayers for Mother Kennedy, Mrs. McPherson's mother."

Reporters swarmed out to Echo Park to interview Mrs. Kennedy, Emma Schaffer, and anyone else who might provide a scrap of information or conjecture. Emma had pulled herself together under Mrs. Kennedy's prodding and briefly described the train of events she had already detailed to the Venice division police at the scene of the disappearance. Drab and lathlike before her questioners, she spoke curtly and positively. Her grief was plain to everybody. Bible under one arm, she repeated over and over, "We must hope and pray." She answered all questions, her face taut with pain, her eyes red from weeping, before hurrying aside to pray.

The evangelist and she, Emma said, had driven out to the beach at about noon; Sister was due back at the Temple for a 4:30 appointment and was later to lead the evening service. They drove to the Ocean View Hotel, which faces the sea at the corner of Rose Avenue and Ocean Front; Sister often came to the beach to swim and the hotel kept a room reserved for her. The manager took them up in the elevator to room 202. Sister quickly changed into her green bathing suit with knee-length skirt and gay flowers embroidered across the chest. She put on a brown bathing cap, but no beach shoes, and slipped a long robe over the abbreviated costume.

They came downstairs and each ate a waffle (Sister was fond of them) in a restaurant at the nearby Lick Amusement Pier plunge. Then they rented an umbrella tent and pitched it on the wide beach almost in front of the hotel. Sister set to work on the notes for her sermon the coming Sunday. "Light and Darkness" was her topic; she discussed it with Emma and for text thumbed open her Bible to the first chapter of Genesis: "And God said, Let there be light; and there was light. . . . And God divided the light from the darkness."

After a while (Emma told the reporters she did not know how long because she said neither she nor Sister had a timepiece) Sister remarked, "I'm going to take a little dip," and went into the water. Emma watched her swimming strongly. After fifteen or twenty minutes she came out glowing. Emma wondered whether the water was cold. "Not a bit," Sister assured her. "Feel me." Emma felt her arm; it was "just as warm as could be."

Wrapping the beach cloak around her, Sister worked on the sermon notes again. Emma observed that she seemed happy, scribbling intently as her thoughts raced her pencil. Suddenly she recollected a message she meant to give her mother about the musical program for the evening's lecture, and she asked Emma to telephone the Temple, and also say she could not keep the 4:30 appointment. "Bring back some orange juice," she called as Emma trotted away.

When the secretary returned with a box of candy and the orange juice in a cardboard container, the evangelist was in the water again, swimming out about half the length of the pier. Emma held up the orange juice; Sister waved and called, "Come on! Bring it out!" Emma laughed shyly: Sister liked to tease her, knowing she could not swim.

She sat on the sand and studied her Bible, checking references for Sister. Gancing up from time to time, she saw Aimee gamboling in the water, diving and surfacing like a porpoise, enjoying herself. Then when Emma looked up, the brown cap was nowhere in sight. Emma stood up and searched the water. She was not alarmed, suspecting Sister might have swum around the end of Lick Pier; she was daring enough to do that. Emma walked up to the pier, a hundred yards north of the hotel, and looked there. Then she came back to the tent, thinking perhaps Sister might have come out of the water meanwhile. She asked two young men swimmers whether they had seen a woman in a green bathing suit and brown cap. They said no, but they swam back out and looked, then reported no such swimmer around; there were very few bathers in the water.

By this time Emma had become fearful. She went to the lifeguards' lookout tower but no lifeguard was on duty, since the Memorial Day start of the official beach season was still ten days ahead. A young man advised her to inquire at the plunge. Emma hurried there; a girl attendant sent her to the man in charge, who said it was very difficult to locate anyone unless they knew exactly where the person was last seen in the water. Emma did not mention Sister's name.

Numb with dread, she went to the hotel and appealed to the manager. Langan reassured her; he could not believe anything serious had happened; he urged her to look in the plunge again, and sent a guest at the hotel, Miss Rosie Miers, to help look. Emma went back to the plunge with Miss Miers, and when they found no trace she hysterically appealed to the man in charge, this time identifying the missing woman as the famous evangelist.

"One life is just as precious to us as another," the man replied, and immediately ordered out lifeguards who put off in a boat; Emma directed them as best she could from the shore. The police in Venice, a mile to the south, were notified at the same time (the call was logged on their books at 4:20 p.m.) and they hastened to the scene. In the beach tent they found Sister's robe, Bible, handbag, and sermon notes with the orange juice and candy. Fred Hoyt, an aviator, was alerted at nearby Clover Field; he flew his plane low back and forth over the water, seeking some trace. A patrol of the shoreline was instituted; some of the gathering Temple workers pushed pathetically into the wavering line of watchers. Soon it grew dark, and the lifeguards repeated that it was very difficult to effect a rescue unless they knew exactly where a swimmer went down. Cramps or a fainting spell were the explanations that the police advanced.

Langan, clinging to hope, suggested to Emma that Sister might have swum or walked to Venice Pier, and Emma desperately plowed through the sand in that direction, searching everywhere. In shivering fright she rode the tram back to Ocean Park, where she proposed to call Mother Kennedy, but Langan and other volunteer counselors persuaded her to wait a while, saying it might not be true and the shock would be too great. Finally she did call Brother Arthur and Langan broke the news to him.

Emma's account gave the newspapers a puzzle within a sensation. That Aimee Semple McPherson should vanish was startling enough. But that a notably powerful, skillful swimmer should disappear almost before her watchful secretary's eyes, within sight and sound of scores of persons along the beachfront, without a cry for help, without a visible struggle in the water, on a calm, sunny afternoon, the sea glassy smooth, wind three miles an hour, temperature 68 degrees—that such a swimmer should vanish from the ocean leaving not a ripple smacked of the miraculous. But many events in Aimee Semple McPherson's crowded life hinted at prodigies.

By the time reporters reached Angelus Temple, the throng expecting to hear Sister repeat her Holy Land travel talk was filling the huge edifice, which seated 5400. The corridors, which customarily rang with "Welcome, Brother!" and "Welcome, Sister!" were subdued. Sobs were audible. Women ushers in white Temple costumes under long blue capes crept to anterooms to cry. Brother Dickey, one of Sister's closest helpers, paced the foyer, eyes brimming with tears which he wiped away mechanically with the back of a quivering hand. Many children were in the crowd, since this was a special service for them; they looked solemn and frightened, but inwardly were excited. "Aimee will come back to her

Temple," was the whisper heard all over the house. Outside on the sidewalks stood thousands of the faithful unable to gain entrance to the packed hall; they would not leave.

At 7:30, promptly on schedule, Mother Kennedy, dressed in white crepe de Chine, appeared on the platform and started the service without explanation. A hymn was sung, then the lights dimmed and colored pictures of Holy Land scenes were projected on the screen. Reporters marveled at the speaker's self-control, forgetting that Minnie Kennedy had been facing audiences since her youthful Salvation Army apprenticeship. Now and then sobs startled the tense listeners. Outside the Temple the newsboys pushed through the overflow crowd shrieking their headlines: "Aimee McPherson believed drowned!" Mother talked on.

After a time the lights came up and the audience sang the hymn "Jesus, Sweetest Name I Know." Collection plates were passed and the tinkle of coins played obbligato to soft organ music. Then the lights dimmed and Mother resumed the narrative. Toward the close, views of Sister were thrown on the screen, intermingled with pictures of Christ on the Cross; they drew tumultuous handclapping. In measured tones, Mother Kennedy then told how her daughter and Miss Schaffer had left for the beach that noon, how she herself went about her work without premonition until "this afternoon, while I was wondering about Aimee," and just then Brother Arthur brought her the news.

"Sister is gone," she concluded. "We know she is with Jesus. Pray for her."

A moan from thousands of throats wafted through the Temple. It was caught up by the throng outside, and over the radio was carried a thousand miles into the night.

After the service, many of the congregation adjourned to the auditorium of the Bible School next door, and there fifteen hundred knelt and prayed until dawn, while on the sidewalks and lawns round about hundreds more prayed fervently.

Caught by reporters after the service, Minnie Kennedy appeared on the point of collapsing, but she braced herself with an effort. "I must stand up and make the best of it if I expect others to," she said. "This Temple, the Bible School, are not paid for," she added with businesslike factualness. "Everything Sister had is tied up in the Temple and the work."

At the beach, Sister's followers clustered on the sand, testifying to each other about their conversion or healing. Some sang, in quavering voices, "Have Faith in Me" and "The Lord Is My Redeemer." Several times police were compelled to restrain enthusiasts from rushing into the surf; the wind was rising. Long after midnight they still knelt, prayed, sang, or stood in stunned bereavement, peering into the darkling waters. So the evening and the morning were the first day.

O Sea, Give Up Thy Dead!

West and a little south of downtown Los Angeles, at a distance of about thirteen miles, the Pacific Ocean is bordered by a broad, sandy beach (the longest man-made beach in the world) that ripples from the tangled hills of Malibu and Topanga to the Palos Verdes headlands fourteen miles to the south. Along this unbroken beach front lie many towns: Santa Monica, Ocean Park, Venice, Playa del Rey, El Segundo, Manhattan Beach, Hermosa Beach, and Redondo Beach at the southern tip. Some of these are, or in 1926 were, separate municipalities; others, like Ocean Park, lay in unincorporated areas of vast Los Angeles County. Venice, a turn-of-the-century real-estate fantasy laid out complete with Grand Canal and imported gondolas, by 1926 had become a sort of Sheepshead Bay–Coney Island on the Southern California shore. The Grand Canal was dust-filled (in 1957 the city considered its utility as a sewer) and the gondolas had been replaced by honky-tonk dance halls, which, by grace of a recent election, were open seven nights a week. Fishing and amusement piers jutted into the ocean between Venice and Santa Monica, north of Ocean Park, and along the paved promenade plied little open tram cars. This was the stage on which the drama beginning Tuesday afternoon, May 18, was played.

Before dawn on Wednesday, volunteers were pouring into Ocean Park to recover the body of Sister McPherson. All night lifeguards had patrolled offshore, while police tramped the beach. Most of the arriving volunteers were Angelus Temple workers, dazed by grief; soon five thousand were congregated. Mother Kennedy did not appear, but she sent the pastor of the Pasadena branch of the Temple, the Reverend D. V. Alderman, to spur the search.

A dozen rowboats with divers moved back and forth; farther out motor launches swept the deeper reaches with grappling hooks. Two airplanes dipped and droned, their pilots peering hopefully into the

LOS ANGELES AREA

depths. Police boats using seine nets raked the sandy ocean floor. Whenever one of the boats returned to shore, Temple followers crowded around it, begging for word of hope.

As the day wore on and no trace of the evangelist was found, fear was expressed that her body had been borne by the current (which was setting strongly northward on Tuesday) under Lick Pier into the tangle of iron and wire left by a roller coaster that had burned two years before and plunged into the sea. The surf built up heavily during the forenoon and one by one the rowboats returned to the beach, some spilling their occupants into the water.

Along the shore thousands of watchers stared at the waves through binoculars, telescopes, and opera glasses. The Temple faithful kept vigil in prayer circles and impromptu testimony meetings. Mrs. Eunice Wickland recounted Sister's last words to her: that when her time came to go to the arms of Jesus, she prayed she might go "by way of the sea." Now and then the chanting of prayers and crashing of the rollers were rent by frenzied shrieks beseeching Sister to come back. One aged man sprang up, trembling arm pointing seaward, and shouted he had seen Sister rise from the ocean in robes of spotless white; she beckoned to him, then sank beneath the waves. Police forcibly prevented him from wading into the surf.

As morning merged into afternoon the crowd grew less demonstrative; they appeared to await a miracle. A rumor spread that Sister would rise and speak at exactly 2:30. Many stood up, expectant, but the hour passed.

All day police and sheriff's deputies were kept running from spot to spot to check false alarms. There were near-riots when Temple followers overheard bystanders express doubt that the evangelist was drowned. Mrs. Mae Werning, of El Centro, said she was on the beach all day Tuesday and she never saw Mrs. McPherson in the water. Police had to rescue her. Another woman who audibly doubted Sister's death they escorted to a streetcar and cautioned not to come back. And the whole city buzzed with the report that Minnie's first concern, when informed of her daughter's disappearance, had been for the safety of Aimee's automobile.

Early Wednesday morning Detective Lieutenant M. O. Barnard of the Culver City police made known that he and his wife had seen the evangelist in an automobile with another woman passing the Metro-Goldwyn-Mayer studios in Culver City at 3 o'clock Tuesday afternoon, headed not toward the beach but toward Los Angeles. They recognized her by her features and by the Temple costume she was wearing. This report by a reputable witness stirred the immediate attention of the Los Angeles police and Sheriff William I. Traeger. Los Angeles Chief of Detectives Herman Cline and Captain William J. Bright of the sheriff's homicide squad interrogated Emma Schaffer at the Temple. Did Mrs. McPherson seem unhappy or distressed? Not at all, Emma assured her questioners; on the way to the beach Sister mentioned how happy she felt, how she "loved everybody, even those who had persecuted her."

Cline publicly disputed Barnard's identification, pointing out that the time did not jibe with the secretary's positive statement; and even if Barnard were mistaken about the hour, street repairs around the M-G-M studios would force a car headed for the beach to detour back toward the city several blocks; and finally that the evangelist was not wearing the white uniform with blue cape she wore in the pulpit, but a yellow silk sports dress.

Mother Kennedy placed no stock in Lieutenant Barnard's statement. "Aimee is gone. I have no hopes of ever seeing her alive again," she said positively, and announced plans to offer $500 for the recovery of her daughter's body.

Angelus Temple remained shrouded in gloom. Thousands of devout milled through its rooms from dawn to dawn. The Temple leader's home was a place of mourning and confusion: attendants and friends came and went, swollen-lidded, faces dismal, speaking in whispers. Telephones rang constantly, reporters prowled through the house, inspecting its expensive furnishings. Condolences arrived from all over the United States and Canada, from England and Australia. One of the first was from Paul Rader, a Chicago evangelist who had substituted for Sister at the Temple during her absence abroad. With lordly disregard for telegraph tolls he wired: SHOCKED, GRIEVED AND STUNNED BEYOND MEASURE AT REPORT OF EVANGELIST MCPHERSON'S DEATH! WHAT A TERRIBLE, TERRIBLE LOSS! SURELY IT CANNOT BE! THE LOSS IS TOO GREAT FOR HUMAN WORDS! ONLY GOD KNOWS WHY! BUT OH, WHAT AN ABUNDANT ENTRANCE! WHAT AN ABUNDANT ENTRANCE, HALLELUJAH!

From Barstow, California, the Reverend J. Whitcomb Brougen, former paster of the Temple Baptist Church of Los Angeles, hastened to testify: A CALAMITY ONLY GOD CAN UNDERSTAND! And from Arkansas City, Kansas, where once Sister bade the rain clouds disperse and they obeyed, Ada Carleton telegraphed: PRECIOUS MOTHER, IS IT TRUE THAT OUR BELOVED SISTER IS DROWNED? WIRE ANSWER IMMEDIATELY. Mother wired the sad confirmation.

Amid the turmoil Minnie Kennedy moved with tight-lipped composure. The Temple activities continued in their accustomed rhythm at her insistence. In the Prayer Tower women knelt in the usual two-hour shifts. Classes continued in the Bible School, where three hundred students chanted: "O sea, give up thy dead! O thou mighty waves of the

ocean, send us a message from the beloved dead! O Thou God who reign-
est over all and abidest in all, hear the cry of Thy stricken children!
O God, be with Sister McPherson!"

The regular Wednesday services were not interrupted. The afternoon
meeting was a healing session, and Mother Kennedy chokingly told the
three thousand present, "Aimee is gone. Pray for her. There is no hope
of her coming back."

On returning home she wavered; friends induced her to drink a little
broth, her first food in twenty-four hours. But she rallied and appeared
at the evening service, her hair freshly marcelled, and informed the
hysterical congregation that Sister had left a will; she did not know its
contents, but it disposed only of her personal property—"The House
That God Built," the home out West Adams Boulevard way that was
donated to Aimee soon after her arrival in Los Angeles, and other personal possessions. The Temple, Mother explained, was owned by the
Echo Park Evangelistic Association, a non-profit religious corporation,
of which Sister was president, Mother vice-president, and Emma Schaffer
secretary. Sister carried no insurance, a $300,000 policy on her life
taken out the previous August, before she flew to San Francisco to address a radio convention, having lapsed after three months. The future
of the church organization would be discussed at a meeting of the board
of trustees, Mrs. Kennedy said.

"Aimee is dead," she told the flock emphatically. "Whatever you read
in the newspapers—unless it is about the finding of the body—do not be
alarmed."

Her final words were an urgent appeal for funds to buy a new carpet
for the Temple's Five Hundred Room.

That evening the Temple radio station went off the air—the first time
its programs were interrupted.

Among the evangelist's intimates a feeling spread that Sister had received a premonition. Emma Schaffer recalled that the last Sunday evening, after her sermon, Sister stepped to the front of the platform and
asked the congregation, "If something should happen to me, how many
of you would carry on the work? Please show me by rising in your
seats." The entire audience stood up, and Aimee led them in singing
"Blest Be the Tie That Binds." Two days before that she had quizzed
her Bible students: "If I should die soon, you will be sure to carry on
the work?" And someone remembered a remark Sister made shortly after
returning from her vacation in Europe: "I am weary, weary. I think only
Christ could have been as tired as I."

At the beach the search was not relaxed. At sunset hundreds of silent believers lined the water's edge and extended their arms toward the west, mutely beseeching. From nearby film studios huge floodlights were brought and played on the uneasy waters, and Sheriff Traeger assigned a hundred deputies to the all-night patrol. Beach points miles from Ocean Park organized separate searches. At Redondo two hundred Temple followers tramped the beach all night—young and old, men and girls with babies in their arms. Farther north, at Hermosa, lifeguards, police, and Boy Scouts searched. When dawn rubbed out the chalky glare of the kleigs, it was the morning of the third day.

"*Oh, Paddy Dear, and Did You Hear . . .*"

The interest of the public—and the newspapers—increased with every fresh rumor. Fifty reporters and news photographers competed with the best police brains to unravel the mystery. The evangelist was reported to have been slain by "rings" of various kinds. . . . Rum runners or vice barons were responsible for her disappearance. . . . She had been kidnaped for a huge ransom that would necessitate mortgaging the Temple. . . . Amid the torrent of speculation and innuendo, the Burns Detective Agency was found to be quietly investigating on behalf of the Temple, at whose instance it was not known.

Witnesses came forward. Jack Cowan, the beach-tent concessionaire, related that when Mrs. McPherson rented her umbrella she inquired about the lifeguards, their stations, when they came on duty. Two women reported they were in the lobby of the Ocean View Hotel and saw Sister get out of her car, one remarking, "There's the famous Aimee!" They said a man stepped up to the evangelist, handed her a letter, tipped his hat, and walked away quickly. Mrs. McPherson seemed perturbed by the letter, the women said, and hurried into the hotel and upstairs. Manager Langan did not see any man or letter, but said Sister did seem to be in a hurry.

A woman member of the Temple, Mrs. Emily M. Finley, reported that while she was sitting with a friend on Lick Pier Tuesday afternoon she noticed a woman swimming strongly; later she heard a scream, which at the time she attributed to children scampering on the beach. Three men and a woman appeared at Los Angeles police headquarters and stated that Mrs. McPherson was seen standing in front of her beach tent in earnest conversation with a pretty blond girl, who was holding "either a baby or a dog in her arms." And Mrs. Sylvia Oberman, who lived at 67½ Rose Avenue, a few doors from the Ocean View Hotel, told police that she was sunning her baby on the beach Tuesday afternoon and saw Mrs. McPherson talking with a man at about 2 o'clock; as he started to walk back toward the promenade, Aimee called after him, "Good-by, Denny" or "Benny" or some such name. Mrs. Oberman described Sister McPherson's bathing suit accurately, and fixed the time at just after 2 o'clock because her baby was becoming fretful, and at 2:20 she took it back to the house for a feeding. When she returned to the beach at 3:20, she said, the evangelist was nowhere in sight. She described the man as tall, about thirty years old, wearing a gray suit and Panama hat; and she stressed that he walked with a peculiar gait through the deep sand.

The police were convinced that Mrs. McPherson was dead. On a possibility that she might have been poisoned with a drug that took effect while she was in the water, they analyzed the orange juice and candy found in her beach tent; the analysis showed no contamination. Eddie Barry, the bellboy who procured the orange juice for Emma Schaffer, disappeared; an all-points bulletin went out. Three days later he was located in San Diego; he had merely eloped and was working in the Salvation Army hotel there.

Among Sister McPherson's followers the scandalous rumors aroused bitterness. All day hundreds sat dolefully in the great auditorium of Angelus Temple, weeping silently, gazing at the empty platform. Women kneeling at the altar railing chanted, "Sister is with Jesus—pray for her." Hundreds camped in Echo Park across the street, waiting for news. Many of them were women in Temple costume. A blackboard was set up on the sidewalk in front of the Temple entrance and bulletins were posted hourly. At 11 a.m. the board read: "Nothing new. God bless you." At 11 p.m. it read the same.

Like Mother Kennedy, the faithful were sure Sister had been taken by the Lord. Some blindly hoped for a miracle. William Walberg, a redeemed sinner and Temple guard whose duty was to keep the crowds from rushing the altar at the healing services, prophesied; Sister, he said, had come to him in a dream, informing him that she was in Buenos Aires, that "everything is all right, there is no need for excitement."

"A miracle of God is at hand," he declared. "Mark me, if her body is found the third day, and if it is brought to the platform of the Temple and all her followers pray, she will be revived. She will preach as one returning from the dead Sunday night."

Mother Kennedy was scandalized by such talk. "No," she said emphatically. "Sister's spirit is with God and cannot return. Nor have we any wish that it should, even if it were possible. We would not bring her back if we could."

Minnie Kennedy had at last found release in tears. Young Gladwyn Nichols, the Temple's music director and ardent worker on Aimee's behalf, arrived after an all-night drive from Oakland. When he and Mother Kennedy met, their tears mingled for five minutes as they clung to each other, incapable of speaking. So shaken was Mother she had to be put to bed and Temple guards were stationed around the house to insure privacy. But by afternoon she was herself again. The weight of the Temple organization was on her shoulders now; she could not afford to luxuriate in unproductive grief.

She allowed reporters to interview Roberta Starr Semple, who at fifteen showed promise of inheriting her mother's good looks and something of her glowing charm. Roberta said her mother always expected her to take up the work. " 'You are a child of God,' Mother used to tell me. After meetings she would take me on her knee and fold me in her arms and tell me that. I haven't had much experience as a preacher. 'Your time will come,' she told me."

Roberta stammered under excitement or stress. The habit had worried Aimee; she blamed the privations of her early days when Roberta was small and they lived in tents. She had asked Gladwyn Nichols to give the girl corrective speech exercises, because a preacher cannot stammer.

Outside the house newsboys were hawking another extra. Roberta slipped down the stairs and had the front door open before her grandmother saw her.

"Where are you going?" called Minnie.

"There is an extra," Roberta whispered, tossing back the long curls from her face. "I thought there might be news of finding Mother's body."

"No," said Mother Kennedy, "there is no news. Just remember always, Roberta, your mother's body is in the sea—but her spirit is with the Lord, shouting victory."

During the afternoon Minnie Kennedy took reporters on a tour of the still uncompleted Bible School building to show that no serious financial difficulties of the Temple would account for her daughter's disappearance. The building had been occupied only since the first of the year, when Aimee dedicated it with prayer on each of its five floors and penthouse.

"The Echo Park Evangelistic Association is in no more financial difficulty than any other organization," Mother explained with solid confidence. "This building cost about three hundred thousand dollars, and naturally such a sum of money is not turned over without some financial strain. We do need money to complete the work that has to be done, but praise the Lord, we will carry on." Complacently she added, "As a businesswoman I have yet to fail in a business undertaking."

The persistency of the rumors that her daughter was not dead outraged her mother heart—the way the newspapers were printing "every scrap of tittle-tattle and senseless speculation."

"If only the public could see the situation in its sane and sensible light!" she protested. "It's a shame that all these unfounded reports should gain circulation!"

But the public wondered why a mother would give up hope so quickly and so assertively: everybody, it was reasoned, in such a crisis clings to hope desperately.

That evening J. W. Buchanan, manager of the Burns Detective Agency, over the Temple radio reported to Sister's following everywhere the result of his investigations. Every rumor, every hint, every slightest apparent clue had been sifted, he said, and nothing pointed to any possible conclusion except drowning. Never had he encountered a case where so many rumors flew so fast. One rumor had it Sister died in an underwater struggle with a sea monster; a woman in Venice excitedly telephoned she saw a whale. Another rumor was that a man was seen standing on the sidewalk across from Angelus Temple for several nights "with a sneering expression on his face."

"The air is full of wild rumors and that is all there is to it," said Buchanan. At Mother's request, his agency was dropping the wild goose chase.

By the next morning—the fourth day incredulous observers were asking, "Where was Aimee when the tide went out?"—Mother Kennedy had shifted her ground somewhat; foul play, she now believed, was the explanation of her child's translation:

> I believe a blow on the head caused her death. She was such a strong swimmer, I cannot believe she was drowned by any ordinary current or tide. Anyone who ever saw her drive a car in traffic, or

deal with the crowds that gathered almost everywhere she went, always remarked her coolness and ability to keep her head in any situation.

Before the April 30 election, Aimee told me she was going to tell the truth about the Venice dance halls. When I sat and heard what she said, that she would rather see her own daughter dead than in a Venice dance hall, I realized she was taking her life in her hands. Often last summer after evening service we would drive out to the beach, and my daughter would almost weep at the scenes there. We often talked about the young girls there, many younger than Roberta.

Had Sister received threats?

"No," conceded Minnie, "but the underworld never warns before it strikes. It would be so easy for something to happen at the beach she preached against."

There was only one other possibility that Minnie could suggest; she summed it up ambiguously as "relentless persecution" by unnamed elements. "No one, except the Lord, was ever persecuted as relentlessly as my daughter."

Later, addressing the weekly rally of the Crusaders, the Temple's young people's organization, she veered closer to the target. Sister had only two enemies in the world that she knew of, she told the twenty-five hundred sobbing listeners: one was "the dance-hall crowd"; the second was "a certain church" where only the Sunday before it had been said, "The skids are being put under Angelus Temple." Everyone knew she was referring to Trinity Methodist Episcopal Church, whose fighting-cock pastor, the Reverend Bob Shuler, had been the loudest of Aimee's churchmen antagonists in Los Angeles. Shuler was in Memphis attending the General Conference of the Southern Methodist Church and could not reply at once.

All told, it was another unnerving day for Mother. At noon a green bathing cap was brought up from under Lick Pier by the athletic coach of Venice High School. After diving as deep as forty feet in the clear water, he reported that the ocean floor was smooth, with nothing to snag or hold a body. He had ventured into the dangerous area under the pier and come up with the torn cap. An elderly Temple worker, trembling with emotion, begged that he might have the relic. "The church will prize it, I assure you," he quavered.

The treasure was borne to the Temple in an automobile procession. Mother and Emma Schaffer took one look and said it was not Aimee's:

her cap was brown. But the incident visibly affected Minnie. With a despairing gasp she cried that her daughter's body must have been swept under the pier and would never be found. "Oh, what shall I do? What shall I do? Tell me!" she implored those around her.

A Coast Guard cutter joined the search and cruised back and forth while sailors put off in small boats to drop grappling irons. In the bow, heedless of the spray, knelt the Reverend D. V. Alderman, praying, "O sea, return to us our champion! Give Sister McPherson back to us!"

Two airplanes hired by newspapers skimmed the ocean's surface fifteen miles out, on a theory that the body had been carried far offshore. Handbills appeared along the promenade offering $500 for recovery of the body, with the thrifty stipulation that the offer held good only if recovery was effected by diving or definite search, not if the body washed ashore. And ships five hundred miles out at sea were instructed by radio to be on the lookout for a body.

Offers of help natural and supernatural deluged the Temple by letter and telegram. Most of these obviously came from cranks; they were tossed aside as mere clutter. One of the telegrams, dated May 21, from Oakland, and addressed to "Mother Kennedy, Angelus Temple, Echo Park, Los Angeles," read: DAUGHTER O.K. DO NOT WORRY. COMMUNICATION PROVEN. AM SENDING FOR J.A. WHOM I BELIEVE SAFE. DETAIL IN MAIL. DR. MERTON.

Mother said later that she dismissed this message with others as "spiritualism."

The evening of the fourth day a judge of the Superior Court, Carlos S. Hardy, over the Temple radio denounced suggestions that Mrs. McPherson had disappeared voluntarily. Standing with bowed head before the microphone, the judge told how his wife and he had enjoyed the evangelist's friendship and loved her, although they were not Temple members; they were Baptists. Just one week previously Sister had attended a housewarming at the Hardys' new home on Lafayette Park Place.

"Her body lies in the great Pacific Ocean," the silvery-maned jurist declared, "and her spirit is with God, and all other reports and rumors are false. As Christ was crucified on the Cross, in like manner such rumors as these crucify her name!"

The work of the Temple would go on, he added; at that moment two leading evangelists—Dr. Charles S. Shreve of the McKendree Methodist Church in Washington, D.C., and the Reverend Watson B. Argue, a

Canadian evangelist—were speeding to the city to take over her pulpit. Brother Argue, who was twenty-two, had been devoted to Sister McPherson ever since he led the singing at her campaign in Winnipeg six years before, when she had startled the city by touring the red-light district, praying with inmates and distributing Bible mottoes for the bedroom walls of the brothels.

Judge Hardy had long been a friendly counselor of Mother Kennedy and her daughter in their business affairs. He helped found the Crusaders and often spoke over the Temple radio. During the search for the evangelist's body he had caused several flurries, once announcing from the bench that the body had been recovered; but that rumor proved to be another of the thousand false leads, a report his wife had heard and telephoned to him excitedly.

While five thousand persons lined the beach that fourth evening, many with cots, camp stools, blankets, lunch baskets, and even tents, Captain of Detectives Cline announced he was going to the beach himself on twenty-four-hour duty to clear up the mystery. He scoffed at the notion that Mrs. McPherson was not drowned, but he promised that every lead would be traced down. Also, he wished to be on hand when the body was found, to inspect it immediately for evidence of foul play.

"Revengers"
and Half a Million Dollars

Herman Cline had earned a reputation as a sound and capable police investigator. Police work was his career. He had joined the Los Angeles force in 1909, had risen through promotions to head the homicide squad, and in February 1926 had been appointed chief of the detective bureau. In 1924 he awed psychologists at the University of California at Los Angeles by his showing in experimental tests given to him and another police officer in an effort to determine standards by which a really superior mind might be rated. The secret report on the tests sent to the Police Commission read: "Cline got each point in the minimum of time without error. In the induction test he would explode with the answer every time. It seems he gives every evidence of a very superior intelligence, particularly in initiating and carrying through a rational process."

Such a mind is not easily diverted by red herrings. Cline was convinced Aimee McPherson was drowned, and that her body would be recovered. But he was determined that no suspicion of scamping the investigation should fall on him. For the benefit of reporters he explained why no theory except accidental drowning appeared to him to be tenable. There were six possibilities:

First, murder. This was impossible because the last time the evangelist was seen she was in the water with no other bather near her.

Second, kidnaping. Impossible for the same reason.

Third, suicide. No motive for self-destruction was known, and it was absurd to think a woman would go to the trouble of changing into a bathing suit in order to drown herself.

Fourth, poisoning. This was impossible because the only thing the evangelist ate before she went into the water was a waffle, in a public restaurant.

Fifth, lapse of memory. If a woman in a green bathing suit wandered out of the water and strayed off somewhere, how far could she go without being seen?

Sixth, voluntary disappearance. No motive for this had been advanced. And if Mrs. McPherson had wished to vanish, she might easily have slipped away while she was in Europe only a few weeks previously, or she could go away quietly at any time.

Captain Cline believed in Emma Schaffer's truthfulness. Emma's horizon was limited but her loyalty to Sister was unbounded. Her literal-mindedness and lack of imagination had even led Aimee to sigh to friends that the constant company of so colorless a person sometimes became a burden. Emma's story never varied. Day after day she gave the lie to all rumors and witnesses. To Lieutenant Barnard she denied that Sister drove to the beach by way of Culver City; to Jack Cowan she denied there was any talk with the concessionaire except about the umbrella and where they wanted it placed in the sand; to Mrs. Oberman she denied that Sister conversed with any man at the beach.

The first fresh clue struck by Cline seemed to confirm Emma. A man who had been observed swimming at the same time as Sister McPherson was traced; named Jose Astengo, he worked for the Hayward Hotel in Los Angeles. He and his wife spent Tuesday afternoon at the beach, he admitted readily. He went swimming in front of the Ocean View Hotel. The water was so cold he came out quickly after a first dip, and while he lay talking with his wife he noticed a woman in a green bathing suit nearby drop her beach robe and enter the water. He was impressed by the way she waded straight in, without hesitation, until the water was up to her chin, when she started swimming with powerful strokes. He remarked to his wife that the woman certainly had nerve to wade into cold water like that. A little later he followed the woman into the water and swam out to a float, where he rested for about fifteen minutes, then swam back. He paid no attention to the woman during this time, but he was always close enough to have heard a cry for help. He saw floating timbers in the water; one of these might have hit the bather. Just before the woman entered the water, he added, a woman in the tent with her got up and walked away, saying she would be back shortly.

Mrs. Astengo noticed that the woman in green walked down to the ocean in an odd manner, swinging her bathing cap in one hand and several times stopping as if thinking about something. "I believe she went straight out but I do not know," she said, "for I did not see her again. I remained in my chair and so am sure she did not come back." Neither of the couple saw any man around.

The other principal development on the fifth day of search, which was Saturday, was the organization of a Temple patrol to form a human chain along the entire fourteen miles of ocean front. Volunteers were instructed over the radio to report to Captain Joseph (he preferred Joe) Taylor, Cline's assistant, who marshaled the force in four-hour shifts and assigned sectors to each squad. More than two hundred determined men and women responded. A headquarters was set up in a vacant store at 507 Ocean Front, a few steps from the Ocean View Hotel, where coffee and sandwiches were provided at all hours under the supervision of Blanche Rice, acting as Mother Kennedy's deputy. A direct telephone line was opened to the Temple.

Sunday was a day of sensations. At the Temple three services were held, the auditorium jammed every time. The streets around the building were filled hours before the doors opened. Thousands were unable to get in. Women fainted in the crush; others collapsed inside. Mother Kennedy, bearing up with remarkable vigor for a sorely beset woman of fifty-five, spoke at all three meetings.

In the morning she explained to the sobbing congregation the status of the church property. It was in her name and Sister's, she said, because "the leaders and contributors wanted it so." Before their pastor left for the Holy Land in January Aimee and she had signed a deed transferring the property to the Echo Park Evangelistic Association, but this deed had not yet been recorded. On Thursday night, at a meeting of the "church backers," she said, she had suggested the deed be recorded to make the transfer binding and legal, but "the business leaders of the corporation asked that the property remain in its present status." The "business leaders of the corporation," of course, were Aimee, Minnie, and Emma, a hired employee; there were no other members or officers. The newspapers were not backward in pointing out that once Mrs. McPherson was legally dead, Minnie Kennedy would own outright the Temple and its appurtenances.

Roberta was greeted with a storm of applause when she arose unexpectedly from her seat in the front row, stepped on the platform, and delivered the altar call. Garbed in white, she prayed earnestly that all would give their hearts to Jesus. To the accompaniment of weeping by men, women, and children, she concluded, "I am sure Mother is looking down from Heaven and sees this sight." The entire audience arose, lifted right hands, and prayed.

At the afternoon service Mother announced plans to form the Aimee Semple McPherson Choir of 1000 voices as the first memorial to their departed founder. Also, May 18 henceforth would be a church holy day, with commemorative services to be held annually at the Temple and at the beach.

While these obsequies were unfolding, the ferment at Ocean Park reached riot proportions. The day began with an alarm to the sheriff's office that a group of men, armed with clubs, had been sighted just before dawn scurrying across the sands, with what intention no one knew. Then a report seeped through that some of the Temple following planned to spirit away the body to an unknown hiding place to prevent official profanation. Deputies were scattered through the crowds to forestall such violence, and typewritten instructions were hastily distributed to all members of the Temple patrol. They were cautioned not to stray beyond their assigned stations; to refuse to enter into controversy or argument with anyone "concerning the matter most sacred to our hearts"; when the body was sighted, to pass the word quietly to the guard at the next station and make no outcry; to try to shield the body and keep back the crowds until they could get the assistance of "our own people" or the police; and to "keep constant vigil: do not leave your post without notifying those in charge. God bless you."

The sheriff's office feared that Sunday souvenir seekers might tear the corpse to bits before it could be hustled away. From earliest morning throngs of morbidly curious poured in by electric train and automobile. The Venice dance halls opened at an unheard-of hour. All day they beat out jazz, which Sister's faithful countered with hymns. An enterprising concessionaire displayed a life-size wax figure of Sister, robed in white, extending one hand in blessing; furious Temple believers mobbed the booth and the riot squad was barely able to save the proprietor from serious manhandling. He took down the waxworks. All along the beach were hawked composite photographs depicting Aimee rising wraithlike from the water. Her followers protested and fought and threatened, in vain.

Above and below the ocean's surface grim search went on. Three airplanes patrolled. On the wing of one poised daredevil Al Jennings, prepared to parachute into the water at the spot where the body was sighted and shroud the hallowed figure in his chute until boats could arrive. A dozen divers kept active offshore. Amateur assistants plunged excitedly into the breakers time and again, only to find that the object they glimpsed was a log or a patch of kelp. At Manhattan Beach, a young man named Robert Browning, who had come to the seaside with his wife for a day's outing, swam out nearly a mile in the rough chop, believing he saw the body. He sank, and an hour later his body was washed ashore. Where he went down lifeguards found two dead seals floating.

That Sunday evening, at Westlake Presbyterian Church, the Reverend Gustav A. Briegleb, a preacher fired by good will who had often been driven into criticism of Mrs. McPherson, spoke on "Aimee Semple McPherson's Disappearance—Its Meaning and Message." The service, well advertised, brought an overflow congregation.

The next day the Ministerial Association of Los Angeles conveyed its condolences in a resolution adopted unanimously. Sister had had more than one set-to with her fellow (her adherents used the adjective "jealous") pulpiteers in the city and had resigned from the Ministerial Association under caustic attack. But the tragedy obliterated Christian differences, and members of all churches were memorialized to "remember in their prayers the sorrowing mother, the bereaved children and shepherdless flock."

Rolf Kennedy McPherson, Sister's son by her second husband, had finally been given the news officially by his grandmother. The boy (he was just turned thirteen) was a boarder at the James Pleasants ranch at Winters, in Yolo County in the northern part of the state, not far from Sacramento; he had been there two years in an effort to build up his health. His glamorous mother frequently visited him there. Reporters found the ranch isolated, guarded against intruders by its remoteness and by an alert German shepherd dog named Peter, Sister's present to her son; around the ranch the dog was called "Aimee's pet." Everything a boy's heart could desire, including a $350 radio receiving set, had been lavished on Rolf.

The lad's reserve struck the reporters; "cautious" was the word they used. Mrs. Pleasants confessed she was mystified. "Maybe she had a mental breakdown and just wandered away from the beach. We still hope there will be some solution of the mystery other than her death."

"I hope my mother is alive," Rolf echoed solemnly; and quickly head-lines blazoned that Mrs. McPherson's son doubted his mother's death. The Temple's indignation flared.

A splintered plank with a mop of reddish hair on it was fished out of the surf. Mother Kennedy said it was not Aimee's; it was too long for her daughter's. In fact—Minnie sniffed—it looked suspiciously like the hair on that waxworks dummy.

On Tuesday, May 25, the acting head of Angelus Temple repeated, "There is absolutely no hope on our part that Sister is alive on land or sea."

All the crank letters and messages coming in by the dozens could not make her change her mind. One nameless tipster suggested that Cline "look behind locked and unlocked doors of the Ocean View Hotel." There was even a letter which boldly purported to be from kidnapers who were holding Sister for a ransom of half a million dollars. This let-ter was mailed in San Francisco the day before it reached the Temple. Written on a torn scrap of paper, apparently in a disguised hand, it ran:

San Francisco May 24

Angelus Temple
Los Angeles

We have with us your beloved Aimee McPherson and will free her on payment of $500,000.00 in currency, to be paid at once, in this manner.

She has injured us and must pay in money or blood.

Select your man and have him take a seat in the Palace Hotel lobby next Saturday and wear this badge on the lappel of his coat and he will be approached by one of our men and instructed what to do. He must be secretive or we will not be responsible for his life. No dicks must follow him.

Get busy at once. We mean business.

Saturday at 11 o'clock.

REVENGERS.

Mother Kennedy gave little credence to this communication; she attributed it also to "spiritualism." Nevertheless she told Cline, who notified the San Francisco police. Two detectives, wearing white Temple badges, one holding a bundle done up to look like money, were posted in the Palace Hotel lobby that Saturday. They remained several hours. Nothing happened.

Months later, when the State of California wished to produce this document as evidence, it was found to have been stolen from the locked secret files of the Los Angeles police detective bureau.

When a Body . . .

The police confessed they were baffled. The evangelist whom they believed to be dead was being reported seen in a dozen places. A rumor that she was in Denver prompted Captain Cline to query the chief of police there; he replied that Sister McPherson bore the highest reputation since the revivals she had conducted there four and five years previously, and there was no sign of her in that city. Obviously nothing could stop the spate of rumors except recovery of the body.

At the request of Sheriff Traeger, Captain Ed Harrison, constable of Avalon on Santa Catalina Island, came over and dove off Ocean Park beach. Harrison held the world record for remaining under water; he was the diver who performed aquatic acrobatics under the glass-bottomed boats of Catalina. Harrison went down five times and explored thoroughly; he reported the ocean floor was clean and unobstructed; there was a strong undertow seaward. The water felt cold to him after the warmth of the Catalina coves.

Preparations for deep-sea diving under Lick Pier got under way. Air-hose and oxygen tanks were assembled, the Los Angeles Fire Department lending ladders and other equipment. The firemen loved Sister for the help she had given them in their election campaign for more pay; they had named her an honorary battalion chief and pinned on her badge at the Temple, where she had preached in a fireman's uniform on "Fireman, Save My Child!"

Mother repeated her belief in foul play and quoted a letter from the insurance agent who wrote Sister's policy the year before, saying the physical examination showed that Mrs. McPherson was in almost perfect health.

On Monday the public was piqued by the news that the City Council had secretly considered a request for permission to bury Sister's body in a marble crypt under one of the stained-glass windows in the Temple. Judge Hardy had telephoned the request to the president of the Council, Boyle Workman, and fifteen councilmen in caucus were inclined to grant it, but could take no action because there was no body to bury. Amendment of the city's cemeteries ordinance would be required.

"She was always taken up by the windows, especially the one portraying Jesus healing the woman," Minnie Kennedy said in corroboration. "She said she would like to rest under that window."

Newspapers published photographs of the window (the first on the right-hand side as one faces the platform) with its legend, "Thy faith hath made thee whole," an arrow pointing to the proposed burial spot.

On Tuesday, May 25, the day of the "Revengers" telegram, Mother Kennedy finally visited Ocean Park. All week she had avoided going near the place where her daughter vanished, and the gossips had commented cynically on this. This Tuesday she appeared somewhat refreshed, and she telephoned Manager Langan at the Ocean View Hotel that she would be there at 1:30 to pray in the last room that had held Sister alive. There was an air of expectancy among those around her when she eluded reporters and was driven to the beach in the automobile of a close friend, Mrs. Elizabeth Frame. Langan took her directly to room 202, where she begged to be alone. Reporters had followed her, and through the closed door they heard her sobbing and praying. After a while the cameramen asked permission to enter. Sitting at the window, gazing across the sunlight-dappled Pacific in whose depths her darling daughter lay, eyes misty with tears, Minnie posed for the photographers, holding Sister's Bible opened at the last passage she was known to have read. "Seven long days have gone by and Sister McPherson's body has not been found," she murmured. "What can it mean?" The intrusive press respected her grief and tiptoed out.

From the hotel Mother visited the beach-patrol headquarters, served coffee to the disheartened but dogged volunteers, and thanked them as each came off duty. Aimee's body, she said, she was almost certain now had been carried under the pier, but they must keep up the search.

A flash from El Paso, Texas, at about the same hour, put federal agents into the hunt. Deputy Sheriff Boquor there reported that a woman resembling the evangelist had been seen crossing the border into Mexico in a California car owned by a person known to Mrs. McPherson. Mexican authorities launched their own massive investigation: the honor of Mexico was involved.

Police were exhausted chasing down false leads, while a newspaper learned that the Burns detectives, supposed to have withdrawn from the case, were active again and had taken Thomas S. Melville, doorman at the Clark Hotel in downtown Los Angeles, to the Temple for questioning about a story he was spreading that he saw Mrs. McPherson enter the Clark lobby on the morning she vanished, take an elevator upstairs, and emerge after about fifteen minutes. He knew her well, having often attended Temple services with his wife. He described the yellow sports dress she wore, and said she was carrying a briefcase with "Aimee Semple McPherson" stamped in gilt letters.

"Fiddlesticks!" said Mother Kennedy. Aimee had gone downtown on the 18th, yes, but it was to buy a toy for Rolf. Her daughter owned no briefcase; sometimes she carried one belonging to Roberta.

But it was reported that a woman, unidentified, had observed the evangelist in the ladies' parlor of the Clark Hotel on May 18, talking with a well-dressed, middle-aged man.

As the caldron of rumor bubbled, District Attorney Asa Keyes (the name rhymes with "tries," "lies," and "dies") entered the case. He announced that unless the body were found within twenty-four hours, "the circumstances are such as to warrant an investigation on my part to determine if any other elements entered into the disappearance than the fact that Mrs. McPherson was last seen in the surf." Among the first persons he proposed to question, Keyes said, were Emma Schaffer and Kenneth G. Ormiston.

Ormiston's was a new name injected into the tangle. Keyes explained that there was nothing to indicate Ormiston had any connection with the disappearance, but it was hoped he might be able to shed some light on Mrs. McPherson's movements since the first of the year.

Keyes was led to take this action by newspaper pressure. Kenneth Ormiston had formerly been the operator of the Los Angeles *Times* radio broadcasting station, serving also as radio editor. Before that he had been a ship wireless operator. He left the *Times* early in 1924 to install the radio equipment at Angelus Temple, whose station KFSG was the third to go on the air in Los Angeles. Since then, until January 1926, he had worked as chief engineer of the Temple station. He was not a member of the church, but was on friendly terms with his employers, Aimee McPherson and Mother Kennedy. The *Times,* printing his background, mentioned that he was married, separated from his wife, and the father of a four-year-old boy.

The interest of the *Times* had been aroused when somebody recalled that in January, about the time Mrs. McPherson sailed for Europe, Ormiston had disappeared from his Temple job, and his wife, Ruth Peters Ormiston, registered a missing-person report at police headquarters. She told the police in an emotional interview that "a certain prominent woman" was responsible for her husband's disappearance; he had written her a letter saying he could no longer live with her, and urging her to obtain a divorce. His car was found abandoned a day later in Pasadena. The police, after a desultory check, decided this was purely a domestic altercation and dropped the matter.

Mrs. Ormiston, it was gossiped, carried her grievance to Angelus Temple and threatened Mrs. Kennedy with naming Aimee Semple Mc-Pherson in a divorce action. Then Ruth Ormiston abruptly sailed back to Australia with her father, who was a wealthy ice-cream manufacturer in Sydney, taking along her child.

The *Times* reporters did not know that, a few days after Mrs. Ormiston's departure, shocked Emma Schaffer brought word to Mother Kennedy that a Hollywood gossip magazine planned to publish an article saying Sister was traveling in Europe with the missing radio operator. Minnie, alarmed for her daughter's reputation and the good name of the Temple, cabled a warning to Thomas Cook and Son, the travel agency arranging Aimee's tour, requesting that a guard be assigned the evangelist. The guard was posted as requested. The article never appeared.

The ferreting reporters did find out that on March 15 Ormiston was in Seattle, where he bought a blue Chrysler coupe for $2500, making a cash payment of $1500 which had been wired to him from Venice, California. Reporters traced the money order; it was dated March 15, signed "James Wallace," the sender's address being given as a hotel close by a home where Mrs. McPherson often visited. The hotel register showed that no James Wallace was there March 15, although a Mr. and Mrs. James Wallace of Glendale had stayed there overnight on February 20, while Sister was still abroad.

Ormiston had next appeared in Venice on March 26. He checked into the Waldorf Hotel and remained until April 9, when he told the desk clerk he was going back to Seattle. During that time he returned to the Temple to handle the radio controls for one broadcast. On May 9 or 10, he was said to have been seen at the Temple again. On May 12 he called on his parents in San Francisco, telling them when he left the next day that he was going to Seattle. On May 21 he was in San Francisco, where he applied at the State Motor Vehicle Department office to have his Washington state license plates changed. His parents did not see him that day. His father ridiculed the notion that Kenneth had been in Europe, saying his son had gone to New York in February to visit an uncle, and had written from Seattle in March. The newspapers described Ormiston as about thirty years of age, tall, dapper, and attractive, with a noticeably receding hairline, and he was lame.

This assortment of facts, which might or might not hold any significance, laboriously assembled by the *Times* staff, was handed to District Attorney Keyes with an intimation that he might do something with it. Admittedly it offered no tangible clue to Sister's disappearance—but then, every theory of the case was tenuous. Keyes was reluctant to become involved; he had no reason to doubt the belief of every police investigator that the evangelist was drowned and neither kidnaped nor in hiding. But newspaper good will is important to an office holder, and in view of the prominence of the woman concerned, the unabating, almost rabid public interest, and also the *Times'* natural eagerness to have its lead thoroughly tested, Keyes understood that his staff could not afford to appear negligent. He issued his premonitory statement. That same day the newspapers got wind of the "Dr. Merton" telegram of May 21 ("Daughter O.K.") and brought that also to the district attorney's attention.

What Minnie Kennedy felt when Kenneth Ormiston's name was tossed into the boiling pot of speculation she did not publicly say. Whatever she may have felt or thought was unimportant, because on May 27, twenty-four hours after he was first introduced to the public by the newspapers, Ormiston appeared in Los Angeles, ready to do everything in his power to resolve the mystery.

"*Let Silence Reign*"

The meeting between Mrs. Kennedy and her one-time employee was affectionate.

"The lost has been found!" cried Minnie when Ormiston, natty in a gray suit and Panama hat, limped into the Temple beach headquarters. "I am so glad you have come to us again!"

Ormiston called her "Mother." They kissed.

"I am glad to be here with you and to do whatever I can to clear things up," he said. Turning to observant reporters, he decried the linking of his name with that of Mrs. McPherson as "a gross insult to a noble and sincere woman," and said it was news to him that he had either disappeared or was mysteriously hiding.

Mother had been at the beach since an early hour. She had been advised that the ninth and tenth days are critical in the recovery of drowning victims, and she issued a radio appeal for all church members and friends, for Boy Scouts and other volunteers, to augment the patrol. Cardboard identifying badges were distributed among the beach detail and automobiles were used to change the shifts.

Cline had discussed all aspects of the case with her at the Temple the day before. Emma Schaffer was present during the two-hour interview, weeping copiously; she was not questioned. On this Thursday morning Minnie appeared really rested and her energetic self for the first time since the blow fell. She said Aimee had appeared to her in a dream, which she interpreted as a good omen. In her dream Minnie seemed to be working at something with her hands, when a thorn pierced her finger. The more she tried to extract the thorn, the more painful it became, until she cried, "I can never work with that thorn in my hand!" Then Aimee appeared, consoled her with "poor Muzzy," and gently, skillfully pulled out the thorn. Instantly the pain ceased and the wound healed. The apparition was exactly like Aimee in manner, action, and tone of voice, Mother said. After the dream she slept soundly.

Ormiston, having arrived in the city from the north by train that morning, had checked into the Rosslyn Hotel and from there telephoned the district attorney's office. Keyes was not in; Ormiston identified himself and left word that he would like to have a talk. Then he hurried to the Temple, where Emma Schaffer told him Mother was at the beach. He got a ride out there and found a welcoming committee at 507 Ocean Front, comprising, besides Mother and other Temple figures, Detective Captain Joe Taylor, Captain Steckel of the Venice division police, Lieutenant Allen of the missing persons bureau, and Deputies Hanby and Humber. After the embrace with Mother Kennedy, the official party adjourned to the Ocean View Hotel and the visitor was interrogated privately by the police delegation, Mother Kennedy being present.

Taylor did most of the questioning, along general lines, and Ormiston replied in a friendly, open manner. He said he had read in the newspapers in San Francisco the evening before that he was wanted for questioning, and caught a train south at once. He reviewed his employment by Angelus Temple and his estrangement from his wife. Incompatibility of temperament alone was the cause, he said; his wife was "insanely jealous." They had been separated since January 22. His relationship with the Temple pastor was simply that of employer and employee; it certainly had nothing to do with his domestic difficulties. He had been moving up and down the coast in recent weeks doing radio work. Yes, he was in Seattle on March 15, and he had used several aliases recently, among them James Wallace ("I used that one a lot"), because friends had warned him that his wife intended to sue for divorce, and, "knowing her frame of mind," he expected "a nasty action" and he did not want newspaper publicity.

"Speaking of Wallace," digressed Taylor, "did you receive the money that was mentioned in a press report—the fifteen hundred dollars—in Seattle?"

"I certainly did not receive anything like that," replied Ormiston.

Had he heard that his wife was going to name Mrs. McPherson in a divorce action?

"No, not directly."

"Did you ever receive any correspondence in reference to this divorce action from Mrs. McPherson?"

"Of course not! Certainly not! I never received any correspondence on any subject from her."

Taylor turned to Mother Kennedy, who was listening intently. "Did you ever hear anything about this divorce action?" he asked.

"No," said Minnie, "I did not, any more than, I believe—that Mrs. Ormiston said it would be her object."

"Did it ever come to your knowledge that she might name some-one?"

"The only conversation I had with her was that Mr. Ormiston had left—or was leaving—her; she told me about their troubles then as she did another time when he left her."

The letter that Ormiston had written to his wife in January came under discussion.

"I wrote her and gave her a means of saving her pride," Ormiston explained candidly. "The basis was that I could not participate in the things she enjoyed, such as dancing, tennis, and so forth."

"That on account of your leg?"

"Yes. I said I knew she could not be happy under the circumstances and I would remove myself from the scene."

"Didn't you tell her that you had seen a doctor in Pasadena and he told you you had a tuberculosis leg? And that you were going to Europe to see if anything could be done there?"

"I told her," said Ormiston, "that a doctor had told me it was tubercular and that I could leave; also, an examining physician of a life-insurance company in San Francisco had told me that was the case."

"Without any mention of going to Europe?"

"No. Anything else is rot!" He glanced sharply at Taylor. "Did she show you that letter?"

"I don't know," the detective searched his memory. "She told us something of the substance of the letter, one page of it, to that effect."

"It is an absolute lie," Ormiston broke in.

He confirmed his movements as they had been traced by reporters and said he was in Venice under his own name in April, as the hotel register showed. On May 19 or 20, just after Mrs. McPherson's disappearance, he was in Salinas, where he went to pay a traffic fine. Salinas is a town roughly one hundred miles south of San Francisco. He said he telephoned Mother Kennedy immediately on hearing the news, and had written her several letters of consolation and sympathy since. The last time he saw the evangelist, he said, was on Sunday, May 9, after the evening service, when he greeted her briefly as she stood on the platform while the congregation was filing out. Mother Kennedy also was present.

Captain Taylor reported to the waiting press that he could find no reason to connect the radio operator with the disappearance; in fact, Ormiston's secretiveness and use of assumed names seemed plausible if he expected his wife to accuse him of infidelity and name a third party; adultery in California is a statutory crime, and is rarely invoked in a divorce action.

Ormiston explained his motives to the reporters cordially. "I am here," he said, "to help in the search for Mrs. McPherson. I know absolutely nothing about her disappearance except what I have read in the newspapers. I believe with Mother Kennedy that Sister McPherson is dead, drowned in the ocean. There is no foundation for any theory that I know anything about her disappearance."

Mother was equally assertive. She characterized Ormiston as "a nice boy" and a good radio technician. "He certainly behaved himself while he was with us at Angelus Temple. I had a telephone message from him several days after Aimee's disappearance; I think it was from Salinas and he was on his way to Seattle." At the persistent rumors of a "romance" Minnie scoffed: "Aimee was nobody's sweetheart! Mary Pickford is the Sweetheart of the World, but Aimee was the World's Sister. Of course, my daughter was perfectly free to form any association she wished, so far as the law was concerned, but she did not have the desire. My daughter led a spotless and blameless life, and all reports to the contrary are absurd and simply an attempt to besmirch her reputation!"

Captain Taylor asked Ormiston whether he would talk with Cline, who was not at the beach. The visitor expressed complete willingness and rode into the city in a police car. Cline was busy when they reached headquarters and they waited. When the detective chief finally was able to see them, Ormiston, it developed, had wandered away. A call to his hotel brought the information that he had checked out. Cline heard Taylor's report and shrugged; so far as he was concerned, Ormiston was eliminated as a possible source of help. He told reporters so.

The Ormiston lead was not the only one exploded that day. The Culver City identification of the evangelist by Lieutenant Barnard also was shaken when Miss Irene Hillstrom, pastor of the Temple's Venice branch, revealed that she drove past the M-G-M studios on May 18 with another Temple worker, and said she was positive that Lieutenant Barnard and his wife had mistaken her for Mrs. McPherson. Demonstrating how easily such a mistake could be made, she posed at the Temple in her pulpit uniform, her hair combed, like Sister's, high on the head, holding an open Bible, in a strikingly McPhersonesque attitude. She offered no explanation as to why she had not spoken up sooner.

That evening, over the Temple radio, Mother Kennedy struck boldly to squelch the gossip that was doing her daughter's reputation—and potentially the Temple—so much mischief. She posted a reward of $25,000 for her daughter's safe return, not in expectation that it would ever be claimed, she explained, but "to set at rest the rumors and call the bluff of irresponsible persons and publications." The announcement continued:

> Never for one moment have we the slightest hope or reason to hope that she is alive. We believe her body is in the sea and her soul is with her Savior, Whom she loved. . . . To the person or persons who will bring my daughter, Aimee Semple McPherson, to the Angelus Temple unharmed and as well as she left us Tuesday the 18th instant, we will give a check for $25,000. There is the offer, and until it is claimed let silence reign.

That day, while Kenneth Ormiston was being questioned in the Ocean View Hotel, beach police picked up John F. Arbuckle, apparently a member of the Temple patrol. The aged man was wet with sea water, shivering with cold, and crying. He told police he had been out of a sick bed only two weeks, after a siege of double pneumonia. The police took him into custody for his own good.

Phantasmas in the Phantasmagoria

But silence did not reign; instead, the clamor became polyphonic. Mother Kennedy fulminated in statements too long to be printed except in brief part, and this led her to fulminate again against "irresponsible newspapers."

The newspapers were interested: circulation figures were up. But the respectful attitude of the press was changing as rumors became more insistent that the evangelist's disappearance was a colossal publicity stunt. The headline writers, coerced by the rigid necessities of their trade to use the short, graphic word, had quickly dropped "evangelist" and the clumsy "Mrs. McPherson" and all over the West newsboys shrilled "Aimee!"

The first newspaper openly to express disbelief in the Foursquare Gospel pastor's demise was not in Los Angeles. On May 28, the second Friday after Aimee had gone swimming, the Sacramento *Union,* five hundred miles north of Echo Park, declared, "Confidential information enables the Sacramento *Union* to state that Aimee Semple McPherson is not dead." This blunt statement was elaborated cryptically:

> Information was received yesterday that an automobile belonging to a man under suspicion of being implicated in the mysterious disappearance was found and identified at a point in the [Central] Valley. From the inception of the search for the body of Mrs. McPherson, the press of the state and local authorities have been dubious about the drowning of the pastor.

The *Union* telegraphed Sheriff Traeger in Los Angeles asking that he request Yolo County authorities to search the Pleasants ranch in nearby Winters. Traeger referred the wire to his homicide department, who reported there was insufficient evidence to justify such a move, and informed the *Union* that Los Angeles authorities were satisfied Sister McPherson was drowned.

Secretive strangers prowling the ranch at Winters (most of them were reporters trying to interview Rolf McPherson; others were private detectives hopeful of collecting the $25,000 reward) so frightened Mrs. Pleasants that she hurried to Sacramento and appealed to Governor Richardson, fearing a kidnaping plot. Mother Kennedy ordered Rolf to be brought home. The boy was convoyed by Harry D. Hallenbeck, a close friend of the Temple leaders, in a hair-raising flight from pursuing reporters. The news hawks even resorted to spreading a kidnaping alarm until they discovered that Hallenbeck was a deputy sheriff and packed a pistol. At the Temple, Rolf was interviewed just once, then was isolated under the jealous surveillance of Emma Schaffer. For the interview Rolf proudly wore his first long pants, sent to him by his mother just before she vanished.

The focus of interest shifted suddenly to San Francisco when a private detective said he had seen Mrs. McPherson, on the previous Saturday, leave the Southern Pacific Railroad station at Third and Townsend Streets and get into a closed car without license plates, driven by a man. The detective followed the car to the California Hotel, 1390 California Street, where the driver went inside and returned with a second woman, dressed in brown. The detective slipped into the hotel to ascertain the identity of this woman; when he came out, the car and its passengers had disappeared. The California Hotel was the residence of Kenneth Ormiston's parents.

Mother Kennedy snorted at this report, lumping it with the "thousand and one wild rumors."

"For people who are so sure they see Sister McPherson," she dared

AREA OF THE HUNT

the scandal-mongers, "there is now the reward of $25,000. They ought to look well and then step up and take her, for that is what we want—our girl. Money is no object. We know she is with God."

The probable source of the reward money she indicated by her confidence that the sum would be "oversubscribed."

Cline revealed that the police had traced only one bank account maintained by Mrs. McPherson in her own name, a savings account in a Venice bank. The balance was $540, and the bank manager said there had been no recent withdrawals, and the balance had never been larger. Angelus Temple accounts were found in two other banks; during the year the balances fluctuated between $500 and $10,000 as receipts from church collections and other sources were deposited and paid out immediately against loans and running expenses. Everything was in order.

Mother made two trips to the beach on Friday the 28th, the day after she had greeted Ormiston there. On the first trip she was upset to find reporters cross-examining Mrs. Oberman about seeing Sister in conversation with a man. Mrs. Oberman was firm in her account; she said the man was tall, dressed in gray, and she noticed a peculiarity in his gait. She said Aimee walked backward toward the water and waved to the man; he waved back, then stepped on a tram going toward Venice. Shown a photograph of Kenneth Ormiston, she studied it carefully and seemed very interested, but she declined to make any identification from a photograph.

"But I am positive," she said, "that I can identify this man if he is brought back to the beach and is allowed to walk through the sand to the point where he talked to Mrs. McPherson."

Mother and Emma both declared her story absurd.

At noon R. C. Crawford, a deep-sea diver employed by the city, descended under Lick Pier, but the heavy ground swell soon forced him to come up. Mother Kennedy was disappointed, and she returned during the afternoon, hoping the search could proceed. Again disappointed, she remained at beach headquarters and personally thanked the members of the patrol as they came off duty at 6 o'clock. The devotion of this band of about a hundred, who were scanning twenty-five miles of coastline, so touched Mother that she had all but collapsed, and with tears streaming down her cheeks was driven back to the Temple barely in time to conduct the evening services.

Her entrance was dramatic. As she appeared in the doorway at the head of the ramp leading down to the platform, there was a crash and roll of drums (a set of timpani for which she had grudgingly paid $385 years previously) and the white-robed choir arose with the four thousand Crusaders in the audience, holding up their right hands in salutation. Down the ramp marched Mother, her right hand held high, Bible clutched under the other arm, her silken robes billowing. Amid a storm of applause she took her place at the pulpit, radiant and smiling. "Carry on!" was her watchword to the Temple's youth.

That day the Reverend Bob Shuler, Sister's gadfly critic and closest competitor as a pulpit spellbinder, returned from Memphis. Tersely he pointed out that he had not been in Los Angeles on either of the two Sundays immediately before Mrs. McPherson's disappearance, hence he could not have said from his pulpit "the skids are being put under Angelus Temple," as insinuated by Mother Kennedy.

Saturday afternoon diver Crawford descended into the debris-littered water under Lick Pier. Mrs. Kennedy, wearing earphones, listened to his report of progress step by step while spectators pressed around. Crawford found no clue, but Mother expressed confidence that the sea would yet give up its victim.

That day a telegram came to the Los Angeles police from Ocala, Florida: HAVE JUST HEARD OF AIMEE SEMPLE MCPHERSON'S DISAP-PEARANCE. WAS HER HUSBAND BUT NOW DIVORCED. I WAS FORMERLY IN THE WORK WITH HER AND WILL BE GLAD TO GIVE INFORMATION OR ASSIST IN ANY WAY. PLEASE MAIL ME LOS ANGELES PAPERS FOR THE PAST WEEK. HAROLD S. MCPHERSON.

The emergence of the former grocery clerk, the all but forgotten ex-husband of rich, glamorous Aimee, was as transitory as it was surprising. Captain Cline could think of no help to be had in Ocala, Florida. Mother Kennedy pursed her lips: "I have nothing to say about my former son-in-law's kind offer."

Immediately there circulated rumors that McPherson would claim custody of his son Rolf. Mother Kennedy hotly denied this, and defended her daughter as a good mother who regularly kept Rolf's father informed of his son's welfare.

Encounter in the Night

The motor car mentioned by the Sacramento *Union* as having been identified in the Central Valley became the focal point of a puzzling development in this second week of the evangelist's disappearance. The machine was a blue Chrysler coupe, California license number F-31052, registered to Kenneth Gladstone Ormiston. On the evening of Wednesday, May 26, it was in the Highway Garage in Salinas, having been brought in for washing by a man with a limp; he said he would pick it up in a day or two. Thursday, May 27, Kenneth Ormiston spent in Los Angeles talking to detectives. In the late afternoon of Friday, May 28, the car was claimed by the man who left it. Several hours later the same man returned in the car to fill up the gas tank; beside him sat a woman wearing large sun glasses or goggles. The car drove away southward, the driver having declined to say where he was heading.

Around dawn the next day the blue coupe stopped at the Andrews Hotel in San Luis Obispo, a town some hundred miles south of Salinas. The driver and his companion registered for a room at 6:15 a.m. as "Mr. and Mrs. Frank Gibson of Sacramento." They remained in the room all day, and checked out at 5:15 p.m., an hour so unusual the desk clerk particularly noticed the man as he paid the bill. The woman acted furtively both on entering and on leaving the hotel, but such behavior was not without precedent in the clerk's experience and he gave it little heed.

At about that hour, a tip reached the Los Angeles *Times* that Kenneth Ormiston was headed south with a woman. That paper called its correspondent in Santa Barbara (which lies about halfway between San Luis Obispo and Los Angeles) and told him to pick up a policeman or highway patrolman and stake out the road; if the blue Chrysler showed up, they were to bring it in for identification of the occupants.

The correspondent, Marshall Selover, city editor of the Santa Barbara *Morning Press,* was tied up with other work; he turned the assignment over to a young reporter, Wallace Moore, who had covered Mrs. McPherson's revival in Fresno in 1922 and was confident he could recognize her.

Moore set out alone in his Dodge brougham; he did not pick up a policeman. After leaving the office at 8:30 p.m., he drove three and a half miles north of the city and parked on the Modoc Road, a crossroad joining the Coast Highway. He waited two hours. At a little before 11 o'clock, a blue Chrysler, license F-31052, came into sight; it was a new car and its smart jauntiness drew his approving attention. A man was driving; a woman sat beside him.

Moore followed the car three or four miles, then hailed the driver and asked him to stop, which he did at Pedrogosa and Bath Streets, just inside the city's northern limits. Moore got out, stepped over to the driver's side of the coupe, and identified himself. "Who are you?" he asked through the open window.

"Frank Gibson. Why?" replied the stranger. His manner was pleasant and relaxed.

"Where are you from?"

"I'm a hardware man from Sacramento. Why?"

"Where are you going?" said the reporter.

"Going to Los Angeles. We're going to the Alexandria Hotel there; reach us any time after nine o'clock tomorrow morning if you want to ask any more questions."

The man wore an overcoat buttoned up, Moore observed, and either a hat or a cap. By the dim glow of the dash light and a nearby street lamp the reporter studied the woman, sitting stiffly as far as she could draw away from him. She wore a narrow-brimmed red hat with a high crown, dark glasses, no gloves, and either a coat or a cape, he wasn't sure which, fastened to the chin. He hesitated; in general build the woman seemed to resemble the evangelist as he recalled her, but this woman appeared older, although the dark glasses and the semi-darkness made it difficult to judge her features.

He nodded and said, "How do you do?"

The woman neither stirred nor spoke a word.

"Well," the reporter told the driver, "you are driving a car fitting the description of the machine Kenneth Ormiston and Mrs. McPherson are supposed to be riding in."

"My God!" exclaimed Gibson. "We'd hate to be mistaken for those two people!"

Moore edged toward the ticklish question. "Is this companion—is this woman your wife?"

Instantly the manner of the driver changed; he grew tense, seemed to relax with an effort, grew tense again, and for a moment Moore thought he was going to open the door and lunge out fighting. The reporter backed off. The man finally snapped angrily, "Of course!"

"Oh, well," said Moore hastily, "I guess this isn't Mrs. McPherson," and went back to his own car, parked just ahead of the blue coupe.

In his windshield mirror Moore saw the Chrysler start up, suddenly swing into Bath Street, and double back northward.

That was the last seen of that blue coupe until the next December.

Moore went back to his city editor and reported that the woman, in his opinion, was not Mrs. McPherson. The *Press* carried the story in its morning edition, stating, "The woman did not resemble Mrs. Mc-

Pherson except in general build." Emphasizing this point, the copy editor inserted a boldface subhead above this sentence: "Does Not Resemble Aimee." The driver of the mysterious car, however, was said to resemble closely photographs of Ormiston. Within twenty-four hours furtive women wearing dark glasses and red hats, riding in blue automobiles, were being sighted all over northern California.

Wallace Moore's encounter in the night occurred at about 11 p.m. on Saturday, May 29. At 10:48 p.m. on May 29, the hopes of the Temple searchers at Ocean Park soared when the highest tide since May 18 came in; but no sea-battered remains washed ashore. Also on May 29, Captain Ed Harrison, the Santa Catalina diver, died in a Los Angeles hospital of a ruptured appendix and pneumonia, induced, doctors believed, by his strenuous diving in the cold water off Ocean Park in search of Aimee McPherson's body. He was mourned by a widow and two children.

Last Farewell

Sunday taxed the police all along the ocean front. The Memorial Day holiday brought a crowd of 25,000, and intricate plans were laid for handling the morbid throng in case Mrs. McPherson's body was recovered: the body would be brought to Lick Pier and the pier cleared, until an unmarked hearse could transport it to a mortuary. Meanwhile, an airplane would fly over Angelus Temple and waggle to inform Mrs. Kennedy.

Mother presided at Memorial Day services in the Temple before overflow crowds, preaching from the "Light and Darkness" sermon notes left by Sister on the sand. While she was preaching an airplane hired by the Temple scattered red and white roses over the spot where Sister was last seen. Reverent followers lined the water's edge, kneeling, heads uncovered, while a loudspeaker tuned to the Temple service brought the sobs of the congregation there as basso Thomas Johnson sang "Asleep in the Deep." When Mother's voice uttered the words "light out of darkness," a heavy mist rolled in rapidly from the ocean, blotting out the entire scene. This was accepted as a supernatural omen, the curtain of oblivion closing over the tragedy.

There was no oblivion. Two days later, thousands in the city were startled by the report that a lawyer in Long Beach was in contact with Aimee Semple McPherson's kidnapers.

R. A. McKinley was a cousin of the twenty-fifth President. He had been blinded by a gun explosion in Cuba in the Spanish-American war, came to California from Idaho, and in 1916 was admitted to the bar. In 1926 he had a scratch practice in Long Beach, a seaside city flanking Los Angeles on the south; his clients ran mostly to bootleggers and petty offenders.

On Monday, May 31, at 9:30 a.m., Long Beach Detective Captain Worley received a telephone call from McKinley, who asked Worley to come over to his office in the Pacific-Southwest Building because he had some important information. Accompanied by another detective, Lieutenant Alyea, Worley went right over. It was the Memorial Day business holiday and McKinley was alone. The blind lawyer greeted the policemen with, "Worley, you know I get more information from the underworld than any other man in Long Beach."

Worley agreed this was true. McKinley then told him that two men, calling themselves Miller and Wilson, had come into his office half an hour before. After assuring themselves that he was really blind, they said they had come to him because he could neither identify nor follow them. They were holding Aimee McPherson, they said, for a ransom of $25,000. They wanted McKinley to go to Mother Kennedy and arrange for payment of this sum and obtain her promise of immunity from arrest, no questions to be asked; for this they were willing to split with him, giving him $5000. He could inform the police if he liked and they expected he would, but if he tried to double-cross them neither his life nor Mrs. McPherson's would be "worth a nickel."

Worley declined to make any move until they talked with District Attorney Keyes and Captain Cline. However, he did call Mother Kennedy and imparted to her a little of what McKinley related.

"I don't believe it," was Mother's response. She was on her way to attend Ed Harrison's funeral; she had contributed a wreath.

On their way out of the building, Worley and Alyea asked the elevator operator whether he had brought up two men that morning. Yes, he had; he couldn't remember what they looked like, but he thought they got off at the second floor. McKinley's office was on the second floor. The gate at the foot of the stairway was locked, as was customary on Sundays and holidays, so the only entrance to or egress from the building was by the elevator.

The next morning, June 1, Worley, Alyea, and McKinley were at Keyes' office by appointment; Cline and the district attorney were waiting. McKinley retold his story. Cline was not interested, said he didn't believe there were any kidnapers, it was all a myth, Mrs. McPherson was drowned. Besides, Mrs. Kennedy would never put out $25,000 without absolute proof that her daughter was alive.

Alyea protested. Didn't they think the lead worth investigating?

"It would be a terrible thing," the detective admonished, "if this woman was bound and gagged and being tortured, it would be a terrible thing not to investigate and try to apprehend the criminals and get her away from them."

Cline repeated, "There's nothing to it."

Worley suggested that Mrs. Kennedy might write out some questions which only she and her daughter could answer correctly and these could be passed along to McKinley's contacts; if they brought back the right answers, that would be proof they were holding Mrs. McPherson.

Keyes listened to the discussion in silence. Finally he told Worley to go ahead; there would be no comeback on him if the scheme misfired. Cline then called Mother Kennedy at the Temple and explained the stratagem to her.

"I don't believe it," Mother said again, but she would do anything to stop the wicked rumors.

McKinley went back to his office in Long Beach. Cline, Worley, and Alyea went to the Temple and were handed four questions which Mother jotted on a slip of paper:

1—Describe hammock at home in Canada and where it was.
2—Describe my dog at home on farm and give name.
3—Describe dining-room stove at home.
4—Who was Wallace at our home?

Cline looked hard at the name Wallace, but said nothing. Worley and Alyea drove to Long Beach and gave the questions to McKinley. The attorney cautioned the policemen not to hang around, saying he was blind and helpless, and the kidnapers, if they suspected a trap, could shoot him down with impunity. Bernice Morris, McKinley's secretary, who perforce had been told what was afoot because she served as his eyes, was thrilled. Excitedly she begged, when the kidnapers brought back the answers, to be permitted to take them to the Temple herself.

The mysterious Miller and Wilson did not appear at the appointed time. But late that night, between 10 and 10:30 o'clock, they slipped into the office and took the questions away with them, McKinley reported. The elevator operator confirmed that two men got off at the second floor at about that time.

Mother Kennedy was of two minds. Harassed by the public clamor, but strong in her persuasion that her daughter was dead, she turned to the one person whose friendship and counsel she leaned on, Judge Hardy. The judge was inclined to discount the whole episode, but on an off chance he called the Burns office and hired operatives to shadow McKinley and his office day and night, in the hope of getting a glimpse of Miller and Wilson. Judge Hardy told the police nothing about this private enterprise.

The day after McKinley's revelation, the kidnaping theory was given a fillip by a police officer's finding on the street a scribbled note in a woman's handwriting, apparently thrown out of a moving car. "Help. They took me to cabin in Bouquet," it read. Search of Bouquet Canyon, beyond Saugus forty miles northeast of Los Angeles, revealed a shack that showed signs of having been occupied recently: there were two beds, one in each room of the shack, made up with clean linen but tousled; on one bed was a pink crepe de Chine nightgown.

The crank letters were raining. One Minnie showed to reporters with relish. "Mother darling," was its succinct message, "pay the money." Mother laughed. That was the last thing Aimee would write, she said. To prove to Temple followers, if not to the public, that there were no "new witnesses," she took statements from Emma Schaffer, hotel manager Langan and the Temple woman who had heard a cry while sitting on Lick Pier, and released them in affidavit form. They added nothing. She took no statement from Sylvia Oberman.

To clear the record, Captain Cline started a final, sweeping investigation by questioning Mother Kennedy and Emma Schaffer all over again. Mother said she welcomed his action: "I hope he will look into everything. He will find we are not people who owe money, that we pay our bills and conduct our business affairs along business lines. Our finances are all right. We are not broke. Oh, why," she blurted as tears welled in her eyes, "can't they let Sister alone! If the President of the United States had gone in swimming as Sister did, it would be said he drowned! We know she is with God!"

Suddenly Cline departed northward for San Francisco, to look, he said, into two mysteries: the whereabouts of Kenneth Ormiston, and a statement given to the newspapers by Mrs. Francis B. Marshall, of the Wayfarers Pentecostal Mission in San Francisco.

Mrs. Marshall, who had long known Mrs. McPherson, said that on Saturday, May 29 (the day "Mr. and Mrs. Frank Gibson" spent in a hotel in San Luis Obispo), she saw Sister in a car with several other people on Market Street. She was startled and called out to the evangelist, but the car sped away. The next day, she said, she received a telephone call from a man whose voice she recognized as that of one of Sister's high-ranking assistants; he dictated a message which he requested her to give to the press "to stop ridiculous rumors." The message:

> Aimee Semple McPherson is not dead. She is not kidnaped. She was not drowned. She is not sick. There is a reason for her remaining in seclusion which must not be known now. She has a right to live her own life in privacy. She will return to Angelus Temple about June sixteenth with reasons for her actions.

Cline got no further information from Mrs. Marshall, but she stuck to her identifications.

The elusive Ormiston had been sending letters to Captain Taylor since he wandered away from the Central Police Station in Los Angeles on the 27th. The first, mailed in San Francisco at 3 p.m. on May 28, under a special-delivery stamp, reached Los Angeles at 9:30 a.m. on the 29th. It announced:

> I returned to S.F. and have been thinking that perhaps those two worthy gentlemen from the Sheriff's office [Deputies Hanby and Humber] or some of the ambitious newspaper boys will feel that I have again mysteriously disappeared. Kindly assure them that such is not the case—that I had your assurance that nothing further was desired of me—that I was free to return.

Having explained his casual leavetaking, the writer went on to say that he expected to continue to use assumed names for reasons Taylor was aware of, and would be moving around, had no fixed address, "but in consideration of your very kind treatment of me, I feel that the right thing to do is to keep in touch with you." He hoped Taylor would not inform the newspapers and put reporters on his trail again; because he wished to avoid the San Francisco press; he was not staying with his parents, but was in communication with them.

The second letter, on the stationery of the St. Mark Hotel in Oakland, across the bay from San Francisco, was mailed later on the 28th, at 11:30 p.m.

The letterhead is self-explanatory. "The name is K. Gladstone—
these being my first two names. I see the Frisco crowd has gone crazy,
too. Poor Sister (according to the papers) has been seen in half a
dozen places there today. I do hope her body is recovered quickly.

On May 31, Taylor received a third letter, dated "Hotel St. Mark, May
30th, 1926. Sunday morning." (This was the morning after Wallace
Moore's night adventure with a blue Chrysler coupe and its two occupants.)

Newspapers say I drove through Salinas southbound yesterday with
a "strange woman." It's just movie bunk. I loaned my car to my
good friend Gibson & he took his wife south—I think as far as L.A.
—so there's your "strange woman." As for me, I'm still here in Oakland but think I will move on tomorrow to a fruitful territory for my
radio work.

This letter, mailed at 4:30 on the afternoon of the 30th, was followed
on May 31 by a special-delivery letter considerably longer and more
vehement in regard to the Santa Barbara incident. It fumed:

It is utterly absurd the way the newspapers continue to use my name,
and the mass of lies they print concerning me and my movements.
Apparently they have absolutely no regard for the truth. . . . The
famous "mystery car" and the mysterious "veiled lady" and all the
gibberish these newshounds have cooked up—my gosh! I think yellow
journalism is committing one of the greatest crimes of all time. I
have sent a brief statement to several of the papers which I hope
they will have the decency to print.

On the day this energetic communication reached Captain Taylor
(June 1) the San Francisco *Chronicle* received a letter signed by Ormiston appealing for "a little fair play. I have not 'mysteriously disappeared'
nor am I missing."

Cline's researches confirmed that "K. Gladstone" had been registered
at the St. Mark Hotel on May 28, 29, and 30, but nobody at the hotel
recalled what he looked like. The senior Ormiston told Cline he had not
heard from his son for a week and did not know where he was. The
detective chief appealed to Kenneth through the newspapers to come
forward and be questioned. Receiving no response, he left a letter at
General Delivery and returned to Los Angeles. His temper was wearing
thin. He announced that the police investigation was at an end. "We're
through. We believe she is drowned and will not run down any more

wild rumors and clues," his ultimatum said. In his opinion the "Re-vengers" letter and the McKinley contacts were simply attempts by somebody to bunco the Temple out of money.

District Attorney Keyes confessed that he was mystified, but, having thought it over since his threat to intervene, he had decided that until some evidence of a crime was produced he did not propose to take action.

"If by any chance Mrs. McPherson is alive," he pointed out, "she is perfectly at liberty to do what she wishes and go where she chooses."

Mother Kennedy, also, was eager to close the dreadful incident. On June 3 she described herself as resigned to God's will, if her daughter's body should never be found. She took Rolf to the beach that day, and together they cast white carnations on the ocean from Lick Pier, stand-ing midway between the Fun House and the Giant Flip.

On June 4 Minnie said the beach-patrol headquarters would be closed, but the search would continue. And at the urgent solicitation of Cline, she announced that the $25,000 reward offer would be withdrawn at midnight; Cline was concerned with shutting off the cranks.

The next morning the city was shaken by a report that Mrs. McPher-son was in Edmonton, Alberta, located there by "Inspector Middleton of the Royal Northwest Mounted Police."

"Oh," wailed Mother Kennedy, "now a million Aimee McPhersons will be seen over the country within a month!" But, she added on second thought, "If Mrs. McPherson is in Edmonton, I want her brought back here right away!"

The excitement turned out to be a farce of mistaken identity; Miss Zelma Argue, sister of the Reverend Watson B. Argue, interviewed the stranger supposed to be Aimee and reported with authority that she was not the evangelist.

Said Cline again, "She is dead." But stung by allegations that the Temple was becoming afraid to risk its money, Mother Kennedy hastily renewed the $25,000 reward offer—for one more week only.

Thereafter for nearly two weeks lassitude overcame the press and public. After the lapse of a full month since her daughter had disappeared, Mother announced plans for an elaborate memorial service to be held at the Temple on Sunday, June 20. This day of rejoicing for Sister's victory won (so Mother decreed it should be viewed) was organized and advertised with enthusiasm. There were to be delegations from the branch churches and special music at three services, morning, afternoon, and evening.

In the midst of the preparations, the newspapers picked up the thread again fleetingly in a dispatch from Coos Bay, Oregon, where a badly decomposed body had washed ashore; authorities hoped to establish the identity through the fillings in the teeth. Mother Kennedy went about her business; Coos Bay, she said, was a thousand miles away, and Aimee had no fillings in her teeth.

On June 18, exactly one month after the pastor had vanished, Coroner Frank Nance for a second time turned down a request that he issue a death certificate. "I am yet to be convinced that Mrs. McPherson is dead," he ruled formally. "I also doubt if Miss Schaffer has told all she knows."

On June 19 in the daily batch of unsought communications reaching Angelus Temple was a special-delivery letter, addressed to Mrs. Minnie Kennedy. It had been mailed the day before on a railroad train between El Paso, Texas, and Tucson, Arizona. It was dated June 18. Two pages long, closely typewritten, it was signed "The Avengers," and it referred to the May 24 "Revengers" ransom note and renewed the demand for $500,000. Minnie was told she had one week to raise the money; another letter would instruct her how to make the payment by a method that was a "corker." There were allusions to developments in the case which anybody might have read in any one of hundreds of newspapers, but the letter also contained two startling elements: (1) a lock of reddish auburn hair, said to be Aimee's, and (2) answers to two of the four test questions that Mother Kennedy had given to Attorney McKinley.

To "Describe hammock at home in Canada and where it was" the answer was, "A woven wire one between two apple trees." The answer to "Describe my dog on farm at home and give name" was, "The hound was black and named Gyp." Both answers were correct. The letter also said, "Her middle right-hand finger has a scar on it you ought to recognize," and the kidnapers suggested that they might chop that finger off and send it along if Minnie needed any more convincing. When she was a child, Aimee's right middle finger had been accidentally gashed by a corn hook in the hand of a hired man on the family farm near Ingersoll, Ontario.

The "Avengers" reassured Mother that her daughter, although "suffering with hysteria and the heat," was well, having "been taken good care of by a woman who has been with her constantly." If the ransom was not forthcoming, the kidnapers said, their only alternative would be to "sell her to old Felipe of Mexico City. We are sick and tired of her infernal preaching, she spouts scripture in answer to everything."

To the thousands gathering at Angelus Temple early in the morning of Sunday June 20 this letter was not divulged. The turnout for the final farewell to their beloved founder, asleep in the bosom of the Lord or in the tenebrous recesses of the sea, was worthy of her who even in death proved a champion crowd-getter. An estimated seventeen thousand persons sorrowed under the hand-painted, sky-blue, cloud-flecked dome of the Temple during the day, and millions followed the three services by radio.

At the morning session five thousand white satin badges emblematic of the spirit of the lost leader were distributed. Mother recapitulated the unparalleled effort made to recover Sister's body, and consoled the weeping flock: "We did not think it would be recovered. Her young body was too precious to Jesus."

The delegations from the branch churches swelled the afternoon attendance, each led by its pastor, in many cases a woman. They brought masses of flowers which they banked around Sister's pulpit chair; Mother said the chair would remain empty permanently. In the evening she told emotionally of Sister's early struggles, and displayed Sister's blue pulpit cape as a relic. A photograph of Sister hung above the pulpit, and Roberta and Doctors Shreve and Argue assisted in the eulogies and the hymn-singing. Memorial music was furnished by the Temple band, quartets, choir, and soloists.

A memorial collection was taken, to defray the expense of completing the Bible School building. One by one the heads of the departments— the ushers, the orderlies, the Prayer Tower group, the Foursquare City Sisters, the Brotherhood, the elders, the commissary, the Cradle Roll officers, the choir, the orchestra, the Bible School students, the cleaning squads, the praying janitors, the book store, the publications office, the radio staff, the Children's Church members—one by one they stepped forward and pledged their offerings. The branch churches each gave their bit. By telephone from radio listeners, by mail from every state and overseas, came gifts. Rumor had it that $40,000 was collected during the day. Somber amid the great rededication, faithful Emma Schaffer, grim-lipped, hollow-eyed, sat swathed from head to foot in funereal black.

Sensation-sated Los Angeles read accounts of the farewell and turned with relief to fresher topics. The delicious lull lasted three days.

At 7:30 a.m. on Wednesday, June 23, Captain Herman Cline was ringing the doorbell of the Temple residence. What, he demanded of sleepy Mother Kennedy, did she know about the news he had received that her daughter had escaped from kidnapers in Arizona or Mexico?

Minnie heard in a daze. "I don't believe it," she said firmly. "I just can't believe it!"

The telephone rang. Cline had arranged the call. It was long distance, from Douglas, Arizona. Minnie took the receiver while Cline listened in.

Five minutes later the household was in an uproar, Rolf tearing into his sister's room to wake her and tell her the news, Roberta stammering in amazed excitement. Hovering on the stairs, Emma Schaffer wept silently.

What Minnie heard, coming over the prosaic wires of the Pacific Telephone and Telegraph Company, was the undeniably living voice of her daughter, Aimee Elizabeth Kennedy Semple McPherson.

THEME II

Resurrection and Ribaldry

"If an angel should come down from Heaven and tell my people that Sister is not the child of God—they wouldn't believe it."

—AIMEE SEMPLE MCPHERSON

A Truancy Report

Frederick Conrad Schansel was the custodian of a slaughterhouse a mile and a half outside the border town of Agua Prieta, Sonora, Mexico. The day had been hot, the temperature hovering around 100 all afternoon, and Schansel had turned in peeled down to his underwear and little of that. Shortly after midnight he was awakened by the barking of his dogs. Stepping out of the shed that was his home, he dimly made out a woman, pressed against the gate.

"Do you have a telephone?" she called.

Schansel shook his head. "No phone. Who you?"

"Can you tell me where I can find a telephone?" the woman repeated. "I must reach the police."

"What's matter? What you done?"

"I haven't done anything! I want help—the police! Do you have an automobile? A horse?"

The puzzled caretaker had neither. "Who you?" he queried again.

"The world knows who I am."

Schansel grunted derisively. He was used to American women who crossed the line to get drunk. Nevertheless, she seemed to need help.

"You come inside, rest," he suggested in guttural English. "It'll be morning pretty soon."

His midnight caller eyed the Schansel underwear unfavorably. "Do you have a wife? Are there ladies in there?"

"No," replied the stolid German. "You come in. I get dressed."

Yelling to the dogs to stop their din, he went inside. When he returned in the full propriety of overalls, the woman was struggling up the road toward the village. He saw her stumble once or twice. When she entered the town, where the lights of the saloons were still blazing, Schansel turned around and went back to his interrupted slumber, never imagining that this midnight summons was to carry him and his underwear into international renown.

55

Ramon R. Gonzales of Agua Prieta—former barber, former *presidente* or mayor of the town of Cananea, former dealer in cattle feed, now proprietor of the respectable O.K. Bar purveying wine and beer to thirsty visitors from prohibition-arid Arizona—closed up his place at 1 a.m. on June 23, 1926, and walked to his home a few blocks away on Second Street. The electric light in the hall was turned on; his wife Theresa always left it on until he came in; it vaguely illuminated the pleasant fenced garden in front. Gonzales undressed and lay down on the bed. Theresa was in bed but awake. Ramon smoked a cigarette while listening for a friend who had promised to drop by and let him know when they should start on a trip to an outlying rancho in the morning. The hall light was left burning.

Out of the night Gonzales heard a woman calling. "Hello! Hello!"

"Hello!" called back the startled Gonzales, adding in Spanish, "Come in!"

A dim figure appeared outside the window, and a woman's voice asked whether he had a telephone. The Gonzales home had no phone.

"Do you think I could find a telephone in the next block or close by?" the stranger asked. Her voice sounded excited.

Ramon answered, "You wait here. I get dressed. I come out."

A minute later, when he came to the front door, the woman was not in sight. Theresa, noticing that the garden gate was ajar, went to close it, and gasped, "She is here!"

Running out, Gonzales saw the woman prone on the garden path, half in and half out of the gate, her head toward the street, one arm thrown up. She appeared to be unconscious.

Gonzales lifted her; the body was cold and limp. He could feel no pulse. To his staring wife he said, "I think the *señora* is dead!"

The best course in such an emergency obviously is to notify the authorities. The town presidente, Ernesto Boubion, lived across the street. Gonzales ran there, but the mayor was not at home. Gonzales ran back and called to his wife to fetch a lamp; by its light he observed with relief that one of the woman's eyes was half open and the eyelid twitching.

The couple lifted the inert form to the porch and Theresa placed a pillow under the head crowned by a mass of auburn hair neatly confined in a silk net. She wore no hat. They threw a quilt over her, and Theresa set to work rubbing her arms with alcohol. For an hour she worked; finally the woman revived.

In his limited English Gonzales asked where she was from. Los Angeles, she replied weakly. Thinking she might have come in a party, he asked whether she had a husband. No; she shook her head. Any family? Yes, mother and two children in Los Angeles. Then she broke into a rapid monologue that was lost on her Spanish-speaking hosts.

Sighting Presidente Boubion entering his house across the way, Gonzales called him over. By now it was well after 3 o'clock.

"What shall we do with this lady?" asked the worried Gonzales. "She seems to be a stranger here."

"Get an interpreter," ordered Boubion, whose English was no better.

The American bartender at the Gem Saloon spoke Spanish, but he refused to come over while there were still customers to serve. Get Johnny Anderson, the jitney driver, he suggested. Gonzales hunted up the taximan who made a business of carrying tourists back and forth from Douglas, on the Arizona side.

Anderson found the strange woman lying on the porch, covered with the quilt, her hair disheveled. After some conversation in English, the jitney man informed the three Mexicans in Spanish that this woman was saying she was Aimee Semple McPherson, the evangelist in Los Angeles who was supposed to have drowned in the Pacific Ocean five weeks ago; she said she was kidnaped and had escaped from her abductors somewhere in the desert about noon the day before and had been walking ever since.

As the crow flies, with a brisk tail wind, across mountains and deserts, from Ocean Park to Agua Prieta is five hundred and fifty miles inland.

Boubion instructed Anderson to take her across the line into Douglas and let her talk to the police there. Gonzales and Anderson lifted her into the jitney and it drove away.

The presidente turned to Ramon. Had the señora drunk any water? Yes, said Ramon, when she first came to, she asked for a drink and Theresa brought her a glass of water. She drank it.

"One glass?" asked Boubion.

No, corrected Theresa; while Ramon was hunting the jitney man, she gave the lady another glass.

"Two glasses." Boubion regarded his neighbors in thoughtful silence, turned on his heel, and stalked to his own house.

Aimee Semple McPherson? To Gonzales the name meant nothing. He was thinking about those two glasses of water.

At 3:45 a.m., June 23, 1926, George W. Cook, night watchman, truant officer, and special policeman on duty from midnight to 4 o'clock, was standing in front of the Douglas police station waiting for his relief. Johnny Anderson drove up in his jitney and parked across the street. He came over to Cook in considerable excitement and said he had a woman in his car who claimed to be Aimee McPherson. Cook stepped over to investigate: women picked up in Agua Prieta in a dazed or uncertain condition at 3 o'clock in the morning were not unusual; he put them down on the report sheet as "drunk" or "full of dope."

Slumped on the front seat of the car, in apparent collapse, was a woman with auburn hair strewn over her shoulders. Weakly, nervously, she identified herself as Mrs. McPherson, and said she wanted to get in touch with her family in Los Angeles as quickly as possible. Anderson interrupted with sketchy details of her asserted escape from kidnapers in Mexico and her flight across the desert until she hit Agua Prieta. To Cook the woman seemed to be speaking the truth, and she certainly looked dead beat; he told Anderson to take her to the city's only hospital, the Calumet and Arizona; he would go along in his own car and arrange for her admission.

Just then O. E. Patterson, Cook's relief, drove up, was given the facts, and followed the jitney to the hospital in a city car. On arrival, Patterson stepped to the door of the taxi and with Anderson helped the exhausted woman out of the car. Cook, walking slowly behind them as they supported her, one on either side, saw her ankles give way two or three times as she stumbled the thirty feet up the drive; each time she would "brace up" and take a few steps, then her ankles would buckle again.

As police officer on duty, Cook accompanied the group to a private room where he saw the woman deposited on the bed by her escorts. The men then stepped into the hall while Nurse Margaret Attaway undressed the patient. Then Cook went into the room again to get the facts for his report. Apologetically he told the patient he would have to smell her breath.

With a smile the woman in bed opened her mouth wide and puffed into the patrolman's face. No smell of liquor there, he assured her. (Later he was to specify that the breath smelled like "I don't know whether you call it a constipated breath, but like my own breath when my stomach is empty or a person is upset.") He picked up a pair of dusty kid slippers under the bed and asked her if they were hers. Not hers, the woman said, but shoes given to her by Rose, one of her kidnapers, and she had been wearing them. Cook looked them over and noticed scuff marks on the soles. He looked around for the clothing the woman wore into the hospital, but it had been taken away. The patient held out her wrists and Cook saw red splotches or welts which she said were marks caused by the rope with which she had been tied. Nurse Meriba Shinn then entered with a glass of lemonade the patient had asked for, and the woman drank it. Cook departed to make his report.

The drama of Aimee's restoration to the world seemed to be getting off to a depressing start—her first landfall a slaughterhouse and the first policeman she encountered a truant officer who smelled her breath. But as in any well-knit play, with the entrance of the star the pace quickened.

While bathing her patient, Nurse Shinn removed two or three cactus thorns from one ankle and remarked two small blisters on her toes; otherwise her physical condition seemed good—no sunburn, lips not parched, cracked, or swollen, tongue not swollen, color normal, no signs of emaciation or dehydration. The medical chart showed her temperature 98, pulse 72, respiration 20.

By now other police officers were reaching the scene—Chief Percy Bowden and Sergeant A. B. Murchison, as well as Patterson—and a reporter, William McCafferty, editor of the Douglas *Daily Dispatch*. McCafferty had covered Sister McPherson's revivals in Denver, and all doubt as to her identity was dispelled when he positively recognized her, and she him. They shook hands delightedly.

To the police clustered around her bed she told her story in greater detail, begging them to get in touch with the Los Angeles police at once and ask them to break the news gently to her mother; she feared the shock would be too great if she called direct. Also, warn Los Angeles that from remarks she had overheard while a prisoner she believed the same gang planned to abduct other prominent citizens, including Mary Pickford. And please, please, tell them to guard Roberta. All the officers noted that she appeared exhausted and nervous, but spoke clearly and energetically. Bowden and Patterson confirmed the welts on her wrists.

At 6 o'clock a telephone call was put through to the Los Angeles police; Captain Cline was aroused and took the news himself, dressed, and hastened out to Angelus Temple. Just after 7:30 a connection was made with the Temple residence and Mrs. McPherson spoke with her mother; McCafferty listened to the conversation at one end while Cline listened at the other.

Weeping and repeatedly becoming hysterical and incoherent, Aimee assured her mother that she really was alive and unharmed, mentioning facts of family history, should there be any doubt of her identity: that Minnie Kennedy had had a sister named Nickerson; that Minnie's maiden name was Pierce; that Aimee's childhood pets were a black cat with a white tail called White Tail and a pigeon named Jamie; and how Aimee as a little girl was cut on the finger with a corn hook in the hand of a hired man. Minnie Kennedy, from the moment she heard the familiar voice, was never in doubt.

By 8 o'clock McCafferty had an extra on the street screaming the biggest news story Douglas ever had, and Aimee, abundantly identified, had finished her breakfast of poached egg, oatmeal, and an orange, and was sitting up in bed curling her hair with an iron borrowed from Nurse Shinn. The one certainty the returned evangelist could look forward to during the next few hours was an onslaught of reporters and photographers; and while the Lord had blessed her with beautiful hair, He had neglected to put a natural wave in it.

The Story of a Crime

The reporters descended, literally from the sky, in chartered airplanes. From the west, the north, the east, by train and automobile. Aimee's disappearance at Ocean Park had happened just too late for the last editions of the afternoon papers; her reappearance occurred just too late for the morning papers, and the afternoons had their sweet inning. From Maine to Saskatchewan, from Miami to Walla Walla, all day the extras rolled out as details of the famous evangelist's harrowing experience were relayed from her willing lips.

"Let the reporters in!" she remonstrated with the nurse when the latter protested she should rest. "I just can't refuse to tell them my story. They will tell it to hundreds of thousands." Again and again fresh waves of cameramen and news writers surged into her room, and again and again she dramatically recounted her astonishing ordeal.

Douglas, a copper-smelting town of 13,000 in the Arizona desert, declared a holiday. The thrilled townsfolk drenched Calumet Hospital with flowers. Mayor Kenton was photographed at Sister's bedside. Throngs milled in and out of the hospital until the nurses could hardly move about their duties. Outside hundreds of curious loitered in the blazing sun, watching the coming and going of peace officers and state and city officials. On the veranda outside Aimee's front room groups knelt and sang hymns or chanted prayers of thanksgiving. The telegraph companies and the railroad hustled in extra telegraphers and cleared circuits to transmit a deluge of words. And everywhere went up a surge of sympathy for a woman cruelly used, and of wrath against her abductors. Newspapers from coast to coast headlined her agony. WOMAN EVANGELIST ESCAPES ABDUCTORS, read the front page of the New York *Times*. AIMEE TORTURED FOR HUGE RANSOM, cried the Los Angeles *Examiner*. EVANGELIST RELATES STORY OF TORTURE BY KIDNAPERS; ANXIOUS TO GET HOME, headlined the Los Angeles *Times*.

Los Angeles reporters, the first big-city newspapermen to reach the scene in numbers, found Aimee reclining against a pile of pillows on a tiny white cot. Her hair streamed around her shoulders, her face was pale and rather drawn, but she appeared cheerful. The room was banked with flowers. The evangelist wore a pink silk dressing gown over a white silk negligee, gifts of Douglas friends. As the reporters pushed into the room, she was telling callers kneeling beside the cot, "God has resurrected me from the dead."

She greeted the news delegation cordially, and her first questions were for her family and Angelus Temple. "Angelus Temple is my life!" she exclaimed. "Nothing else amounts to anything."

From what she had overheard, she was convinced that her abduction was part of a plan by a billion-dollar crime syndicate to kidnap movie stars for ransom. She exhibited burns on her fingers inflicted, she said, with a lighted cigar when her kidnapers tried to compel her to divulge information that would help them collect $500,000. Her feet, the reporters gathered, were covered with blisters raised by her long flight from a shack somewhere in Mexico, while her ankles, reposing snugly under the sheet, were said to be bruised and torn by ropes. The *Examiner* staff man excitedly wired, "Her shoes were virtually cut to shreds!"

Facing the cameras, the evangelist feared she had aged and looked haggard. Reporters reassured her.

"Why, I look twenty years older!" she protested. "Just look at the wrinkles and circles under my eyes! Aren't they terrible?"

To the reporters deep lines were more apparent around her mouth, and they recorded her statement that she had lost weight during her captivity.

Pressed to tell her story, she stipulated that she be allowed to tell it straight through, without interruptions, and warned that she would not be able to account for dates, times, or places, because she had been chloroformed, gagged, blindfolded, and kept locked up entirely out of touch or communication with the outside world. The story, the reporters agreed, pictured one of the most sensational abductions in police annals.

The evangelist started with her going to Ocean Park on May 18, and told the incidents leading up to the time when she went in swimming, confirming what Emma Schaffer had told again and again. At that point, her story diverged from Emma's.

While the secretary was making the telephone call to the Temple, Aimee said, she swam out almost to the end of Lick Pier, circled, and swam back. A lifeguard class was being drilled just where she came out, she said, and she paused, standing about knee-deep in the water. (Emma had said there were no lifeguards on the beach.) Suddenly she heard a woman call, "Oh, Mrs. McPherson!"

She was surprised, because she believed nobody knew she was at the beach except the Temple. Her accoster was a woman with black hair and brown eyes in a full face, husky, weighing about 180 pounds, and dressed plainly. There was a man beside her, heavy-set, clean-shaven, with brown hair and fair complexion.

"Oh, Mrs. McPherson," the woman pleaded. "My baby is dying. I would be ever so happy if you would just come over and pray for my baby." She said the baby was in an automobile parked by the bathhouse, and they both urged her to come right away.

"I told them I must first go to the hotel and get my clothes," she continued. "This seemed to disturb the man and woman. They told me they could not wait. But before I went further, I wanted to know how they had found out I was at the beach. They told me they had gone to the Temple and I had just left. They said Mrs. Kennedy had told them I was at the beach and that she was certain I would be glad to administer to the dying baby.

"This sounded so much like Mother Kennedy I believed them. The woman had a large black coat over her arm and this she threw around my shoulders. We walked across the sand over to the boardwalk that runs parallel to Lick Pier. Just as we neared the bathhouse, the woman left us and ran ahead to a sedan automobile parked alongside the bathhouse with the engine running. When I reached the car there was another man in the front seat at the driver's wheel. The woman sat far back in the rear seat with a bundle of blankets in her arms. This, of course, I thought was the baby.

"I was barefooted with only my bathing suit and the coat around me, and I hesitated about getting into the machine. I placed one foot on the running board.

"Just as I did, the man stepped up behind me and pushed me headlong into the machine. Before the wink of an eye, the woman had thrown the blanket over my head. I didn't have time to make any outcry, and the first thing I realized a sponge was pressed against my nostrils. It gave forth a sickly odor.

"That was the last I remembered until I came to, desperately ill, perhaps hours and hours later. It seemed to be dawn.

"A woman was bending over me. I recognized her at once as the same woman who had approached me at the beach. I was lying on an old iron bed, vomiting severely. It was a terrible room, a small one. There was only one window, boarded up almost to the top. The only furniture was a chair, the bed, a table, and a dresser. I imagined we were somewhere near Calexico, as I heard them speak of the place. It was a two-story house, as I heard footsteps above me. The only light was from a kerosene lamp.

"Then I heard the woman call, 'Steve,' and a man walked in. It was the very same man who was with the woman on the beach and who pushed me into the auto. He did most of the talking and appeared to be the ringleader. He told me frankly what had happened and that I was being held for ransom, although he did not tell me the amount at that time.

" 'You've taken enough of our girls, and turn about is fair play,' he told me. I imagined he was connected with the white slavers or dopesters.

"From overhearing their conversations I gleaned that they were holding me for $500,000. I begged them to take me home or telephone my mother, but they scoffed at me. I paced the floor like a tiger. It was terrible—the suspense and worry about Angelus Temple and Mother and the children. Then one day they came into the room with a piece of paper."

In an aside, the evangelist explained, "The woman was always there. She was called 'Rosie' and she always called me 'dearie.' "

Thus disposing of the proprieties, she resumed her narrative.

"They asked me to write a letter to my mother and told me they wanted $500,000 ransom. I told them it couldn't be raised.

" 'Why, you've got a million dollars,' Steve told me. I told them I didn't have that much money, that the money was tied up in Angelus Temple and all I had was a deed of trust. They began to question me. They wanted me to describe our hammock in Canada and I told them it was a wire hammock between two apple trees. Then they wanted me to describe our dog. They also wanted a description of the dining-room stove and a description of Wallace. I refused to give them these descriptions, as I had broad suspicions and was afraid if I answered more it would only further their scheme."

Then it was they tortured her. " 'I'll make you talk!' Steve told me." One of them grabbed her and Steve burned her fingers with a lighted cigar. The evangelist held up scarred fingers to attest to this barbarity.

"I told them to go ahead and burn me," she continued. "I never moved my hand. When they saw they couldn't frighten me, they stopped. That was the only time they mistreated me. Once I screamed, but they gagged me and threatened me with violence if I did it again. But they didn't harm me."

Days passed in nightmare procession while she lay on the cot in the white nightgown she had on when she came to; her bathing suit had vanished. Finally the woman gave her an old dress to wear, much too large. The weather, she said, was unbearably hot. Most of the time she was bound hand and foot, but Rose was always in the room with her. One day two men came to the house. They appeared to be elated, and Aimee surmised that they had established contact with her mother.

"It was night when they came," she recounted. "I was blindfolded and taken outside. They threw me into the rear of an auto, bound and gagged, and placed a blanket over me. We drove for hours. I heard another machine following. Finally the auto stopped. They took me to an old shack with one poor room in it. They threw down soldiers' cots for us to sleep on. Rosie slept on a cot next to me.

"Two days later I saw the two men again. They once more demanded that I write a letter to my mother. I refused, and they cut two locks of hair from my head.

" 'If this doesn't convince your mother, then we'll cut off your finger with the scar on it and send it to her,' Steve told me."

She never saw the two men again, but before they left they brought to the shack an old Mexican whom they called Felipe and threatened to sell her to him if she remained stubborn. Rosie stayed in the shack with her, and kept assuring her that she would be restored to her mother on Friday.

Tuesday afternoon she was left alone for the first time, when Rose went for supplies.

"She bound me with straps and rope and left me on a cot. She left." Aimee described the scene to the rapt listeners. "As I lay on the cot, I noticed a tin can on the floor with a jagged lid. It was square like the cans we use for maple sugar in Canada. I rolled off the cot to the floor and managed to squirm to that can. By rubbing the straps and ropes against the jagged edge of the can, and pulling and tugging, I managed to cut them.

"Then freedom for the first time! But I could hardly stand when I got to my feet. Strength finally came to me. I prayed for help and it came. I got through the window, it wasn't much of a drop, and I started running. I imagine, from the position of the sun, this was about eleven o'clock in the morning. It was hot. I stumbled, as I ran, many times. Finally I sighted a mountain, which later I learned was Niggerhead. You see, all the time I thought I was in the Imperial Valley. I ran on for hours. Finally I came to a fence. My hope went up when finally I came to a road.

"Night descended. I was afraid to sleep, but many times I dropped from sheer exhaustion. Big blisters came on my feet and the pain was terrific. After a while I came to a little shack with a tin roof, and I went to the door and knocked and called. My voice sounded so little. It was vacant, so I came back to the road, and it was getting cold, so I put my dress over my shoulders and wrapped it around me and I lay down. I scraped the dust up in a little bundle for a pillow, thinking I would sleep, and then I would hear a rustle and I thought it was a rattlesnake and I would get up and go on.

"I went on and on until I saw a glow in the sky and thought it must be a village or town. It looked like Heaven in the distance. I saw lights flashing. Finally I saw a shadow, and as I approached it I saw it was a building. Habitation at last! A man came out, attracted by the barking of his dogs. He was dressed in BVDs. I begged him to help me."

There followed details of her slaughterhouse interview, her staggering into Agua Prieta and collapsing in Ramon Gonzales' front yard, and her arrival in Douglas.

"That's all there is to it," she concluded. Just then another reporter arrived, and she started her story over again with tireless verve.

Evincing distress at the rumors that had linked her name with that of Kenneth Ormiston, she implored the correspondents please to do everything in their power to "clear up any misapprehension" that might exist in the public mind. Of course she had not seen Ormiston, she said; he was merely the radio operator at the Temple, that was all there was to it.

A reporter asked a stock question—did she expect to marry again?

She shook her head; she did not believe in remarriage for divorced persons. "My life will always be for Jesus," she said.

Again she inquired anxiously about her family and the Temple. Were the crowds holding up? Told that the crowds were as large as ever, she seemed pleased. "If everything is all right at the church, now I can rest easy." She beamed. "Do you think I will be welcomed back?" A questing glance accompanied the sudden query, then she turned to the heap of congratulatory telegrams that was steadily growing higher.

Newspapers published this account in a thousand towns and cities. The radio spread it to the remotest corners. But there was an ominous footnote. Amid the nationwide rejoicing and calls for swift retribution on the criminals, the sheriff of Cochise County, J. F. McDonald, told a reporter for the nearby Bisbee, Arizona, *Review* that the clothing worn by the evangelist on her estimated fourteen-hour flight across the Sonora wastelands puzzled him.

The country Mrs. McPherson crossed was hilly, composed of rocks and shale, covered with mesquite, cactus, and a plant suggestively named catclaw. Now catclaw, the sheriff pointed out, is hard on clothing; it tears and clings to anything it touches. The sheriff and his deputies had been over in that cactus-bristling region and they came back with their boots scratched and clothing covered with dust. But the clothing worn by Mrs. McPherson was not torn and bore no dust or perspiration stains. He had the clothing, the sheriff added in his soft, desert-man's voice. Yes, he had it, locked in the vault of the First National Bank.

Footprints by the Wayside

Sheriff McDonald had been in Tombstone when his deputy, Walter Morris, telephoned the news at 10 o'clock on the morning of June 23. Cattle rustling, bank holdups, and barroom mayhem the sheriff had coped with for years, but the kidnaping of a famous woman preacher was something new in border lawlessness. He jumped in his car and hustled over to Douglas, reached Calumet Hospital at 11:30 and found the evangelist receiving a stream of callers. He questioned her and picked up her clothing from the nurse. Then he drove into Mexico and scouted.

Before sun-up Sergeant Murchison of the Douglas police, assigned to the case by Chief Bowden, had started into the desert by car with policeman Patterson. In Agua Prieta they were joined by Sylvano Villa, the chief of police there. Their objective was to pick up the trail of the kidnap gang and make quick arrests, and they were armed for action. At about 9 o'clock they were followed by another desert rat, C. E. Cross, mine employee, who had ridden that country as a cowboy since 1889. Murchison himself had punched cattle in Cochise County for twenty years, since before Douglas was built. With Cross were Jack Moore and George Spear, Bisbee newspapermen.

Murchison had made one significant discovery: prints of a woman's shoes leading from the road toward the Schansel slaughterhouse and back again to the road, about a mile and a half east of Agua Prieta. A couple of miles farther east on the road paralleling the international boundary, more prints made by a woman's shoes were found; these led eastward on one side of the road, crossed over and led westward (toward Agua Prieta) on the opposite side for a short distance, then stopped. In their erratic wandering they led to a rough wooden shack with a tin roof used as a rain shelter by Mexican *rurales* patrolling the boundary. This shelter was called a *garita,* which means a sentry box or outdoor privy; it was not much larger.

Toward noon the trackers returned to Douglas, and Cross met Aimee in the hospital for the first time; he noted the red welts on her wrists. Murchison questioned her more closely, this time eliciting two significant details: first, that in her estimated twenty miles of flight she did not at any time *cross* either a road or a fence; second, that the adobe shack from which she escaped had a wooden floor.

The statement about the road and the fence narrowed the field of investigation sharply. Eastward from Agua Prieta ran the international border fence, six to seven feet high. This extended to Niggerhead Mountain, a landmark rising five hundred feet above the mesa some ten miles east of Agua Prieta. Aimee said she made her way *toward* the mountain at first, later turning her back on it when she encountered a road, which she followed and which ultimately conducted her to Agua Prieta. Meandering alongside the border fence, on the Mexican side, was a well-defined road called the Gallardo Road.

From Niggerhead mountain running directly south was the Gallardo Ranch fence, barbed wire, four strands high. This ran to the Cenesas Ranch, a distance of eight or nine miles; it was broken by a gate and cattle guard at that point, then continued on southward. Beside this fence ran a blurred trail, called the Old Road, hardly more than a cattle path in the scrub.

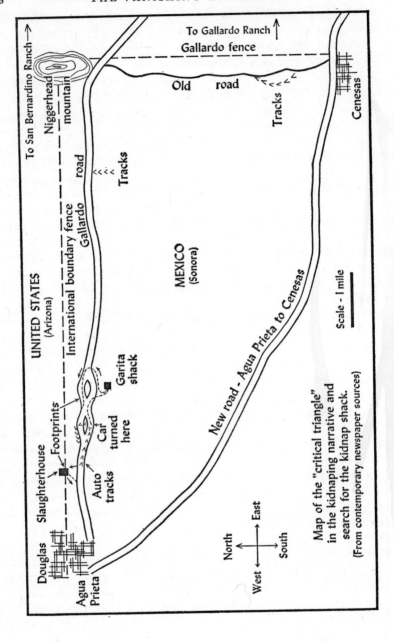

Map of the "critical triangle"
in the kidnaping narrative and
search for the kidnap shack.
(From contemporary newspaper sources)

A good road, plainly marked and frequently traveled, ran from the Cenesas Ranch northwest to Agua Prieta.

Thus the shack from which Aimee escaped must have been inside the triangle enclosed by the international fence on the north, the Gallardo fence on the east, and the Cenesas–Agua Prieta road on the south. Had she approached Agua Prieta from either directly south or southwest, she would not have had Niggerhead Mountain at her back at any time. Had she *entered* the triangle from the east, north, or south, she would have had to *cross* either a fence or a road. The only point at which she could have entered the triangle without crossing either fence or road was—Agua Prieta.

The hue and cry was raised: apprehend the kidnapers! But now, instead of tracks in the dust, the search turned to locating the kidnap shack, around which the abductors were certain to have left telltale traces. Murchison set out again at 1 p.m. with Harold Henry, a reporter for the Douglas *Dispatch;* but first Murchison went to the First National Bank and got one of the shoes Aimee had been wearing. He went back with Henry to the slaughterhouse and compared the imprint of the shoe with the tracks in the fine, clinging sand of decomposed granite. The shoe fitted the tracks perfectly; even the trademark "New Era" on the rubber heel was duplicated in reverse in the footprints, sharply and clearly. The heel was not worn down.

They tried the same test on the tracks around the garita, two miles farther along the border road, but here there were no heel marks that could be identified; otherwise the prints and the shoe appeared to match, both size 5. West of this point they observed tire marks of an automobile that had turned around at an island in the road and headed back toward Agua Prieta; the tracks looked like the latest on the road, Murchison thought, but he attached no significance to them; probably some rancher had driven out that far and turned back.

Meanwhile Cross and Sergeant Patterson were scouting along the border road clear to Niggerhead Mountain. At a point about seven miles out of Agua Prieta, in a sandy wash, they found tracks which appeared to have been made by a woman's number 5 shoe, but there were no identifying heel marks.

Thus all day Wednesday, June 23, the search went on for a Rose and a Steve and their unnamed accomplice. Peace officers on both sides of the line formed posses, cowpunchers and ranchers and miners and reporters rambled around on their own volition, Mexican authorities called in Yaqui Indians, reputed to be the keenest desert trackers in the Southwest; no more tracks were found and no shack fulfilling Aimee's description.

This did not surprise Sergeant Murchison. Before he set out armed with Aimee's statement that her prison hut had a wooden floor, he knew there was no such shack in the area. Inside the triangle were only three isolated huts—an occupied adobe house belonging to a Mexican *vaquero* named Francisco Perez, an old mescal plant built of poles with a thatched roof, and the line riders' garita. An adobe shack with a wooden floor simply did not exist in the architecture of that countryside; Mrs. McPherson's description must be wrong. Nevertheless the search went on: Murchison was not going to risk criticism on the score of want of zeal, especially in view of the prominence of the lady in the case and her undoubted command of the channels of publicity.

The lack of progress was reported to Aimee in her hospital bed; it failed to dampen her spirit. "Won't it be a glorious day," she cried to the reporters, "when Mother and the children arrive here tomorrow!" She fingered a telegram that had just come in from Merle Armitage, a Los Angeles impresario, offering her $10,000 for an appearance in Hollywood Bowl.

"Coming Back, Back, Back . . ."

The return to life of her daughter stunned Minnie Kennedy. There could be no doubt that the person speaking from Douglas was Aimee. But how? What had happened? Minnie groped for an answer.

"I can hardly believe it!" she repeated several times to Captain Cline. "If they kidnaped her and held her for ransom, why didn't they come forward when we offered the $25,000 for her return?"

The reward offer, once extended, had expired finally on June 12; the public pounced on the intriguing fact that nobody in Douglas or Agua Prieta could claim a dime.

"It doesn't seem possible they could snatch her up unseen," Mother went on. "She never listened to strangers, much less carry out their wishes." She was shaken by a fit of trembling, and for a moment Cline thought she was about to collapse; but she recovered, and with the familiar Kennedy determination said, "How she was enticed into the hands of kidnapers is something she alone can explain to my satisfaction!"

From her desk she took a letter and handed it to the detective; it was the "Avengers" ransom letter. There it was, she said, a lock of hair, the answers to two of the questions relayed through McKinley, it tied right in with what Aimee said.

"When did you get this letter, Mrs. Kennedy?" Cline asked.

"I just received it last night, the 22nd," she replied.

Cline's trained eye caught one peculiarity: the letter had come by special delivery, the post-office stamp "Fee Claimed" was on the lower left-hand side of the envelope; but there was no special-delivery stamp. In the space overprinted by the cancellation stamp were two two-cent stamps. They did not quite match the gap and the wavy cancellation lines on them did not join up with those on either side. He put the letter in his pocket.

"Tell me, Mother Kennedy," he said, "who is James Wallace?"

"Well, I will tell you, Captain," Minnie answered, "only I did not want the public to know. James Wallace was Aimee's half-brother. He has been dead many years."

By now reporters were flocking in, telephones were jangling, jubilant church members were arriving at the house and massing in the Temple. The Temple residence was flung open to everybody as Mother snatched a bite of breakfast with reporters surrounding the table.

"Those gypsies!" she exclaimed. "Aimee knew a Steve and a Rose. But they loved her; she had done a great deal for them. They would never have done a thing like this!" She thought a moment. "That other gypsy—I don't know his name—he came to the house, to the back door, when Sister disappeared and there was so much excitement. How he knew about her disappearing I don't know. But he asked, 'Has Sister disappeared?' His face was white and he was scared. Later he came back and asked whether she had been found. I just wonder. . . ."

She told the reporters about the "Avengers" letter. "It made the statement that they had really kidnaped Sister out of spite for the Temple, and wanted to break the work of the Temple and ruin Sister's reputation. We thought they might have telegraphed to Canada and got the information to answer the questions. Our workers advised me not to pay any attention to it.

"I recognized her voice on the phone immediately," she chattered on. "I said, 'What happened?' But right away I knew that was the wrong thing to say, for she broke down and couldn't speak. How they got her into that car and away without attracting attention is something I cannot explain. She is strong and she has a powerful voice."

Yes, she was going to Douglas on the noon train, she and the children. "And when Sister gets back," she called to the press crew, "we are going to have every one of you out to the house for a big dinner, and don't you forget it!"

Rolf and Roberta seemed bewildered by the turmoil; shyly they avoided questioners. Flitting in the background, Emma Schaffer, still in mourning, eyes reddened by tears which reporters attributed to excess of joy, hovered like a symbol of grief.

Mother Kennedy headed off the newsmen. "No, you just can't talk with her. She is so nervous and she just can't talk very well. She isn't that sort, you know. She doesn't know anything."

"Did she see the man and woman who kidnaped Sister?"

"No, she did not. She never saw them at all," was Mother's firm reply.

One reporter did intercept Emma in the alley behind the house. Did she see the two kidnapers described by Sister?

Emma turned a startled face. "No, I never seen them," she blurted, and darted away.

In the Temple, workers were busy removing funereal trappings left from Sunday's memorial service and decorating the auditorium with fresh flowers. The streets were black with autos. The bulletin board reappeared on the sidewalk, this time with a telegram reading: MINNIE KENNEDY. YOUR DAUGHTER IN GOOD HANDS AND EVERYTHING BEING DONE FOR HER. WE ARE AWAITING YOUR COMMAND. DOUGLAS CHAMBER OF COMMERCE.

Bible School students danced up and down Lemoyne Street. By afternoon four thousand frantically happy Temple workers were gathered in the auditorium. Paraphrasing the words of the Pentecostal hymn, "Coming down, down, down, the glory of the Lord is coming down," they clapped hands and sang:

> Coming back, back, back,
> Our Sister in the Lord is coming back!
>   There is shouting all around
>   For our Sister has been found,
> There is nothing now of peace or joy we lack!

Shouted choir leader Nichols, "She has been delivered out of the hand of the enemy by the Lord Himself! No one else could have done it!"

Sheriff Traeger broadcast a description of the kidnapers and dispatched deputies to the San Fernando Valley to interview a gypsy named Steve who lived outside Glendale. Everybody in the district knew and liked Steve Uwanowich and his daughter, Mrs. Rosie Moreno. They were followers of Sister; she had baptized Rosie's two boys, naming one Robert Semple after her always mourned husband who had died in China.

Steve took the deputies inside his neat house. The walls were covered with photographs of Sister, garlanded with artificial roses; Steve was proud of the display. Sister used to visit them in the early days after the Temple was built, he recalled. "The last time Sister came to our house was on Saint John's Day, our holy day, January seventh, nineteen-twenty-four. I haven't seen her since she got back from Europe. When I heard she was drowned, I went over to the church right away and saw Mother Kennedy. She cried when she told me about it, and I cried, too. 'Brother Steve,' she said, 'you must stand by us now that Sister is gone.' I promised I would."

He recalled that he donated $1000 for one of the windows in the Temple, and with other gypsies gave the evangelist a plot of ground in Elysian Park valued at $7000 to $8000; she held Easter sunrise services there.

"No gypsies harmed Mrs. McPherson," he said. "They loved her too much. Why, two hundred of us bought chairs in the Temple for twenty-five dollars each." Besides, there were no gypsies around Los Angeles except himself and his family; there hadn't been for six months.

Federal authorities could not understand how a woman bound and gagged in an automobile could be smuggled across the border under the eyes of the authorities on both sides. Governor Abelardo Rodriguez of Baja California, the state in Mexico bordering Sonora on the west, said he had assigned special police to the border as soon as the evangelist disappeared, and he was positive she could not have been carried by force into his territory. The Mexican consul general in San Francisco, George A. Lubert, announced that a check of all identification tags since May 18 failed to show that any woman resembling Mrs. McPherson had crossed the Mexican border in a car at any point. In his opinion she could not have been smuggled across by force under the eyes of immigration officials and two other government agencies that patrolled the boundary. "I hold her story of her escape and subsequent arrival in Douglas to be without good foundation," was his conclusion.

These wayside utterances in no way deterred the Los Angeles authorities. District Attorney Keyes, shocked as was all the city by the crime, said the full power of his office would be employed to bring the kidnapers to justice. He ordered a deputy, Joseph Ryan, to accompany Captain Cline to Douglas and investigate "to the bottom." On an hour's notice Ryan packed a suitcase and hurried to the Southern Pacific Railroad station, where he found reporters harassing Cline. Did Cline believe Mrs. McPherson's story?

"Well, boys," the detective conceded, "it sounds impossible. But experience shows that sometimes the impossible happens."

Ryan swung aboard the special Pullman and joined fourteen reporters and newsreel men, under the escort of the Southern Pacific's news bureau chief. Mother Kennedy and Rolf and Roberta occupied a stateroom. Ryan brushed aside the newsmen; as he entered the station, he had been handed a written message from his chief, Keyes, reading, "Make no statement."

The Law Takes a Look

Like most Angelenos, Joseph W. Ryan was born elsewhere: in Brooklyn, where he attended the Schermerhorn grammar school. He graduated from high school in Los Angeles, took his law degree there, and in March 1923 was admitted to the bar, just three months after Aimee McPherson opened Angelus Temple. He was twenty-nine, keen-witted, energetic, and ambitious (some of his colleagues felt he was too ambitious), had his hopes set on a political career, and was married to the daughter of Captain Herman Cline.

Ryan had never met Mrs. McPherson, although like everybody in Los Angeles he had heard all about her. On the train, Cline introduced him to Mrs. Kennedy, and the three reviewed the situation from all angles.

"It's too bad Sister couldn't have returned a couple of days earlier and saved the necessity of taking that memorial collection," said Mother Kennedy; she didn't know what to do with the money now.

The ransom letter was discussed, and Minnie told Cline she was satisfied that the lock of hair was her daughter's. Mrs. Kennedy appeared to Ryan to be taking the development with singular equanimity, neither elated nor apparently nervous. The phlegmatic attitude of the two children also drew the deputy's attention.

"Aren't you glad your mother is alive?" he asked them.

"Uh-huh." They nodded.

"Aren't you glad you are going to see her again?"

"Uh-huh."

A reporter wondered what Roberta intended to be when she grew up.

"Oh, I suppose we'll be evangelists," the girl answered listlessly. "We don't want to be evangelists."

Such bland indifference struck Ryan as suspiciously odd. What the young deputy could not appreciate was that from babyhood Rolf and Roberta had lived in a world of drama as part of the background furniture of two strong-willed, assertive women—their mother and their grandmother. Drama was an everyday commodity with them. They were being taken to another scene and it was bound to be dramatic and that was that; they could not work up any special display of emotion about it at the bidding of curious adults.

When the train reached Douglas at 8 a.m. Thursday, a crowd was gathered at the station, singing hymns and praying. After speaking a few emotional words to the greeters, Minnie, with the children, was driven in a waiting car to the hospital, Cline and Ryan and the reporters following in jitneys. Behind them streamed a long caravan of the automobiles of the citizenry.

The evangelist had been awake and busy since an early hour. At 5 a.m. she telephoned the editor of the Bisbee *Review* to protest against the printing of Sheriff McDonald's statement about her clothing. His description was not true, she said, and she must correct their use of the word "mystery." There was no "mystery" about her experience and therefore it would never be "solved." With a glowing "God bless you" she rang off.

The hospital physician, gratified that she had slept well, placed her on full diet. She ate everything offered for breakfast.

The first member of the Los Angeles party to enter her bedroom was her mother.

"Mother! Mother darling!" Aimee cried, holding out her arms. Choking back sobs, the older woman flung herself into her daughter's arms and they both wept, at the same time carrying on a whispered conversation. The rest of the group hung back tactfully during this reunion, and although Ryan and the reporters later admitted that they tried their best to overhear, they caught nothing; Minnie's white hat with broad yellow ribbon obscured Aimee's face, and Mother's was buried in Aimee's hair. Then Aimee held out her arms to her children, waiting at the foot of the bed. Obediently they stepped to either side and received hugs and kisses. Roberta seemed embarrassed; Rolf looked bored. Bedside photographs followed, the cameramen refusing to wait; then Aimee was introduced to Cline and Ryan.

"Oh," she cried, extending her arms eagerly, "if you knew how I have longed to see a policeman! Now I know I am safe!"

Briefly she retold her story to her mother. During the recital Minnie sat beside the bed, clutching her daughter's hand, staring at her. Aimee was eager to talk; she wanted to tell everybody everything. When Cline asked whether she would repeat the entire story with a stenographer present, she assented gladly. A shorthand stenographer was borrowed from Camp Jones, a nearby United States Army cavalry post, and for three hours Cline and Ryan were taken through the absorbing narrative of abduction, torture, and flight to freedom that had already enthralled millions of newspaper readers. In all essentials, the account was unchanged; there were more details, and some were amplified or altered slightly.

Cline interrupted with questions now and then. He was curious about the nature of the anesthetic used to produce unconsciousness from 4 o'clock in the afternoon until the next dawn. Aimee could tell him only that she was familiar with the odor of chloroform from having been given it once in China, but she could not say that chloroform was used by her kidnapers.

Cline wanted a description of the room in the first house to which she was taken, where she was confined most of the time.

"Well," answered Aimee readily, "the wallpaper had a small border running around the top. The ceiling was not papered. It had some cracks in it. There was an iron double bed, a dresser, well used, brown-colored with the varnish pretty well worn off, and a mirror, a rather wide mirror, and a rocker and a chair. That was all, except the cot."

"Did you place any mark or writing of any kind in the room?"

"No."

"There was a rug on the floor?"

"There was no rug on the floor. There was one door and one window and the bathroom door. There was no clothes press, just a little curtain over the corner of the room."

"Was it a modern house?"

"No, I would not say so, but it did have a small bath."

"And a lavatory?"

"Yes."

"With a flush toilet?"

"Yes. But no electric light, only kerosene lamps."

This gave Cline one positive clue: the house was unusual in that, having no electricity, depending on oil lamps, it was nevertheless equipped with indoor plumbing.

Ryan was realistically inquisitive about the all-night and all-day ride to the second shack, during which, the evangelist insisted, she was never allowed to get out of the car. There were "other arrangements" provided on that trip, she replied with some hauteur. Ryan did not press his query.

Aimee estimated she was in the second shack only three or four days. That shack had no bathroom—"other arrangements." The floor was wooden. The woman, Rosie, tied her hand and foot before she went to fetch supplies on the last day, in spite of Aimee's plea that she was too enfeebled to stand. Rosie bound her hands behind her, although she begged to have them tied in front. She heard the car drive off; it sounded like a small car, not a Ford, more like a Chevrolet.

Dramatically, acting out the narrative while sitting up in bed, Mrs. McPherson described how she rolled off the cot and agonizingly sawed through the bonds on her wrists against the jagged edge of the can.

"Then I got the feet undone myself and left the rope right there and did not stop in the manner of my going, although I could hardly stand. Strength came to me and I got out the window. I didn't stop to look at anything; I saw it was the desert, but I didn't stop to look which way I went, I just went."

"Did you try to get out the door?" Cline interposed.

"No."

"Do you know whether the door was locked or not?"

"It was closed."

"Do you remember when Rose left whether she locked the door?"

"I do not know."

"Was the window up or down?"

"The window was open."

"There was no screen on the window?"

"No, no screen."

"It was just the desert you saw?"

"Just cactus."

And so on to her reaching Agua Prieta, which means "dark water."

One addition to this final portion of her narrative was the inclusion of the words, "I began to get very thirsty." It was the first time she had alluded to thirst in telling of her escape.

Cline endeavored to obtain an accurate description of her three captors, without marked success, and also brought up the subject of Ormiston. Mrs. McPherson denied ever having sent him $1500 to buy an automobile in Seattle; the only money ever paid to Ormiston, she said, was his salary as radio operator. She never heard her abductors say anything about having made arrangements to collect the ransom through an attorney in Long Beach, although from what she had been told it seemed to her now that her jailers must have been the same two men who called at McKinley's office. She did hear them say once, "They must think we are a couple of fools to go to a place like that and get caught," and something about a man wearing a badge or ribbon. This appeared to tie in with the rendezvous that fizzled in the Palace Hotel in San Francisco.

Ryan asked whether she had seen the "Revengers" letter of May 24; she replied she had not. Nor had she seen the "Avengers" ransom letter of June 18. And she had not seen any newspapers while she was held prisoner. Ryan asked whether she realized that many of the matters she was telling them, such as the threat to cut off her scarred finger, were also in the June 18 ransom demand. She knew nothing about the ransom letter except what he told her.

The interrogation was typed up into thirty-five pages of questions and answers, and was telegraphed word for word to the nation's waiting press. At the close Ryan and Cline posed for photographs standing genially beside her bed. Then they went to the First National Bank and examined the clothing.

The dress was gray gingham, an almost shapeless house dress, new, and had never been washed. The inside of the white collar and white cuffs was barely soiled. One pocket was torn. From the other pocket Ryan drew a silk hair net.

The shoes were cheap black kid slippers, each fastened with one button; the buttons were intact. The uppers showed slight wear and the soles were scuffed; the leather on the insteps was bright and bore markings like grass stains. For the rest, there were lisle stockings, a cotton princess slip with a blue bow at the neck, a cheap combination undergarment, and a corset, size 37, stamped with the name "Bon Ton" and a serial number. Ben Levy, proprietor of Levy's department store in Douglas, was unable to identify any of the clothing as coming from his stock. He pointed out that everything was new; the stockings showing creases from lying folded in the box. The corset appeared to be the only help toward providing a clue: the serial number might be traced. Cline had his photograph taken holding up the clothing for inspection.

Ryan had been sent to Arizona as the representative of the People of California to get the facts, and the facts were becoming extraordinarily complicated. The "Avengers" letter fascinated him. Time and again he read it, weighing every word. Two pages long, it was typed inexpertly:

June 18, 1926.

Mrs. Minnie Kennedy,
Angelus Temple,
Los Angeles, Cal.
Dear Madam:—

Exactly one month has elapsed since we grabbed Aimee McPherson and now is the time for action. We nearly bungled it once, but we've moved her to a safe place now and have doped out a plan of ransom payment that is absolutely safe to us. You wont be able to trap us if you act in bad faith. We doubt if you will attempt any funny business though when you are convinced this is no hoax or Sunday school picnic and that we really have your daughter. Do what you like with this letter (we realize you got to use it to raise the dough) but the next one must be kept absolutely to yourself and its instructions followed exactly or there will be grave consequences to your daughter.

First, in order that you may know without doubt that Aimee is alive and in our hands, we are enclosing a lock of her hair. We tried to get answers to your silly questions but because she knows about the half million ransom she wont answer them. Says she would rather die than cripple the church to such an extent. But before she knew what it was all about we tricked her into a couple fool answers something like 'A woven wire one between two apple trees' and the hound was black and named Gyp. She shut up then realizing what we were after but if you insist a lighted cigar against a bare foot often gets results. Her middle right hand finger has a scar on it you ought to recognize, suppose we chop it off and send it along to kill your doubts? Weve got her alright and trust by now youll believe it and know that we mean business. She has been taken good care of by a woman who has been with her constantly, an ex-nurse who knows her business. She is suffering with hysteria and the heat and is pretty weak but physically and mentally theres nothing wrong with her that wont mend soon once shes home. But though we've treated her respectfully in fairness to her position and value to us, what the future holds for her is entirely up to you. Our alternative is to sell her to old

Felipe of Mexico City. We are sick and tired of her infernal preaching, she spouts scripture in answer to everything.

We took her for two reasons—: First To wreck that damned Temple and second: to collect a tidy half million. We have held her for a month during which time her name and standing have been just about ruined. We had to fight hard to kill that 'drowning' idea of yours but a little palm-oil brought forth plenty reports of her being seen all over the place and the newspaper hounds were only too anxious to play it up. They seem to have an axe to grind too and sure helped us grand. You've taken some of our girls Damn you, and given us many a jolt, but guess we are square now eh?

Now as to the ransom. We've been stumped for a method of collecting that would be safe, because you spilled it to the police before. Its plain no ordinary methods will work with you, so weve sure doped out a corker, and while it has taken time and delayed things a bit it is apple pie for us. You got a week to raise the money, and on June 25th you will get the final letter with the instructions how to proceed to get the money into our hands and how to get your darling daughter into your hands.

It might interest you to know just what happened on the beach a month ago today. Well we had inside workers who kept us informed as to her whereabouts, and that day she went to the beach looked like our chance. We watched until she was alone, then a man and woman stepped up to her with a heart-breaking tale of a deathly sick baby in a car across the street, and that Mother Kennedy had sent them down to the beach to find Aimee and ask her to pray for the kid. She kicked and insisted on going to the hotel to dress first but the argument of dying kid together with the use of a long coat the woman carried persuaded her to come as she was. When she got into the car to pray for the imaginary kid, a quick shove, a gag with some dope on it and a couple of blankets thrown over her, and away we went. Simple, wasnt it?

Now get busy. Have the $500,000 ready in big bills. Watch for the final letter of instructions which will reach you next Friday. That letter you must keep absolutely confidential but you will alright when you read it. Follow the instructions exactly and on that same night you will have your Aimee back and we'll have the dough. If anything slips Felipe gets her.

> Till Friday,
> THE AVENGERS

This prolix missive, with the account of the beach events laboriously appended, seemed odd to Ryan; criminals usually avoid strewing clues wholesale or wasting words in their desperate communications. Some phrases—"grave consequences," "in fairness to her position," "her name and standing," "absolutely confidential"—and the occasional imitative snatches of slang sounded like no thieves' lingo he had ever heard around city jail. The reference to a previous demand for $500,000 sent and received, the statement that the prisoner would be released Friday, the McKinley questions answered (these questions, like all the anterior events mentioned in the letter, had been published in the newspapers)— sentence by sentence Ryan picked the note to pieces and laid the fragmented bits beside the narrative Mrs. McPherson had told to the newspapers and to him. That bit about "Mother Kennedy had sent them down to the beach to find Aimee"—what was it Mrs. McPherson had interjected at this point in her statement to Cline, when she turned to Mrs. Kennedy with an aside? "Mother"—that was it—"you have always told me that they should always bring a card with your signature, and I should always ask for it; if I had, it would have been all right." Was this an allusion to something long understood between the two women— or was it perhaps a cue? . . . Ryan grew excited as he reflected. "A heart-breaking tale of a deathly sick baby" . . . "would rather die than cripple the church to that extent" . . . He seemed to detect a familiar rhetoric. Or did he?

Papa Cline counseled the young man to keep an open mind; there was still a lot they didn't know.

"Why," asked the experienced crime analyst, "should a woman in Mrs. McPherson's position say she was kidnaped if she wasn't? What could she gain by it? How long could she make her story stand up? The supposition is fantastic."

"Well, I'll ask you a question," parried Joe. "You saw those shoes, the grass stains on the instep. I ask—what is so rare as a blade of grass on the desert in June?"

Belief and Disbelief

Ryan and Cline had come back to the hospital after examining the clothing in time to witness Mrs. McPherson holding court for the newsreel cameras on the front lawn; she insisted they get in the picture. The newsreels of those days were silent, and there was much movement. Aimee emerged from the hospital wearing a gray silk dress and white shoes and stockings (clothing brought by her mother) and walked slowly to a wicker chair placed before the cameras. She smiled wanly and waved to the cheering crowd; it was explained that these were her first steps out of bed. (The nurse, a few minutes before, had entered on her medical chart: temperature 99, *pulse 118,* respiration 20.) Aimee assumed affectionate poses with Mother Kennedy and the children and spoke a few words in pantomime. Then she stood up and collapsed in a faint. Police Officer Gordon Newman earned supporting-role billing by gathering her in his arms while the newsreels cranked and carrying her into the hospital, where she was put back to bed.

Mother supplied a patter of comment for the newspapers. "I can't help but feel our years of hard work will be hurt as a result of what has happened," she said. "We were always so careful and conservative. It is so unfortunate it had to be Sister. If I had been at the beach, this would never have happened!"

"I can't realize it," she told another interviewer. "The shock just numbed me. It was like a blow that knocks a person down; it seemed a dream, just like she was resurrected from the dead. [Mother Kennedy accepted her imagery readily from her word-resplendent daughter.] Here is Sister a wreck! She will probably never be the same!"

Minnie's first move was to get her talkative daughter into her custody, in a suite at the Gadsden Hotel. Aimee joined her family there in the afternoon, explaining that the turmoil she caused at the hospital was unfair to the patients. Also, reporters could be excluded from the suite.

In high spirits, she headed her own search into the desert for clues to her trail of flight. Cline and Ryan accompanied her, as well as a posse of police and newspapermen. They crossed into Agua Prieta, and Aimee insisted on first visiting the Gonzales house, where she graciously thanked the good Theresa for her kindly ministrations; the good Ramon was tending bar, so Aimee could not thank him. Then they drove, by easy stages and frequent halts, to investigate the terrain toward Niggerhead Mountain. The feeling was friendly all around; Ryan got out at one point to have his photograph taken with a Brahma bull which he misnamed a yak, but the bull proved camera-shy.

Aimee recognized the gullies around the slaughterhouse and pointed out familiar objects as far as the garita, where footprints matching her shoes led eastward a short distance, crossed the road, and went back toward Agua Prieta toward the point where the automobile turned around. Beyond the footprints she could recognize no landmark except Niggerhead Mountain in the distance. Driving to that elevation, the party was overtaken by dusk, and as the moon rose Aimee wandered vaguely over the lower slopes of the mountain endeavoring to identify some feature in the bleak landscape which she said she had traversed in the same moonlight forty-eight hours before. The flinty monotony of hill and arroyo meant nothing to her. She confessed candidly to Ryan, "It all looks alike to me."

On her return to Douglas she thought she might be able to trace the cabin in the morning, but frankly she wasn't sure of anything.

"I have been wondering," she mused, "if that house into which my captors took me last could have been a camping outfit of light canvas or wood?"

A reporter handed her a piece of burlap. She shook her head.

"No, it couldn't have been that. I can see through this, but I couldn't see through the walls of that house."

Plans were laid to start out again at 4 a.m. Mother Kennedy had returned from an independent but equally fruitless search of the desert, on which she took Rolf; the boy showed tremendous enthusiasm for the game of shack hunting.

The next day, Friday, Aimee made three exploratory trips. The first, in the company of Ryan, Cline, her mother, Cross, and Mexican police officials, was on the American side as far as the San Bernardino Ranch, sixteen miles east of Agua Prieta. There she was shown two huts; she could identify neither.

The party then returned to Douglas and crossed into Mexico, where they covered an area of thirty-five square miles, east and southeast of Agua Prieta. Aimee could recognize none of the scenery, and although she was shown a number of crude shelters, both inside and outside the critical triangle, no adobe shack with a wooden floor was found. At the outset of this trip she had offered to demonstrate that she could walk twenty miles without water and suffer no harmful effects, but reporters maliciously observed that after three-quarters of an hour of desert heat —although she left the car and walked only a few yards now and then— she reached for the canteen. Mother Kennedy several times ostentatiously scuffed her white shoes in the dust to show they were not soiled.

At noon the party returned to Agua Prieta for lunch. Cross, the desert tracker, suggested that possibly Mrs. McPherson was confused in her directions. He had examined every foot of ground over which she was supposed to have walked around Niggerhead. The country was rolling, with outcroppings of flat rocks and earth baked hard as cement, on which no tracks would appear; but in between were little gulches, or washes, with sandy soil at the bottom into which a person's foot would sink and leave tracks visible for several days, unless the wind obliterated them. No such tracks were found, he said. As for the shack: "I do not know of an adobe house such as the one described by Mrs. McPherson within a hundred and fifty miles of Agua Prieta, and I know every house in this vast area."

Pedro Demandivo, chief of the Mexican border patrol, said he did not expect to find such a cabin as Mrs. McPherson described. Probably, he said with courteous shrug, she was too hysterical to note the cabin carefully. Anyway, he had sent out his men looking for the kidnapers, on the orders of Presidente Boubion, within one hour after the evangelist's identity became known; they searched all Wednesday and Thursday. "These men know every foot of ground within fifty miles," said the chief, "and none of them knows such a cabin. If one did exist, we would know about it within two days after it was built."

And Antonio Gabiondo, chief of the Mexican customs guards, was scornful. "I have three sons and they all own large tracts of land around Agua Prieta," he said. "Almost all the land over which the search has been conducted is owned by my family. Do you think that if such a shack existed we would not know of it, we who have lived here all our lives? It is a preposterous assumption!"

A woman reporter for the Los Angeles *Examiner* talked quietly with Ramon Gonzales and was impressed by his intelligence and gallantry. She asked him candidly whether he credited Mrs. McPherson's story, and he replied, through an interpreter, "I do not wish to say anything against the lady, but I think the lady is a liar."

Reporters questioned the nurses at the hospital. Nurse Shinn told about Aimee's nervousness, which the truant officer Cook also had noted. "She was all right when she was talking," said Nurse Shinn, "but when she stopped talking she would close her eyes and twitch and jerk." Her rapid pulse just before she faced the newsreel cameras also was mentioned. But her complexion, in the nurse's opinion, was little affected. And after she entered the hospital, except for a glass of lemonade she did not drink anything or ask for water; in fact, the nurse particularly noticed that no drinking water had been placed in the room half an hour after Sister was admitted. As for the collapse that morning: "I know she fainted, or appeared to faint, but she came right out of it when we got her inside, sat up and undressed."

Upon her return to the hotel, Aimee was informed of the rising cloud of doubt. She flushed with resentment, and turning to the correspondents trailing her, with Cline standing at one side, she read them a lecture on the ethics of their business.

"I am a good woman," she exclaimed in a voice pulsing with emotion. "My heart and soul are tied up in Angelus Temple! There is nothing in the world I wouldn't do to stop these untrue and soul-searing rumors!" She appealed to the reporters' good sense. "Please tell me your feeling about my story. Doesn't it sound logical? Isn't it a picture that could be visualized only by someone actually passing through it and not merely in imagination? Why, how in the world could I ever accomplish such a thing as hatching this up? Isn't it true that I am probably the best-known woman in this country, after spending seventeen years campaigning as an evangelist around it, and there is hardly a man or woman who wouldn't recognize me?" Trembling with anger, she threatened to "file several libel suits" when she got back to Los Angeles.

"Before the God in Whom I have every faith and utter belief," she declaimed, "every word I have uttered about my kidnaping and escape is true! If I have been unable to answer any question propounded by a score of newspapermen, detectives, attorneys, friends, even my own mother, I have told them 'I do not know' or 'I do not remember.' My story is true! I have permitted every reporter to ask any question and where I knew the answer, I gave it!"

At about 3 o'clock that afternoon, Sister set out a third time with Ryan, Cline, her mother, and the usual entourage of reporters and policemen. They traveled along the road from Agua Prieta clear to Cenesas Ranch to explore another possibility. During the early hours of her flight, Aimee said, she headed toward Niggerhead Mountain; after she came to a road, she turned left on it, putting the mountain behind her, and followed this road until the lights of Agua Prieta came into view. Hence, if she was facing Niggerhead until she struck the road, she must have been walking northward from somewhere in the vicinity of the Cenesas Ranch during the first stage of her escape. The distance from Cenesas to Niggerhead and thence westward to Agua Prieta was about twenty miles, the distance it was estimated she covered in her fourteen hours of wandering.

This expedition, however, proved fruitless like the others; no shack meeting her specifications was found around Cenesas, no tracks or other clues, and she returned to the hotel at about 8 o'clock visibly dejected.

A few minutes later, Ryan, entering the Gadsden, met her jubilantly waving a sketch that had just been brought in by Leslie Gatliff, a Douglas policeman, and Constable O. E. Ash.

"They have found the shack!" Aimee cried.

"God bless them," echoed Ryan, "if they have!"

"Oh, I hope and pray," continued Aimee, "that they may be right! Oh, if only they are!"

This shack, closer examination was to reveal, was not the one demanded by Sister's occasion. Situated south of the Cenesas Ranch, it had four rooms, a galvanized iron roof, and a dirt floor jointly tenanted by chickens and Mexican children.

But what Ash, Gatliff, Deputy United States Marshal T. F. Sims and the Douglas newspaperman Henry had found in a private exploration, and was of far greater moment, was a trail of footprints seemingly made by a woman's number 5 or 5½ shoes on the west (Agua Prieta) side of the Gallardo fence, about three miles north of Cenesas Ranch. These tracks, discernible in the sandy bottom of the gullies, would disappear on hard ground, then reappear in a wash farther along. They pointed toward Niggerhead. They straggled along about three hundred yards, then ceased altogether. Sims estimated they were two or three days old.

The Southern Pacific's Golden State Limited pulled out of Douglas at 9:13 Friday evening with Aimee Semple McPherson an additional occupant of the special press car. Just before entraining she posted a $500 reward for finding the prison shack, a gesture the Los Angeles *Examiner* immediately topped with the offer of $10,000 for capture of the kidnapers and another $1000 for locating the shack. Police Chief Bowden of Douglas deplored these rewards; they were bound to set off a rash of identifications, he felt. Not that he doubted Mrs. McPherson's story, he made plain. On the contrary, he believed it "because I don't see how any woman could create such a startling sequence of events in her mind."

Two thousand persons congregated at the station to bid the Temple party good-by. Aimee was sprightly in a light gray dress and brown hat, with corsage of sweet peas and rosebuds. Mother Kennedy had put off her usual white silk for a black and white traveling suit. Both women, and Roberta, too, carried huge bouquets, the gifts of local admirers. In an automobile behind this flowery femininity rode Cline and Ryan, saying nothing except that as far as the Los Angeles police were concerned the hunt for the shack was ended.

Eight railroad detectives surrounded Aimee's automobile and herded the crowd away from the steps of the Pullman; there had been rumors of threats against her life. From the rear platform Aimee turned her smile upon the throng and in the voice known for its tingling rasp and throb thanked them superbly for their many kindnesses, promising that she would build a church in their city, a choice of building sites having been offered already. She introduced her mother and her children, and then Ryan and Cline, telling the applauding townsfolk that they had been "simply wonderful." Then she led the singing of a hymn, read a Bible passage, and prayed until the train pulled out.

"Oh, Douglas, God bless you!" was her farewell as she leaned over the car railing, clasping the crimson roses that were the town's last tribute. Behind the receding crowd she saw the lights of Agua Prieta, those friendly beacons that had guided her out of darkness to the gate through which she re-entered life. Not until weeks later did she realize that those friendly beacons were the glare of Agua Prieta's cabarets, barrooms, and dance halls.

The summer had been very dry around Douglas. The day after Aimee departed, rain fell in torrents, and all traces in the desert were obliterated.

Entry into Jerusalem

Disenchantment had no place along the right-of-way of the Golden State Limited chugging through the night. At every stop, crowds pressed around Sister's car, clamoring to see her. When the train halted at Bisbee Junction, twenty miles from Douglas, she was already fast asleep. But she was told that a crowd was waiting, and in three minutes was dressed and out on the platform, giving her audience the joy of her radiant presence. By snatches through the night, she slept. At 1:10 a.m., when the train pulled into Tucson, she was awakened by Captain Cline.

"Are some of my people here?" she responded eagerly. Cline asked her to dress and step into the car.

There B. P. Greenwood, a building inspector of Tucson, was waiting.

Cline asked whether he recognized the evangelist. Greenwood, a cautious man with a strong sense of probity, studied her, then asked her to walk along the car aisle. Aimee complied. Could Greenwood identify her? Cline asked again.

Well, replied the inspector, she certainly looked like a woman he had given a ride to, on the Tucson-Douglas road, last Sunday, and also like a woman he saw on the street in Tucson four weeks previously.

"If it wasn't Mrs. McPherson," he concluded, "she was close enough like her to be her twin sister."

Aimee was flabbergasted. She had never been in Tucson in her life, she protested, except to pass through in a train. She reminded Greenwood of the element of uncertainty that hovers over all identifications. When he refused to change his opinion, she appealed to his chivalry.

"You must realize," she said, clasping and unclasping her hands, "that I am fighting for my life!"

Greenwood was unshaken. What clinched it, he said, was her thick ankles. He recognized them.

Instantly Aimee ceased to fight for her life and rallied to the defense of her ankles. "That is preposterous!" she gasped. "My ankles are not thick!" And an hour after the train had left Tucson she was still telling the newspapermen and women how absurd such an allegation was, as they could see for themselves. The reporters, who wished she would go away and let them sleep, thought the identification well founded; among themselves they said Aimee's ankles *were* heavy, some even maintaining she had barrel legs, which in an era of short skirts was a blemish quickly noticed.

At the next halt, Maricopa Junction, at 3:24 a.m., a crowd was waiting, but Aimee did not appear. But at Yuma, in the morning, where the train halted eighteen minutes, she accepted a frantic ovation from a crowd that struggled hysterically to touch her hands or clothing.

"Praise the Lord," she shouted with an all-embracing smile, "the hour of resurrection has come!"

At Colton, near San Bernardino, five thousand persons scrambled to get close to the car while she spoke over the radio, hooked up to every station in Los Angeles and many up and down the coast. For radio listeners the last vestige of doubt as to her identity was dispelled when she stepped to the microphone and announced briskly, "This is Aimee Semple McPherson, of Angelus Temple, Los Angeles, California."

A roar went up from the crowd. She shouted back, "Praise the Lord! God bless you all! I am just bubbling over with joy!"

A telegram was handed to her. It was from Douglas and said the shack had been found. (This was a new development and a new candidate shack.)

"Praise the Lord!" she screamed again and read the message to the crowd. "Oh, dear friends, it was bad enough to go through the ordeal, but to have your word doubted is worse! There couldn't be any thinking person who would think for a minute that these stories doubting the report of my kidnaping are true. How many in this crowd believe my story? Those who do, raise your hands!"

A forest of arms shot up.

Emotionally she prayed for "all the police officers who have stood by me so loyally," and asked forgiveness for her kidnapers. "Dear Lord, ever bless these wicked people who have caused these things to happen and bring them to repentance. Oh, this is a glorious day!"

Then the train sped on, with cameramen, reporters, crowds and hallelujahs and waving of flags marking every mile of the triumphal route. At Shorb Station, hysterical welcomers rushed her car, and Ryan, Cline, and the reporters caught every word when the slender, alert evangelist, who looked surprisingly tiny beside her burly railroad guards, announced her plans for a round-the-world speaking tour:

> It won't be a vacation. The world has been hearing about me for a month, reading a great many things that were not true. I feel that if I go myself and meet these people, talk to them, they will know I am just a woman who has been led by God's providence through a terrible experience, and who is still devoting her whole life and soul to the work.

In Los Angeles, railroad officials had prepared for a crowd at the station that might, it was thought, exceed the twenty-five thousand who had welcomed Sister home from the Holy Land in May. Every precaution for safety was taken. Besides the guards on the train, a pilot engine preceded her locomotive. Aimee, it was believed, would be too weak to address a crowd. But by 1 p.m. a thousand persons were on hand and the street was cleared of automobile traffic. At 1:30 four thousand were gathered, and the multitude swelled by the minute. Thousands of Foursquare Gospelers arrived in chartered buses. Sixty policemen formed a cordon around the siding where Sister's car was to be shunted. Battalions of firemen, assisted by a dozen cowboys from the Temple's mounted posse, regulated the throng, which by 2:45 numbered fifty thousand, packing the pavements for two blocks around. For a mile along the track approaching the station, rooftops and fences were black with spectators.

Twenty minutes before train time, the crowd grew overwrought with anticipation, men and women laughing, weeping, praying. The friendliness in the air was electric; scoffers were in a minority, or sagely were keeping silent. "Aimee!" was on everyone's lips. Venders wormed in and out peddling ice cream and little American flags. Cameras appeared everywhere.

When the train came into sight, bells, horns, and sirens mingled with the human roar. Several hundred Temple members, drawn up inside the train yard as an honor guard, fluttered gold and yellow banners. The Angelus Temple band and choir struck up "Wonderful Savior." The train halted: Aimee's Pullman was detached and slowly shunted into position. When Aimee appeared on the platform, a shout went up and the throng surged forward, pushing over an iron fence. "Aimee! Aimee!" screamed thousands. A man running beside the car made a flying leap to grasp her hand, missed, and barely saved himself by clutching the handrail.

"God bless you!" cried the startled evangelist. "Please don't get yourself killed just to see me! Come up to the Temple any night, I'll always be there!"

Standing beside her daughter, Mother Kennedy wept. "They love her so!" Overhead an airplane droned, dropping roses. As the Pullman halted, the Fire Department band blared "Praise God from Whom All Blessings Flow."

Waving, shouting, excited, the Titian-haired preacher appeared worn but glowing. Her costume was a gray georgette crepe with a green and white knotted tie, gray stockings, and low black shoes. First to greet her was Emma Schaffer, garbed in white, toying nervously with a bouquet. They kissed tenderly; Emma seemed on the point of bursting into tears. Next in line was a fire captain who pinned on Sister a gold badge emblematic of her rank as honorary chief. A delegation of firemen handed her an armful of American Beauty roses. Several times she tried to speak, but cheers overpowered her voice. Finally she held up her hand in a gesture for silence, and the crowd around the car hushed; farther off they kept cheering.

"I am so, so happy!" she yelled. "This wonderful demonstration! God be praised! I have never had people look so good to me as you do! You are wonderful! God bless you all! Everybody has been wonderful to me!

I want to thank everyone—the police officers and the firemen and God, from Whom all blessings flow!"

Standing just inside the car door, the fat Pullman conductor rocked from side to side and wheezed "Hallelujah!"

Aimee drew Captain Cline forward. "Captain Cline has been wonderful!" she told the crowd. "He has helped me. I want you all to know it, and I wish to thank him!" Cline bowed and smiled.

Clasping Ryan's elbow she edged him into view. "He also has been wonderful!" she cried. "He has been a rock to which to cling!" Ryan bowed to the applause. "I wish to thank him, and I wish to thank the newspaper men and women. They, too, were kind to me! They have my gratitude! Praise the Lord! Everyone now— Praise the Lord!"

The response boomed back: "Praise the Lord!"

Sister was ceremoniously enthroned in a high-backed wicker chair laced with red roses and carnations. Four stalwart firemen lifted this *sedia gestatoria* to their shoulders and bore her along an aisle formed by members of her Pasadena and Long Beach churches; her disciples, carrying Bibles and waving flags, strewed flowers in her path. Behind the leader came Emma, then Mother Kennedy and the children, Brother Arthur, representatives of the Temple departments, and the two pulpit substitutes, Argue and Shreve. The delirious crowd almost overwhelmed the chair, clutching at Sister's dress and snatching the blossoms; rose petals stuck like beauty patches on the sweating faces of her bearers.

At last Aimee stepped into her automobile, covered with flowers, followed by Mother Kennedy, Roberta, and Rolf, and the parade to Angelus Temple got under way. North on Central Avenue to Fourth Street, to San Pedro, to Aliso, to Los Angeles Street; into the Plaza district, where the Chinese and Mexicans set off firecrackers and other noise-makers in her honor (the first branch of the Temple she established was in the Plaza quarter); past densely packed sidewalks into Sunset Boulevard and westward to Echo Park. More than one hundred thousand onlookers viewed the procession, many of them just curious, some scornful, but most of them enthusiastic well-wishers. Inside Angelus Temple five thousand persons were waiting, while another five thousand stood outside Sister's home. With difficulty forty policemen opened a path from the car to the front door; and thirty-nine days almost to the hour after she vanished in the ocean, Aimee stepped tremulously across her threshold. The time was 3:15 p.m.

The crowd called for her, and in a moment the French window of her upstairs bedroom parted, and Sister stepped on the balcony.

"Oh, I love you so much!" she gasped in a voice husky with repressed tears. "I am so glad to be back! My voice is still a little weak and I need rest and food, but I can't resist your appeal."

She read a Bible verse, then asked, "How many have been faithful and believed through all this?" A sea of hands appeared. "Praise the Lord! God bless you!" she breathed thankfully. "I have come back to you—I know you will not let them take me away again!" She swayed, caught herself, and called, "I'll be with you in the Temple in just a few minutes!" Two policemen supported her tenderly back to the arms of her mother and the window closed.

Sister did not keep her people waiting. Ten minutes later she entered the Temple, carrying the customary sheaf of red roses in her arms, and strode down the ramp to the platform. The audience of nearly six thousand stood and cheered, shouted, stamped, screamed hallelujahs. She led the singing of "Old Hundred," then fell on her knees beside the microphone and offered a prayer of thanksgiving. After more singing, she told everybody, "Turn to your neighbor and say, 'Happy day!' " Then came the great moment when she recounted for her own people her harrowing experience.

The narrative was the same as that given to the newspapers, but now it was acted out with drama, humor, and pathos. The comical embarrassment of the Douglas truant officer who smelled her breath for liquor was good for the mimicry at which she excelled; she demonstrated how he paced up and down beside her bed, getting up courage to ask her to blow in his face.

" 'Well, that's that!' " she quoted him as saying. " 'Whatever they say, they can't accuse you of *that!*' " The audience howled.

She ridiculed the rumors spun about her disappearance and her return. She poured vials of sarcasm on the Tucson building inspector, and told how reluctant even the Douglas police were to accept her identity because she had been falsely reported in so many places. " 'Are you really Aimee?' " she gasped as she said they gasped; then she commented with smiling resignation, "I guess I'll be 'Aimee' from now on!"

At the close she asked how many present believed her story. Almost every hand went up.

Other auditors had to be satisfied. Just after 5 p.m., Sister emerged alone from her home and got into a car with Cline and Ryan; she was wearing a heavy coat with a large hat pulled down over her face, and she appeared exhausted. The car drove out to Ocean Park beach. At Washington and Rimpau Streets she asked the driver to stop while she bought the evening newspapers flaunting pictures and headlines of her triumphal entry into the city. The newspapers' account of the reported discovery of the captivity shack (about which she had received the telegram on the train) specially interested her. The shack was said to have been found by the Douglas newspaperman Henry and Constable Ash.

"The windows of the cabin were barred," Ash was reported as saying. "One window showed evidence that it had been broken. The cans of which Mrs. McPherson spoke were found inside, and the one on which she said she cut the ropes with which she was tied is believed to have been a forty-gallon drum. The bonds were not found, however." Photographs were said to be on the way to Los Angeles.

"Just as soon as you receive those photographs, let me know, Captain Cline," Aimee said. "I want to see if I can identify them."

Noticing a statement that her clothing was not damaged during her desert trip, she appealed sincerely to the detective. "You know, if I had been a bad woman and had some motive, I would have faked this thing, wouldn't I? I would have walked through the brush and rolled down on the ground and torn my dress and scuffed up my shoes. That would have been the thing to do if one was faking, wouldn't it?"

Cline nodded and said nothing.

A cold fog hung over the deserted beach when they pulled up in front of the Ocean View Hotel. In the doorway stood a news photographer. "Don't notice me," Aimee told him brusquely, as she led Ryan and Cline over her route stage by stage. Her movements were never hesitant, there was no reluctance, her gestures were prompt and vigorous. She walked across the sand about halfway to the water, sat down, motioned Ryan and Cline to sit beside her, and spoke earnestly for several minutes. Then she arose and walked toward Lick Pier, gesturing and explaining.

Suddenly a woman screamed, "There's Aimee!" Immediately people came running, from the houses, the shops, from side streets; in a few minutes two thousand spectators were crowding around. Aimee continued her description of the kidnaping with animation in their midst.

"The man stood about here," she said, "and the woman [she reached out and pulled an onlooker out of the crowd] about here. It was here they placed the coat over me. The coat was too large for me. I could feel the sleeves dragging down—you know how that feels."

Ryan and Cline were surprised when she led them to where the kidnapers' car was parked. The location was in front of 22 Navy Street, two blocks from the hotel, about a hundred feet inland from the promenade, on the south side of the street, in front of an occupied beach cottage with a veranda. Houses were all around. In Douglas she had said the car was parked beside Lick Pier—in an area that turned out to be a no-parking zone.

A man introduced himself as in charge of the lifeguards who tried to recover her body. Aimee shook hands and thanked him fervently: "May God bless you!" Then she returned to the hotel and with Cline and Ryan drove back to the Temple. As the car pulled away, people were still sticking their heads inside and endeavoring to touch her.

Reporters noted throughout the day that she showed the effects of an ordeal. Her voice lacked vibrancy and power, although it could still fill the Temple; her face was lined, and frequently she seemed harassed and fretful. But there was no want of assurance in her manner.

Thoughtful observers, catching their breath after the torrential emotionalism unloosed by her joyful reappearance, wondered, that evening, at the ambiguous pledge given by Captain Cline, the city's chief of detectives, to conduct an investigation "that will be fair to everybody." This seemed a surprisingly restrained statement from a police officer on the trail of a gang of kidnapers. Also thought-provoking was the two-edged encomium bestowed by Judge Hardy on the Los Angeles *Examiner* for its offer of rewards for apprehending Sister's abductors and locating the kidnap shack. "The public wants the truth, and I think they will get it now," said the judge. "If left to the law-enforcement agents alone, I am afraid the truth might not come out."

That Saturday evening Aimee repeated her story to another overflow audience in the Temple, with the same effectiveness. District Attorney Keyes instructed his deputy, Ryan, that he desired a meticulous report, with Cline on hand—not at his office, but in the privacy of his home, secure against the obtrusion of meddlesome reporters—on Sunday night.

Strike the Lyre!

The Sunday newspapers carried columns of description of Sister Mc-Pherson's recapture of the city and center of her evangelistic influence. No Hollywood premiere, costing thousands of dollars, ever received one-tenth as much attention. The imprimatur of sheer bigness was stamped by M. F. McCarthy, Southern Pacific special agent in charge of the security precautions at the railroad station; the reception, he said, outdid anything known in Los Angeles, including the visits of President Wilson, former President Taft, and King Albert of the Belgians. The police could recall no equal turnout of people in the streets.

Aimee did not appear at the morning service in the Temple, although thousands waited for hours; it was explained that she was saving her strength for the afternoon and evening, after passing a fairly restful night. Brother Argue dispensed the morning message, cracking ministerial jokes and disdainfully dismissing the rumors that were again filling the city.

"We here at Angelus Temple know our Sister is back, and that's sufficient for us," he cried. "We know the joke is not on us, and it is not on Sister McPherson!"

At the afternoon service the city's reporters and news photographers gathered in phalanxes. Six thousand devout adherents jammed the building, and ten minutes after Mother Kennedy opened the divine office, Sister made a dramatic entrance with Roberta and Rolf on her arms. The congregation stood and applauded minute after minute.

Her appearance had improved, although subtly she seemed changed from her pre-disappearance presence. She was thinner. In face, however, she looked ten years younger overnight; tell-tale lines of strain and fatigue had been eradicated—by the beauty specialist, she confided with a smile that seemed to embrace each person individually, "so I might look my old self again for you." Instead of her customary roses, she wore a corsage of lilies-of-the-valley.

Energetically she took charge of making room for some small fraction of the throng standing hopefully in the hot sun outside; she requested

Temple workers to give up their seats, and marshaled standees until seventy-five hundred were crushed in the space designed to hold fifty-four hundred. In the Bible School next door sat fifteen hundred more, listening to loudspeakers, while several thousands lingered on the pavement behind police ropes.

During the opening hymns Sister sat idolized, enshrined in her pulpit chair under a canopy of flowers. At intervals girls brought glasses of orange juice, which she drank thirstily; once she closed her eyes and seemed about to faint, but she looked up and smiled brightly when one of the girls approached, while seventy-five hundred pairs of eyes focused on her solicitously.

Her sermon was "The Conquering Host," and to her followers it sounded a call to man the battlements against hellish dangers. From the opening words, the reporters sensed she was pouring her immense forensic powers into a studied effort: the burden was like an impassioned appeal to a jury. Point by point she buttressed her tale of abduction and escape with plausibilities; point by point she tore into the innuendoes and falsities she credited to her critics and to those others who, without malice, simply refused to believe, and step by step she swept her auditors resistlessly toward the foreordained conclusion: "My story is true!"

"I think perhaps it would be unwise to give a lengthy sermon this afternoon," she started huskily; "not until I get a few more beefsteaks inside of me—I haven't had any yet—nothing but orange juice. I find my breath a little short. I am not sick, I am just weak from loss of sleep and worry."

The congregation stirred sympathetically.

Striking poses obligingly for the photographers, she thanked the press for its coverage of her welcome home. There was a time, she said, when she feared adverse publicity. "But that's all over now. We are alive from the dead! The work is going on! Praise [flashlights boom] the Lord!"

Comparing herself to Job and to Daniel, who were betrayed by false witnesses, she shouted, "Daniel was saved from the lions' den, but not from the lyin' tongues! There's a lot like that going on today! It's bad enough to be kidnaped without having lions roaring at you! Daniel was surrounded by lions—the lion of unbelief—the lion of persecution—the lion of opposition, slander, falsehood! The Devil has lots of lions—either way you spell it!"

To satisfy doubters who believed it was impossible to walk twenty miles across a desert without suffering sunburn, Sister showed how she shielded her face from the sun by pulling her skirt over her head to form a sunbonnet, "just like we do in Canada"—a precaution which she could not have taken decently, even alone in the wilderness, but for the fact that "I had been furnished with a long slip."

As for stories about her garments' being undamaged, her shoes not scratched by cactus and thorns, she pointed out that desert cactus grows in clumps, and it is a simple matter for a person to step between the plants and avoid catclaw. She dramatized how she fell in the road, how she vainly called for help, how ominous sounds in the darkness terrified her. Her tongue became swollen, she said, her lips cracked, she was tormented by thirst. Why, she went on, this whole business—her kidnaping and the scandals circulated during her absence and since her return—was a plot hatched by the Devil, not to extort dollars, but to wreck Angelus Temple.

"For three years there has been a great revival. Thousands have found their way to Jesus. You have seen big, strong men stumbling down the aisles. The Devil had lost his grip—just standing there, pulling his mustache (if he has one) and saying, 'What am I going to do to stop this revival?' If I was the Devil, I would sure put on my thinking cap to see how to stop this revival! He never could get into this church because we loved each other too well and stood too closely together. So he finally said, 'If I can get hold of Sister McPherson, if I could just get her away, the thing would crumble!' He said, 'There she is, and I have caught her alone—the secretary has gone to telephone.' He said there was a little child sick and dying, and would the undershepherd come and pray.

"So the little shepherd covered her dripping swimming suit with a coat. The little shepherd lifted up her foot and put it on the car. A blanket is thrown over her—something is pressed to her face. Then the Devil called all his wolves—and she is reported in sixteen different places at once! Well, if they say they saw her in sixteen places, the more the merrier! How many of you have ever been stopped on the street by a stranger and asked, 'Aren't you so and so?' I thought so—practically all of you."

Pausing just long enough to let her hearers yell agreement, she hurried on.

"Then came the wolves—the hounding pack—tongues lolling out, just ready to lay hold on the sheep! 'We've got her bound and gagged! We're going to stop this revival! We've got them on the run!' "

Dramatizing, darting from side to side, she was all over the platform; her audience sat fascinated.

"I thought of those three others in that conquering host—Shadrach, Meshach and Abed-nego. Those three Hebrew boys loved the Lord. The Devil began to lay his plots against them. They were cast into a fiery furnace and their shoes weren't even scorched! I have been in a fiery furnace too! Daniel was delivered. Job was delivered. The three Hebrew boys were delivered. And the same God that delivered them is the same in this present year of the Lord! Hallelujah!"

Why, she demanded, should she run away and hide? "In all this surmise about me there has never been one logical motive advanced to explain any voluntary disappearance on my part. There was absolutely nothing that I wanted my followers would not give me gladly. I was a queen in my kingdom, and I am not boasting."

The audience were lifted out of their seats; they stood and shouted for joy in the same place where just seven days before they had mourned her as dead. Confident and smiling, Sister rode the gale, fresher, more electric, more glowing, than when she stepped on the platform. The waves of adulation beat on her thrillingly. Whatever the world might say, the press could report that this jury was convinced; her people were secure.

That evening, in fine form, in the again dangerously overcrowded auditorium, she repeated the performance. She assured her flock that she was recuperating rapidly; she had eaten half a sandwich, she said, and drunk a glass of orange juice that evening, her first solid food for many days. The congregation murmured in sympathy.

The Reverend Bob Shuler, in crowded Trinity Church that evening, picked up Aimee's self-comparison with the Three Holy Children who passed through flames without singeing. Well, he subjoined, when a person can walk twenty miles in the desert without being sunburned, that was either a miracle or—something else. Ryan and Cline he challenged to make "a real investigation," and he categorically denied he had ever said, anywhere, "the skids are being put under Angelus Temple." When a woman, he went on, "can produce the mayor of the city, the sheriff's men, the fire department, the police department and fifty thousand people to greet her," why . . . And he discoursed darkly about mob psychology. "Aimee Semple McPherson," he warned solemnly, "was born knowing all there is to know about mob psychology."

Clues and Misclues

The next morning (Monday) District Attorney Keyes announced curtly that his office was doing no investigating. He had received Ryan's report, and the deputy would be on loan temporarily to the police. The prosecutor declined smilingly to amplify this apparent kiss-off of a subject that the whole town was arguing about, and caught the train for San Francisco.

Promptly Monday morning Cline turned over the "Avengers" letter to the United States Attorney's office. Ryan, the press found out, was endeavoring to trace Aimee's corset through the serial number, and EVANGELIST'S CORSET VITAL CLUE made a newspaper headline calculated to induce any passer-by to delve for details.

In Douglas, Chief Bowden scotched all reports that he had ever said the captivity shack had been found; that story was Constable Ash's; Bowden had no part in it. But a fresher, satisfactorily vague and exciting rumor, to the effect that Mexican police had a "Steve" and a "Rose" under surveillance in Nacazarra, Sonora, deflected attention from Bowden's denials. This report said Mexican authorities would convoy the undesirable pair to the border, where they would be picked up by United States agents. Within a couple of days this lead also fizzled out. And day after day the photographs of the shack supposed to have been located by Constable Ash and a reporter failed to reach the police in Los Angeles.

Aimee spent Monday morning with Detective Captain Taylor in her home, running through more than three thousand rogues' gallery photographs in an attempt to identify her captors. She was unable to recognize any face, although the photographs of herself and Taylor poring over heaps of assorted miscreancy made excellent illustrations for the newspapers.

The persistency of the papers in alluding to "clues" to her "mystery" nettled the pastor. Since her tale had been ratified by the votes of innumerable upraised hands, why did the press and the public remain obtuse? Her people believed her; why shouldn't everybody?

"Instead of making such an exhaustive investigation of my story," she suggested with asperity, "why don't the officials make an investigation of my possible enemies? The statement made a few weeks ago from a certain pastor's pulpit that 'the skids are under Angelus Temple' might easily be construed as a threat."

The sinister inference was plain: Shuler had a hand in her abduction.

"Why should I disappear?" she went on. "To rest? I was not tired. Amnesia? I never suffered from that. Publicity? That is absurd. Love?" She laughed. "The man I would marry hasn't appeared on the scene as yet, and Mr. McPherson would have to cash in before I ever marry again; I do not believe in marrying with a previous husband alive." Verbally she sketched her ideal mate. "He must be tall—six feet or more —good-looking—must be a preacher—a good and holy man—and he must play the trombone." Her fate was not at stake, certainly, she continued, but she was demanding a clean bill of health for the sake of her children and her work. "My character has always been spotless. My life has always been the church. I will not rest until I convince even the doubters of the truth of my story in its every detail!"

Meanwhile, the work of the Temple would go forward under her direction. Briskly she announced plans to construct a seven-story hotel for Bible School students, with a penthouse home for herself on the roof. Then she set out for an overnight rest at seaside Palos Verdes with her mother and children. Just as she was stepping into her car, a message arrived that Police Chief Sterling Oswalt of El Centro had "partially identified" Sister as a woman who was found wandering in El Centro June 11. Aimee laughed scornfully. "Another of those wild rumors! I have heard hundreds of them since I returned home, and I suppose there will be many more!" She whirled away.

At the Temple, three hundred and fifty disciples gathered for an allnight prayer and jubilee meeting conducted by Brother Arthur, assisted by Brother Argue. At midnight the meeting was going strong.

Aimee's luncheon guests at La Venta Inn at Palos Verdes on Tuesday were—reporters. The luncheon was on the heavy side. "First square meal I've had in more than a month," she explained as she topped off with two helpings of strawberry shortcake. Betraying increasing annoyance at the rumors persistently circulating, she challenged her critics to step up and accuse her in person.

"These blackening insinuations against my character must end! I challenge any person who thinks he or she is in possession of any scandal about me to meet me face to face and tell me what he or she knows.

Otherwise I shall take legal action to shut them up! I will not stand by silently and see my character besmirched."

Already two $100,000 libel suits were being drawn by her attorneys, she intimated, although she would not name the parties under fire.

Mother Kennedy revealed she was hiring detectives to investigate independently of the police. The solution of the crime, she predicted, would be found "right here in Los Angeles. Rose and Steve were only tools in this thing." Reporters fancied they heard an echo of Judge Hardy's expression of faint confidence in the law-enforcement powers.

Yet all was not acrimony during the sojourn by the sea. Aimee posed for the cameras on a windswept cliff overlooking what one newspaper caption termed "the kindly sea that did not claim her."

"It is so long since I have seen the ocean! It thrills me!" said Aimee. Barefoot Rolf dogged her steps happily; Rolf adored his exciting mother.

No shack photographs reached Captain Cline that day or later, but unknown to the watchful press a document of more than nominal import did arrive in the city. It was addressed to District Attorney Keyes, and was a confidential memorandum from Sheriff McDonald of Cochise County.

When he arrived at Calumet Hospital from Tombstone on June 23, McDonald wrote, Mrs. McPherson was receiving callers, and it was impossible to get a complete and definite statement on account of the interruptions:

> I did, however, question her very carefully regarding the appearance of her abductors, but could get nothing more definite than the following descriptions:
>
> Number one, woman named Rose, age 40 to 43 years, weight 185 pounds, large arms, black bobbed hair, eyes dark brown, even teeth, deep voice, businesslike.
>
> Number two, man named Steve, broad shoulders, weight 200 pounds, height six feet, ruddy complexion, dark clothes.
>
> Number three, name unknown, flat-chested, dark complexion, bushy eyebrows, upper gold tooth, gray clothing.
>
> I thought possibly that as Mrs. McPherson is a public speaker and must have a considerable knowledge of English that she would be very apt to remember their manners of speech and detect any slang expressions or grammatical errors by her abductors. She could give no information along this line. . . .
>
> The day on which her hike was made was hot and she should have perspired freely. She wore corsets which should have showed signs of perspiration, yet I found no indications of excessive perspiration on

her clothing. Furthermore, I cannot understand why she did not discard the corsets. The heat would have made their presence known to her and however excited she may have been it would seem she would have thought of taking them off and throwing them away. . . .

I have helped revive people who had been exhausted on the desert and have been near the point of exhaustion myself. One symptom is always present—INSANE CRAVING FOR WATER. [The sheriff underlined his own capitals.] In no part of her story does water seem to play an important part. In my opinion the first request from Schansel at the slaughterhouse would have been for water.

Finally, the shack in which she was said to have been held captive has never been found. . . . I have no desire to cast any reflections on anyone, but my conclusions are that Mrs. McPherson's story is not borne out by the facts.

This letter Ryan added to his thickening dossier.

Just before noon the next day, which was Wednesday, Cline received a telephone call at his office. Speaking rapidly, Minnie Kennedy told him that Aimee and she were boarding the train for Arizona. She gave no reason for the sudden departure. So far as Cline was concerned, the women had a right to go anywhere they wished. But Ryan was furious; Cochise County lies outside the jurisdiction of California authorities, and just across the border lies Mexico.

Locked in a Pullman drawing room with the shades pulled down, Aimee and Minnie slipped out of the Southern Pacific station where four days before fifty thousand frenzied welcomers had cheered her.

At the same hour, in San Francisco, jovial Asa Keyes was telling reporters, "Our office has dropped the case."

Transmontane Thunder

At Angelus Temple nobody would admit that Sister was on the way back to Douglas. All reporters learned was that Aimee had returned from a horseback ride a few minutes before she and Minnie Kennedy departed for the station; that they had been on the long-distance telephone, presumably to Douglas; and that Aimee appeared jubilant. Reporters boarded the train at way points after the word got out. Sister denied there was any mystery surrounding the trip; at the urging of friends in Douglas, they were simply going back to have another look for the shack. Several shacks had been spotted as likely possibilities, she asserted, but only she could identify the right one. She would cross the border into Mexico and search, and she wanted no retinue this time, she added sharply.

"My only wish is that when I start across the line again all the newspapermen in the world don't trail along. I'll be glad to announce it if I find the shack. If I don't, I'll announce that, too. I believe the shack will be found some time, although this trip may not produce anything. I feel the newspapers in Los Angeles have been very unfair to us."

This was a sudden change toward the press.

At Douglas, although their approach had been well heralded, the Temple leaders detrained at 7:30 Thursday morning before fewer than a hundred gawking spectators, most of them depot loafers down to watch the train come in. There were no hymns, no hallelujahs, no roses. Reporters were present in force and in earnest, but Aimee elbowed past them to the waiting car of the Reverend J. E. Howard, pastor of the Baptist church, and closed the door with a bang. "I do not wish to be molested," she snapped.

The press men pounced on Mother Kennedy and queried her about the "Avengers" ransom letter, which the United States prosecutor's office was hinting would cause a grand-jury inquiry. Minnie waved the letter aside as inconsequential; she knew nothing about any "tampering" with the stamps. When she first saw the letter, on June 21, it was opened and there was no special-delivery stamp on the envelope, she was sure. She didn't hand the letter over to Captain Cline until Wednesday, June 23, because everything she had given him had immediately appeared in the newspapers. As for the memorial service, it wouldn't have made any difference had she seen the letter sooner. Anyway, the Temple received dozens of special-delivery letters every day, so why pick out this one for special attention? Minnie smiled in deprecation: probably the postal inspectors had it confused with some other special delivery. The hair in the letter looked like Aimee's, yes, but she couldn't prove it.

"I looked everywhere in her room, on her combs and brushes, but I could find none of her hair," Mother said. "If I had thought Aimee was alive, wouldn't I have waited and taken up the collection after she came back? She could get ten dollars to our one any time."

Aimee sat stiffly in Howard's car until all other cars had left the station. Even then she did not go directly to the Gadsden Hotel, where

Mother had reserved rooms, but drove around town for half an hour in an attempt to elude reporters and spectators. Unsuccessful in this, she flatly refused to cross the border if any reporters followed her. How could she concentrate, she said, with a lot of crazy reporters tagging along asking fool questions? She was quite rude to the representatives of the press whom she had praised fulsomely one week before. Finally she relented to the point of permitting one reporter and one photographer to accompany her, on the condition that they pool their material with those left behind.

First stop in Agua Prieta was at the office of Presidente Boubion, where Aimee was received courteously and closeted with the mayor and an interpreter for half an hour. Then the party moved into the desert and cruised nearly ten hours, scouring over a hundred and sixty miles of rough terrain. No cabin that Aimee could identify was found. She looked over several possibilities, and partially identified two: one was a six-room building on the Cenesas Ranch, half of it occupied by a Mexican woman, four children, and twenty-four chickens; the second was a one-room shack on the Mills Ranch, on the United States side, with a beaten-earth floor. At both places Aimee demonstrated how she climbed through the window. She also posed for photographs with her skirt draped over her head. The sun was sweltering.

Before starting out, she announced she would drink nothing, but observers saw her help herself several times to the Thermos jug of ice water in the car. Twice, at points more than twenty miles from Agua Prieta, she offered to walk back, just to show she could, but Mother and others dissuaded her. Minnie plainly suffered from the heat. Several times she remarked on the curious softness of the voices of the dwellers in that enormous solitude. Empty the desert was of corroborating signs to bolster Aimee's story. Most of the time she seemed confused, unable to identify any landmark more than three miles from Agua Prieta. During the brief halts of the caravan, she left the car and walked perhaps half a mile altogether, and she returned to the hotel at 7 o'clock in the evening looking haggard.

Mother had announced they would remain two days, but shortly after 8 o'clock she canceled their train reservations for Friday and they hurried to the station to catch the Golden State Limited leaving at 9 p.m. Aimee went directly into the sleeper without acknowledging the thin crowd assembled beside the track. There were no railroad guards this time. Mother Kennedy turned on the car steps and maundered through a few words. Sister might return soon, she suggested. "I believe her return would be a lovely thing. All of you who believe with me that Sister McPherson's return to Douglas would be lovely, raise your hands."

Five hands went up, the one held highest being the hand of the jitney driver who had collected $30 for chauffeuring Sister all day. The whistle blew. Mother struggled up the steps and the train pulled away.

The cause of this precipitous retreat was evident to the reporters left behind: one hour before train time, the evangelist had received alarming news from Los Angeles, where two grand juries were looking into her disappearance. Assistant United States Attorney J. Edward Simpson, in charge of mail-fraud prosecutions, was being quoted publicly as saying that suppression of the "Avengers" letter, with its clear proof that Sister was alive when the memorial service was held, was a plain case of fraud. Regarding this and similar letters which Minnie Kennedy had received, he permitted himself to be quoted:

> Whether genuine demands for ransom, the work of a crank, or whatever they may be, these letters were clearly written and sent for a fraudulent purpose.

The Los Angeles *Examiner,* publishing this statement, printed beside it, without comment, the text of the statute on mail fraud. At the same time, with not wholly unperceived irony, it retained on the front page its offer of rewards for finding Sister's kidnapers or the shack.

The Los Angeles County grand jury had entered the picture unexpectedly, calling in Keyes (just back from San Francisco), Ryan, and Cline. The first intimation of this development was a statement by Ryan, made in the district attorney's office, that sufficient evidence was in hand to warrant going to the grand jury. Keyes was out of the room when Ryan said this; on his return he contradicted his deputy, saying there was no evidence that any crime had been committed. Ten minutes after this minimization, the prosecutor nimbly entered the grand-jury room with Ryan and remained half an hour. On emerging, Keyes was smiling.

"As far as I am concerned, this is not an important case," he said. "At least"—his smile broadened—"until the kidnapers are caught."

Tight-lipped and tense beside his chief, Ryan kept silence.

The action of the grand jury had been initiated by the foreman, William H. Carter, who told reporters that so many rumors were flying around that the jurors wanted to get the facts so some report could be made to the public.

Not only the city but half the state (with the rest of the nation looking on in amazement) was in a welter of confusion. Police had to be stationed around Angelus Temple to break up the fights constantly flaring between Sister's adherents and those whom they denounced as her detractors. And Ryan came in for much guying professionally, City Hall laughing over a rhymed squib composed by a court clerk, in which the joke was aimed at impetuous Joe. Irreverently this jingle ran:

THE INTERVIEW

Joe Ryan down to Douglas went,
Where he by Asa Keyes was sent,
And told to solve a mystery
Unmatched in modern history.

Joe opened up the interview
By saying, "Aimee, howdy-do;
Your mother swore that you'd been drowned
And recently with Jesus crowned."

But Aimee, not to be outdone,
As quick as lightning sprang this one:
"Yes, I've been dead, as she suspected,
But I have just been resurrected!"

And Aimee took Joe by the hand,
Said, "Joe, you're my rock in a weary land!"
And Joe replied, "Fine, Aimee, but—
Where in the hell can I find that hut?"

Then Aimee said, "Don't doubt me, Joe,
That hut's somewhere in Mexico—
An adobe hut with a wooden floor,
And a flushing toilet, furthermore!"

Joe scratched his head and kind of sighed,
And then distrustingly replied
(Quite sure that tale was bound to totter):
"Where in the hell did they get the water?"

But Aimee wasn't to be caught
By Ryan's sudden, wise onslaught;
She shouted, with a burst of glee:
"They got it from the Holy See!"

Joe paused and meditated then
Before he started in again:
"How could you keep so clean and pure
In blistering desert temperature?"

"Oh, Joe, that's easy," Aimee said,
As she tossed back her auburn head;
"As I was strolling through the night
God bathed me in a flood of light!"

Poor Joe began to feel downcast,
He saw he'd met his match at last;
Posthaste he asked, ere she could think:
"Where in the hell did you get a drink?"

But Aimee was all primed to shoot,
And answered Joe as he sat mute:
"You must be lacking, Joe, in brains—
You ought to know that Jesus reigns!"

Still, with exuberance of youth,
Joe kept on seeking for the truth,
And said: "Please tell me, if you choose,
Where in the hell did you get those shoes?"

Then Aimee kind of hemmed and hawed
As at her petticoat she clawed,
And finally, with heat, she raved:
"I made them from some souls I saved!"

Yet Joe was not quite satisfied
With all that Aimee had replied,
And so he ventured, with great stress:
"Where in the hell did you get that dress?"

So Aimee tossed her head once more
And said (beginning to get sore):
"Joe, I would have you understand,
I got it in the Holy Land!"

Joe then appeared somewhat confused
As he sat there and softly mused:
"I'd not precipitate a row—
But surely 'tis not holy now!"

Strong-hearted Joe, still much dismayed,
As Aimee bowed her head and prayed,
Inquired once more, quite cold and calm:
"Where in the hell's that corset from?"

And Aimee then, with flash of fire
Revealing her long latent ire,
Said: "That's hidden from your view—
A thing you'll never look into!"

The interview was o'er at last,
Joe saw that he was far outclassed;
He felt his trip had been in vain,
As he rushed down to catch a train.

And here's the wire he sent to Keyes
When he abandoned desert skies:
"To solve this riddle you had hope—
But where in the hell did you get that dope?"

Frame-up!

Hardly had the Golden State Limited cleared Douglas that evening of July 1 when Ernesto Boubion released to the press his report on the activities of Mexican authorities in the case. He had been shut in his office alone with the evangelist for half an hour that morning, no other person present except an interpreter—and the interpreter was an American. The *presidente municipale* may have sensed that he was in an exposed position, hence his haste to make his report public. With unruffled dignity he divulged that during the morning conference he had informed Mrs. McPherson plainly that Mexican officials did not believe her, whereupon she implored him to withhold or entirely suppress his prepared statement "because it differs so materially from my story." Differ it did.

Police Chief Sylvano Villa, born and reared in Agua Prieta, started trailing at daybreak on the day of the evangelist's reappearance, the mayor's report set forth:

A woman's footprints were first picked up at the Gonzales house. Backtracking, Chief Villa and his men read the tale in the dust in the early hours before anyone else had passed over the road. . . . Only one automobile had passed over the road. These tracks led to a wash slightly less than three miles east of Agua Prieta. Here the dusty road again told the whole story. Footprints of a woman led from the automobile to the *garita*. Then the tracks returned to the automobile, where the woman must have entered the machine, as the tracks stopped and the automobile started out again back in the direction of the city. Some distance from the slaughterhouse where Mrs. McPherson was first seen, the automobile stopped again and the woman's tracks again began. For one hundred and seventy-five yards they were followed by my men to about the spot where Mrs. McPherson says she stopped and called for aid. Then the tracks left the slaughterhouse and headed for Agua Prieta, where they were lost.

The automobile followed by my men came from across the line. It was driven to the *garita* and there turned around. A woman got out and walked to the shelter, and, as the footprints showed, went into the shelter for some reason. . . . The tracks and footprints found by my men in the dust of the road were the only tracks on the road where Mrs. McPherson says she was. I therefore believe that they were her tracks. If she did make them, then she could not have been wandering around all over the desert here, but would have been the passenger in an automobile which drove her across the border and from which she got out and walked back from a point near the slaughterhouse, after having left the machine once before several miles beyond.

With this summation in their hands, Douglas Police Chief Bowden, Sergeant Murchison (elevated to the grade of assistant chief), and Mayor Hinton went into a huddle to draft their report; it was learned that it coincided wtih the Boubion statement in every respect, and added details which did not come within the Mexicans' purview.

This was grist for the press, and at Yuma reporters piled aboard the Golden State Limited. They found the doors of the McPherson Pullman locked and porters on guard to repel boarders. Indignant representations to the Pullman conductor finally gained the press men permission to enter the car, and persistent banging on the locked door of Aimee's compartment caused it to open a crack. Minnie Kennedy peered out. She was taken aback at the number of the interviewers and answered questions through the slit.

No, nobody could talk with Sister. Yes, they had heard about the grand jury's interest. "We will be willing to go before the grand jury any time we are wanted." The ransom-letter investigation while both she and Sister were out of town was very unfair. As for Boubion's ungallant conclusions, Mother slyly rubbed the palm of her hand, smiled, and said, "That's Mexico, Mexico. . . ." Then the door clicked shut.

A few minutes later, as the reporters continued to pound, they were told they could speak to Sister.

Aimee sat staring stonily out the window. Mother did most of the talking. Now and then Aimee glanced at her mother and checked a reply forming on her lips. She seemed docile, a trait no reporter had ever seen in her before. Minnie sniffed at the suggestion that they had planned to run away; Captain Cline knew all about their departure. How could their trip possibly interest the Los Angeles authorities? Minnie urged the reporters to look carefully at her daughter's white silk poplin dress— the same dress she had worn all day on the desert, and it was hardly soiled. Her shoes were not scuffed, she was not sunburned, and there were no perspiration stains on her clothing, Minnie pointed out.

"Stand up so these men can see," she instructed her daughter. Aimee stood and turned slowly, letting the reporters inspect her, front and back, head to foot. She endured their stares silently, then sat down and looked out the window again. Minnie prattled on, until Aimee flashed righteously, "I can tell you one thing—we are going to clamp down on reporters from now on! Our work is too important!"

At last Minnie pushed the reporters out the door, where from other passengers they learned that the two women had remained secluded during the entire trip, taking their meals in their stateroom. Only once— at Bisbee Junction, first stop out of Douglas—did Aimee show herself. About fifty members of her Foursquare Church of the Air were on the platform, and the evangelist threw up the car window and spoke a few words to them rather ungraciously.

The reporters speculated: belabored on so many sides, was Aimee losing her nerve? They could hardly credit that; her whole career was an exemplification of her oft-shouted slogan: "In the vocabulary of a Canadian, the word 'can't' does not exist!" She had never shrunk from any contest or opposition; she had been rash to the point of folly, but never uncourageous. Now she appeared not defeated but frightened, like a whipped child. The same reporters she had loaded with gratitude a week before she glared at with hostility.

A crowd of several hundred persons waited at the station in Los Angeles Friday morning, but the evangelist and her mother hailed a taxi and hurried to the Temple. There Minnie telephoned Captain Cline and he drove over at once. A conference among the three lasted more than an hour, and Cline, on leaving, repeated that the women had a right to go anywhere without consulting him.

To reporters waiting outside the barricaded front and back doors of the Temple home, Minnie passed a mimeographed statement regarding the ransom letter:

> The letter was given to me either Monday afternoon or Tuesday morning, I am not sure which. There were two two-cent stamps on it when it was handed to me. I had been disturbed with many letters containing all manner of messages—some purporting to have word from my daughter in the spirit world, others with information she was here, there, everywhere. I noticed with distress the answers to the questions, but figured they were questions anyone could have answered had they lived in our Canadian neighborhood.

Formal denial was entered that any "memorial fund" had been raised; it was just a "carry on fund."

> Absolutely no money was asked for a monument—it was all for the Bible School. I cannot remember the exact sum in cash, but it was small compared with the amount quoted in the newspapers, the bulk being in pledges which anyone is at perfect liberty to withdraw and cancel if he is not pleased that Sister is alive.

Mother appended the bland statement that she was "glad to welcome a grand-jury investigation." Pinned to the mimeographed release was a typewritten slip:

> Mrs. McPherson says her statement given to Captain Cline is correct and other stories are not so. We realize there are many and will continue to be many stories played. Over that we have no control.

The Los Angeles Ministerial Association, acutely embarrassed by the abrupt annulling of their condolences over the supposed death of a former colleague, debated issuing a retraction in form. Jumping the gun, eight pastors publicly tossed a series of questions to the authorities, prompted, they said, by "insinuations that perhaps this whole matter might be covered up, dropped, or in some subtle way eliminated without the facts being delivered to the public." Among the points raised were the exact time when the kidnapers sought out Mother Kennedy at the Temple and were directed to the beach; why Mrs. Kennedy never mentioned this incident all during the time her daughter was believed to be drowned; whether the statements made in Douglas by police and desert experts were to carry any weight; and to which store Mrs. McPherson sent her kidnapers to buy just the kind of corset she preferred?

In conclusion there were two shrewd thrusts:

> The fact that Mr. Ormiston dropped from sight during the reported drowning of Mrs. McPherson is still in the public's mind. Is this fact of such trivial importance that it needs no official attention?
>
> When our district attorney states that he has received no evidence of a kidnaping, is the public to take that statement as meaning he does not accept Mrs. McPherson's story as evidence?

This lashing-out flung into the open rumors that were convulsing the city. Bob Shuler added to the excitement by reading, in crowded Trinity Church, ten similarly embarrassing questions addressed to the district attorney, which concluded:

> Is it customary for a district attorney to remain passive and inactive when it is charged that three kidnapers lured a woman into an automobile . . . demanded ransom of $500,000 for her release, and defied the laws of the State of California and the County of Los Angeles?

If Aimee was supposed to be on the run, her appearance in the Temple Friday evening put an end to that supposition. Before she spoke, Mother Kennedy cleared up, to her own satisfaction, the matter of how much money really was collected at the famous memorial service by bringing to the platform faithful Brother Arthur. He was introduced to the audience and radio listeners as the Temple's auditor and chairman of the board of directors. Resting a ledger on the pulpit lectern, he read the entries for the June 20 love offering—$4690.56 in cash and $29,500 in pledges, payable in one year, making a grand total of $34,190.56. That, Mother Kennedy said, smiling sadly, was a long way from the $40,000 the newspapers kept talking about, and she repeated that anyone was free to withdraw his pledge if he was not truly pleased that Sister had been restored to them.

Aimee followed the financial statement with an incandescent sermon, during which she likened herself to Joseph and her kidnaping to his sale into bondage by the jealousy of his brethren. "Joseph was the victim of a frame-up, a real frame-up—as good as some people know how to make today!" she screamed.

Her disciples looked at each other. Aimee had extended a handle and they seized it. Frame-up!

Martyrdom!

With Saturday came a lull. True, the Foreign Ministry in Mexico City received an agitated telegram from Agua Prieta authorities recommending that representations be made to the United States government regarding "the shadow that has been cast on the treatment of distressed Americans in Mexico." And in Douglas, Chief Bowden mailed a bulky envelope to Cline, containing the stenographic statements of five witnesses, including the nurse who attended Sister in Calumet Hospital. While from Albuquerque, New Mexico, United States Attorney Mc-Nabb, who had been in the East on business and was hastening back to Los Angeles, intimated that he had a clue as to the whereabouts of the typewriter on which the "Avengers" letter was written. (Later he said that the machine he had in mind was one of four spotted, but when his investigators tried to borrow it for testing, it had vanished.)

Also on Saturday the foreman of the county grand jury assured Los Angeles through the press that the district attorney had promised not to shelve the case. Ryan's mail, that day, amid the clutter of self-serving letters signed and anonymous, yielded a page torn from the Los Angeles *Times* of June 25 (a day Ryan had spent hunting shacks in Mexico) showing a photograph of Mrs. McPherson taken in the hospital in Douglas on June 24, in which a wrist watch appeared on her arm. Had the kidnapers given her a watch as well as a corset to fit? "A listener in Radioland" wondered.

During Saturday morning the evangelist and her mother remained cloistered, sending out two brief communiqués. One, by Aimee: "Although we spent hours in the desert we were unable to locate the shack. However, I recognized a good deal of the country as that through which I ran after I escaped." The other, by Minnie, served notice that they could not receive interviewers "because of the attitude of the press. We have been constantly annoyed by telephone calls and have hardly had time to perfect our plans for the Sunday services." Toward noon the alert reporters caught Minnie clandestinely re-entering her home and flabbergasted her by inquiring why she had just visited the downtown office of the Nick Harris detective agency, a firm which had a reputation for gathering evidence in divorce cases.

"You found out?" grumbled Mother, and stumped into the house, flinging back, "If only the investigation would center more on trying to find the kidnapers than on the details of Mrs. McPherson's experience! The longer the delay, the farther they may be getting away!"

Saturday morning Arthur L. Veitch, a lawyer, accompanied by Nick Harris, showed up at the United States Attorney's office for a conference with the mail-frauds prosecutor, Simpson. They identified themselves as Mrs. Kennedy's representatives and remained for a two-hour discussion. Simpson betrayed his annoyance; he had invited Mrs. McPherson and Mrs. Kennedy to his office, not a lawyer and a detective. Minnie confirmed that she had hired Veitch that morning. Sister's personal lawyer, Roland Rich Woolley, was seen entering and leaving the Temple home. A dull day, Saturday.

But Sunday brought compensations to the hundreds of thousands of partisans who had adopted the scrimmage as a new spectator sport. United States Attorney McNabb reached Los Angeles full of prosecutor's talk about "startling evidence." A rumor that kept thousands of listeners glued to their radios was that Aimee planned to appeal to Kenneth Ormiston to get in touch with Cline. This aroused Aimee to retort that for her personally to appeal to Ormiston would be "ridiculous and out of the question"; nor, she said, had she promised Cline or anybody else, during the halcyon hours of her early thankfulness, to assist in any such way.

Cline half admitted he was hunting the radio man, and Nick Harris (employed, he put it, by the Temple to make "an impartial investigation, let the chips fall where they may") made known that he too was seeking Ormiston, because the sooner that fugitive was forced to tell whatever he knew, the sooner the rumors would be squelched.

The star of the Sabbath performance was, of course, Sister. She preached three times at the Temple, addressing overflow audiences and thousands more by radio. At the morning service she made no mention of the kidnaping, but both afternoon and evening she tore into her critics, the newspapers, and rumor-mongers in a virtuoso performance marked by all the high spirits of a dog fight.

That hullabaloo about a letter, she scoffed—"It is peculiar what silly little things the newspapers can quibble over! Somebody says somebody changed a stamp on a letter—that's worth at least four columns! How did it get changed? Perhaps a little child wanted the stamp for a collection. Who knows? At least, we do *not* know how it got changed—if it was changed. When a letter comes into your hands, it is your own letter. You can take the stamp off if you like—although nobody knows about the changing of this certain stamp here!

" 'Did it come Saturday or Sunday?' someone asks. It might have come in on Saturday or Sunday and never been opened until Monday or Tuesday, for we have too many letters to care for the instant they arrive. 'Did you hold that letter up to raise $40,000?' No! Not at all! To begin with, $40,000 was not raised. Furthermore, the money was not raised for a monument to Sister McPherson—some great marble shaft with an angel poised on one toe on top; but it was all for the great Bible School. Boo! That's good for four columns! It seems so utterly absurd!

" 'I know,' someone says, 'but there was the presidente who saw an automobile's tracks that turned around.' I don't care if a thousand cars turned around! I know my story is true! Folks," she snarled, bringing her lips close to the microphone, "are paying more attention to the word of one Mexican than I have ever known them to! Things seem to be just turned around!"

Hallelujahs steamed up to the dome and over the air.

" 'But he did say it,' " she hurried on. "Yes, he did, according to all reports. That's the word of one man. On the other hand, here is a beautiful blueprint [an usher lugged forward a king-size map of the Agua Prieta vicinity on an easel] drawn for me by the deputy United States marshal, the chief of police in Douglas, and the sergeant of police who formed a posse and backtracked immediately and found the footsteps, as nearly as they could, of my pathetic journey but my escape, for which I thank Jesus!"

With a pointer she indicated markings which were indistinguishable to the audience. Why couldn't she find the shack? Naturally she couldn't recognize the outside of any hut, because "when I left I had no time to admire the architecture or landscaping, I was in a hurry. 'Sister, darling,' some are saying, 'haven't you any sense? Don't you realize that anybody clever enough to plan that crime could do away with the shack and any evidence?' That is true."

A shiver ran through the congregation. Of course the shack could not be found! The kidnapers had destroyed it!

How foolish to imagine she could slip out of sight, she went on—she who was known to millions by sight and voice. "How foolish it would be to think that Sister McPherson would leave her beautiful Temple, leave her school, the administration building, the plans for the new Bible hotel, her beautiful mother who is the finest little lady on earth, and her own two beautiful children! Come here, Roberta and Rolf, stand beside me!"

Emotionally she told how her daughter was born just one month after her father's death as a missionary in China. She exclaimed over Rolf, standing shyly, embarrassed, "who has grown so, he is almost grown up, my son! . . . I think now I realize what it is. The old Devil didn't want the money so much as to discredit Sister McPherson's story, cast a reflection on her integrity and her character! I think he's a pretty slick old fellow—and I suppose the same hand that planned this thing in the first place is the same hand that is feeding the criminals now!"

Amens reverberated. Smiling, one hand upraised, Aimee stilled the outburst. Then, speaking quietly, with womanly sweetness and candor, she delivered her climactic stroke. "I had not meant to say a word about this today. My business is not to say anything about it, but to preach the gospel of Jesus Christ and get just as many souls saved as I can. I realize that I am a good big target for the Devil and that I am in the front-line trenches. I shouldn't be surprised if the old Devil tried to finish me off, one of these days—that I should be picked out to be a martyr. Praise God if I should be counted worthy of such a grave!"

Thousands, in the stillness that followed, were ready to shed their blood, if need be, to defend Sister. And thousands listening by radio wondered whether their ears were functioning: from doubting a person's word to martyring her required a grandiose mental leap.

Sales of radio sets boomed. And a lively parade of new witnesses and mysterious clues quickstepped past the fascinated eyes of the public. On Monday morning Cline received the police report from Douglas, looked it over, and forthwith locked it in his files. To clamoring reporters he refused to divulge any inkling of its contents beyond saying, "The information in it is the kind that you wouldn't dare to print at this time."

The reporters would have felt twice as aggrieved had they guessed that in the report was a positive identification by the railroad ticket agent in Douglas of Harry D. Hallenbeck, the friend of the Temple family, who owned a ranch in Arizona, as the man who bought a ticket for Los Angeles on the Golden State Limited in Douglas on June 22. Mrs. Mc-Pherson appeared in the desert across the border a few hours after that train left. A Tucson haberdasher identified Hallenbeck as the man to whom he sold a Panama hat on June 20. And the movements of a closed blue automobile in and around Agua Prieta on June 21 and 22 were being checked, with the ardent assistance of the Mexican authorities.

These border worthies were wroth at Mrs. McPherson's slur from the Angelus Temple platform, and protests to Mexico City doubled; the Foreign Ministry there compiled a full report for President Calles' personal consideration.

Nick Harris spent the better part of the day sifting through letters with Mrs. McPherson and Mrs. Kennedy. Sister was said to be under close guard by her followers, who feared another attempt would be made to kidnap her.

"This isn't the last of it," said Minnie with a bob of her head. "This plot goes deeper than has been revealed. Why don't the authorities look for the real ringleaders?"

At the United States Attorney's office, an assistant prosecutor received over the telephone a threat of death unless the office dropped its investigation. McNabb's retort was to request that the outgoing federal grand jury be held over to consider the case.

In Tucson the chief of police released a statement by an automobile dealer, C. A. Pape, identifying Sister McPherson as the woman he saw leaving the International Club, a saloon in Agua Prieta, five days before her reappearance. The woman's furtiveness drew his attention, he said, and out of curiosity he particularly observed her and her companions, a woman and two men, as they got into a blue Hupmobile and drove away.

On top of this, Sheriff McDonald in Tombstone released a signed statement by two men, named Jones and Bermond, who were positive that they saw Mrs. McPherson in a blue Hupmobile near Esqueda, Sonora, with another woman and a man, on June 21. Their statement was filled with circumstantial details, such as their remarking the woman's hair—brownish in color and piled high on her head, so unusual a contrast to the bobbed hair in fashion that one said jocularly, "Four or five years from now, if you see a woman with that much hair you'll think she's crazy." Later these men saw Sister McPherson in Douglas and recognized her. McDonald also published the statement of the nurse together with the hospital chart, and the statement made by the watchman at the slaughterhouse, which stressed that Aimee did not ask for water.

Aimee chuckled over Pape's story. "Isn't it ridiculous that anyone should say they saw me coming out of a roadhouse?" she scoffed. "It seems almost useless to deny these rumors—I have no positive way of disproving them."

Reporters uncovered the interesting detail that a blue Hupmobile was registered to Harry D. Hallenbeck. They found the contractor on his ranch thirty-nine miles northeast of Yuma and received his denial of any connection with the affair. His movements during the time of Sister's absence could be verified by witnesses, he assured them, and he was in Los Angeles, in the sheriff's office, on the morning on June 23, when he first heard of her reappearance; he telephoned to her from there at about 3 o'clock that afternoon. Reporters noted that the Golden State Limited reached Los Angeles at 2:45 p.m. on June 23. Everybody at the ranch backed up Hallenbeck, who said he was willing to come to Los Angeles and testify, if there was a grand-jury investigation, but he didn't see how he could contribute anything worth while.

A two-pronged grand-jury investigation—federal and county—definitely loomed. Tuesday, pricked by rising pressure and bombarded by questions embarrassing to a conscientious public servant, Keyes took Ryan before the county grand jury and requested the jurors to investigate. The panel voted unanimously to oblige. Subpoenas were issued for Aimee, her mother, Emma Schaffer, Brother Arthur, Hallenbeck, Roberta, Rolf, and Temple workers, and Douglas and Mexican officials were invited to appear.

Immediately Sister and Mother went into virtual hiding. Process servers were unable to trace the evangelist at all; she was resting somewhere with Emma, they were told. Mother sent out word that she saw no point in going before a grand jury; Aimee and she could only tell the same story all over again, and it had been told and retold. Maybe later they might go, she didn't know. Hallenbeck started for Los Angeles. Presidente Boubion said he and his police chief were willing to make the journey (Mexico City immediately granted them official permission), provided, of course, that their expenses were paid.

The real spur in Keyes' flank and the action that notified the Temple's embattled leaders that they faced a fierce crisis was a resolution voted by the executive committee of the Church Federation of Los Angeles—and circulated to every possible publicity outlet:

Whereas, there has arisen throughout the nation an intense interest in the story related by Mrs. Aimee Semple McPherson, in which she claims that she was kidnaped and held for practically thirty days in a Mexican cabin, and

Whereas, it is apparent to all that either a crime of the most terrible nature has been perpetrated against Mrs. Aimee Semple McPherson, or else a fraud and hoax that is a shame to Christianity have been attempted and the Christian religion is being criticized and even condemned as a result of conflicting stories that are being circulated to right and left;

Now, therefore, be it resolved: First, that the executive committee of the Church Federation of Los Angeles declare itself absolutely neutral as regards the supposed and reported differences of opinion that may exist between Mrs. McPherson and those whom she terms her 'enemies'; Second, that we solemnly affirm that the district attorney, the sheriff, the police department and the grand juries empaneled in Los Angeles County should make an honest, sincere and thoroughly adequate investigation of this whole matter, without fear or favor, and report to the people their findings. . . . We go on record as demanding of the officers of the law that they do their duty in this matter irrespective of consequences.

Mother Kennedy was prompt in rebuttal. "These ministers issuing this statement didn't build Angelus Temple, and it will take care of itself! If they have any information, the place for it is before the grand jury!" Defiantly she capped the *Examiner*'s reward offer with another $5000 for the arrest and conviction of the kidnapers, or $1500 for the arrest and conviction of any one of them. Temple workers offered $500 for finding the shack, although Mother didn't think highly of this gesture. "We've about given up all hope of ever finding the shack," she explained. "It was probably destroyed by the kidnapers."

Secretly she called a caucus of her legal staff to decide on the least disadvantageous course of action. The meeting was held in the Temple home. Present were Woolley and Veitch, Mother and Aimee, and, as chairman and final authority, Judge Hardy. The judge, Minnie felt, was the only real friend to whom she could turn; lawyers she thought little of, except that they were shamefully overpaid. Hardy she trusted. (Years later, under questioning, Aimee was "unable to remember" whether an additional person present at this highly secret council was H. H. Kinney, secretary to Mayor Cryer of Los Angeles.)

The issue was whether Aimee and her mother should testify before the grand jury, or decline to repeat their stories under oath. Minnie was dead set against testifying. Woolley was equally firm in opposition; he felt that testifying would be a major mistake. Veitch rather thought they should answer questions freely. Hardy, exhibiting a degree of naïveté seldom encountered even among judges, counseled that their best course was to tell everything; if they declined to testify, even though they had every right to do so, the public, already stirred by a thousand and one derogatory rumors, would be bound to get a "wrong impression."

The dilemma was sharp. As chief counsel, Woolley (a Mormon who was destined to hold positions of trust and esteem in his church) submitted his opinion that the furor would die out if Mrs. McPherson would simply drop the discussion. There was no legal complaint against his client (that was preposterous; she was the complainant), and the best course for her would be to withdraw into impregnable silence; she had told her story, and whether the public believed it or not was a matter for its conscience. The newspapers, an admitted irritant, depended for their material on her continued actions or statements, or on those of the law; if she would shelve the whole matter, leave her kidnapers to divine justice if human agencies should fail, the press would soon be stymied, and the public clamor would die away for want of fuel.

Hardy still believed that the evangelist should testify. His participation in the debate was, of course, nonprofessional; a judge is forbidden to practice law. His view was expressed merely in the form of the solicitude of a family friend. In the end his view prevailed.

Aimee was elated. While she was ready to accept the decision of her advisers, she welcomed the bolder, more dramatic course, accepted the challenge gladly, and announced she would go before the grand jury and tell them everything. Her first action was to ask Sheriff Traeger and Undersheriff Eugene Biscailuz for an armed escort to the Hall of Justice. Then she mapped out the staging of the performance in which she intended to be the shining star—a show such as the legal corridors of California never saw before and probably never will behold again.

What Goes On
in a Grand-Jury Room

Los Angeles' imposing, gray Hall of Justice stands on Temple Street. This was merely a fortuitous similarity of names; yet on the morning of Thursday, July 8, some persons among the crowd that blackened the sidewalks for a block around wondered fleetingly whether the jurisdiction of the Temple on Echo Park had been extended overnight into the very center of town. Temple adherents were out in force; a corps of uniformed workers armed with Bibles lined a hundred-foot lane from the curb to the main entrance in readiness for Sister's appearance.

Inside the building the district attorney's office was unusually animated. Messengers scurried along corridors, deputies spoke gravely, clerks checked through folders. An air of expectancy penetrated nearby courtrooms, where bailiffs tiptoed to the doors now and then for a hungry peek. Keyes showed up at 9:30 and went into a huddle with Ryan; they were still conferring when sirens wailing in the distance announced the approach of Mrs. McPherson promptly at the scheduled hour of 10 o'clock.

Three sheriff's deputies, heavily armed, escorted the evangelist. As she swept between the files of her saluting followers, cries of "Hallelujah!" broke from the crowd. From the windows of nearby buildings hundreds of spectators craned. Aimee seldom wore pulpit regalia on secular occasions, but this day she was in her preaching costume—white dress with starched collar and long blue cape lined with gray. She appeared pale, but her eyes sparkled and she lacked none of her customary vitality. Surrounding her as a guard of honor were seven women, dressed identically like their leader even to the hair piled high on the head; none of them wore hats. In flying-wedge formation they ran interference for the pastor through the milling corridors. In the midst of the seven look-alikes, the evangelist was difficult to distinguish; many onlookers picked the wrong woman. The utility of this maneuver to illustrate the doubt inherent in all identifications, should the need arise, was not lost on the press.

Aimee insisted on having a word with Ryan privately, and did not reach the grand jury room until 10:31. Pausing at the door, she quoted, "I am like a lamb led to the slaughter" (ignoring the continuation of the

passage, "he openeth not his mouth"), and then entered the legal holy
of holies. Briskly removing her cape, she sat down in the witness chair.
Keyes administered the oath to tell the truth, the whole truth, and nothing else. The prosecutor then started to administer the oath of secrecy by
which grand-jury witnesses are bound, but Aimee would not promise
not to tell.

"On what ground?" asked the startled Keyes.

"On advice of counsel," was her quick reply.

The district attorney fumbled and yielded. "All right," he said, "I
won't hold you to that oath."

Keyes invited her to tell her story in her own words, straight through,
without interruptions. Sitting forward in the chair, Aimee began, in
a composed distinct tone. The seventeen men and two women, seated in a
semicircle around her, listened gravely. The dramatic narrative was a
repetition of what she had told elsewhere, differing in no essential from
the first statements she made in Douglas.

Reporters, who in spite of all taboos contrived to learn what was going on in the sacrosanct chamber, accosted Veitch, Aimee's attorney,
in an antechamber about his client's refusal to be bound by the secrecy
rule. The lawyer contended that since her story had been told and retold
secrecy would be pointless, she had nothing new to impart, and the oath
would debar her from reporting to her people at the Temple and over
the radio; it might even preclude consultations with her mother and
counsel.

Aimee's guard of honor prayed in another room while their leader testified. At noon they escorted her back to the Temple (the deputy sheriffs
had quietly melted away) and all returned at 1:30, when Aimee picked
up her narrative at the moment of her miraculous escape. Through the
open door as she entered the jury room, reporters glimpsed beside the
witness chair a diagrammed blackboard and blueprint showing the
Ocean Park area and the desert around Agua Prieta.

A recess was called at 3 p.m. Aimee hurried to a conference with her
battery of lawyers—Veitch and Woolley had been reinforced by Leonard
Hamner, a former deputy district attorney—then returned for two hours
of searching cross-examination by Keyes and Ryan. This passage of
arms was extraordinary. Almost from the start, the alert, studiously
polite, and cleverly suspicious prosecutors diverged from the events of
the kidnaping as she told them to fish in the grab-bag of public conjecture, rumor, and scandalous innuendo. Mrs. McPherson was before the

grand jury as the injured party, asking for the simple justice of indictment of her abductors, whoever they might be. Under the urbane and relentless probing of the district attorney, she was almost jockeyed into the position of a defendant; almost, but never quite, for the prosecutors were opposed by a will stronger than their own—the will of a woman who knew just what she wanted to say, and would not be led astray.

The questions put to her covered a multitude of lateral issues. Among these were: what about the hair net found in the pocket of her dress; what about the wrist watch; was the dress she wore June 22 new or a hand-me-down; during her kidnaping did she sleep in her clothes or a nightgown; did she see the newspapers; did she quarrel with her mother; had Mrs. Ormiston accused her of over-friendliness with her radio operator; did she send him money; did she ever threaten to fire Emma Schaffer and meet with the bluster that she didn't dare because Emma knew enough to "blow up the Temple"; was Mrs. Hallenbeck jealous of her; what kind of a car did Hallenbeck drive; was she seen coming out of a saloon?

Perhaps she could give them some idea of the ages of her three kidnapers, Keyes began. Aimee explained apologetically that she was not good at guessing ages; he might test her on the grand-jury members. There were no volunteers.

Now, regarding the length of time she was under the influence of the anesthetic: "You can't give any estimate of the time that had elapsed prior to your becoming conscious again?"

"I would be delighted if anybody could tell me how I could estimate that."

"By the way, when you went in swimming, Mrs. McPherson, did you have any jewelry with you?" Keyes was disarmingly digressive.

"I never wear jewelry."

"I see you have a wrist watch on now."

"Yes."

"And a ring."

"I always keep my wedding ring on."

"Did you have it on this day when you went in swimming?"

"I did. I have never had it off."

"Did you have your wrist watch on after you left Angelus Temple to go swimming?"

"I don't remember."

"Did you have it while you were in this particular house you have described?"

"Oh, no, sir. I was in the water swimming; I wouldn't wear my watch swimming."

"Do you remember if you left it any particular place?"

"If I wore a watch that day, which I do not remember, I would most certainly leave it in my pocketbook."

"Is this the same watch you have always had?"

"Yes."

"Where did you get it?"

"Miss Schaffer gave it to me, or Mother, I don't remember. I can easily check on that if it is material."

"Well, it is quite material."

"I believe I got it when I returned home. I think it was on the dresser."

"You don't believe, then, that you had it while you were in Douglas?"

"Oh, no, sir!"

"In the hospital?"

"I don't believe I did. I am not positive, but I don't think so, that— I am quite positive that I didn't."

"The reason I am inquiring about this," said Keyes with an assumption of straightforwardness, "is this: that if my memory serves me right, I saw a photograph of you taken in the hospital while you were in Douglas, and on your wrist apparently was that wrist watch."

"Then Mother must have brought it, if she did. I didn't have any watch myself when I was found. Mother must have brought my watch."

"You are positive of that?"

"Oh, I am positive of it. Mother must have brought my watch. She brought all my clothes, and probably she did that. I don't remember— it is not important. But I didn't have a watch with me when I was away, positively not."

Regarding the second shack and its wooden floor, Aimee twice said the hut seemed like a temporary camping outfit rather than a permanent structure. On the issue of the floor, she qualified her description to the extent that while her impression still was that the floor was wooden, on her latest trip to the desert she had been taken into a hut that had a floor which to her seemed to be wood, but she was later told it was hard-packed, darkened earth, "smoothed and hardened with some preparation they have."

The food given her during her captivity, she said, was canned goods, bread, and potatoes.

The desert she walked through she described as "not a rough country that would chop your shoes off by any means. As Mr. Ryan said, he could walk two days on it without his commissary shoes being marked."

"Do you perspire freely?"

"I very rarely do," replied Aimee coolly. "I was hot, though; my fore-head was moist with sweat."

"Was there any perspiration on your body?"

"I don't believe I noticed, Mr. Keyes."

The subject of Steve's hat got the prosecutor nowhere.

"At any time while you were with these people, Mrs. McPherson," said the district attorney, "did you see Steve wearing a straw or Panama hat?"

"Not to my recollection."

"Well, weren't you taking particular notice of these people?"

"Not of the hats."

"You expected sometime, didn't you, to come back to Los Angeles and tell the story of your kidnaping?"

"Yes, but I didn't notice his hat."

"Weren't you careful to see the clothes and characteristics and some peculiarities of these people so that you could give a description of them?"

"Yes, I was; but I didn't notice the hats."

Keyes decided to try a different hat himself. "Now, during all that time, Mrs. McPherson, from the time you left this cabin that morning, had you any water to drink?"

"No."

"Were your lips parched at all?"

"My lips were cracked."

"Was your tongue swollen?"

"It felt swollen, yes, and dry, very dry."

"Could you talk readily?"

"I don't remember."

"Didn't you talk at all, or cry out?"

"I cried for help at night, yes. I said, 'Help!' I don't consider that a great length of time to go without water."

Keyes wanted to know why she failed to ask Schansel, at the slaughter-house, for water.

"My thought was to get on. He was a man of a strange-looking face—as you will see when he comes, if he comes—dressed in his underwear, his BVDs, and I was backing away."

"Did you ask Gonzales for water?"

"No—I—just as soon as they came out to me I did—as soon as they were dressed and came out and I could see, the first thing I asked for was water."

"Now, you passed several houses, did you not, from the time you entered Agua Prieta until you came to the Gonzales house? Why didn't you stop at some of those houses and ask for water?"

"Because everyone was in bed; there was no light; and because there were dogs barking and growling in every one."

"Did you ask for water at the slaughterhouse?"

"No. I was not dying for water. I was not in agony for water."

"Don't you know it is practically an impossibility for anyone, particularly a woman, to walk over the desert in Mexico in the broiling sun from noon until practically midnight without water?"

"Yes, I was very thirsty, but I do not say I was dying for water, and I can only say for the grand jury, if there is any doubt along that line, please permit me to go with anyone you want to send and permit me to take the same journey again."

"You don't know the same journey, do you?"

"I know the same desert, Mr. Keyes."

Keyes parried the thrust and feinted for another lunge. "I am going to ask you rather a personal question. Is that hair that you have in sight all yours?"

"Yes."

"You don't wear a switch?"

"No."

"Have you got a hair net on now?"

"I have."

"Had you one on that night when you got to Agua Prieta?"

"Yes."

"Where did you get the hair net?"

"I had it under my bathing cap. The cap was gone, but I still had the net."

"You wore that all the time you were held prisoner?"

"No, sir, I wore it at different times when I needed it."

"You had only one net all the time you were in captivity, is that right?"

"Yes, sir."

Turning abruptly to rumors of quarrels at the Temple, Keyes asked, "What had been the relations between you and Mrs. Kennedy just prior to your disappearance?"

"The same as they always have been—deepest love and confidence."

"Is it a fact or is it not a fact that you and Mrs. Kennedy for some time prior to your disappearance had been having a great many difficulties over financial matters in connection with the Temple?"

"Absolutely never! No difficulties whatever, let alone finances."

"Had you been having difficulties over anything?"

"No, sir, absolutely not. Mother and I were never more in love with each other."

Mrs. Ormiston, Aimee admitted, had shown jealousy—totally unwarranted—because of her husband's association with the Temple; she was temperamentally jealous. Aimee had heard gossip, she had even heard the name of Brother Nichols, her choir leader, linked disparagingly with hers, just because he was often on the platform with her, leading the singing. "But I understand that as to my being mentioned in any connection by Mrs. Ormiston, she denies that, and that must be a mistake, and I have that on very, very good authority; and we have a letter very recently from Mrs. Ormiston, a very friendly letter, thanking me for all my interest and kindness."

Under the far-ranging inquisition Aimee assured the jurors that she slept in a nightgown, and she didn't know whether the dress given to her was new or one worn by Rose; she did not know who tore the labels off. Newspapers she did not see, any they had around the kidnapers kept from her. As for threatening to fire Emma, she scoffed: "Miss Schaffer is like one of the family."

Keyes shifted to whether Mrs. McPherson had ever telephoned to Ormiston from the Rosslyn Hotel, in downtown Los Angeles, during the previous November.

"I have no recollection," she replied. "It might be possible. I usually take a little portable radio set with me in my car wherever I go, that I may keep in touch with my work, and it might be—I cannot recall at the moment, but it might be—that if 10:30 came and I would—if there was nothing coming in—call up and ask why we were not on the air."

Hallenbeck, she had been told by Ruth Culp ("one of my guard who came down to wait for me and pray today"), once owned a Hupmobile, but had traded it two years before for a Chrysler. As for trouble with Mrs. Hallenbeck, there was none whatever, and she sharply corrected the prosecutor's wording with a curt "Mr. Hallenbeck was *not* seen with me on 'innumerable occasions.' "

Of course she had never sent Ormiston $1500, nor had any representative of hers. "To begin with," she explained patiently, "I could not possibly get hold of money like that. I received for spending money twenty-five dollars a week."

"You don't handle the finances?"

"I don't handle the finances, no. If I want any money, they give it to me like a child."

The unaffected statement intrigued the jurors: was this the woman whom malice pictured as a high priestess of avarice? They watched intently as Keyes tried again.

"Whether or not the Temple had ten or twelve different bank accounts you are not prepared to state?"

Aimee looked at him with disdain. "Pardon?"

"I say, whether or not the Temple had ten or twelve different bank accounts you are not prepared to state?"

"No." The word was coldly final.

Ryan took over the questioning and broached the corset riddle. "How soon, would you say, after you arrived at this first house, was it until this corset was brought to you?"

"Probably a little more than half the time."

"Now, did you give them a description of the kind of corset you wanted?"

"No."

"Now, isn't it a fact, Mrs. McPherson, that the kind that you did get, which is a Bon Ton corset, is similar to the kind, character and description, weight and quality, to the kind you ordinarily use?"

"It could not be more different, positively! Absolutely different in every way! The one I had is such a corset as I would give to my little girl to wear to school. I wear a long one."

"What is the name of that?"

"Campo. They could not be more dissimilar, because I never wore anything like that, like a little child's."

Ryan rested on that point and veered to the report that she was seen in Agua Prieta on Monday June 20, in a car with a man resembling Hallenbeck. Was this true or untrue?

"Untrue," came the steady response.

"Were you there by yourself—"

"No!" Aimee cut in sharply before Ryan could finish his question. "I have given a complete breakdown of my whereabouts."

Ryan's excursions seemed less to irritate than to baffle the witness, who with strained patience tried to cooperate. Keyes spelled off his rebuffed deputy. When Mother Kennedy rushed into her daughter's arms in the hospital room in Douglas, there was a whispered conversation between the two women. Did that have to do with her kidnaping?

"Yes," replied the witness. "I can tell you just what she said—the first question, I guess, any mother would ask her daughter at a time like that. She said, 'My dear, did they injure you in any way?' And I said, 'No.' She said, 'Are you certain that you are not injured in any way?' And I said, 'No, Mother, thank God, no.'"

Ryan was up again with a question as to whether any threats against the Temple had been made before her disappearance. Aimee said she knew of none, and her matter-of-fact reply opened a door on the monotony of her life as the leader of a cult. "I know that from time to time crank letters come in, but they are taken up through regular channels. I don't hear of little crank letters coming in. I don't mingle a great deal with the general public except at the prayer [healing] meetings. I go from my house to the platform and from the platform to my house."

One of the jurors had a question. "Did you ever refuse to pray for a woman's sick baby because that woman was not a member of your congregation or your church?"

"No, sir!" Aimee's eyes flashed.

"You never did refuse to pray for a baby?"

"No."

"Did you ever turn anybody down who came to your church and asked for prayer and relief from sickness because they were not a member of your church—"

In her earnestness Sister interrupted. "No!"

"—or a member of some other doctrine?"

"No." Aimee's answer was warm. "We would go out of our way to meet them, because of that. I am sure that could not be." She turned with an easy movement to the district attorney. "Would I be granted a moment to speak to the jury, Mr. Keyes?"

Before Keyes could reply, foreman Carter assented. "I would be pleased. Go right ahead."

But the prosecutor fended her off with a question suggested by a juror. "How is it that you can recollect in such complete detail some of the episodes that happened during your absence and other matters you are not sure of or don't recall?"

Which episodes? Aimee countered.

"Well, for instance, whether you crossed the fence or not."

"Such things I am sure of."

"You are sure you were pushed in an automobile."

"That was at the first, when my health and my mind and my strength were all clear."

"You are sure that Rose, so called, gave you some clothing on that day you departed from the cabin; you are sure of that."

"I know there were clothes laid out for me to put on."

"Certain things that occurred on this day you escaped from the cabin and were wandering on the desert you are not so sure of; is that true?"

"Well, I was running."

"The direction or distances?"

"No, sir; I was not looking for directions or distances. One mountain or hill didn't mean any more to me than another and today I can't recognize—they moved me twenty miles, and one twenty miles looks just the same to me as any other twenty miles. You could lose your way unless you are a trained desert man."

A juror wondered how much money she had collected in London during her appearances there in April. At her meetings in the Royal Albert Hall she received about $500 a night, she said. This was not a fee, but a love offering. "I never charge for my lectures; it is on the free-will-offering plan."

Keyes nodded that she might proceed. Facing an audience on whose emotions she might work, Aimee was in her element. She spoke as a woman, feelingly, with the ring of sincerity. The surface implausibility of her misadventure she readily conceded.

> I realize that this story may sound strange to many of you, may be difficult for some of you to believe. It is difficult for me, sometimes, to believe. Sometimes it seems it must have been a dream. I would to God that it was, that I could wake up and pinch myself and know that it was not true. I realize that, and whether it was a part of the plan of it all—

She paused, seeking suitable words, while the thought of kidnapers who concocted an unlikely technique for carrying out their scheme in order to nullify her word sank home.

> I want to say that if character counts a little, that I want you to look back: my mother gave me to God before I was born; my earliest training had been in Bible and religious work; I lined up the chairs and preached to them as early as five years of age, and gave my testimony; I was converted at seventeen, married an evangelist, preached the gospel in my humble way at home and then sailed for

China, never expecting to come back to this land, but willing to give my life for Jesus. They buried my precious husband there. I came back with my little baby in my arms, born a month after her father died. I took up the Lord's work as soon as I was able to go on.

I had no great denominations back of me, but I began very humbly. Until this crushing thing that none of us can explain why even God would permit, although we cannot question that—it would be wrong to do that—I was on the pinnacle of success so far as my work for God was concerned, but I have not always been there. I began preaching to farmers, ranchers, under the trees to farmers in their blue overalls sitting on the grass and using the piazza as a mourners' bench. But from there, with the sixty dollars that came in the collection, I bought a little tent, a poor little tent very full of holes, and from that I saved my money and bought a bigger one, and that has been the history. I drove my own stakes, patched the tent and tied the guy ropes almost like a man; and then came the times when we began to get bigger buildings and theaters and buildings costing sometimes as much as a hundred dollars a day, in buildings where I have preached to as many as sixteen thousand in a day.

Then came the building of Angelus Temple. I came here to a neighborhood that had no special buildings in it, got a piece of land and hired horses and scrapers and bossed the men myself and went out to build the foundation with my little capital. I told people my dream to preach the gospel as God had given it to me, and they came to help me, not here, but from other cities, through the *Bridal Call,* my little magazine. I have never put my money in oil wells or ranches or even clothes or luxuries. My great thought has always been— and this can be absolutely proved—for the service of the Lord and my dear people.

"My dear people." To the jurors the words had a regal ring: not of arrogance or condescension, but of duty and love loyally rendered and received. Aimee adverted to possible enemies.

Naturally, I have preached a gospel which made some enmity: I have gone unmercifully after the dope ring, gambling, liquor, tobacco, dancing, and made the statement that I would rather see my children dead than in a public dance hall. I have perhaps laid myself open in these lines about evils in the schools, et cetera; but in everything, I have tried to live as a lady and a Christian.

Perhaps you are skeptical. I don't blame anyone who should doubt my story, because it does sound absurd. But it did happen, ladies and gentlemen. I would not work with one hand seventeen years, and, just as I saw my dearest dream coming true, sweep it over!

She listed and demolished the theories of motives—sickness, fatigue, amnesia, publicity, love. She brought into the open a rumor that had circulated persistently, that she had gone away for an abortion.

There might be a baser motive—I almost blush to mention it here in the jury room, but some might think of it. They say the waters of the mind are like the waters of the sea, that cast up strange things; and that I might be in trouble of some sort and had to go away and come back. I would like to say, although I apologize for having to mention such a thing, that I had a thorough examination upon coming home, although that was not necessary, as the history of my case for twelve years back would show that such a thing would be absolutely out of the question. . . .

Had I gone away willingly, I would not have come back. I would rather never have been born than to have caused this blow to God's word and His work! I had rather than I had never been born or seen the light of day than that the name of Jesus Christ, Whom I love, should be crucified and people would say, "There is Sister; she has been preaching, and if her story is wrong—" That is the sad part to me, not only that my children should go through life and have people say, "See what her mother did," but the blow to my work is the greatest thing.

I pray, I don't need to ask that you will give your most earnest consideration, and that you will pray about it on your knees, because it concerns the church and concerns Christ, and the eyes of the world are on a religious leader and upon this case; and people may come and say, "I saw Sister McPherson here," "I saw her in a dance hall," "I saw her in a saloon there." Just look at me. Look at my children and my family.

Of course, there is one thing: I am powerless, my hands are tied. I don't fear the most rigid investigation of my story, for my story is true. The only thing I fear is—I don't say a frame-up—I don't think people would do that—but mistaken identities. I don't think anything like that will be found to be true, but I would like to have you call me and ask me; and I do thank you for these few words.

She had arisen and stood as she stood on her platform. The jurors sat silent: if this was prevarication, it was prevarication on a courageous scale. Ryan's dark eyes snapped aggressively: histrionics!

With the cool dispassion of the courtroom, Keyes snipped the spell. "Will you please be seated a moment?" he requested. There were several questions suggested by her statement, he went on. For one, had she ever been run out of Denver?

Aimee all but laughed. In Denver the mayor, the famous juvenile court advocate Judge Ben Lindsey, and a host of notabilities had sat on her platform; she was showered with roses.

What about other cities, Keyes asked negligently, Oakland, perhaps, or Fresno; had she started her movement elsewhere and after a time been obliged to leave? Never, Aimee replied, her astonishment growing. "I have always been an evangelist. I think I have rarely been in one city more than three or four weeks at most."

"Now, I have noticed in the press a statement from you—although, knowing the press, I don't place credence in it"—the district attorney smiled sagely—"but they have made the statement from you, and I would like to know whether it is a fact that you intend to make a world tour?"

That, cried Aimee, why, that all started when she was in England and people asked her to come back, and she promised she would, if possible. "But since this has come up, I don't want to leave here and leave this town, but to regain the confidence of the people. My mother was in agony when she said that there was doubt of me, really. She said, 'Darling, I think you will have to make a world tour.' But there is nothing to it."

"Well, one of the reasons that you might have for pulling a stunt like this is for the purpose of getting worldwide advertising or publicity for the sake of helping you in your work." Keyes' manner was jocular, his tone cynical.

"That"—Aimee snubbed the suggestion with complete calm—"would not be necessary."

A juror interposed with a final question. "Mrs. McPherson, did you ever hear or have knowledge of one or two men being drowned in trying to find your body at Ocean Park?"

"No, I haven't."

"You know nothing about a deep-sea diver being drowned or losing his life?"

"Someone said something to me," Aimee answered vaguely. "Was it you, Mr. Ryan?"

"I started to tell you," Ryan concurred, "but your mother looked at me, and I didn't ask you."

"That is the only thing I have heard," Aimee told the juror. "Is it really true?"

"That is what is supposed to have happened."

"I am very sorry, if it is true," murmured Aimee.

Other jurors had questions jotted down, but she pleaded it was bap-

tismal night at the Temple and begged to be allowed time to prepare
for the service. Keyes cut short the session with, "I think that is all, Mrs.
McPherson." The hour was 5:30. Her day-long interrogation under oath
was ended.

That evening the Associated Press correspondent, reporting the day's
events for a thousand newspapers, confidently commented, "With her
story before the grand jury, a feeling prevails that the last phase of the
case is in sight."

Far from being in its last phase, the case was to pre-empt the attention
of the press and official investigators for the next six months.

There was one sour note in the symphony. While Sister was on the
stand before the grand jury, a man in clerical costume circulated through
the crowd waiting outside the Hall of Justice with a fistful of green tickets
which he sold readily at two dollars each. The printed ducats read:

LOS ANGELES COUNTY GRAND JURY
ADMIT ONE

This ticket entitles the bearer to enter the Grand Jury room
during the examination of witnesses in the Angelus
Temple case. Proceeds from ticket sale divided
among six worthy Temple charities.

More than twenty indignant and disillusioned purchasers protested
next day in the district attorney's office, demanding their money back.

A Tangled Web

Aimee emerged from the grand-jury room looking worn. Her plump
and prayerful guard clustered at the portal. Sister saluted each with a
ritual hug and kiss, while flashlights exploded; through the open doorway,
foreman Carter was seen to pause in his remarks to the jurors and observe the giddy spectacle with a nonplussed smile. Aimee posed willingly
for the photographers, but bade them be quick, because "there are

thirty people waiting to be baptized at the Temple tonight." Then she bustled through the crowded corridor, calling greetings right and left —"God bless you!" "Why, hello there, brother!"

On his departure, foreman Carter assured the reporters that Mrs. McPherson had answered every question "and in all made a very pleasing witness."

Sensations were not confined to the Hall of Justice. Reporters pelting after the evangelist's homeward-speeding car were greeted at the Temple by Mother Kennedy with a statement by "the first eyewitness of the kidnaping." This proved to be a vegetable huckster named Harry C. Swift, who offered a detailed account of how, while his truck was parked near Lick Pier, he saw Sister snatched, although at the time he did not realize a crime was being perpetrated. Considerable wind was taken out of his tardy testimony when it was learned that he had been trying to peddle his story to a newspaper for cash, but the paper, upon investigation, did not think it worth buying; by the peculiarity that he had not spoken up sooner; by his placing the time of the kidnaping an hour later that Aimee placed it; and by his locating the kidnapers' car several blocks from where the evangelist had placed it during her re-enactment before Ryan and Cline.

Aimee was smiling happily when she appeared on the Temple platform to conduct the evening worship. Informing the congregation of Swift's verification of her story (as she insisted it was), she shouted, "Thank God! The truth seems to be coming out!"

Then, standing squarely before the microphone, she told her people and the world everything that had taken place behind the closed door of the grand-jury chamber that day.

"I suppose you want to hear something about what happened today," she started breezily. "The grand jury has begun a real investigation of the kidnaping, and at last an effort is under way to get the facts and apprehend the kidnapers."

A hum ran through the congregation.

"If I were a trained investigator—which I am not," Aimee went on, "one of the first things I would want to know, if I didn't believe the story of my kidnaping, would be the motive for my not telling the truth."

Again she enumerated all imaginable motives and found them all untenable. As for love, she laughed. "If I fall in love, it will have to be with someone who is a better preacher than I am!"

The audience roared at the thought.

Listening to this broadcast, at the end of what for him had been a long and incredible day, was Judge Arthur Keetch of the Los Angeles Superior Court, the judge who (he had supposed) was in charge of the grand jury whose secrets were being hurled to the winds by the jaunty evangelist. Judge Keetch possessed an Englishman's veneration for the law and for the dignity of judicial process. Born in Liverpool, as a poor boy he ran away to sea, and after adventurous years arrived in the United States, where he studied law and eventually attained the eminence of the bench. He was scrupulous, conscientious and able; he detested rant and sham. While Mrs. McPherson was before the grand jury, reports of successive affronts to the sanctity of the proceedings had percolated to his chambers and greatly disturbed him; listening at home that evening to the crowning outrage against legal propriety, he was infuriated. The next morning, hastening to his office, he dictated a bristling statement to the jurors and all others concerned:

> The present matter under consideration by the grand jury should be treated just exactly as any other matter that comes before that body. If this is to be a criminal investigation, it should be just that and nothing else. I think it unwise, also, that the grand jury should be tied up indefinitely in this matter unless it is to be treated with the seriousness it deserves.

Then he called in a deputy district attorney and through him conveyed to Keyes a salty lecture on legal decorum.

Mother Kennedy had her own statement prepared for the newspapers, even before Judge Keetch released his. That watch, she said—she intended to learn the truth about that watch. If photographs showed a watch on her daughter's arm at the time of her reappearance, she wanted to see the photographs and find out when they were taken. Veitch said Sister left her watch with Emma before she went swimming May 18 and he could produce five witnesses to the fact.

Aimee herself had a statement ready amplifying her contentions of the night before, as given to the world by the radio:

> Yesterday I appeared before the county grand jury. I raised my right hand and before the God I love and revere swore to tell the truth. All day long I sat upon the witness stand and told how I was taken by force and false pretense from my home, my children, and my work. The entire responsibility at last is safely and officially in the hands of the grand jury. Now it is there, my silence can be broken. . . .

Religious persecution is no new thing in history. Not because she led the French armies, but because she flouted bishops, was Joan of Arc burned at the stake. The same spirit of intolerance and cold-blooded cruelty is rife, though more secretly, today. Its hand is against me because I preach a gospel that interferes with its ambition. . . .

The plot was devilish in its cleverness. It was carried out in such a way that when I told the naked truth of what happened, the truth sounded absurd. It was planned and done so that when I told the truth, the truth might sound like a lie. . . .

There was no lack of witnesses to give false testimony when the Inquisition dragged helpless women from their homes and loved ones to the rack. There has been no lack of witnesses who saw me here, there, everywhere, now that my story has been told. But I feel I am not helpless. The investigation has really begun. To this investigation I look for vindication.

But popular skepticism merely intensified when it was found out that less than thirty minutes after Aimee left the grand-jury room on Thursday, Joseph Ryan, without waiting even to pack a suitcase, had caught the train for San Francisco. He was on the trail of Kenneth Ormiston.

Saturday morning District Attorney Keyes issued two subpoenas, both signed by Judge Keetch, ordering Ormiston to appear before the grand jury. Keyes' order to his staff was, "Get Ormiston." To reporters he said, "Ormiston is the key to the entire mystery—we are certain of that now. We must locate him." The basis for this sudden certainty the prosecutor declined to discuss. And locating the missing radio man was the one thing the combined forces of press and prosecution seemed powerless to do.

There were clues enough. For instance, that day a telegram addressed to Ormiston was delivered at the Mission Inn, in Riverside, east of Los Angeles. The unsigned message read: SIT TIGHT. CERTAIN PARTIES LOOKING FOR YOU. GO DUMB.

The telegram was not claimed. Keyes scented a trick to communicate with Ormiston through the press; if so, the trick worked perfectly, for hundreds of newspapers all over the country printed the mysterious wire.

The sender was run down and proved to be a Los Angeles attorney who had no connection with Angelus Temple or the case in any way. He told a curious story. A person unknown to him, he said, telephoned him at his office and asked him to send the wire as a legal service. He thought the commission a bit irregular, but he sent the telegram. The next morning an envelope containing money for the tolls and a fee was pushed under his door. "I have absolutely no knowledge of its meaning," he said.

Several pastors that week end announced their intention to preach on the consuming topic, Bob Shuler, as usual, topping the list with a triple-barreled inquiry: (1) Why hadn't the official report of the Arizona police been made public? (2) Was an effort being made to cover up the facts? (3) Why be afraid of the white light of publicity?

Sister Aimee advertised that her sermon would be on "Light and Darkness," and she would preach from the scribbled notes she left on the sands that famous 18th of May.

All the embattled ministers had good turnouts, but Aimee's was spectacular. Morning, afternoon, and evening crowds were turned away, more than two thousand that night, after eighteen hundred managed to squeeze into an overflow meeting in the Bible School. At the altar call, more than a hundred converts came forward.

Aimee was glowing. Cooing into the microphone, she promised her abductors forgiveness and immunity from prosecution if they would only reveal themselves to her. "If those people are listening in, I want to say to them: I hold no animosity toward you; I freely forgive you."

If she was aware that granting immunity to a criminal was not in the power of a private citizen and would, in fact, be compounding a felony, she did not show it.

Mother's announcement from the platform was practical: $1500 donated in the afternoon collection, she said, would go toward paying for a better amplifying system for the Temple. Altogether the improvement would cost $5000, and the evening congregation was urged to contribute handsomely.

Ryan, in San Francisco, marked the Sabbath by showing Ormiston's parents a letter which Mrs. McPherson had handed to him a few days previously. Dated June 21, mailed in Oakland at 11 p.m. June 22, it was addressed to B. Ernest Ballard, an elder of Angelus Temple, and was signed "Ormie." It disclosed that the writer had been actively smuggling liquor, hence his fear of the spotlight and necessity to hide. "I would have just about given my worthless life for Sister or the Temple, or even Mother," the letter mourned. Aimee accepted it as genuinely from Ormiston, Ryan said, and felt that it explained how he happened to have money to buy an expensive automobile. The senior Ormistons spurned the document as a forgery, saying the signature was not their son's, the language was unlike him, he never was a bootlegger, and he was innocent of any connection with the Temple case.

"We believe Mrs. McPherson's story of her kidnaping," they added stoutly, "and know Kenneth knows nothing about it."

Ryan did not find Ormiston.

Letters generally were in the news. The newspapers, the police, radio stations, public officials, and almost every person mentioned in the case were deluged with them. The newspapers found their mailbags heavily weighted in favor of the evangelist. Many of the writers commented on the unedifying spectacle of other churches and pastors rushing to condemn her. One minister arose to count himself an exception: "Not all the ministers of the Church Federation are neutral. We are with you and stand ready to help in any way we can at your call."

An attorney wrote: "Any person who reflects on the character of Mrs. McPherson shows himself devoid of decency."

A woman told of her experiment in trying to cut a rope off her tied wrists: "It is impossible to cut any rope in that fashion WITHOUT CUTTING UP YOUR WRISTS VERY BADLY. Also, how in all commonsense can any Mexican shack have a bathtub and a lavatory?"

A woman in Calexico contributed a perspiring note: "Right here in Calexico, with an electric fan running, we are changing our gowns twice and even three times a day because of perspiration."

A businessman wrote gloomily: "There is a larger issue in this case, and that is saving the face of Los Angeles, if that is possible."

And an astute lawyer piqued the editors of the city's newspapers with a round-robin letter saying: "I am satisfied that I can prove from the oral testimony of the past few weeks that the city editors of the leading dailies combined and kidnaped Mrs. McPherson, and staged her comeback so as to make copy."

The East Coast had a flurry when a telegram addressed to Ormiston turned up in Taylorsville, North Carolina. Signed "Harry," it read: MEET MAC OCALA. TREE IS FALLING. EVERYTHING OK. MUM THE WORD. APPEARANCE G. J. FLOP. WIRE ME UNDER SAME NAME. JONES STANDS PAT. A SAYS TELL MAC NOTHING.

The oddity was that Ocala, Florida, was the home of Aimee's divorced husband, Harold S. McPherson. The telegram was not claimed and inquiries at Ocala produced no clue, McPherson revealing nothing except an abiding bitterness toward the woman whom he had once married. "Kenneth G. Ormiston will be dropped like a hot penny by Aimee as soon as she has obtained all the help from him he is able to give her cause," the former grocery clerk, now remarried, told a reporter.

The Taylorsville wire was followed by one from Norfolk, Virginia, signed "Ormiston." It was addressed to Asa Keyes, and explained that inasmuch as the sender stood to "clean up $100,000 in Norfolk real-estate boom," he could not spare the time to return to Los Angeles. Keyes guessed a smart real-estate operator wanted to advertise Norfolk. But a few days later the district attorney received a letter undoubtedly from Ormiston, mailed in New York City. The cockily impudent missive contained denials that the writer had been inquiring for Mrs. Mc-Pherson in Riverside, as reported in the newspapers; that he had any connection with "the greaser mayor's story of the 'mysterious car and mysterious persons' who, he claims, dumped Mrs. Mac out on the 'burning sands' "; or that he had any information about the case to impart. On June 23, the day Mrs. McPherson reappeared, Ormiston wrote, he was in Oakland, registered at the Harrison Hotel as "J. F. Duffy," and that day he took his Chrysler car out of the Dalma Garage on Webster Street, where it had been stored since May 29. This stale lead proved out, with slight differences: "J. R. Duffy" registered at the Harrison Hotel June 22 and checked out June 24, and a Chrysler coupe carrying license plates issued to Ormiston was at the Dalma Garage from May 31 to June 21.

> As for your desire for me to appear before the Los Angeles grand jury [Ormiston informed Keyes], I am afraid I cannot oblige you. I can afford neither the time nor the money to come to Los Angeles on what would be nothing else than a worthless errand, as I have no knowledge that could possibly assist the jury in its investigation. And I can assure you that I am getting sick and tired of all this rubbish.

The day the letter was mailed, the Los Angeles *Times* received a telegram from New York signed "Ormiston" referring them to the letter, in case Keyes should not publish it. A similar telegram, addressed to Mayor Cryer and the grand jury, threatened civil action if the "stupid stories" about him in connection with the case were not stopped.

These goads in the flanks of the authorities were from the East, but where was the fugitive? Reporters and detectives in New York found no trace. Ormiston obviously had no intention of being "led like a lamb to the slaughter," although Aimee's attorneys said the evangelist felt he should come forward and tell what he knew—or be arrested and prosecuted as an accomplice to the kidnaping.

Ryan did strike what might be pay dirt in Oakland when he obtained the original of the "Dr. Merton" telegram sent to Mrs. Kennedy on May

21, three days after Sister's disappearance. The signature on the scribbled message was all but indecipherable, and might be read "Dr. Merton," "Dr. Miston," or "Ormiston." The address given by the sender was fictitious. Ryan established that the sender behaved mysteriously, honking his horn in front of the Western Union office until a messenger came out, then taking the boy around the corner and writing out the telegram in his car, with the explanation that he was a Secret Service agent and did not wish to be observed. He gave the messenger money for the telegram and drove away. The messenger was unable to recall the kind of car or identify photographs of Ormiston.

Ryan hustled back to Los Angeles and submitted this find to Milton Carlson, an authority on disputed documents. Carlson identified the handwriting on the telegraph blank as Ormiston's; newspapers published photographs of the telegram beside Ormiston's known handwriting to let readers make their own comparisons.

Carlson also positively ruled that the "Avengers" letter was not a bona-fide ransom demand. The letter and the address on the envelope were typed on different machines, he brought out, and he explained his reasoning in regard to the spuriousness of the letter. It is obviously impossible, he said, for an uneducated person to write in a style or vocabulary beyond his capacity, but it is possible for an educated person to imitate the limited vocabulary and faulty grammar of an ignorant person. "The letter is too long for kidnapers who mean business," Carlson said. "The spelling is too accurate, and numerous high-sounding words are used grammatically correctly. Yet there are a few words such as 'doped out,' 'now get busy,' and 'apple pie.' Why should kidnapers use two different typewriters to write the epistle, as was done in this case, giving investigators the double chance of finding one of the two machines?"

Fat was thrown in the fire when Judge Keetch gave out word that the grand jury would not be permitted to make any report on their investigation; they should either indict or not indict, he insisted, that was all; there would be no public statement.

A storm of protest erupted. Vitriolic cries of "gagging the jury" were shot at the unfortunate Keetch. Bob Shuler plunged into the fray with a three-page open letter to the jurist that put into words the charge of "whitewash" being heard all over the city, but which had not hitherto appeared in print. Professing esteem for Keetch, the fiery pastor expressed his surprise that the grand jury was to be "muzzled and prohibited from giving out any report on the McPherson case unless actual indictments are returned." As "a man who voted for you," Shuler vigorously objected to the judge's "policy of silence." The decision, he said, boiled down to this:

> If Mrs. McPherson was kidnaped, and any evidence is produced that would justify the indictment of her kidnapers, action by the grand jury will be taken. On the other hand, if the evidence presented tends to disprove her story, there will be the whitewash of silence. . . . That efforts have been made to cover up and protect, I am aware and the public is not deceived. . . . There are two of the judges of this county who have been personally identified with the movement of Mrs. McPherson's and their interest and concern are well known. . . . One of the greatest crimes that can now be committed against this community is to whitewash the situation that has arisen, or fail to give it the honest and thorough investigation which it merits.

This impertinence, instructing an upright member of the bench in his duty, angered Keetch further. But he contained himself, appealed to two fellow judges for support (Judge Hardy was not one of them), then issued an amplifying statement justifying his action on the ground that the business of the grand jury is to hear evidence and act or not act; the jury is not an open forum for the expression of opinions or discussions. To put force into his determination to keep the investigation within proper bounds he visited the grand jurors in their chamber before they resumed deliberations on Tuesday and read the riot act on their limitations. During the morning he conferred twice with Keyes; the district attorney said he and Keetch agreed perfectly. The jurors smarted under their tongue-lashing and made plain they had nothing to do with Aimee's vaudeville. Veitch, the evangelist's attorney, feeling the edge of the storm, said the Temple witnesses would not discuss their testimony hereafter. Yet when Mother Kennedy appeared to testify that day, Keyes did not even ask her to take the secrecy oath; in fact, his staff intimated that the formality had been practically abandoned for the case.

Mother on the Stand

Mother slipped into the Hall of Justice by a side door, disappointing a crowd waiting at the main entrance. The large police detail that was on hand controlled the spectators smoothly. There were no reserved seats sold.

For the public, Mother's testimony was not the stellar attraction her daughter's had been, but the jurors were keenly interested. Throughout the city Mother Kennedy had become almost as legendary as Aimee, and the jurors were impressed by her practical, businesslike, forceful, unlettered capabilities; she seemed to be composed of tenacity and canniness in equal parts.

Minnie settled dumpily into the witness chair and faced Keyes without visible nervousness. At one point, while describing how Brother Arthur broke the news of her daughter's disappearance, she sobbed; repeatedly she bemoaned her ordeal during the weeks when she believed her daughter to be drowned.

"Did you believe she was drowned?" asked the curious Keyes.

"I did, yes, sir."

"And on what evidence did you base that belief?"

"Why, I believed she had gone into the water and hadn't come out of the water. I didn't know what had happened, but I knew that was—nothing else ever entered my head."

Keyes returned to this point. "You believed she was drowned?"

"I either believed," Minnie said slowly, "that she was drowned or that God had taken her."

"What do you mean by that?"

"I don't know whether I can explain it. I believe that God has taken people, according to the Bible, whose bodies have never been found."

"Well, you don't believe, do you, Mrs. Kennedy, that God or any other supernatural power would take a person up out of the water—pick up a body and take them away? Do you believe that?"

"Well, I know that in the Bible He did, because that is—"

"The Bible says that?" Keyes was incredulous.

Minnie was unruffled. "Of course, I don't want to bring any Bible chapters here, but we do believe that there have been times when God took people and that their bodies have never been found, such as Moses. Not that Sister would be compared with that, but when we couldn't find her body we knew not what to think."

"Is it your belief now, Mrs. Kennedy, that your daughter was really kidnaped?"

"It certainly is."

The "Dr. Merton" telegram was gone into exhaustively. Minnie denied she had attached any importance to it when it arrived, and repeatedly affirmed that she had turned it over to Captain Cline.

To refresh her memory, Keyes read the message: "Mother Kennedy, Angelus Temple, Echo Park, Los Angeles, California. Daughter O.K. Do not worry. Communication proven. Am sending for J.A. whom I believe safe. Detail in mail."

"Who," asked Keyes, "is 'J.A.'?"

"I couldn't say."

"What are Arthur's initials [referring to the chairman of the Temple board]?"

"Why, J.—"

"J.W.A., isn't it?"

"I couldn't say, his second initial."

"You never did receive any message in the mail, or through the mails, that to your mind followed the sending of this telegram?"

"I didn't communicate with anyone."

"Did you believe or connect the sender of this telegram as Mr. Ormiston?"

"No, I never thought of that."

Mother could not recall anybody's having come to the house on May 18 inquiring for her daughter. Nor had she known of anyone's threatening Sister before her disappearance. "She was as carefree as a child. Everything was happiness and joy."

As regards Aimee's watch, Minnie could speak only from hearsay, but she believed it was at the jeweler's all the time Sister was away.

"After she returned to Douglas, you went down immediately, did you not?"

"I did."

"And did you take that wrist watch with you and give it to her?"

"I don't think so."

"Did you notice whether she had a wrist watch at that time?"

"No, I don't think she did."

"You wouldn't be sure of that, though?"

"I wouldn't be sure about that. I know Mrs. McPherson has a habit of borrowing a watch, even around the Temple, if she hadn't one; but her watch, I believe, was in the jewelry shop."

The "Avengers" letter brought the positive assertion from Mother that she received it Monday afternoon or Tuesday morning. "They tell me it was Tuesday morning."

"Who tells you that?"

"Well, different people. I spoke with Captain Cline about it and he says I told him it was Tuesday morning, and Miss Schaffer said it was Tuesday morning. I have no special reason to fasten the hour in my mind."

"Well, you know the letter was delivered at the Temple on Saturday?"

"I only know when the letter came to me."

"Who received the letter?"

"Miss Schaffer gave it to me."

"Do you know who received it?"

"No."

There was no special-delivery stamp on the envelope when it was handed to her, Minnie repeated under oath.

"Well," Keyes said, "there were some answers to certain questions which convinced you, did they not, that she was really alive?"

"No." The response was firm. "I knew very well that anybody in Canada would know our hammock, because it hung for years between two points and was an odd—I know of nobody else that had a hammock of loose woven wire, and it didn't mean anything, and the name of my little dog was well known, because it was Gyp, and we had had him for many years, so I didn't think that meant anything, and the other questions were not answered."

"Well, in this letter there was a lock of her hair, was there not?"

"Well, it seems it was her hair. I couldn't recognize it as her hair."

"You didn't recognize it?"

"No, I didn't."

"Well, as I understand you, Mrs. Kennedy, when you read this letter it didn't impress you very much and didn't cause you—"

"It distressed me," Minnie interposed.

"—cause you to believe that your daughter was alive?"

"No, it distressed me, Mr. Keyes, and other letters had distressed me."

"Did it strike you, Mrs. Kennedy—" The district attorney groped for

the right word. "Did it strike you that the general tone of this letter was
—sounded like your daughter?"

"No," replied Mother. "Something about the letter sounded to me
like somebody was trying to personate—somebody—it didn't sound—
some of it sounded like underworld, and some of it sounded like somebody had listened to our conversation, our mode of speaking, and was
trying to imitate her; and I spoke to Mr. Cline about that and I said, 'The
letter doesn't sound entirely sincere.' "

"Weren't there some of the words and phrases peculiar to Mrs. Mc
Pherson's line of talk?"

"Well, I don't think peculiar to her any more than to the rest of us,
but it didn't sound to me like a kidnaper's letter."

"Mrs. Kennedy"—Keyes assumed his blandest manner—"have you
any suggestions that might assist this grand jury in apprehending the people whom you say—who, you say, you believe kidnaped Mrs. McPherson?"

"Of course, everything—" Minnie fluttered her hands and smiled
wanly. "We have just been surrounded and harassed ever since the
eighteenth of May with newspaper reporters, and I have never even had
one twenty-four hours I could even think clearly, but even if one needs
sleep, it has been at the front door and the back door and the telephone
constantly, and I didn't know what to do. I didn't call an attorney, I
didn't—I just was distressed beyond everything. I think it is wonderful
that I have even kept up as I have, but you—there are so many things
come in that I have had no chance even to have them looked up. We
are endeavoring to do that now."

Keyes turned to the Temple finances. Here Minnie was not at a loss.

"Mrs. Kennedy, is there a large mortgage on the property out there?"

"On the Temple? No."

"Eighty-five thousand dollars?"

"No."

"No such mortgage as that?"

"No."

"Is there any mortgage on that?"

"Well, we have some property that we are buying that is not fully paid
for, but that has nothing to do with the Temple."

"Isn't it a fact, Mrs. Kennedy, that you and Mrs. McPherson had
many quarrels shortly before she disappeared over money matters?"

"I don't believe anybody could quarrel with Mrs. McPherson."

"I wish you would please answer my question."

"No, there was no quarrel over money matters or anything else that I know of."

"What were the relations between you and Mrs. McPherson just before she disappeared?"

"Splendid."

"Your relations have always been friendly with Mrs. McPherson, have they?"

"Absolutely. I boss her around considerably and try to keep her from getting into trouble."

Keyes shifted to another issue.

"At the time of her disappearance, Mrs. McPherson had no life insurance at all?"

"Not a penny, and I sure thank the Lord she didn't!"

"Who was handling the financial end of the Temple out there?"

"Why, I don't know what you mean by 'the financial end.' "

"Well, there was a good deal of money collected, wasn't there?"

"Yes, sir."

"Who handled that money?"

"I handled the checking out."

"You have several different banking accounts, have you not?"

"Yes, sir."

"Was the institution out there in good financial condition at the time Mrs. McPherson left?"

"Yes, fairly good. Sound, I should say."

Keyes asked about the financial structure of the Temple, and Minnie warmed to the subject.

"We are incorporated," she said, "and first we purchased the property knowing no person here and having no financial backing. The property and whatever Sister has come from her own hard work, her life—the cream of her life—and instead of putting it into trips and dress and all sorts of oil wells, as other evangelists do, the little thing has worked for seventeen years. This trip to the Holy Land was the first real vacation that the child ever had; and when we purchased the property—and it was just from the love offerings and what we had saved and from people who believed in us—and the only thing that many of the people in our campaigns who gave us money asked me to see was that while Mrs. Mc-Pherson lived I see that she never let any bunch of men get it in their hands, that she was to preach the Foursquare Gospel, and I have stood by that. But we have incorporated, and as we incorporated we made a deed of trust, so that in the event of anything happening to either of us it could be recorded at any time in the name of the association, and we both signed."

"Who has that deed of trust?" Keyes asked.

"Pardon?" Minnie looked at him doubtfully.

"Who has that deed of trust?"

"We have it."

"That trust deed is not recorded?"

"No."

"It is in your possession?"

"Yes, sir."

"Well, there would be nothing to prevent your destroying that trust deed, would there, and then disposing of the property as you wanted to?"

"No, we couldn't do that."

A juror interposed. "Is it recorded?"

"No," Minnie replied stubbornly. "The—the attorney who drew it up advised against recording it."

Keyes resumed. "The question is suggested, Mrs. Kennedy, for you to name the members of the board of directors of this corporation."

"The trustees of it are Mrs. McPherson, myself, and Miss Schaffer."

"If the property were sold, Mrs. Kennedy, who would get the money?"

"It could not be sold."

"Well, it stands in your name and Mrs. McPherson's?"

"Yes, but it is for the work of the Lord and could not be sold."

"The grant deed went directly to you and Mrs. McPherson, does it not?"

"Yes, we purchased it before the Temple was built."

"And paid for it with your own money?"

"Paid for it with the money of our hard earnings."

Keyes gambited again. "How much does Mrs. McPherson take for her living expenses a month?"

"Why, there is an offering the first Sunday of each month that is given to her. We never bother with that. We just let her use it at her own discretion."

"She has no stated amount paid her each week?"

"She has this offering. It has only been recently, though, that it has been hers absolutely."

"What becomes of the money taken in?"

"Which money?"

"The money taken in, the offerings or pledges."

"To pay for the expenses of the work."

"And that is handled by you?"

"No, not altogether. I don't handle the incoming money, but I handle the outgoing. I write the checks and watch the amounts."

Keyes finally informed her that was all, and Mother left the room with a tight smile. In the corridor the inescapable press crew hovered. Minnie posed, asking brightly, "Is my hat on straight?" Then she made a quick trip to the county jail on the top three floors of the building to look into the estimated cost of installing radio receiving sets that would pick up the Temple services, which was a current Temple welfare project.

Keyes emerged from the grand-jury room smiling enigmatically. "The kidnapers are as elusive as ever," he said. When he was pressed to disclose whether the evidence to date seemed to confirm Mrs. McPherson's story, he repeated, "The kidnapers are as elusive as ever."

"That Is the Woman"

Back home from her grand-jury interrogation, Mother unburdened herself. "Perhaps the only way Sister's name can be cleared absolutely and forever," she said, "is for the kidnapers to be caught or come forward voluntarily with a complete confession. The only mistake Sister made in this whole terrible affair," she went on with a rush of practical sense, "was to talk at all, to make any explanation of her disappearance, though her story was every word true. If she had declined to explain her absence, little would have been thought of it. But because she did tell her story, because she told exactly what happened, she has made herself the target of enemies and unbelievers. Of course, she had no way of knowing it would turn out this way. It was her faith in human nature that trapped her into this awful situation."

Minnie herself was reposing solidly on the wisdom of not talking about the "Avengers" letter. The federal authorities continued to rumble ominously but it was apparent that they had no case. Even if it could be proved that Mrs. Kennedy read the letter before the memorial service, only she could testify competently regarding her state of mind at that moment, whether she believed the letter or not. If she would not talk, the federal authorities were helpless, and they knew it.

The drama of the county grand-jury sessions extended into the next week. Regarding the "Dr. Merton" wire, Cline swore it had never been given to him; he had never seen it. Mother said the telegram was all part of the plot to ruin Angelus Temple, and if Ormiston sent it "he must be found at once." Woolley, the Temple attorney, pointed to "communication proven" as "typical medium talk," justifying Mother in dismissing it as "spiritualism."

Ryan startled the jurors with his statement that a night mechanic in the Highway Garage in Salinas, Dennis Collins by name, positively identified Kenneth Ormiston as the man who drove a blue Chrysler coupe into the garage on May 29, and the woman in the car as Mrs. McPherson. Identification was made by photographs. But Collins, in Salinas, quickly denied that he had identified the woman, although he did identify Ormiston. The woman in the car, he said, looked younger than Mrs. McPherson in her photographs.

Hallenbeck, Emma Schaffer, Blanche Rice who had bossed the Temple's beach patrol during May, and even Rolf McPherson, Aimee's son, were paraded before the grand jury. McKinley, the blind lawyer, and Bernice Morris, his secretary, were called; Carlson testified on the handwriting; Mrs. Oberman, who said she saw Aimee with a man at the beach, and Langan, the manager of the Ocean View Hotel, told their stories. A Venice haberdasher said he saw Sister a mile from where she said she was kidnaped, two hours after she said she entered the water; he hadn't spoken up sooner, he said, because he didn't want to get mixed up in the case.

Then came a day of sensation, when Pape, the automobile dealer from Tucson, in a face-to-face meeting identified Aimee in the most positive terms as the woman he saw in an automobile in Agua Prieta on June 20, and Hallenbeck as one of the men with her. He volunteered that he also did not want to get mixed up in the case and had said nothing at the time the evangelist reappeared, because he feared the effect it might have on his business; but since that time he had sold his agency in Tucson and left that town, so he felt free to talk.

After Pape had made his identification from photographs, foreman Carter telephoned Mrs. McPherson at the Temple and asked her to come to the jury room. Half an hour later the evangelist appeared, dressed in Temple costume and wearing a wide-brimmed black straw hat. No honor guard attended her, although Carter said he had requested that they come, too, dressed identically with the pastor just as before. Aimee said she had misunderstood, and went into a huddle with her three attorneys in a side room; then Keyes came out of the grand-jury room and instructed her to enter the room, say nothing, but stand in a corner where she would be plainly visible.

Aimee followed his directions exactly. Pape stood on the opposite side of the room. After a long, searching interval, a juror told Aimee she was excused, and she departed. Keyes turned to Pape. "Can you now sub-stantiate your identification?"

"Beyond any question of a doubt," responded Pape, "that is positively the woman I saw in front of the Club International in Agua Prieta three days before Mrs. McPherson came into that town. Of that I am certain." He noticed particularly, he added, the woman's auburn hair and "pierc-ing eyes."

That evening the newspapers carried photographs of Aimee with Pape superimposed at the side, pointing to her and exclaiming, "That is the woman!" Woolley, on behalf of his client, simply said Pape was mis-taken. The evangelist, appearing before one of the biggest week-day crowds ever to fill the Temple, baptized a hundred and thirty-four men, women, and children. Standing waist-deep in the tank, assisted by Brother Arthur, she worked more than an hour immersing candidates, two and three at a time.

That evening Ryan received a death threat signed "Steve and Rose." And an anesthetist proposed not only that the kidnapers should be granted immunity, but that a public subscription should be taken up for them as benefactors of mankind, if they would only reveal by what won-derful technique of anesthesia they kept a woman unconscious for four-teen hours, clad all the while in a dripping wet bathing suit, without permanent ill effects. In reply to which one Temple member, a man of sixty, challenged Sister's detractors to meet him at sunrise at six paces.

The day after Pape's damaging testimony, the lawyers in Aimee's camp struck back with two affidavits. One was by Hallenbeck, giving his movements day by day. The second was by a Mrs. V. R. Umphrey, a person as far as was ascertainable in no way associated with Angelus Temple, who said she probably was the woman seen by Pape. She said the incident occurred on June 15 and her Hudson car was blue. Her statement was given to Nick Harris. Reporters commented that Pape, who as an automobile dealer presumably was thoroughly familiar with the appearance of different makes of cars, had identified the car he saw as a Hupmobile.

Hallenbeck personally visited Ryan's office with apparently iron-clad proof of his whereabouts all the time Aimee was absent. Hallenbeck assured the deputy that he believed Ormiston was hiding right in Los Angeles, and if given proper authority he would undertake to flush him out.

The McPherson attorneys supplemented the affidavits with a bitter attack on the prosecutor's office. "The alleged inquiry into the kidnaping of Mrs. McPherson," they protested, "is but an attempt to discredit her and destroy the great church and work which have been founded through her efforts." They were making every effort, they said, to find Kenneth Ormiston.

That Sunday Bob Shuler held forth in pulpit tones on the topic, "Is There an Effort to Stifle the Grand Jury?" Aimee, at the Temple, took a fling at the scurrility of the press in printing, she said, whatever damaging evidence they could find.

As the time approached for the grand jury to vote on indictments, the suspense became feverish. Aimee's camp produced an affidavit by the interpreter who had sat with her and Presidente Boubion, accusing the Agua Prieta mayor of soliciting a bribe to withhold his report. The district attorney's office discredited the affiant by publishing his record: he had been convicted of robbery in Arizona, and in 1915 had been found guilty of a morals offense against a young girl in California and had been banished from the state for ten years. Ryan visited Bechtel's, a dry-goods store in San Pedro, trying to get a line on Bon Ton corset number 872. Mrs. Bechtel said the only place she knew where that number was carried was a store in San Diego; the model was ten years old. Nick Harris operatives were reported to be on the trail of a mysterious "double" of the evangelist. Police staked out every road leading into Los Angeles in the search for Ormiston, although a district attorney's investigator was told by a stranger over the telephone, "You are wasting your time. Ormiston is out of the state and far away." Investigator Burgess of the district attorney's homicide squad nearly lost an ear in the general excitement. A Negro barged into Burgess' office and wildly claimed a reward for having captured Aimee's abductors. In the process of forcibly removing him to the psychopathic ward at General Hospital, Burgess was painfully bitten: his damaged ear was treated at the hospital, too.

Each night found Sister mentioning the case less and less in her sermons, but the Temple remained jammed. On the eve of the grand-jury vote she revealed that she was working out an "animated sermon" in which she would portray, with elaborate stage effects, the full attempt of the Devil to discredit her story. The finale would show, she promised her faithful, an angel descending from Heaven "sweeping away the clouds tainted with innuendoes, rumors, and lies and setting forth in the brilliant sunshine the indisputable truth as I have told it."

On Tuesday, July 20, Keyes gave the grand jurors the letter he had received from Ormiston, laid before them blank indictments naming Steve Doe, Rose Roe, and John Moe, explained the law, and retired. The jury debated all day until 5 p.m., then voted. The ballot was fourteen to three against indictment. A thirty-two-word report was filed with Judge Keetch, saying:

> The county grand jury had presented to it for consideration the evidence in the alleged kidnaping of Aimee Semple McPherson and finds there is insufficient evidence to date to warrant an indictment.

Foreman Carter amplified this tersely. "As far as the grand jury is concerned, the case is ended, but if Mrs. McPherson cares to continue her efforts further to substantiate her story, this body will be open at all times to receive such evidence as she may submit."

Ryan shrugged, half content. "The evidence was presented to the grand jury absolutely from an unbiased viewpoint," he commented, "and the action of that body explains fully the weight of the evidence in this case."

Said Keyes, "The report of the grand jury covers the case very well."

As far as the prosecutor's office was concerned an embarrassing, thankless involvement had been shelved. The grand jury, politely but scathingly, had declined to swallow the evangelist's desert yarn. If tacit condemnation could do it, Aimee stood stripped of veracity—discredited. But the legal agencies failed to take account of the excitability and relentlessness of one section of the public, for whom Bob Shuler hastened to speak in an outraged communication to Judge Keetch. Mere refusal to indict would not satisfy these partisans: they demanded point-by-point analysis of the evidence against the truth of Mrs. McPherson's story. Shuler prepared to hold a mass meeting in Trinity Church the following Sunday, at which "there will be a formal protest lodged against the suppression of facts now known to the grand jury or evidence that has been produced before that body." He invited Keetch to attend and answer questions from the platform. A copy of his scorching letter to the judge was sent to Keyes, but for the prosecutor there was an extra question: "I have noted your statement through the press that a full and fair investigation was to be had and a complete report of the findings given to the public. When did you change your mind?"

Such effrontery threw Judge Keetch into a passion. He consulted colleagues again—the presiding judge of the Superior Court and representatives of the State Bar. The possibility of contempt action against the Trinity pastor was canvassed. Incensed as the conferees were, they agreed that the best thing would be to bury the case with the grand jury's epitaph; the city was on edge, orderly process in the matter having been flouted constantly. A statement was drafted defending Keetch's action, and the judge issued it without verbal elaboration. The statement quoted the law that a grand jury's sole duty is to investigate alleged crimes, consider the evidence in secret, and indict or not indict. "It is not its purpose to give information to the public, or to influence public opinion, in regard to unresolved questions, however interesting or important." The grand jury is prohibited by law from reporting or divulging any testimony given before it, Keetch concluded, and he advised the jurors and the public that the McPherson case was no exception. Shuler stepped up his preparations for the biggest rally Trinity Church ever held.

There was also a letter from Ormiston to the Los Angeles *Times* which promised: "You will continue to hear from me until my name is omitted from the affair." The letter was mailed in New York City. Simultaneously a testimonial to the pastor of Echo Park came from citizens in Douglas, giving their opinion that her story was true and that no proof against it had been produced. The letter was signed by the mayor, the president of the Chamber of Commerce, the president of the Southern Arizona Ministerial Association, the British vice-consul, and several bankers and well-known businessmen. Douglas was enjoying a tourist boom; the Chamber of Commerce printed windshield stickers for automobiles reading, "Aimee Slept Here." Wags quickly competed with rival stickers: "Aimee Slipped Here."

Sister McPherson seemed to require no assistance. Immediately after the grand jury's finding, through her attorneys she issued her undaunted rejoinder:

> The close of the official investigation into the abduction of Mrs. McPherson marks the end of the first phase of the search for her kidnapers. California, Arizona, and Mexico have been searched, not for the criminals, but for evidence against the evangelist. And after the combing, there is no such evidence. Mrs. McPherson's story, related

time and again, to officials and others, remains as firm and unshaken as the first time it was told. . . . The official investigation not only bears her story out and proves it true, but reveals her to the world as a truthful, upright woman, who has withstood the attack in a religious, God-fearing manner. Today she stands vindicated and unafraid.

THEME III

Confoundings in Carmel

"Ten thousand difficulties do not make one doubt."

—CARDINAL NEWMAN

The Old Spice Trail

Three days after Shuler hurled his thunderbolts and Aimee struck her victory pose, a Los Angeles newspaper printed this doggerel contributed by a reader:

> While I hold no brief for Aimee,
> I'm admitting, all the samee,
> That she might have "rose" alrighty,
> Like another Aphrodite,
> From the deep where she lay soaking
> For a month or two—no joking!
> Then again I haven't tracked her
> From the hut wherein they shacked her,
> Where fair Rosie gagged and tied her,
> With that two-edged can beside her. . . .

The same newspaper, that same day, also published an ambiguous minor dispatch from Monterey, a town in Northern California three hundred miles from Los Angeles, reporting that new clues to Ormiston's movements during May had been unearthed by Monterey Police Chief William A. Gabrielson, and the information had been sent to Prosecutor Keyes. The district attorney's staff disparaged the report, saying that as far as Los Angeles County was concerned, the McPherson case was closed. Ryan disclaimed knowing anything about the fresh information; he doubted that anyone would be sent north to look into the rumor.

But the next morning, unknown to the press, Ryan surreptitiously boarded the train north. At the same time, unknown to Ryan, reporters headed toward Monterey. Both parties smelled something important pending.

Thus sounded the first ruffle of thunder in the cloud that hung over the pastor of Angelus Temple. It was to burst in a storm of such fantastic complexity as to make all that had happened up to now appear, by contrast, as mild as a meeting of dancing masters.

On the evening of July 22, two days after the grand jury returned its finding, a woman walked into the office of Police Chief Gabrielson in Monterey and asked whether he would like to know where Aimee Semple McPherson and Kenneth Ormiston were from May 19 to May 29. She offered to tell him if he would promise not to ask her name or reveal the source of his information. Gabrielson was interested. His caller related that she was from San Diego, a transient visitor in nearby Carmel. The evening before, a man whose tongue had been sufficiently oiled by liquor told her the story; it seemed to be no secret around Carmel. If Gabrielson could overlook the prohibition law and buy this man a few drinks, he probably would be told everything also. She identified the man and walked out, still without giving her name. Not until years afterward did Gabrielson reveal her role in the drama, and he never learned her identity.

Gabrielson followed up the tip. After an adequate number of rounds the chatterer rambled freely. The story he told sent Gabrielson in a hurry to a bungalow on Scenic Drive, a squat, crate-shaped stucco structure facing the ocean. The chief rang the bell and was answered by Henry C. Benedict, a prosperously retired insurance adjuster, owner of the property. Gabrielson began to put questions about tenants who had rented the house in May.

Benedict, who was not a man to be pushed, spoke up. "Just a minute. Let me ask you a question. Who are you?"

Gabrielson identified himself. Benedict then invited him inside and talked to the point. The chief was shown certain belongings that the tenants had left in the house. He also interviewed the couple next door, the realty agent who rented the cottage, and men who delivered wood and groceries to the place. Then he telegraphed Asa Keyes that he possessed information of the highest importance, and offered to come to Los Angeles and present it in person.

Gabrielson realized that he had stumbled on the greatest break in a policeman's career: apparently he had solved a mystery that was setting the state by the ears. By every rightful expectation he should acquire professional fame overnight. Keyes, however, preferred not to trust the acumen of a small-town cop but to send a member of his staff to Carmel. Ryan was the man. Ryan was ambitious, too.

Mrs. Ryan accompanied the deputy on the train ride north. As they traveled they talked about the time they had called on Sister four days before the grand jury's vote. Ryan had received an anonymous letter which he wished to show to the evangelist, and Mrs. Ryan was eager to meet the glamorous celebrity. Mrs. McPherson came into the foyer of the Temple residence to greet them; her manner was cool. Ryan explained his purpose. He was asked to step into a side room, where he confronted a panel of lawyers staring in undisguised unfriendliness. The astonished deputy, thrown on his guard and mentally marveling at the array of talent assembled to protect an innocent woman, quickly took himself out of there. Ryan's mood on the train, as he riffled through a pile of photographs he had borrowed from a newspaper, was not placatory.

They arrived in Monterey at 8 o'clock in the evening, Saturday, July 24. Gabrielson told Ryan what he had learned. Together they went to the bungalow on Scenic Drive, but the house was dark. Early the next morning Ryan took over and Gabrielson was shunted aside, although he continued loyally to give every assistance requested. During Sunday, July 25, the following facts were established by the industrious deputy.

On May 14 a man calling himself George McIntire (or McIntyre—he spelled it both ways) applied at the office of the Carmel Realty Company to rent a cottage for his wife and himself. He explained that his wife was in San Diego recuperating from an illness; quiet and isolation were imperative, so he wanted a cottage in the most secluded location available. He had just driven down from Seattle, he said, where he had bought his blue Chrysler coupe. Mrs. Daisy Bostick showed him several places but none suited. Finally they reached the Benedict cottage and he accepted it immediately, partly because of the high stone wall around it. He rented the bungalow for three months at $150 a month, and put down a deposit of $100 in cash which he took from a large roll of bills. He asked Benedict, who with his wife was living in the cottage, how soon they could move out, and was assured they would be out by May 18. McIntire said in that case his wife and he would arrive from the south, driving up, late on the 18th or in the early hours of the 19th. Mrs. Bostick and Benedict described McIntire as about thirty years old, possessing a pleasing, active manner, and walking with a limp. When they were shown photographs of Ormiston, they identified them without hesitation: George McIntire was the missing radio man.

Mrs. Jeannette Parkes, who lived next door to the Benedict bungalow, recounted that at 4 a.m. on May 19, when she got up to feed her two-weeks-old baby, she noticed that the new neighbors had arrived; they were standing in the kitchen, a man and a woman, getting a drink of water. Mrs. Parkes noticed favorably the woman's "very beautiful hair piled on top of her head." Then the newcomers drew the curtains together and Mrs. Parkes saw no more. She was positive of the day and hour, because, as later she testified in court, "Your honor, we always keep track of the baby's birthday."

The next morning she observed that the curtains in the bungalow were still pulled together tightly and pinned. They remained that way for ten days. Piqued by this demonstration of secretiveness unusual in Carmel, Percy Parkes made a point of watching for the elusive neighbors his wife had glimpsed, and was rewarded with a good view of them in the yard. Both Parkes and his wife identified photographs of Ormiston and Mrs. McPherson as the man and woman in the bungalow.

Benedict, in a breezy interview, told of McIntire's free-and-easy way with money. On May 19 he paid the balance of the three months' rent, $350, also in cash, and signed for the light and water without quibbling. "I thought we had a damn good tenant," was Benedict's recollection. He said he left the lights turned on the evening of May 18, and food in the icebox, so that if the couple should arrive during the night they would find the house lighted and could "make a scratch at breakfast." Dropping past on the morning of the 19th to see whether they had arrived, he noticed a green bathing suit hanging on the clothesline. The next day he came around to plant some bulbs that needed to be set in at once, and while he was troweling in the garden McIntire brought a woman out of the house and introduced her as his wife.

"She was rigged up in a kind of afternoon tea outfit," Benedict said. "I mean by that she had on a silk waist and silk skirt and white felt hat, one of these bucket or scuttle-shaped things, pulled well down over the back of her neck and eyes, and had on a pair of black goggles. All she would say was, 'How do you do,' in a very subdued voice, and she didn't say a word beyond that. I noticed she had on satin slippers, and you know Carmel is a rough-and-ready place, and I said, 'Those slippers won't last long around here.' But she didn't answer, she turned and went into the house."

Pleased with his tenants and wishing to put them at their ease, Benedict tactfully remained away from the house thereafter. On May 29, he received a letter postmarked in nearby Salinas at 6 a.m. that morning; it was typewritten, and the signature was typed "McIntyre." Addressed to "My dear friends, Mr. and Mrs. Benedict," it said their tenants had been called east suddenly by the illness of Mrs. McIntire's mother. Benedict might reach them in care of the Hotel Pennsylvania, New York City. "Please use the groceries while they are fresh," the note added. "Needless to say, we enjoyed every moment of our stay in your cottage."

Benedict went around to the bungalow and found that the couple had left behind, by oversight or intending to pick them up later, some personal belongings. These included a battery-powered portable radio receiving set (a novelty in those days), a bottle of witch hazel bought in Salinas, groceries in the cupboard, two kitchen aprons, a can of ground allspice and one of pepper, two cleaner's checks, newspapers from Los Angeles and San Francisco, a dozen hairpins scattered through the house, a new, small Bible, five other books, and two coat hangers from a San Francisco dry cleaner. Ryan was permitted to impound these articles; after a quick test, he said that fingerprints showed on the allspice can. The titles of the books indicated weighty reading for the seaside: *The Pleasure Buyers* by Arthur Somers Roche, *Unmasking Our Minds* by David Seabury, *History of France* by Jacques Bainville, *Why I Am a Christian* by Dr. Frank Crane, and *Science Remaking the World* by Otis W. Caldwell and Edwin E. Slossom. Each book was marked, inside the front cover, with a small cross.

Benedict wrote to the Pennsylvania Hotel, but his letter was returned unclaimed; the return postmark was dated June 21. But a letter mailed to him in New York on June 21, dated June 18, on Hotel Pennsylvania stationery, signed "McIntire," contained the information that the couple would be unable to return to the West Coast, and a request that one month of the rent money be returned, the landlord by custom being entitled to the first and last months. Benedict told Ryan that he had mailed a cashier's check for $150, which had not yet been cashed and had not been returned. This irregularity upset the meticulous insurance man. "It looks to me like this was an outstanding obligation of the bank from now until Doomsday," he complained. "I am out $150 that McIntire did not get, or as we may say now, Ormiston did not get. There is not a shadow of doubt in my mind about that."

When pressed to identify the woman, Benedict balked. He was once the victim of a mistaken identification in New York, he told Ryan, and "in the rig she had on I would hate to attempt to identify my own sister." Ryan pressed for half an hour, but the peppery old gentleman stood pat. "Ryan tried his damnedest to get me to say I could identify her," he said later.

Among other witnesses interviewed, several positively identified photographs of Mrs. McPherson as the woman in the bungalow. Ernest A. Renkert, who delivered wood to the cottage on May 24, said emphatically, in the presence of Ryan, Gabrielson, and Harry Marks (a friend of Gabrielson and a former New York City detective sergeant), when shown a picture of the evangelist, "That is the woman." On the back of the photograph he wrote, "This is the woman I saw in the garage of the Benedict cottage at Carmel, May 24, 1926, when I delivered wood." All three investigators witnessed the signature.

Ralph S. Swanson, who brought groceries to the cottage, wrote on the back of a photograph of Aimee, "This looks like the woman in the Benedict cottage on account of her hairdress." Swanson said he called at the bungalow every day to pick up the order for groceries, which the woman in the house left on a little pad hanging beside the back door. McIntire had explained that his wife was ill and didn't wish to be disturbed, and instructed the delivery boy to leave the groceries inside the door. Twice Swanson encountered the woman in the house while making deliveries, he said. "Once the bill was a dollar sixty-nine and she gave me a five-dollar bill. I started to make change; but she told me to keep the rest of it for myself."

A woman witness described the woman in the cottage as having "great masses of hair." Several witnesses said the woman was "five feet six or seven inches, with thick ankles." All stressed that McIntire made no attempt at concealment, drove freely in and out of town for ten days, and was acquiring friends; the woman did not leave the house for several days, but later made short trips, always wearing goggles and a tight-fitting turban pulled down over her head. William McMichael, a carpenter working on a house being built next door, saw the couple in the back yard. He was positive about the man's being Ormiston, but vague in his recollection of the woman. "They were holding hands and seemed to be very engrossed in each other," he said sentimentally. The owners of the store for which Swanson worked said the couple tried to buy a Los Angeles newspaper of May 19 date, but were unable to find one. They ordered the San Francisco papers to be delivered to the house as soon as they arrived.

Ryan and Gabrielson were not alone on their tour of research; at every step they were dogged by newspapermen. Reporters seemed to sprout out of the ground—from Los Angeles and San Francisco, local newspapermen, correspondents for the wire services—they were present at the interviews, roamed the cottage, and were put to work by Ryan ransacking the grounds for further evidence. During the afternoon, the search turned up two crumpled grocery-order slips, written in pencil on paper torn from the pad hanging beside the back door. Mrs. Ryan spotted them in a tangle of wild grass near the back steps; Ryan and District Attorney Campbell of Monterey County witnessed their retrieval. The list of groceries tallied with food supplies found in the house after the tenants left. Ryan said the slips would be submitted to hand-writing experts in Los Angeles. The identification of Ormiston was be-yond question, he said, fourteen witnesses having positively named him, citing as identifying features his bald spot, large ears, his pleasing per-sonality, and his limp.

"I have talked with many witnesses," Ryan told the newspapermen formally on Sunday evening, "and many more are being found as the hours pass. I feel what I have found here will do a great deal in solving the mystery."

Twenty-four hours later, to his boss, Asa Keyes, he telephoned jubi-lantly, "There is no doubt in my mind but that Mrs. McPherson and Ormiston were here from the morning of May nineteenth to the night of May twenty-eighth. Handwriting and other evidence prove it beyond a doubt."

All this filled the newspapers Sunday and Monday morning. How, the public wondered, could such explosive evidence have remained con-cealed for two long months in the face of a national hue and cry and the efforts of police from Canada to Mexico, abetted by newspapers every-where? The reason lay in the nature of Carmel-by-the-Sea.

That pretty resort, a hundred miles south of San Francisco, suns it-self just below Monterey, the old capital of Spanish California. A turn-of-the-century project of artists and writers fleeing cramping conven-tionalities, Carmel soon attracted the "arty" and took on the quaintness of a contrived stage decoration, dedicated to tea shops, handicrafts, talk, and curios vendable to well-heeled tourists. Situated in an unrivaled set-ting of ocean, valley, and hilly groves, it had a reputation for exclusive-ness—an asset to which the Carmelites clung tenaciously. The Coney Island touch, sensationalism, they abhorred; Carmel did not want that kind of publicity. This was the reason for the discreet whisperings about the visitors on Scenic Drive; Carmel did not want to become involved.

On Sunday July 25, Angelenos had the sensation of watching a three-ring circus, their attention being drawn back and forth from the drama unfolding in Carmel, to the gymnastics of Pastor Shuler in Trinity Church, to the spectacle of "The Devil's Convention" premiered by Sister McPherson at Angelus Temple.

Shuler's mass meeting brought an overflow crowd. The afternoon was warm. His first act was to take off his coat and invite the men in the audience to do the same. Attacking "this damnable policy of silence" in the grand jury's failure to file a full report of its investigation, Fighting Bob branded Judge Keetch's ruling "a horrible iniquity."

"If Mrs. McPherson's story is true," he shouted, "then an infamous injustice has been done to her, for she is the butt of derision and ridicule, and every humorist in the country is busy concocting jokes and verses! But if her story is false, and if she fabricated the whole affair for purposes of her own, then an outrage has been committed against true Christianity!"

Keetch and Keyes he lashed mercilessly. "Poor Asa Keyes is the most helpless man in Los Angeles County in a crisis. I know him well, and there is mighty little to him!" Political pressure was behind the campaign to stifle any attack on Aimee's story, he charged, one judge, Hardy, being notoriously active in Temple affairs, while another judge, Gates, was "enamored" of the Foursquare movement, and both Mayor Cryer and Boyle Workman, the president of the City Council, were the evangelist's close friends. He concluded his philippic with a collection appeal, to pay, he said, for reprinting a pamphlet in which he examined "McPhersonism" apostolically, Biblically, and dispensationally, and found it and its prophetess a pernicious fraud.

At Angelus Temple the Carmel revelations, heralded in the morning papers, brought a flat denial from Attorney Veitch: "Mrs. McPherson was not in Carmel or its vicinity at any of the times referred to in the story emanating from Carmel—particularly during any of the time she was absent from the city. Mrs. McPherson is not interested in the movements of Kenneth G. Ormiston or the identity of any woman or women, goggled or otherwise, who may have been in his company at any time."

At the morning Temple service, Dr. Howard, the Baptist minister from Douglas, told the out-size crowd he had come all the way from Arizona uninvited to assure them that the search for the shack was not ended. "Only recently they have found four shacks," he said, "any one of which officers admit may be that in which Sister McPherson was held captive." Aimee, introducing Howard, said he came unsolicited, paying his own way. "But I feel the good friends of Angelus Temple will not let it be that way." A few days later Mother Kennedy announced that Howard had been presented with "a beautiful radio set" to enable the people of Douglas to hear the Temple services.

The evening service was the headliner. The auditorium was packed, the Bible School was jammed, and five thousand shut-outs stood on the sidewalks and listened to the sermon over the newly installed, improved loudspeaker system, which projected the evangelist's voice for blocks around. In all, eleven thousand persons heard her preach that evening, as the elaborate drama of the triumph of Truth over Falsity was enacted on an enlarged platform with the help of allegory and pyrotechnics.

From craters spouting red fire leaped seven devils (impersonated by Bible students) to open "Satan's Convention" in a realistically painted Hell. Against the lurid backdrop flickered flames from the "River Styx," casting a baleful glare over the congregation. The convention, Aimee explained, was assembled for the purpose of plotting the destruction of Angelus Temple by an attack on her credibility. She alluded to the jealousy of other ministers, mentioning no names, but it was observed that the hideously grinning demons were made up to resemble some well-known parsons around town. Sister likened her plight to that of Jesus, paralleling plots against Him as recounted in the Bible with those she charged were leveled against her.

" 'Ah!' screamed the Devil as he heard the pastor of Angelus Temple was only a poor little woman, 'that makes it easier for all of us! All we have to do now is puncture the bubble of her reputation and she's gone! Go after her name, that's the way to wreck her!' You know, sometimes I think it was made easy for me to escape my captors so that all this slander about me being seen here, there, everywhere could be circulated!"

At the climax the futility of efforts to discount her story was portrayed by two angels who descended from the dome, one brandishing the sword of truth, the other rattling a chain to bind the Devil and "cast him into the pits of Hell." And, cried the preacher, in the three and one-half years the Temple had been open, forty-six thousand converts had answered the altar call, and nine thousand eight hundred and nine had been baptized. Her final words were drowned out by what Temple workers estimated to be the greatest ovation ever accorded her.

While Aimee preached and devils capered, outside the doors newsboys yelled the Carmel headlines. When asked to comment on Shuler's mass meeting, Aimee retorted, "A dog may bark at a queen, but the queen doesn't necessarily have to bark back."

Woolley, Aimee's chief counsel, first learned about the happenings in Carmel when he read the Sunday newspapers. "All hell is popping!" he telephoned his reverend client, instructing her to say absolutely nothing until he could get the situation in hand. To save time he called his brother, Kenneth, who happened to be in San Francisco, and told him to hurry down to Carmel and hire the best lawyer he could find to take charge temporarily. The brother retained J. A. Bardin, of Salinas, a respected former judge of the Superior Court of Monterey County, who in private practice retained the courtesy title. Judge Bardin drove to Carmel and collected statements, strewing doleful forebodings about the effect all this "bad publicity" would have on the town.

On Monday, Ryan sent for his father-in-law. That day he traced a telegram addressed to "Mrs. George McIntire" that had been delivered to the Benedict cottage on May 28, coming from Oakland and reading: LEASE EXPIRES TONIGHT. The woman in the cottage signed for it. Ryan sequestered the receipt.

Cline reached Carmel Tuesday morning and looked over Ryan's work. Then he picked up the telephone and put in a call for Aimee. Unable to reach her, he talked with Mother Kennedy.

"Things look very black here for Mrs. McPherson," the policeman reported bluntly. "Her place now is in Carmel definitely to prove or disprove whether she was the 'Mrs. George McIntire' who occupied the bungalow. The only fair thing is to have Mrs. McPherson come here immediately. This is the most vital evidence that has been discovered during the investigation, and things look bad for Mrs. McPherson. You tell her attorneys they can bring as many Temple workers as they desire who resemble her to take part in the identification."

Mother didn't know; she would have to talk with her daughter. Cline impressed on her the urgency of the situation. "The only proper thing for her to do is to come and face these witnesses in the presence of her attorneys. The identification process will be made under fair and honest conditions. We will place them all in a room together, Mrs. Kennedy, and I feel this will be a fair test for the witnesses we have interviewed so far."

Mother finally said she would let Cline know by 4 o'clock that afternoon. All day Cline and Ryan checked the evidence gathered, and Cline asserted it stood up. Ryan counted fourteen witnesses who positively identified Mrs. McPherson. At 4 o'clock there was only silence from the Temple. At 5 o'clock Cline said he would wait no longer and he was starting home.

"The evidence here," he told reporters, "is conclusive. An invitation was extended to Mrs. McPherson to come here and prove or disprove the identifications, but neither she nor her attorneys have communicated with me. So far as the police are concerned, the mystery of the asserted kidnaping is solved."

The Bible found in the cottage, Cline reported, was purchased by a man in a Carmel bookstore more than one month previously; the price was $1.75. The store proprietor recognized it because it was the only one of the kind he had in stock. He could not recall the buyer's looks, because the store was a help-yourself place and he paid little attention when he took the money.

Witnesses who had waited fretfully all day were both relieved and chagrined. Mr. and Mrs. Benedict expressed their disappointment. "We want to be absolutely fair in this matter, and have nothing to gain by identifying her if she is not the woman. But we think she is, and would like to have the opportunity of definitely settling the question in our own minds."

Back in Los Angeles, investigators from the district attorney's office, on behalf of Ryan, called at the Temple in quest of specimens of Mrs. McPherson's handwriting, and also her fingerprints. Aimee refused to furnish either. Veitch said he certainly would not subject his client to the indignity of being fingerprinted like a criminal "just for the purpose of exposing another one of the wild and obviously concocted identifications." Woolley denounced the "malpractice of so-called investigators" and said he refused to sanction her making the trip to Carmel.

Amid this brannigan, Carter, the grand-jury foreman—just seven days after the jury voted to drop the case—announced that the jurors were ready to reopen their inquiry on the basis of the Carmel disclosures.

De l'Audace,
Toujours de l'Audace!

Late Tuesday afternoon, the silence of the Temple leader was broken dramatically. She handed to the Associated Press a statement with the request that it be disseminated as widely as possible. The statement was headed "An Appeal to Kenneth G. Ormiston."

> If this should reach you anywhere in the world, will you come forward in the interests of justice and make known the facts of your actions and whereabouts during the time elapsing between May 18 and June 22 of this year? Since May, when I was forcibly taken from my home, children, and work, your name has been constantly before the public in an endeavor to link it with the case and attempt to dis-

honor my name and work thereby. Many believe that you are a party to the kidnaping and received large sums of money, being paid to drive around the country and be seen here and there with an unknown "mystery woman," resembling myself—a woman whose part in the transaction it was to act mysteriously, wear veils and goggles and act in such a secretive manner as would draw inevitable attention to you both. It would seem that any true man who knew the diabolical attempts to assassinate my name and great work by linking it with such a story would come out with a clear statement or communicate directly to our office.

Signed—Aimee Semple McPherson, by Minnie Kennedy

If Ormiston was possessed of the slightest gallantry, surely, it seemed, he would respond. The puzzle-happy public immediately fell to sorting out the known facts about the phantom fugitive, in the light of the newest discoveries. They were summed up something like this:

Mrs. McPherson disappeared from Ocean Park between 3 and 4 o'clock on the afternoon of May 18.

At about 4 o'clock on the morning of May 19, a man and a woman arrived at the Benedict cottage in Carmel, three hundred and twenty-five miles north of Ocean Park, a good twelve-hour auomobile drive. This man was identified positively as Ormiston.

May 19, Benedict saw a green bathing suit dangling on the clothesline at the bungalow.

May 26, word was published for the first time that Ormiston was being hunted for possible information about the evangelist's disappearance. This information was broadcast by newspapers and the radio. There was a radio receiving set in the cottage at Carmel.

The next morning, May 27, Ormiston arrived in Los Angeles from Northern California and talked with detectives. It is an overnight train ride between San Francisco (and intermediate points) and Los Angeles. He took a train north again late that day, and arrived in Oakland the morning of May 28.

May 28, 29, and 30, Ormiston was registered as "K. Gladstone" at the St. Mark Hotel in Oakland.

May 28, a telegram sent from Oakland was delivered to the Benedict cottage, "Lease expires tonight."

Late on May 28, Ormiston reclaimed his Chrysler car at the Highway Garage in Salinas.

In the early hours of May 29, he reappeared at the garage and bought gasoline. A woman was in the car with him then.

Soon after dawn on May 29, "Frank Gibson" and a woman companion, traveling in Ormiston's Chrysler coupe, registered at a hotel in San Luis Obispo, between Carmel and Santa Barbara, checking out that evening.

At about 11 p.m. on May 29, "Frank Gibson" and a woman companion, in Ormiston's car, were stopped by the reporter Wallace Moore outside Santa Barbara. Moore identified "Gibson" as Ormiston.

On May 29, meanwhile, Benedict had received a letter from McIntire, mailed early that day in Salinas, saying he and his wife had been called east.

Since then, although letters and telegrams had been received from him, Ormiston had remained invisible.

Ryan and Cline returned from Monterey and spread the evidence they had gathered before Keyes; the three were huddled for several hours. Rumors percolated from the guarded conference room that perjury action was probable. Keyes declined to be quoted, but it was given out that he viewed the new evidence as "startling." Reopening the grand-jury investigation would entail bringing more than sixty witnesses from Arizona and Carmel, as well as further research in Tucson and Douglas, and this factor, with its attendant cost, was canvassed.

Ryan had no comment to offer on the interview, but he did deny emphatically that he was looking for two doctors in connection with the case—a denial brought on by gossip that the grocery boy in Carmel had said that the first time he saw the woman in the Benedict cottage she looked pregnant, and the second time she did not. (The boy later denied having said this.) This revival of the abortion rumor went so far as to cause the examination of the records of three sputtering physicians and publication of their names, and a challenge was issued to Aimee by a Los Angeles newspaper to submit to a medical examination. Aimee agreed, set the time and place (at the Temple, after the evening service), the doctor to be named by the newspaper, and a nurse, also to be chosen by the newspaper, to be a witness. Convinced she was not bluffing, the editors at the last minute called it off. The insatiable curiosity of the press served Aimee well in this instance: reporters tracked down New York hospital records of twelve years back which established that surgery Aimee underwent at that time precluded her ever having another child. This behind-the-scenes showdown the public heard nothing about; they heard only the bitter surface scandal.

As the district attorney's office reported that the Carmel grocery slips would be turned over to a handwriting expert within a matter of hours, Woolley dashed north, driving all night, to reinforce Judge Bardin. Nick Harris speedily followed. Aimee through attorneys again said she would not go to Carmel.

Mother Kennedy was wrought up. "What are they trying to do to Sister anyway?" she wailed angrily. "It certainly seems inconsistent to me that after several months of linking her name with a radio operator's, these so-called investigators go north and without trouble pick up a radio, and in the next room find a Bible! It certainly looks shady to me!"

The demand that Sister confront witnesses in Carmel Mother denounced as outrageous. "Those people up there are sitting back with a smile in joyful expectation of a publicity harvest they will reap from Sister's visit." Minnie's head bobbed vigorously. "But I'll tell them right now, if they can hear me, that they might as well pack their kit and go fishing, because Sister is not coming!"

And the evangelist? Shielded from the press (Mother absolutely forbade any interview), Aimee prepared her retaliatory answer. Under the storm of attack, she did not retreat; she charged. And with a woman's blazing unconcern for the male flummery of rules, she struck where the blow would hurt. Let her opponents strive by rules; she was fighting to win. The press seeming to be the tool of her enemies, she seized a counterweapon which she controlled—the radio.

That evening she handed to the newspapers and read over her radio a blast which one morning newspaper printed under the headline, FLOODGATES OF RIDICULE AND ANATHEMA UNLOOSED BY EVANGELIST ON HER DETRACTORS. In a voice vibrant with conviction, at times quivering with pathos, and always fired by passion, she read the statement over the air:

> The time at last has come for a showdown. Another dastardly attempt to assassinate the character and chastity of a defenseless woman has fallen of its own wickedness. And now comes the showdown. It is a showdown, not before officials and officialdom, not before judge and grand juries, but before the great American public. If the chivalry of American manhood, the wonderful sympathy of American womanhood will sanction the suffering, the mental and physical anguish which I have withstood, then I am content; but I have held my peace long enough! Now I will reveal a sequence of sinister events, a chain of evidence that will make the motive of the whole damnable conspiracy apparent to every man, woman, and child in the civilized world. Then, perhaps, if no effort still be made

to find my abductors, no further efforts will be made to find me where I never was. . . .

First, however, these new "witnesses" so belatedly discovered in Monterey. Why did they not come forward when I was missing and claim the twenty-five-thousand-dollar reward that was offered for me? Months have elapsed since they saw me—wherefore do their memories return so suddenly and so positively at the instigation of two officers who purport to be investigating not the perpetrators of a crime, but their victim?

And what of the fingerprints that remain for months on a tin can? My fingerprints are everywhere—on my pulpit, on my Bibles, everywhere I go, available to anyone who is sufficiently interested to copy, transfer or forge them—everywhere but on a tin can! Press your own fingers against a tin can and watch the prints dissolve immediately you take your fingers away. Yet those on this tin can endured for months! Seven "witnesses" and a tin can!

Of course they can identify my pictures! Who is there in California, throughout the whole of America, after my photograph has been broadcast for all these weeks in every newspaper of the land, who is there could not identify me? I marvel they did not produce seven thousand! But why didn't they come forward before? They could not! But they can identify me now, and the reason they can goes back to those first days in Douglas after I escaped.

Then she proceeded to trace the "sequence of sinister events" she had promised her listeners. Cline, she asserted, arranged to have his son-in-law accompany him to Douglas for a foul purpose. "Until that time Mr. Cline stated publicly and repeatedly his belief that I was drowned. Then, in Douglas, he stated equally positively his belief that I had been kidnaped. And then, suddenly, he changed completely around and began venomously to attack my story. Since that time both he and Mr. Ryan have been intensely active in the attempts to shatter not only my story of my abduction, but also my character. They have scoured not only California, but Arizona and Mexico as well, in a constant and determined effort to dig up dirt and filth wherever they could and hurl it at me!"

This persecution, she charged, was motivated by her refusal, on her return from Douglas, to hire "a certain person whose name he [Cline] specifically mentioned, to 'save me any possible trouble.' . . . I did not see why I required that person; then I had no idea of the plot. And it was right then that Herman Cline's attitude changed. Since that time I have been constantly besieged, both by telephone and in person, by every variety of impossible personages, all asking preposterous sums for unperformable services. I have been the chosen lamb for every kind of slaughter—but I will not be slaughtered, either financially or morally! . . .

"After the grand-jury investigation had ended, still with their purpose unattained, Mr. Ryan and Mr. Cline immediately began another phase of the inquiry. This time, however, it was Ryan who first went away and found what he wanted to find—and Cline came tumbling after! Between them they found seven 'witnesses,' the Bible, and the handwriting—and the tin can! Nobody else at any time—always just Cline and Ryan, or Ryan and Cline!"

Then came the haymaker. Leaning over the microphone, she said deliberately, with her startlingly incisive enunciation, "Both are Catholics, persecuting a Protestant minister."

In the silence that ensued, the public careers of Ryan and Cline (although they did not realize it) soundlessly collapsed.

Aimee hurried on. "Then they laid their latest trap for me. Yesterday afternoon they telephoned me from Monterey to come up and be identified some more—play lamb again for their slaughter! And submit myself to police fingerprints—I, who was abducted! Let them find my kidnapers and fingerprint them!"

Lunging at another prime enemy, Shuler, she associated him directly with the minions of the Pope in the conspiracy against her:

It is significant, also, that the second outburst of calumny came precisely at the time when a jealous rival pastor began a separate but coordinated attack. On exactly the same day that the [Shuler] letter criticizing Judge Keetch and Mr. Keyes was received by them, Mr. Ryan left for Monterey. Strange, is it not? . . . Must I permit pastors who preach hate against my creed to lead the hordes of darkness against my church? Am I, a woman, to be deprived of the chivalrous protection with which Americans have always guarded every woman's name? Blunderers that they are! They do not see that they are trying to drag down into the abyss not only Aimee Semple McPherson, but Christianity throughout the earth! The Devil's Convention is at its height!

"Are We Down-Hearted?"

With that broadcast, more fat was in the fire. From then on there were no neutrals. Shuler termed her manifesto a call for a lynching bee— with himself the ornament of the noose. The district attorney's office cowered under the uproar; never for one instant had it occurred to anybody there that the religious faith into which Ryan and Cline happened to have been born might have the remotest bearing on the investigation. For years afterward they were to groan over their lack of foresight.

Promptly the next morning Keyes convened his advisers; besides Ryan, eight deputy district attorneys participated in the high council. Keyes then announced that the grand-jury inquiry would be resumed the coming Tuesday. After issuing a batch of subpoenas for the Carmel witnesses, he hustled his own chief of detectives, Ben Cohen, northward to serve them.

"In view of the new evidence obtained," Keyes said with dignity, "it is my duty as district attorney of this county to present the evidence to the grand jury to determine whether perjury has been committed."

Asked whether he included the Angelus Temple pastor in the possible perjury, he snapped, "Yes, Mrs. McPherson or any other witness who testified before the grand jury."

As quickly as a fair sample of Aimee's handwriting could be obtained, the grocery slips would be turned over to experts, Keyes went on; police technicians already were analyzing the fingerprints on the allspice can and on the books found in the cottage. A subpoena was issued for Aimee, but officers were unable to learn her whereabouts.

In the face of this scurrying activity, foreman Carter sounded a minatory note: "We don't want any more beating about the bush. I hope the district attorney has sufficient evidence to indict and convict, or we do not want to handle it."

In Carmel, Judge Bardin and Woolley spent most of Thursday interviewing possible grand-jury witnesses. A third man, unidentified, followed them, reinterviewing the interviewees. The town was jittery with detectives shadowing detectives and sightseers swarming in.

When J. Buchanan, of the Burns detective agency, left for the northern battlefield the spotlight swung in the direction of Judge Hardy. He denied that he had hired Buchanan. "I merely advised Mrs. McPherson to employ the best detectives in the country to dig up evidence to support her story," he explained urbanely. Why should a judge of the Superior Court take so great an interest in the case? Didn't he have confidence in the law-enforcement officials? "Why," the judge replied, "because I felt, judging from all the news accounts carried in the papers—that is all I have to go by—that they are confining their efforts to breaking down the McPherson end of the investigation and are making no effort to find the kidnapers or to uncover evidence tending to substantiate her story. They have been digging up a lot of stuff—but who knows, is it true?" Told that Buchanan had already started north, the judge breathed a fervid "I hope so!"

Aimee took a horseback ride that afternoon, then conferred with Veitch. In the evening she preached to another overflow crowd at the Thursday baptismal service. She alluded to her troubles only twice.

"They may bury my body but they will never bury my soul!" she cried, and again, during an impassioned plea for her congregation to continue their support, "Dear folk, it seems to me that if you ever intended to stand by Sister McPherson, now in her time of trial and persecution is the time!"

A male quartet enchanted the worshipers (and radio listeners) with a ditty, "Ly-in Ry-an Won't Get Her!" And Aimee led the choir in singing:

> "Identifications may come,
> Identifications may go—
> Are we downhearted?"

The congregation roared back: *"No! No! No!"*

Sister's sermon topics for Sunday, she revealed, would be: in the afternoon, "I Am Doing a Great Work and Can Not Come Down [to Carmel]"; in the evening, "Fingerprints."

Early Friday morning she appeared, radiant and vital, at the district attorney's office to accept service of the grand-jury subpoena, having come downtown, she told investigators, because of newspaper insinuations that she was hiding.

That afternoon the police experts reported that the fingerprints on the allspice can were "too blurred" to be identifiable, but they were still trying to develop the prints on the books. In this statement they were not wholly candid: the prints on the allspice can and the books had been identified, but they belonged to newspaper reporters who had infested the Benedict grounds. This embarrassment was kept from the public.

Unable to procure samples of Mrs. McPherson's handwriting by voluntary cooperation, the district attorney ordered Emma Schaffer to bring in the "Light and Darkness" sermon notes. With a glare, but helpless, Emma obeyed. Ryan at the same time procured a police guard for his wife; six men in a sedan had been seen loitering near his apartment at midnight, and during the day a stranger had gained admittance by a ruse and had started questioning Mrs. Ryan about the case; when she telephoned the police, the intruder ran out. Ryan said he had received scores of threatening letters since the Carmel evidence was published.

Woolley and Nick Harris, on returning from Monterey, informed the press that they were trying to find Ormiston. "We feel certain Ormiston is implicated in the kidnaping," declared Woolley.

Mother Kennedy thereupon revealed a telegram that had been received that morning from the missing radio operator. It came from Chicago, was addressed to Mrs. McPherson, and had been in hand at the Temple all day unknown to public, prosecutors, the McPherson counsel, or reporters. The surprise wire read: SWORN STATEMENT TRUTH CONCERNING CARMEL INCIDENT CLEARING YOU EN ROUTE. DEEPLY REGRET RYAN'S HORRIBLE ERROR. K. G. ORMISTON.

"That sounds like Mr. Ormiston as we knew him!" Minnie said.

But question marks shot up like skyrockets when the newspapers learned that while this message lay unannounced at the Temple, the following telegram had been sent from there to the San Francisco *Examiner:* INSERT IN PERSONAL COLUMN SUNDAY EDITION AD: "MCINTIRE—YOUR LETTER RECEIVED. PLEASE WRITE FURTHER DETAILS IMMEDIATELY SIGNING YOUR NAME IN YOUR OWN HANDWRITING." MAIL BILL TO ME. AIMEE SEMPLE MCPHERSON.

To complete the day's telegraphic tangle, late in the afternoon a wire arrived from San Francisco for Asa Keyes. Cryptically it stated: THE WOMAN WITH MCINTIRE AT CARMEL WAS NOT AIMEE SEMPLE MCPHERSON BUT MY SISTER WHO IS HURRYING HOME FROM THE EAST TO EXPLAIN. BELLE OWENS.

Keyes had left his office before the telegram was delivered. Reporters called him at home and asked what the message meant; he assured them he knew no more than they did. Queries north had revealed it was sent from a San Francisco hotel—the Lankershim, on Fifth Street just off

Market—the sender unknown. What did Keyes think of it? Over the wire came a chuckle.

That day was Friday, July 30.

On Saturday, July 31, the city was astounded by the news that Keyes had telegraphed Ben Cohen in Carmel to pull back all subpoenas, including those he had already served, and return to Los Angeles. All activity in the case was halted.

Ryan was dazed. Keyes could not be found. This time the district attorney had disappeared.

"Full of Strange Oaths . . ."

Keyes managed to elude persistent search by reporters and some members of his staff for thirty-six hours. Meanwhile, nothing stood still.

On Saturday morning a telegram reached Keyes' office from Chicago: ASA KEYES, DISTRICT ATTORNEY, LOS ANGELES, CAL. SENDING YOU VIA AIR MAIL ORMISTON'S AFFIDAVIT. YOU CAN COMMUNICATE WITH HIM THROUGH MY OFFICE. H. F. MARTIN.

Inquiry in Chicago brought denials from sixteen attorneys named Martin (including Edward H. S. Martin) that they knew anything about the telegram. In Los Angeles, Hallenbeck telephoned Cline his certainty that Ormiston had shipped as a wireless operator on a steamship that was on its way from San Francisco to New York.

Mother Kennedy was exultant. "Now I think we're getting to the bottom of the thing!"

As for the sudden dropping of the case, her first comment was, "O-o-o-oh?" Then she added, "We all knew God was with her. Not one of her followers or her hundreds of friends could conceive of her in a situation such as the mighty officials have tried to place her at Carmel."

Said Cline, "So far as the police department is concerned, the case is closed unless evidence is produced that will aid them in locating Mrs. McPherson's asserted kidnapers."

Said Ryan, "I do not know what it is all about, but when I do I will issue an unqualified statement."

Said Aimee, "I am so happy! That is all I care to say."

Saturday evening, in the Temple, she improvised on this theme:

The superstructure of falsehoods about my kidnaping is fast crumbling under its own weight and will crash on the heads of those who built it up. Even though I am an honorary battalion chief of the Los Angeles Fire Department, it would take more than a hook and ladder to get to the top of the pile of falsehoods in this case! I have looked to the Lord for help and got it!

Thus the tangle still stood at 5 o'clock Sunday afternoon, when, on the eighteenth green of a golf course, reporters caught up with Asa Keyes. The district attorney refused to explain his *volte-face*. All investigation of the case by his office had ceased, he told them succinctly, and it would not be resumed unless fresh evidence should be forthcoming.

"When the proper time comes," he said with finality, "I will issue a written statement, but at present I have nothing further to say."

Then with a volubility peculiar in a person committed to silence, he tore the Carmel evidence to shreds and tossed it on the dust-heap of false leads. It just hadn't stood up under scrutiny, he asserted, and never had been as binding as the newspapers indicated. Failure to develop the right fingerprints on the allspice can and the books struck a body blow at the State's case, while the affidavits collected by Ryan were "far from being positive identifications either way."

"The case has now reached the point," he said, "where it would cost the county thousands of dollars to carry it on, and after our evidence from the north collapsed, I can't see where anything is to be gained by continuing. I am going before the grand jury Tuesday morning and lay what evidence I have on the table, and it is up to them to decide whether they care to go into it further. But after that, I think it is doubtful the McPherson case will ever be heard of any more."

What about the perjury flurry? He brushed that technicality aside as infeasible. "It takes overwhelming evidence to prove beyond a shadow of a doubt that it was committed, and the evidence from Carmel is far from conclusive."

He wasn't bothering to submit the grocery slips to a handwriting expert, because "any layman can compare the handwriting with Mrs. McPherson's, it is so obviously hers."

About reports that circulated all day Saturday that shortly after he left his office he was seen at Angelus Temple, Keyes would say nothing. Mother Kennedy and Aimee emphatically denied having seen or communicated with him.

A stalwart defender of the evangelist arose Sunday in the person of Mrs. Hardy. She spoke over the Temple radio, from the Temple platform, in a prelude to Sister's evening sermon. Listeners were startled by her assertion that her husband was giving all his energies, when off the bench, to vindicating Sister. This seemed an equivocal occupation, to say the least, for a judge.

"You know, my husband speaks here very often," Mrs. Hardy said, unbosoming herself, "and he would be here tonight were it not that he is in conference, and has been all day, relative to this case. Outside of his heavy judicial duties, he is devoting all his spare time to the unraveling of this case, that truth and justice may prevail."

Urging women everywhere to close ranks and defend one of their sex unjustly accused, Mrs. Hardy cried emotionally, "Are we, as women, not going to profit by the tragedies of the past when all our great women have been persecuted by scandal?"

Again more than twenty thousand persons heard Aimee preach four times during the day, not counting perhaps a million radio listeners. Bursting with suppressed good news, she told her audiences that "a certain judge in Carmel (whom, on advice of counsel, I cannot name) has evidence which will overwhelmingly crush every angle of the case up that way."

On Monday, August 2, rumors flew through the city that political dickering was responsible for Keyes' jumping-jack behavior; no other explanation seemed credible. Denials of double-dealing poured out. Specifically Keyes denied that he had attended a meeting of local political bosses just before he recalled the Carmel subpoenas. But the suspicion lingered and was plainly reported in the newspapers.

Judge Hardy entered his denial that he had anything to do with a deal. As for devoting all his spare time to the case, that was quite untrue, except, perhaps, casually, as a friend. Yes, he had discussed the case informally with Judge Gavin Craig of the Appellate Court, but only casually; that was several days before. Judge Craig was said to be politically influential; he instantly published his denial of any connection with, or special interest in, the McPherson case.

When Keyes showed up at his office late Monday afternoon, he sent for Ryan, and the report got out that he had called in the deputy only because the grand jury was demanding Ryan's appearance; the jurors were incensed by the district attorney's twistings. Foreman Carter made it clear they expected Keyes to appear personally and present every bit of evidence in his possession.

Keyes, on his part, was fortified by the affidavit signed by Kenneth Ormiston, which had arrived in Monday morning's mail. In the affidavit, Ormiston admitted almost every circumstance that had linked him to the case—except being with Mrs. McPherson in Carmel. All the "rubbish" against which he had stormed he now confessed was true—but he was not with Mrs. McPherson in Carmel. He had been in Carmel, yes—but with an anonymous "Miss X," not with Mrs. McPherson.

Keyes accepted the document as genuine; at least the signature was Ormiston's beyond doubt. The affidavit was executed in Chicago on July 31, and was forwarded under cover of a letter from Edward H. S. Martin, attorney, who prepared and witnessed the instrument.

Day by day Ormiston set down his movements during May, starting with renting the Benedict bungalow on May 14. "I used the name of George McIntire. On May 21 I introduced 'Miss X' to Mr. and Mrs. Benedict as Mrs. McIntire." On the evening of May 26 he heard over the portable radio in the cottage that he was being hunted for questioning in connection with Mrs. McPherson's disappearance. He drove at once to Salinas, parked his car there, and caught the night train for Los Angeles, where he was questioned. He caught the train north that evening, found it did not stop at Salinas, and was compelled to ride on to Oakland, where on May 28 he registered at the St. Mark Hotel. The next day he returned to Salinas and picked up his car. His statement went on:

> I decided that since my name had been dragged into the McPherson case, that the Carmel incident had better terminate. Accompanied by "Miss X," I drove back to Salinas, arriving there about 2 o'clock in the morning, and went to the Salinas garage for gasoline. I stopped in front of the garage and was served by the night man, who had delivered my car to me two hours before. We drove south, since "Miss X" desired to be delivered to an address in the south. Arriving at San Luis Obispo at about 6 o'clock in the morning, I registered at some hotel, the name of which I have forgotten, as "Frank Gibson and wife." We spent the day in the hotel and continued the trip at about 5 o'clock in the evening, May 29.
>
> On reaching the outskirts of Santa Barbara, I was stopped by a man who stated he was a reporter on a Santa Barbara paper. He stated that he had received a tip that a man named Ormiston, in a car bearing the license number of the car I was driving, was headed for

Santa Barbara, accompanied by a woman who might be Mrs. Mcpherson. His exact words at this point were: "I know Mrs. McPherson
personally, having covered her meetings when on another paper, and
I can see that your companion is not she." He got back into his car
and went his way. I went mine. I continued on and delivered "Miss
X" to the address to which she directed me.

Then followed his explanation of why he had avoided Cline:

I either had to refuse to answer his questions or discuss the Carmel
incident which involved "Miss X." No doctor or nurse visited the
Carmel bungalow during my occupancy of it. "Miss X" went
swimming daily and we patronized the Carmel or Salinas movies almost nightly. "Miss X" resembles Mrs. McPherson in that she is of
the same general build and has brown hair. The reported "goggles"
were in reality a pair of Krux [tinted] horn-rimmed glasses which
I purchased in Monterey. The two aprons found in the bungalow
I purchased in Salinas. The books and portion of a radio set are
my property. To the best of my remembrance, I opened all tin cans
and the highly prized fingerprints on those are probably mine.

I have not seen "Miss X" since the night of May 29, but I have
corresponded with her. I know her true name and her present whereabouts. She has insisted that I make this statement. She is a trained
nurse by profession. I have sufficient confidence in "Miss X" to state
that I am of the opinion that before any great harm should befall
Mrs. McPherson, who is entirely innocent of the matter and yet
utterly unable to defend herself, that "Miss X" will make an affidavit
supporting mine.

Asa Keyes had confided to a fellow county official, "I'm in a terrible
predicament." To him this affidavit out of the Midwest may have appeared to open a possible avenue of escape from an intolerable impasse.
He was basically a good-natured man who wished harm to no one,
certainly not to a woman of Mrs. McPherson's standing. Tuesday morning, before he took the Ormiston affidavit and the other evidence before the impatient grand jurors, he conferred confidentially in his private
office with Aimee's legal staff. Present at this consultation were Woolley,
Veitch, Hamner, and Judge Bardin, who had hastened south to place
his findings before the prosecutor. Bardin told Keyes he had found nothing in Carmel that he could not offset in court. "I failed to find one witness who even partially identified Mrs. McPherson as the woman who
occupied the cottage. The leading citizens of Carmel take no stock in
the story. Public sentiment there favors Mrs. McPherson decidedly."

One Carmel witness already had tried to shake down the evangelist for favorable testimony, he said.

He brought affidavits. One was by Fred Horton, a carpenter, who said he called at the Benedict cottage on May 24 to ask about some carpentry work to be done on the adjoining lot; the woman who answered the doorbell was not older than twenty-five and had long blond hair. He talked with her later several times, and since he had heard Mrs. McPherson preach in Oklahoma, he could take his oath the woman in the cottage was not the evangelist. Then John E. Considine, of Monterey, who had been employed at a house nearby during May, saw the man and the woman in the Benedict cottage seven or eight times; she was twenty-three to twenty-five, with long medium-blond hair, about five feet seven, weighed a hundred and thirty to thirty-five pounds. He noticed nothing to suggest that she was trying to avoid being seen. He saw a bathing suit and it was not green.

During the conference, Keyes called in Ryan and ordered him to bring into the room every scrap of evidence he held; it was spread out for the inspection of the McPherson counsel. After looking it over, Woolley pleaded with Keyes to "go slow." The prosecutor needed little encouragement. Jauntily he and Ryan strolled off to the grand-jury room.

They had been preceded by a sympathetic statement from foreman Carter (nobody could resist talking to the reporters) indicating that the jury realized Keyes was on a spot, and they were willing to shoulder the responsibility. The session with the jurors lasted three hours. During the presentation of the evidence, keyhole listeners gathered that Ryan and Keyes clashed frequently, and an hour before the jurors adjourned the door of the room was suddenly locked from the inside. The waiting reporters heard angry voices and shouting.

When Ryan and Keyes emerged, the district attorney was taciturn. Ryan's scowling face was the picture of frustration. He had no comment. Carter said the jury had ordered Keyes not to drop the case, "now that he knows he has our support." In fact, the jurors had taken the unusual step of composing a letter to the district attorney underscoring their instructions. Drafting the communication had consumed so much time it could not be typed that day, but Carter conveyed the substance, which contained the following significant warning:

> The grand jury prefers his investigation shall be carried out along as secret lines as possible, eliminating the "brass band" air of last week.

The next day, Wednesday, Aimee and her mother were "too busy with church affairs" to see reporters. At the Wednesday evening prayer meeting Sister told the congregation that Cline and Ryan had deliberately framed her at Carmel; but God put a carpenter at work next door who saw 'Miss X' and she had golden hair and was twenty-five years old. Thirty-five-year-old Aimee, her copperish tresses glancing in the spotlight, invited as many as wished to join her in a testing of the efficacy of prayer in the Bible School after the service. About a thousand responded. They knelt and prayed that Keyes and the grand jury would come out pointblank in the morning and pronounce the case closed.

Echo of El Segundo

Judge Keetch had been trying to enjoy a vacation, but when, on Thursday morning, he read in the newspapers (his swiftest and most reliable source of information regarding the confidential proceedings of the grand jury with whose conduct he was entrusted) about the jurors' letter instructing the district attorney in his plain duty, the judge stormed into town. He had no inkling of the shock he was in for.

First, before the jury's letter could be transmitted to Keyes, Keetch summoned the jurors to his chambers, read the letter, and locked it in his desk. Then he gave the jury a twenty-minute dressing-down, enlightening them again on their duties and limitations. The abashed jurors trooped back to their own room and lamely informed Keyes that their letter could not be presented. Keyes, of course, knew everything that was in it. He marched across to Judge Keetch and let him in on a secret, telling him exactly what had happened in the grand-jury room Tuesday while the door was locked.

There were seventeen jurors present, fifteen men and two women. The entire mass of evidence—affidavits, spice cans, the grocery slips, the telegram receipt, everything Ryan and Cline had gathered at Carmel or elsewhere—was laid out on a table for the jurors' inspection. Ryan had mounted the grocery slips, a prize exhibit (the State considered them the most binding evidence they possessed linking Mrs. McPherson to the Carmel cottage), on cardboard beside the "Light and Darkness" notes, so the jurors might make their own comparison of the handwriting. This exhibit, with the other documents, was passed from hand to hand among the jurors.

One of the women, Mrs. E. A. Holmes, excused herself to go into the adjoining ladies' room, a part of the sequestered grand-jury suite. Shortly after she returned to her seat the jury adjourned. Ryan, collecting the documents, missed the grocery slips. None of the jurors had yet left the room and Keyes was still present. Several of the men recalled that the last time the slips were seen they were in the hand of Mrs. Holmes.

A furious row broke out. Angry jurors accused the woman of abstracting the evidence. Ryan locked the door. The jurors' desks were searched, the men turned out their pockets, both women emptied their handbags. The exhibit was not found. Ryan looked everywhere—everywhere except, as he ruefully admitted later, "at El Segundo," the location of the municipal sewage-disposal plant. Mrs. Holmes stubbornly disclaimed any knowledge of the whereabouts of the invaluable bits of paper. Keyes thundered: destruction of evidence, under the California code, is a felony exposing a public official to fourteen years in prison, a private citizen to five! The jurors envisioned the scandalous necessity of indicting one of their own panel. What if the newspapers found out—and of course they would!

Mrs. Holmes—who was neither a member of Angelus Temple nor an acquaintance of Mrs. McPherson—sat tight while the storm raged around her. After an hour of wrangling, the members were sufficiently calmed to agree to recess until Thursday, at which time Keyes sternly ordered Mrs. Holmes to produce the missing documents. Everybody secretly feared that it probably lay beyond the power of anyone to restore the papers.

All this Judge Keetch heard with unbelieving ears from the district attorney. The jurors, Mrs. Holmes included, had showed up that morning, but the slips were still missing. What, Keyes anxiously inquired, was to be done? Judge Keetch snatched at dignity: he advised that the deadline for restoring the slips be extended to Monday. Then he called his stenographer and composed the first of a rain of pronouncements that was showered on the populace that day, which in the McPherson affair was to go down as the Day of Statements:

> Ever since the organization of this grand jury, I regret to say that the law regarding the secrecy of its sessions has been violated almost continually. . . . A short time ago the grand jury was permitted to make a simple report that the evidence before it [in the McPherson

case] was insufficient upon which to find an indictment. Almost immediately thereafter, the columns of the press were filled with the details of the activities of a deputy district attorney, who appeared to be acting in the role of an investigator in another city. Apparently without waiting to communicate his findings, whatever they may have been, to his chief, he is credited with having given to the world the statement that "the mystery is solved," with such details as constituted a bald and sordid accusation against a woman who has insisted that a crime has been committed against her.

The district attorney was credited by the public press with the statement that he would again put the evidence before the grand jury, and subsequently the further statement that "after further consideration of the evidence submitted to him, the matter would *not* be submitted to the grand jury." Nevertheless, the matter *is* again before the grand jury. It needs no letter on the part of the grand jury to instruct the district attorney to do what his plain duty calls for.

Keyes acted on the judge's recommendation and extended the deadline for returning the grocery slips until Monday. His warning was general, but he eyed Mrs. Holmes bleakly while he spoke. Then he hastened to his office and indited his exculpation, addressed likewise to the public.

The investigation of this matter has been one of the most difficult ever presented to a prosecutor. Because of the prominence of the persons involved, the sensational features of Mrs. McPherson's disappearance and return, and the unfortunate entanglement of religion, this case has been investigated in the full glare of publicity. Excessive zeal in seeking from the slightest clue even a mere suspicion of superficial evidence, and almost hysterical vehemence in reporting ill-considered information as proven facts, has given the public a false impression as to the nature of the evidence in the hands of either the district attorney or anyone else interested in bringing out the true facts in the case. In this case the evidence is not ready or sufficient to sustain a prosecution. . . . Personally I am unwilling to assume the responsibility of incurring the enormous expense of a criminal trial unless and until the grand jury is prepared to justify it. Hasty or ill-considered action in this case would plunge this county into a religious turmoil.

The county already was in a turmoil, political, religious, salacious, sex arrayed against sex. Mrs. Hardy's call had struck fire, and a crusade with feminist overtones against the hounding of a defenseless woman by "filthy-minded" males was being felt in countless households. The reported actions of the woman grand juror were less a symbol than a symptom of a wave of feminine solidarity in favor of Aimee.

Keyes implemented his manifesto to the public with a bulletin to every member of his staff, forbidding them to make any statement to the press on any subject whatever.

Excessive zeal and brass-band effects, together with the circumstance of having a religion, had finally impaled poor Ryan; in his youthful devotion to the logic of facts, he had overplayed his hand. The "open letter" which he addressed to the public was so overwrought it seemed to have been infected by the phraseology of the woman whose "Ly-in Ry-an" chant he heard nightly over the radio.

> I wish to annihilate certain diabolical rumors prevalent since my advent into the McPherson case by stating emphatically that the admiration and respect which I have long held for Mr. Keyes is stronger now than ever before. Like every truly great man, Mr. Keyes has enemies—enemies gained because of envy and malevolence. . . . My work throughout the McPherson case has been under his personal supervision and direction. If I have accomplished anything, the credit belongs to Mr. Keyes. If I have justified his faith in me, I count my work well done, for his commendation has been my goal.

This was handsome of Ryan, because he had just been fired—pulled off the McPherson case that he had built up, and ordered back to prosecuting pickpockets and other petty offenders.

The public was not informed of Ryan's summary shelving, but at Angelus Temple, by some means, the action became known almost immediately, and great was the joy expressed. Asked whether she might wish to add to the day's pronunciamentos, Aimee responded dynamically, "Yes, indeed! Just what I have always said—the story of my kidnaping is absolutely true! All these other reports have been a pack of lies!"

With that she marched into the Temple to baptize five-score candidates for glory before four thousand followers shouting, "Hallelujah!"

Under the balcony, Woolley whispered to a reporter that Ormiston ought to show up quickly now—any red-blooded man would. The lawyer did not mention (he did not know) that, now that Ryan had been administered his come-uppance, the time of Herman Cline was growing short. Private detectives, hired by Aimee McPherson, were shadowing the Los Angeles chief of detectives day and night.

Friday's newspapers carried a report that one or more grand jurors faced dismissal for violation of their oath of secrecy. Saturday the press, still groping for the real story, found out that Keetch, although ostensibly on vacation, was making trips into the city; he would not divulge why. Rumors were rife that something of extreme gravity had happened at the last meeting of the grand jury; half the jurors were said to be ready to resign. As Keetch himself later put it, "the air was full of it."

A maneuver the newspapers did not discover was a secret meeting between Keetch and foreman Carter at a Santa Monica beach club, where Keetch proposed a way out of the dilemma. It might be that the jurors would take a vote of confidence in Mrs. Holmes, with the understanding that she would resign quietly, without scandal, and thus the record could be kept clean. Carter agreed this might be the best way; the jury was about to take a two-week vacation, and when it reassembled their attainted colleague would thus no longer be among them, and the scandal would be effectively suppressed.

But Sunday the newspapers tracked down the whole story and printed it Monday morning in minute detail. Carter was astounded that the information had leaked out. "I have absolutely nothing to say," he said, and slammed the door.

Keetch, Keyes, and Ryan were unavailable for comment.

The shocked *Times* commented:

> Evidence regarded as the most important in the investigation has been destroyed or hidden from the authorities by one of the grand jurors. This amazing situation, believed to be without parallel in local grand-jury history, had been guarded by the closest secrecy since the disappearance of the evidence last Tuesday.

Readers then were regaled with every detail; nothing was omitted; the locked door of the grand-jury room was rendered as of glass.

Grimly Keetch submitted to inquisition by telephone. "If any member of the grand jury has deliberately destroyed evidence placed before that body, it is a serious matter and must be punished accordingly," he said sternly. "If the district attorney has evidence that points to any one person, it is his duty, and his alone, to file a complaint."

On behalf of Aimee's attorneys, Leonard Hamner deplored the lamentable event. "Naturally we hate to see anything occur in this case that is of a suspicious nature," he said.

The following Tuesday morning the grand jury reassembled in a day-long, tense session. Mrs. Holmes was told the alternatives: resign or face criminal prosecution. She left the room while the other members debated the vote of confidence. Three ballots were taken; in the last, seven members voted to take criminal action and nine voted to hush the matter. Mrs. Holmes was recalled to the room and heard the verdict. The next day the jury recessed for two weeks, after appointing an interim committee to study the newest phases of the McPherson affair.

The public's indignation was whipped up by this burlesque of judicial processes, and the letters to newspapers, radio stations, prosecutors, grand jurors, and interested bystanders snowballed, the kidnaping being almost overlooked in the outcry against the grand jury, against Keyes' backings and fillings, and, conversely, against the "slandering" of Mrs. McPherson, of Ryan, of the press. Everybody seemed excited except Aimee. She had returned home from a brief absence from the city, and her viewpoint was given in a statement that Minnie Kennedy put out for them both: "Sister and I just returned from a nice, restful trip and we are having lovely meetings."

Thus the pot boiled for two weeks. On Thursday, September 2, the grand jury reconvened, and ructions broke out instantly, for the expelled woman juror, reneging on her tacit pledge to resign, sturdily took her seat with the others. Before the first business could be started (reading of the report of the special committee on continuation of the inquiry) Judge Keetch summoned the panel to his courtroom and summarily discharged them all.

The outraged jurors handed all their reports to Keyes (demanding and receiving receipts for everything) and nine of them adjourned to a lawyer's office to consider possible retaliatory action. Said one of them, "We would have resigned by noon if that juror had been permitted to remain." They had been under political pressure from the start, they declared, and Judge Hardy's name popped up repeatedly.

The action threw Bob Shuler into a shouting tizzy. Through his personal magazine he vituperated against Keyes, Keetch, Hardy, and Aimee. In discharging the grand jury, Keetch acted to protect Mrs. McPherson because they both were born under the British flag! "This Englishman could not bear to see one born under the British Jack brought to justice by an American jury!" Keyes he scorned as "fat and timid. When a man grows two rolls of fat on the back of his neck, he no longer courts battles of the character that he now has on his hands. . . . As for Carlos S. Hardy, there may be reasons as horrible as hell why he is forced to play the part he has played." He denounced Hardy's "organized effort, through the Superior judges and otherwise, for the protection of a woman whose name has become the brunt of lecherous jest and filthy joke the nation over. Four names loom large in Los Angeles today—Keetch, Keyes, Hardy, McPherson. Behind these names looms the name of *Arnold* and the more hideous name, *Iscariot.*"

Mrs. A. E. Holmes spoke her mind. "It's all dirty politics," she spat out. "You can't put half a dozen clean people in with a bunch of Bolsheviks and make a go of it!"

Weeks later, Aimee and her mother invited Mrs. Holmes out to the Temple for tea. It was a mutually interesting introduction.

Under the Rose

These convulsions were on the surface, but underneath, unknown to press or public, other strands of intrigue were being woven throughout the hectic weeks of July and August.

The day after Sister McPherson returned in triumph to Los Angeles from Douglas, McKinley, the blind attorney, happened to be in Judge Hardy's chambers on court business. McKinley told the judge about the visit of the mysterious Miller and Wilson. Hardy believed McKinley, but he had suspicions about Miller and Wilson; his guess was that they were sharpers horning in on some apparently easy money. He suggested that McKinley let him know if he should hear from the pair again.

On July 11, three days after Mrs. McPherson made her appearance before the grand jury, Roland Rich Woolley showed up at McKinley's office. McKinley was not in. Woolley handed a card to Bernice Morris, the secretary, who read all McKinley's mail and acted in the most confidential capacity for him; it was Judge Hardy's professional card, and on the back was penciled:

> Mr. McKinley, this will introduce Mr. Woolley, who will act for me.
> Please work with him. Carlos S. Hardy.

Two days later McKinley received a telephone call from Mother Kennedy, asking him to see her that evening after the Temple service. The friend driving him lost his way, and it was midnight when he reached the Temple. The mansion was dark. The attorney rang the doorbell. An upstairs window opened and Mother Kennedy peered out. Too late to talk that night, she called down; perhaps they had better not talk just yet anyway, because McKinley was under subpoena by the grand jury. Mc-Kinley testified before the grand jury a couple of days later, and two days after that Mrs. McPherson visited his office in Long Beach.

Almost immediately after the grand jury's refusal to indict, on July 20, consultations between McKinley and the Temple leaders grew frequent. While not confiding everything to his secretary, the lawyer did tell her that Aimee and her mother were urging him to re-establish contact with her kidnapers and procure from them a confession and information as to the location of the shack, which the evangelist needed to convince the world of the truth of her story.

It was assumed between McKinley and Miss Morris that there were no kidnapers; but the lawyer shadow-boxed, tantalizing the Temple leaders with intimations that he was working out a deal, and had talked with the criminals. They were prison-shy, he explained, fearful of being arrested. Aimee begged him to assure them they ran no risk, since she would not sign a complaint, and without a complaint the authorities could not prosecute. McKinley knew the nonsense of this legal moonshine, but he strung along, collecting $1000 in the process, a fact which he did not tell his secretary. On August 15, he and Miss Morris went in utmost secrecy to San Francisco, ostensibly to keep a pre-arranged rendezvous with the shadowy Miller or Wilson in the St. Francis Hotel there. Judge Hardy was told in advance of this trip, and cautioned the attorney that no money should be laid out in expenses unless there was a good chance of success. No kidnaper kept the appointment.

Mrs. McPherson was stipulating, McKinley told Bernice Morris, that the proofs the abductors should provide must be irrefutable—no more shacks inhabited by chickens and brats. At the Temple, in the presence of her mother, she suggested that McKinley get the kidnapers to sketch a road map showing the route over which they carried her; also, couldn't he bring a photograph of whomever he was talking with, or have the man speak to her over the telephone? If he was one of her captors, she was certain she would recognize his face or voice.

McKinley came away from this interview laughing. When he told Bernice, she laughed with him. If Sister wanted a photograph, why not? It would have to be a picture of a man conforming to Aimee's description, so they searched the newspaper files and settled on the nameless "thin, flat-chested" kidnaper whom she had mentioned, who was dark and had a beard so heavy it showed blue after he shaved. They chose this candidate partly because a waterfront character named Joe Watts, part-time oil worker, part-time process server, was in and out of the office nearly every day and he was meager and hollow-chested. Get Joe Watts to pose, McKinley suggested. Joe was willing, but he was blond; so Bernice smudged his face, blackened his eyebrows and painted long sideburns with mascara, and then pulled a fedora hat down over his eyes. In this make-up she photographed him with her Brownie camera. On August 23 McKinley took a print of the picture to the Temple.

Aimee recognized her abductor at once. "Mother," she cried, "that looks like the man that was with Steve!"

Minnie was less enthusiastic; all she could make out, she complained, was one ear. Couldn't they get an enlargement? Aimee grew vehement in her identification.

When McKinley had entered the room, Aimee had guided him to a chair and taken a seat on a settee beside him. From time to time during the conversation she nudged him with her knee, and his acute hearing detected a subtle antagonism in the voices of the two women. Back in his office he burst out in astonishment to his secretary: "You never could have told me—never in the world could have told me before tonight—that the old lady wasn't in this business! Now I believe, as sure as God makes me live, that she is absolutely innocent! Aimee is trying to fool her mother more than anybody else in the world!"

He was never permitted to meet the evangelist alone, he pointed out, Mother Kennedy always being present when they discussed the kidnap houses, both the first and the second, and when Aimee specified what the genuine hut would have to contain.

"Did you say anything about the toilet that was supposed to be in the first house?" Bernice asked.

"Yes, there would have to be a toilet in it," McKinley said, chuckling, "because she said in the grand jury there was a toilet that flushed in this shack."

He was willing to guarantee that anything he cared to mention in connection with the kidnapers Aimee would back up in front of Mrs. Kennedy because she was afraid of her mother.

"Aimee wants to hear one of their voices over the telephone, this man in the picture, she wants to hear him over the telephone. She gave me a telephone number where I can reach her day and night. She said any time I get hold of this man, to call her and have this man speak to her over the wire, that she knows she can recognize his voice. We'll have

Joe Watts talk to her over the phone, and if her mother is standing around, she'll identify his voice."

The morning of August 25 Miss Morris was delayed in getting to the office. When she arrived she found McKinley and Joe laughing.

"Well, Joe, did you talk to Aimee?" she asked.

"Sure did," grinned the sometime process server.

"What did she say?"

"Oh, she recognized me all right."

McKinley took up the story, tears of merriment trickling from his sightless eyes. "Well, I called her at the Santa Monica number and talked to her, and then I put Joe on the extension in the other room, and he said, 'Mrs. McPherson, I'm sorry I caused you such a long walk.' "

"What did she say?"

"She said," Joe Watts piped up, " 'My God, is it really you?' "

"Was that all?"

"That's all she said."

The men discussed a road map of the kidnapers' route; Joe said he knew a place around Blythe, over Imperial Valley way, where he could probably find a shack that would fit Aimee's description.

"Well," said McKinley, "it's a cinch that any shack we find that is anywhere near the description she gave to the papers she will identify."

That afternoon McKinley with much amusement told a friend how Sister McPherson recognized Joe Watts' face and voice as belonging to one of her kidnapers. The lawyer attended a lodge meeting that evening, and shortly after midnight left with two friends who offered to drive him home.

Near dawn the automobile was found overturned in a water-filled roadside ditch. All three occupants were dead. The date was August 26.

One hour after the news hit the streets, Mrs. McPherson appeared at the undertaker's parlor in Long Beach where the body of the blind attorney had been taken. She wanted to see the body, but was refused permission. She drove to McKinley's office building (in Woolley's car, with Woolley, her mother, and a chauffeur), called Bernice Morris downstairs, and took her into the car; they drove around the city for nearly an hour, pursued by reporters in another automobile.

Bernice was weeping when she got into the car and sat between the two Temple leaders in the back seat.

Sister comforted her. "You poor child!"

Soon after Bernice was let out of the car, she visited the undertaker's with an order signed by the coroner to surrender to her the papers found in the dead man's pockets. Much affected by the sight of the water-stained, begrimed documents, she took them back to the office and locked them in the safe.

Reporters who were on her heels dunned her to say what these papers were. For twenty-four hours she resisted, then in a stilted, formal statement explained:

> The papers indirectly deal with the McPherson case. They are correspondence with a third person who was interested in a solution of the kidnaping, and giving them out to the newspapers would only make timid those whom it was necessary to deal with.

Already she had visited the Temple (on the evening of the day of McKinley's death) and had initialed a statement which Mother Kennedy released to the press, carrying the startling disclosure that McKinley had established contact with Sister's kidnapers and had engineered a telephone conversation between one of the men and Sister only a day or two before. Part of the statement read:

> He said he had interviewed both men and was confident they were the right persons. His information included the location of the first house in which Mrs. McPherson was held. He outlined the route followed, and, more important still, the peculiar formula of the anesthetic used, which we never thought of. This we cannot speak of until we have it investigated.

Aimee confirmed the telephone conversation. "Although he said only a few words to me, I feel certain I recognized his voice," she said.

There was action on other hidden fronts. During July, Judge Hardy had persuaded Sheriff Traeger to detach two detectives to investigate an underworld tip about a Steve and a Rose around Mexicali. The deputies brought back word that the Rose in question (in the inner circle she was promptly dubbed Mexicali Rose) had died in Mexico, and the Steve referred to was in the midst of serving a long prison term in Texas. During July also, Judge Hardy was receiving reports, by letter and telegram, from Burns detectives in Carmel, sent there to check on "Mr. O. and car." Operative X-2 (his name was Archambault, but to use his name would have violated the code of professional sleuthing) reported to the judge that he had talked with two of the Carmel witnesses interviewed by Ryan, and there was "nothing to fear" from them. He also talked with Police Chief Gabrielson, who said that he (the chief) was satisfied in his own mind that the Benedict cottage was occupied in May by "Ormiston and client." Operative X-2 also interviewed Ormiston's parents in San Francisco, but got no information about their son; he was unable to trace Ormiston's blue Chrysler.

Hardy had also engaged Buchanan, the Burns agency manager, to accompany McKinley to San Francisco on the August 15 expedition, in the hope that the kidnapers might turn up.

Toward the end of July (while the dealings with McKinley were in progress and just when the furor over the grand jury's failure to indict was agitating the city) a former convict named A. M. Waters, who styled himself a doctor, came to Judge Hardy with a story about a double of Mrs. McPherson whom he had seen in Ormiston's company. Waters said he knew Ormiston's parents. Hardy referred him to Mother Kennedy.

Early in August Mrs. Hardy happened to bemoan the fact to Aimee that the judge and she could not afford a vacation trip, what with the expense of moving into their new home. Aimee suggested to her mother that they really ought to do something for the judge financially, in view of his years of helpfulness. With ill-concealed repugnance Minnie consulted Brother Arthur and they agreed on the sum of $2500. Minnie signed the check, and after some demur the judge accepted the gift on the day the grand jury adjourned for its vacation. He and his wife headed north toward Canada by automobile on August 16.

That evening they stopped at Santa Barbara. Hardy went to the office of the *Morning Press,* introduced himself to the reporter Wallace Moore, and requested a talk privately. Hardy explained that he was deeply interested in Sister McPherson's work, and he wondered what was Moore's off-the-record conclusion about the identity of the woman in the Chrysler coupe he stopped the night of May 29.

Well, Moore replied, if the woman had been a few years younger she would have strikingly resembled Mrs. McPherson as he saw her in Fresno four years earlier.

Hardy complained that the Los Angeles police were spending more time checking Sister's activities than hunting her abductors. Identification by witnesses is a serious matter, the judge continued with fatherly gravity; it is so easy to make mistakes in testimony, and perjury on the witness stand is dangerous. Even if a man identifies a defendant in good faith, if the defendant is convicted and later cleared, he can sue the witness for damages in later life and stands a very good chance of collecting a heavy judgment. He recalled such an instance that occurred in his own court.

It happened that the young reporter was looking forward to inheriting a legacy, and as he listened to this warning by a judge of the Superior Court, he envisioned his inheritance in jeopardy. After Hardy departed, the city editor found Moore incoherent, pacing back and forth, sweating, hands trembling, hair tousled, face contorted, gnawing his fingernails. He was in no condition to work for two days.

During this period when the scandal of the missing grocery slips was setting pulpits aflame, Chief of Detectives Cline was suddenly suspended from duty and ordered to departmental trial. On the previous Sunday, in Azusa, a town east of Los Angeles (it was Kenneth Ormiston's birthplace), Cline, driving a police car, had smacked into the rear of the machine ahead. Nobody was hurt and damage in the amount of about $25 was inflicted. Instantly a cry went up from a car directly behind the chief's: "Stop that driver!" A policeman arrived; Cline was arrested, subjected to a sobriety test, and certified as drunk. He spent the night in the Azusa jail.

The news reached Aimee while she was on the platform in the Temple's evening service. She appeared elated. With easy confidence she assured her auditors, "The story which I told when I returned stands just as true today. The Carmel story will fall, cans and all."

Mother Kennedy hurried to Azusa and gathered details; then she and Aimee telephoned the facts to the Los Angeles newspapers, with barbed inquiries as to how the editors intended to handle the item. The newspapers buried it in a few lines on inside pages. Aimee broadcast a sizzling statement over the Temple radio, and several community weeklies printed lurid accounts, embellished with photographs. One showed Cline dramatically pointing to "Azusa, where men are men and drunks are drunks." Another showed the cell in which the chief rested ("For obvious reasons he had a lower berth"). The jail entrance was pictured under the caption, "Where Is My Wandering Boy Tonight?" A Glendale paper screamed, "Taxpayers Up in Arms over Cline's Asserted Debauch!" and delineated "a drunken chief of a great city's detective force at the wheel of a high-powered official car, careening madly through the streets, wrecking another automobile and endangering lives and property."

In the morning Cline was released in his own recognizance, and eventually the case was dismissed because of conflicting testimony. After his departmental trial, with the help of a sympathetic press, Cline was restored to duty to serve out the few months separating him from eligibility for retirement. He never meddled with the McPherson case again.

Even Fighting Bob Shuler, enemy of strong drink and miscreant public servants, could not stomach the entrapment of Cline. He refused to preach on the subject; instead, Rudolph Valentino having died that week, he joined several of the city's pastors in deducing moral lessons from the passing of the screen lover, posing this pulpit conundrum:

> A) What percentage of women are crazy?
> B) Will the world be 95% insane in 500 years?

A Soul Seared

Meanwhile, on Sunday August 22, the public had been introduced to a fresh set of characters, some visible, some hovering tantalizingly in the wings. Heading this company were a phantom "Miss X" and her very-much-in-sight self-proclaimed sister, Mrs. Lorraine Wiseman-Sielaff.

The evening before, reporters had been called to the office of Roland Rich Woolley, the McPherson chief counsel. There they found a woman who gave her name as Mrs. Lorraine Wiseman, her address as San Francisco, her age as thirty-seven; she said she was the widow of an Army captain killed in the World War, and the mother of a son aged nineteen and a daughter aged seven. She was a legal secretary, she said, and her mission in Los Angeles was to exonerate Mrs. McPherson of any connection with Carmel.

Woolley interposed that the woman was speaking entirely for herself; neither he nor his clients at the Temple assumed any responsibility.

Pacing the floor and wringing her hands, Mrs. Wiseman told a vivid story. On May 18, she said, she received word from her sister that the latter was ill and on her way to Carmel; would Mrs. Wiseman meet her there? Mrs. Wiseman drove down from San Francisco on the morning of May 19 and was introduced to Ormiston under his alias George Mc-Intire, and remained with her relative at the cottage continuously for three days. She did not sleep in the house; she took a room in Monterey, the address of which she had forgotten. Later she called at the bungalow off and on almost every day. Mrs. Wiseman said that she was the woman who was introduced to Benedict as Mrs. McIntire; she signed for the "Lease expires tonight" telegram; she ordered the groceries on behalf of her sick sister.

"I did not know Ormiston," she recounted. "I took for granted his name was McIntire. I understood that as soon as my sister recovered from her illness they would be married. Later we learned that he was Ormiston, and that newspapermen were looking for him, so it was only natural that they left."

"You are positive you were the one who signed for the telegram and also wrote out the list of groceries?" a reporter asked.

"Yes, I am positive; I did all the ordering. However, I doubt whether they really found any grocery slips."

Reporters asked to see a specimen of her handwriting, but she countered that she used three different styles of script and couldn't remember which she used in writing the grocery slips. But she would submit samples to the grand jury; she was going to meet the interim committee Tuesday.

In confirmation of this narrative which placed *two* women in the Carmel bungalow during Ormiston's tenancy, Mrs. Wiseman produced an affidavit signed "Miss X." This statement attested:

> I am the woman referred to as "Miss X" in the affidavit of Kenneth G. Ormiston. . . . I was with Mr. Ormiston at the Benedict cottage at Carmel from May 19 to May 29. . . . While we were there we went under the name of Mr. and Mrs. George McIntire. . . . During a portion of this time my sister, Mrs. Lorraine Wiseman, visited with us. . . . I was wearing my hair long at the time.

Mrs. Wiseman explained that since May "Miss X" had bobbed her hair. The affidavit had been signed in the office of Judge Bardin in Salinas one week before, on Sunday, August 15. Reporters noted that "Miss X" gave no clue to her name, her addresss, or her whereabouts. Mrs. Wiseman explained that her sister had returned to Philadelphia after the fiasco of the Carmel romance, but had been persuaded to come back and clear Mrs. McPherson as an act of justice. However, when they reached Monterey, her sister became frightened, and had consented only to make the affidavit.

Woolley said he met Mrs. Wiseman for the first time in Bardin's office, when she witnessed the "Miss X" affidavit. Woolley had no notion who this "Miss X" might be; he saw her and talked with her, but she refused to divulge her name.

"I told them both," said Woolley, "that they should immediately tell their story to Mr. Keyes; it is a matter that should be handled through his office."

"I have been to the district attorney's office several times and have told and retold my story," broke in Mrs. Wiseman, "and they don't seem to care to make it public. That is why I am telling it to the press. Mrs. McPherson must be vindicated, and knowing what I do, she will be, if it takes my life blood!"

Did Mrs. McPherson instigate her action?

"I called at the Temple and wanted to broadcast my story then, but Mrs. McPherson, in true Christian spirit, didn't want me to drag my name into the mire. She said her shoulders were broad, and inasmuch as her people had confidence in her, there was no need of sacrificing my job and my good name. But I cannot stand by and see another woman suffer for an indiscretion with which she was not connected in any way."

With the "Miss X" affidavit, the newspapers printed Mrs. Wiseman's story in full, then sent reporters scurrying on this new trail. These ferrets were unable to find Mrs. Wiseman at the Los Angeles address she gave or at the YWCA in San Francisco, where she said she had lived. A woman of that name had checked in and out of both places during August, but left no forwarding address. The reporters did notice a similarity of appearance between Mrs. Wiseman and Mrs. McPherson, in that they were about the same age, weight, and height, and had abundant hair of the same copperish hue.

Opening the service at the Temple that Sunday evening, Sister prefaced her preaching with a report on the new development. She said she had promised herself "not to mention this terrible affair again," but she owed some statement to her faithful followers.

"This woman got in touch with me," she explained simply, "saying she must make this public. I tried to dissuade her; I didn't want to see anyone suffer as I have suffered. Nevertheless, she went to the district attorney and gave him her information."

Why Keyes had not honestly and openly revealed this clarification of the whole Carmel misunderstanding she left to the imagination of the wildly cheering audience.

Keyes, as usual, could not be reached for questioning.

Ryan said he never was told that the woman called at the district attorney's office.

The manner in which the newspapers handled Mrs. Wiseman's story incensed the Temple leaders, especially when editorial demands were made for a meeting with "Miss X."

"It certainly isn't necessary to reveal 'Miss X,'" objected Mother Kennedy. "This woman has a fine family and name and we are not going to see her dragged into the mire as was done to Sister McPherson. After seeing how this story was handled, we might as well forget the entire matter and go along as we are, bearing the burden in silence."

Aimee issued a dignified protest:

> Some of the papers carried a statement purporting to come from me that I claim a vindication by reason of the story revealed by Mrs. Wiseman. I have been misquoted. If any vindication were needed to satisfy the mind of any skeptic, it came completely and beyond refutation last week when H. C. Benedict called upon me and after spending one-half hour in conversation with me, during which time the Carmel incident was not referred to, stated to my attorney, and the next day to Mr. Keyes, that I did not resemble the lady who was at his cottage under the name of Mrs. George McIntire and he was positive I was not her.

The disclosure of this Benedict tête-à-tête was a shock to the press, which believed it knew everything that was going on. But Benedict could not be found, although it was established that he had just left a Glendale sanatorium where he had been undergoing treatment for high blood pressure. Keyes declined to amplify. "I'm sitting tight," he said. It would be up to the grand jury, when it reconvened on September 2, to hear "Miss X," if they wanted to.

Mrs. Wiseman haunted newspaper offices. Repeatedly she promised to bring in "Miss X," who earnestly desired to "clear up the name of Mrs. McPherson." She had brought several witnesses and two attorneys from the north at her own expense, she declared, all primed to testify in support of her true account as soon as the grand jury returned. Six times she assured the *Examiner* that she would bring in "Miss X" and six times she reported inability to break down her sister's aversion to publicity.

"I, like Mrs. McPherson, have two children growing into maturity and it would blacken my soul for life to know that I had not aided in clearing an innocent woman when I knew it was I who could do so," she declaimed in the city room of the *Times,* smartly attired in a picture hat of the latest fashion, a black dress, cream shoes and stockings, with her nineteen-year-old son at her side. "I have done nothing criminal. The fact that efforts were made to hound me has caused me to act with the least possible publicity. Also, you can realize the undertaking that I have faced, and see that it is one that sears the very soul; so why should I blazon it to a morbid world?"

The *Times* blazoned her outbursts for her, and she returned with more. Woolley professed repeatedly that he knew nothing about her activities; she was on her own. "All I know in regard to any action taken by the lady known as Mrs. Wiseman is what appears in the newspapers," he emphasized. "Anything she says or does is on her own initiative. I do know, however, that Mrs. McPherson was not in Carmel."

Early on September 2, foreman Carter received a telephone call from Mrs. Wiseman, requesting an appointment to appear before the grand jury. Carter advised her to be on hand at 2:30 that afternoon. At 11:30 Mrs. Wiseman called back and inquired what she should do now: she had just heard that the grand jury was dismissed. Carter was dumbfounded; the word had barely been broken to the grand jurors. He told her she would have to wait for a new grand jury.

Judge Keetch also received a call from the frustrated Lorraine; she wanted to confess to him. At first he was unable to grasp what the woman was gabbling about, and when he did comprehend, he cut her off indignantly with the reminder that he was a judge, not an investigator, and he certainly would not see her. Mrs. Wiseman thereupon told the newspapers that her witnesses—since nobody wanted to hear their testimony—were going home.

The Times *Scores a Scoop*

On the afternoon of September 10 (the Friday after Labor Day), a *Times* reporter complained to Mother Kennedy that Mrs. Wiseman was not keeping her promise to produce "Miss X."

"She must have some very good reason," Minnie said. "You can depend on her, she is a very high-class woman; anyone who has talked with her and been with her would know that."

That evening the reporter telephoned to Mrs. Wiseman. "We haven't been very nice to you," he admitted. "We've acted as if we didn't quite believe your story. But we are skeptical no longer. We are ready now to reverse our position and back the truth to the limit. We might even pay for a series of articles."

Lorraine hurried to the *Times* office as fast as a taxi could carry her. Once she entered the city room, the newspaper lowered the boom. Step by step she was confronted with evidence their investigators had gathered. It could be summarized thus:

Her right name was Villa May McDonald Wiseman Sielaff.

She had a twin sister named Virla, who lived in Oakland.

During May, on the dates when she said she was in Carmel, with her sister and Ormiston, she was living in a furnished room in Los Angeles, working as a seamstress.

On May 17 she received a pay check, for $18, made out to Villa May McDonald.

On May 18 she told her landlady she didn't feel well and stayed home from work.

On May 20 (the day she said she wrote out the grocery-order slips in Carmel) she cashed the pay check in a Los Angeles bank.

On May 24 (when she said she was commuting between Carmel and San Francisco) she rented a sewing machine in Los Angeles.

On May 27 (the day Ormiston was interviewed at Ocean Park beach) she cashed a second pay check in a Los Angeles bank.

On May 28 (the day she said she signed the receipt for the telegram to Mrs. McIntire) she bought an accessory for the sewing machine at the place where she rented it.

That exploded the Carmel fantasy. There was more. Villa May McDonald was wanted up and down the coast on bad-check charges. In Los Angeles she had borrowed money, including $1000 from a crippled woman, to be used to open a dress shop; she stocked the shop with merchandise for which she gave rubber checks. On July 19, the day before the promissory note for the $1000 loan was to fall due, she disappeared. The next day her landlady received a telegram from San Jose: MOTHER AND BABE HURT. TAKING THEM HOME. BE BACK IN COUPLE DAYS. LOVE. VILLA. In San Jose she cashed a worthless check for $50.

While this evidence was being placed before her, the landlady and two of the persons who had been bilked entered the room and watched silently. Mrs. Wiseman retained her composure, denied everything, said her twin sister was the Villa May McDonald of the worthless checks. The witnesses identified her positively; eight others had identified her from photographs. Mrs. Wiseman stuck to her guns: they were confusing her with her twin sister.

"I am not Villa May McDonald," she insisted. "She is my twin sister. The things you say she did I know nothing about. But I will gladly pay back all she owes if you will give me half a chance."

Her sister she described as a trained nurse, "somewhere out on a case"; she had seen her at 2 o'clock that afternoon "somewhere out on the Redondo road." She would not reveal her sister's address.

One of the identifying marks the witnesses pointed to was her missing left thumb. She said her sister also had no left thumb. "It isn't so strange, we are twins, you know. Things like that happen with twins. I lost my thumb by blood-poisoning twenty-one years ago; she lost hers in an automobile accident eight years later. Coincidence? Oh, no."

Detectives were waiting. Just before midnight on September 10, they arrested Mrs. Wiseman on felony check charges. Her handbag was searched and yielded documents linking her with Mrs. McPherson. Among them was a packet of photographs of herself and the evangelist in identical pose and dress, side by side, their hair combed exactly alike. On the parcel was written, "Angelus Temple. Will call."

There was a red notebook on several pages of which were written "butter," "pears," "rhubarb," "meat" and other words appearing on the Carmel grocery slips. On another page was a long list of itemized expenses totaling more than $2000—railroad fares, hotels, taxis, meals, a handwriting expert's fee, long-distance telephone calls. One entry: "Mrs. McPherson gave me 100 for a present and asked me not to tell her mother about it."

The grocery words—Mrs. Wiseman laughed—were written "just for fun. We were talking about it, one night, my son and I, after the Carmel story came out. I wrote the words there just to see how they would look." The handwriting expert's fee referred to "another case, a long time ago, in San Francisco." As for the other items, "They are all old—long before the McPherson affair."

Also in her handbag was a long statement in affidavit form which recounted her secret meeting with District Attorney Keyes and with Benedict at the sanatorium in Glendale. The district attorney, she had written, "put me through a perfect third degree in every sense of the word. Mr. Keyes is that type of man. It was a very trying ordeal. I was exhausted and my nerves so unstrung afterward that I thought I should not be able to get back to my hotel." When she asked Keyes' advice as to what she should do next, he told her bluntly to go home and go to work. This outrageous suggestion moved her to "remind Mr. Keyes that he had accepted and immediately published Mr. Ormiston's affidavit without question, yet when I, the only one who had come forward in person, had told the true story, he was refusing to let the public know about it. At last I became thoroughly indignant and did not even let him see my sister."

Her struggle to overcome Mrs. McPherson's scruples, the discussion with Benedict, "during which I recalled to his mind many minor details which he admitted were correct and which only the party actually staying in the cottage could know," completed the summary. The statement ended: " 'Miss X' is going east tonight. I am going to return to my home and my son is returning to his school tonight." It was to have been released the next morning.

At 1 a.m., September 11, Mrs. Wiseman was jailed and her bail set at $1500, while off the *Times* presses rolled one of the cleanest scoops in Los Angeles newspaper history.

Mrs. Wiseman's first action was to rout Woolley out of bed at 2 a.m. Woolley angrily refused to have anything to do with her. At Angelus Temple there was silence.

All day Saturday Lorraine muttered and swaggered in jail, surly, defiant, and confident by turns. The whole business was a frame-up, she railed, and she could bring Ormiston himself to prove it. "I can get ahold of him inside a few minutes when I get out of this place," she bragged.

The *Examiner,* humiliated by its rival's enterprise, on Sunday morning printed the first rejoinder from Aimee:

> I was never so surprised in my life. I must admit that I believed her and sympathized with her in what seemed to be her deep trouble. She came to me at the Temple and said her conscience would not let her rest until she told the truth about the Carmel incident. I told her emphatically that I did not need her explanation of the Carmel incident to help me because the whole thing was built on a base of untruth. She told her story despite my efforts to dissuade her. I believed her—she was so convincing. I am sorry she is in trouble.

Then, forty-eight hours after the *Times* put Mrs. Wiseman in jail, the *Examiner* bailed her out, conveyed her at 11 p.m. to its office, and there obtained her confession of having conspired with the Temple leaders to perpetrate a hoax. The *Examiner's* readers devoured the tale in installments over the next three days. It was the turn of the *Times* to feel chagrined.

What neither newspaper guessed was that Lorraine Wiseman had once been committed to a Utah insane asylum because of ungovernable lying.

Lunatics at Large

" 'X' CONFESSION—MRS. MCPHERSON ACCUSED!" the Los Angeles *Examiner*'s headline screamed.

The story Lorraine Wiseman related departed radically from the versions she had been pressing on the press, and introduced still more characters to the already overlong roster.

To obtain this story that circumstantially enmeshed Mrs. McPherson in a maze of duplicity, the *Examiner* had employed its own wiles: legal counsel had been procured for Mrs. Wiseman (S. S. Hahn, an ambitious young divorce and criminal barrister who understood the uses of publicity) and, as bait, it was hinted that the bad checks might be made good. Then, trotting tandem with the San Francisco *Examiner* (another Hearst publication), the paper brought south Mrs. Wiseman's twin sister, Mrs. Virla Kimball, who lived with their mother, Mrs. Clara McDonald, and her five children in Oakland.

The sisters met in the *Examiner* office. Virla implored Villa to tell the whole truth, sparing nobody. Mrs. Wiseman wrung her hands, hesitated, wept. She wanted to speak with Mrs. McPherson alone, without Mother Kennedy being around, she said. A reporter offered to telephone the evangelist, and a call was faked from another room, the reporter returning with the supposed message that Mrs. McPherson refused to have anything to do with Lorraine, she was "through." Then, in the presence of her attorney and her sister, Mrs. Wiseman began the narrative, speaking clearly, coherently, and plausibly. She talked for hours, while downstairs, excluded from the confessional chamber, Woolley paced the foyer.

Mrs. Kimball had told reporters her sister's story. Villa and she were twins, Virla being the elder by five minutes. They were born in Des

Moines in 1890 (the same year as Mrs. McPherson); they had been reared in Utah, and Villa had been a "bad lot" since she was a girl. At seventeen she ran away and married C. B. Wiseman; there was a son, and Wiseman divorced her in Pioche, Nevada, three years later. She then married Gustav J. Sielaff, a geologist (in 1926 chief geologist) for the Southern Pacific Railroad. He separated from her after the birth of their daughter because of her inability to tell the truth and her check-book rampages, although he had remained friendly with the family.

Her sister traced Villa's behavior to injuries she received in a rail-road wreck many years before; she had suffered a head injury, besides losing her thumb, and was in hospitals for months. Afterward she developed delusions of persecution and the family committed her to an asylum; technically she was still in her mother's custody. The family had made good her bad-check sprees over and over. Virla had last seen her in April, after she telephoned from San Francisco that her son had died in New York, and had lent her train fare to go to the funeral. The same day Lorraine inserted her son's death notice in the San Francisco *Examiner* (paying $1.75 for it), although he was neither dead nor in the East.

"I'll stick by her," said Mrs. Kimball, choking back sobs, "although I can't imagine her saying these terrible things about me, her only sister! She was paid to do it—she must have been paid to do it! Somebody paid!"

Mrs. Wiseman's account started on July 30. She was sitting in the lobby of the Hotel Lankershim in San Francisco when a stranger approached, gave his name as Martin, and said he knew her. He told her that she had been recommended to him as a trustworthy, capable person who could undertake a job that would be well paid, required little work and only a few weeks of time, and involved principally typing and investigation. It concerned the McPherson case, he said; she would have to go to Los Angeles. What the work entailed she would be told in Los Angeles. First she must send a telegram to District Attorney Keyes, signing the name "Belle Owens," saying that her sister was the woman with Ormiston at the cottage in Carmel. Although she had never seen the man before, knew nothing about him and never saw him again, and did not know what the job might be, with whom she would deal, or how much she would be paid, she accepted the commission, she said, sent the telegram dictated by him, and entrained for the south.

In Los Angeles the next morning, she telephoned to Keyes' office

and was told he was out of town; this bore out a prediction made by
Martin. Then, following his instructions, she went to Angelus Temple
and met Mother Kennedy and the lawyer, Veitch. Veitch was unfriendly,
she said, and she talked vaguely, because she did not know what was
expected of her. Once Veitch left the room, the proposition was unfolded to her: if she could produce "Miss X" to back up Ormiston's
Chicago affidavit, she would be paid $5000 and expenses.

Her first move was to visit Carmel, where she watched the detectives
and got the lay of things. She returned to Los Angeles and assured Mrs.
McPherson and Mrs. Kennedy she could produce "Miss X," but it would
take time. Mrs. McPherson told her to go right ahead, and sums of money
were doled out to her, for which she was required to sign receipts.

To pose as "Miss X," she summoned from Philadelphia a friend,
"Miss Rachel Wells," whom she had known a long time; they com-
municated "through her home address which I don't recall at present."
"Miss Wells" arrived in San Francisco, and Lorraine took her to the
office of Judge Bardin in Salinas, where she signed the "Miss X" affidavit.
An added purpose of this deception, which she asserted was known to
all the conspirators, was to prevent Mrs. Ruth Ormiston from naming
Mrs. McPherson as corespondent in a divorce action.

Lorraine said she brought "Miss X" to Los Angeles to meet Keyes,
but in view of Keyes' brutal reception she decided the introduction
would not be politic until she produced witnesses to buttress her story.
She related her interview with Benedict:

> I knew at the time I was talking with him that he did not believe
> me; in fact, he stated this. That evening when I called on Mrs. Mc-
> Pherson, as I called on her every evening to report what I had done
> during the day, I told her I didn't get by very well with Mr. Benedict.
> There were certain details about the cottage that naturally I was un-
> familiar with. The next day she told me a great deal more of the
> things that were in the Carmel house, such as the small portable ice-
> box, the cedar chest in which the linens were kept, the writing desk
> in which the table silver was kept, the large two-piece chair which
> could be used as a day bed.
>
> During my first talk with Mr. Benedict he questioned me about the
> bedspreads and also about the clothes I wore when I was supposed
> to have been introduced to him in the back yard. [These things she
> had been unable to describe.] The following day we [she and Aimee]
> discussed the different things in and around the Carmel house in de-
> tail. In coaching me, Mrs. McPherson would say, "Don't you re-
> member the pretty spreads they had on the beds?" I would say, "Oh,

yes, but I just don't remember the color." Mrs. McPherson then would say, "Weren't they those fancy spreads—weren't they yellow or old rose?"

Mrs. McPherson also said, "Don't you remember what was said about the black satin slippers you wore? Don't you recall what Mr. Benedict's remark was about the slippers you were wearing when he met you? He said he didn't think they were very appropriate for that kind of country." In coaching me about the dress, she said, "Was it a two-piece dress you wore? Was it a blouse and skirt?" and I answered, "Yes."

The next day Aimee drove her to Glendale to talk with Mr. Benedict again; Rolf was with them in the Kissel.

She let me out at the front entrance and drove around the bend and waited for me there. I was a great deal more successful at this interview than I was at the first one, although I was positive in my own mind that Mr. Benedict knew I was not the woman whom he had met at the Carmel cottage. I also want to add that Mrs. McPherson asked me if I remembered that there were no shades, and that was why the curtains were pinned together.

On a subsequent trip to San Francisco she rounded up witnesses who would corroborate her story, she said, including friends who had driven her back and forth to Carmel. During this visit she was in an automobile accident and telephoned to Mrs. Elizabeth Frame, a Temple confidante and her intermediary with Mother Kennedy, for $50, which was wired within two hours. Back in Los Angeles with her witnesses, she was stymied when the grand jury was discharged; both Aimee and her mother, she said, were present when she telephoned to the foreman, Carter, asking an appointment. Her telephone inquiry to Judge Keetch as to the best course of action, she continued, elicited the advice to "let the matter slide for the time being." The statement continued:

Finally it was decided by Mr. Woolley, Mrs. Kennedy, and Mrs. McPherson that it was a better thing to do to get it before the newspapers and make a final statement and let it go for good and all. This I proceeded to do. I had just arranged my statements and had witnesses and everything ready to go before the newspapers on Friday afternoon. I stated to Mrs. McPherson that I would be through in a day or so, and she told me to be sure to have a complete list of all expenses and everything would be fixed up for me. She also stated that she wanted me to make a trip to the Grand Canyon, the Yosemite, to rest, and that I was to go as her host [*sic*]. I figured out the list of about two thousand dollars but that was not all of it. She expected to pay me Saturday, September eleventh. I planned to leave Sunday or Monday.

Friday night she was arrested.

"The whole thing was a fake," she concluded. "I received only a small part of the money."

Intimate glimpses of life inside the Temple residence were scattered through the confession. Lorraine described Sister as giving up her own bed on several occasions, and the spread on Sister's bed she was in no doubt about.

> I stayed at the house many times. I stayed in her room. This room has a double bed with a yellow cover, and a lace cover on the top. It has a princess dresser, a dresser and a day bed. It has a bookcase in it. It also has her mother's picture at the time she was in her late twenties above her dresser. In her bookcase she had several Bibles and books pertaining to sermons. Off the bedroom on one side is a clothes closet with her clothes in it and her shoes. She has numerous beautiful robes and beautiful underwear. I wore one nightgown while I was there that was very beautiful. While I slept there she slept outdoors in the outdoor swing.

Mrs. Wiseman said she bought a switch and arranged her hair high on the head like Aimee's, and they were photographed together. She was sent to an optician's to get a particular kind of dark glasses to be photographed in. "She had the photographer pose us so I would look as near possible like her."

About ten days previously, Mrs. McPherson had telephoned the lawyer, Martin, in Chicago, the statement went on, asking him to transmit a message to Ormiston to get in touch with her personally. Last Thursday, Sister had excitedly told Lorraine that Ormiston was in Los Angeles; he had telephoned her and would call again Friday; she was sure the call was not a fake. She kept Lorraine waiting around all day Friday but no call came; Lorraine made herself useful by acting as a witness at a wedding Sister performed, signing the marriage register.

Lorraine mailed a letter to Ormiston from Mrs. McPherson (she did not see the contents), she said, and she herself wrote to the radio man in care of the Chicago attorney, requesting him to write or come back and back up her statements identifying "Miss X." She said Aimee assured her Ormiston would be glad to do this; "she said that was all we needed to clinch the whole thing."

Regarding the radio operator, Aimee was represented as being crushingly candid, once quipping, "People ought to know if I was going to take a man I wouldn't take a cripple or one without hair!"

The words on the grocery slips she was advised to practice copying, after photostatic reproductions were published in the newspapers. She and Aimee both copied them, she said, Aimee to show how dissimilar her handwriting was, Lorraine to demonstrate how similar hers was. "We laid across her bed in her room a whole half day while I practiced the handwriting. She would write the list and I would write it." After that Woolley, she said, sent her to a handwriting expert who "stated that there was no question that the handwriting [on the slips] was not mine, and for me not to write any more for anyone."

She described a visit to the Temple by Bernice Morris after McKinley's death, and the secretary's conversation with Mother Kennedy and Mrs. McPherson about bringing a map showing the location of the kidnap cabin; Bernice said the kidnapers were demanding money in advance, $15,000, and while Aimee was all for giving them a substantial sum, Mother balked, pointing out that McKinley had been given $1000 and produced nothing. Finally $100 was advanced to Miss Morris, Lorraine said.

Mrs. Wiseman said "Dr." Waters (whose name and telephone number were written in her notebook) had been in a deal to produce "Miss X," and he once brought his "Miss X" to within a block of the house, but she became frightened. Once, she said, she overheard Mother Kennedy tell Waters over the telephone, "Now, I've given you fifty dollars and seventy-five dollars and you haven't produced. You needn't do anything further, because the lady who is going to produce 'Miss X' is right in this room."

After the long, soul-searching session, Mrs. Kimball came downstairs in the *Examiner* building and passed Woolley. The attorney immediately identified her as the woman who had signed the "Miss X" affidavit in his presence in Salinas.

Mrs. Kimball angrily declared, "I am not 'Miss X' and I am positive I have never been anywhere near Carmel at any time."

"Do you know Judge Bardin of Salinas?" a reporter asked.

"I do not."

"Do you know Roland Rich Woolley?"

"I do not."

"Did you ever hear of him in Salt Lake City while you lived there?"

"No."

On her way back to jail to complete bail, Mrs. Wiseman learned that a man acting on behalf of her estranged husband, Sielaff, had been trying to get her transferred to a psychopathic ward preparatory to having her placed in a mental hospital. She was outraged.

"A Pack of Lies!"

The *Examiner*'s journalistic ten-strike had the effect of a giant firecracker exploding in a flock mattress: the feathers flew and statements rained. Judge Keetch repudiated the scandalous allegation that he ever told that woman to let anything slide. Bob Shuler jumped to it with a pulpit dissertation on "Was the grand jury a bunch of flour-flushers— or is Judge Keetch a four-flusher?" Woolley declared he had always suspected Mrs. Wiseman was a fake, and had told her in Salinas he did not believe her story; he finally became completely convinced of her fraudulence when a handwriting expert said the writing on the grocery slips could not possibly be hers.

"I warned Mrs. McPherson and Mrs. Kennedy from the very beginning that I did not believe the woman's story and cautioned them against having anything to do with her," the lawyer said. "If they were parties to her deception scheme, it was entirely without my knowledge, and I really can only believe that they acted in good faith and were themselves deceived."

Russell A. Swan, handwriting expert, recounted Mrs. Wiseman's coming to him with samples of her calligraphy and copies of the grocery slips. He told her at once it was useless to go through an elaborate comparison process, because the slips could not have been written by her. "I asked her if she had told anyone she wrote them," Swan recalled. "She said, 'No!' 'Well, then, don't,' I said to her, 'because if you persist in this story it can land you nowhere but in jail.' She was not in the least abashed."

Mrs. Frame, in an affidavit drawn up, she admitted, in Sister's dining room with Mrs. Kennedy doing most of the dictating, confessed she acted as go-between during Mrs. Wiseman's trips out of the city; once she lent Lorraine a disguise and spirited her out of town when she complained that she was being followed by reporters and detectives. Mrs. Frame admitted wiring the $50 to Lorraine in San Francisco after the latter telephoned a pitiful story of having been injured in an automobile accident, although Mrs. Frame noticed that a few days later Mrs. Wiseman went swimming with Mrs. McPherson at Ocean Park without any visible sign of injuries. Mrs. Frame was sure the Temple leaders believed Mrs. Wiseman and intended no wrong.

Ormiston Senior in San Francisco expressed his belief that "after reading my son's affidavit Mrs. Sielaff took a chance and made a supplementary affidavit in the hope Mrs. McPherson would be grateful and reward her. Her statements are pure invention. There will be a day of reckoning. I know my son has told the truth."

In Chicago, lawyer Martin cleared himself of being the "Mr. Martin" who first approached Lorraine, according to her account; Martin said he had never been in either San Francisco or Los Angeles, knew nothing about Mrs. Wiseman, and since mailing Ormiston's affidavit had not seen the man again, although they remained in communication.

Reporters hurried to Waters' apartment, for this was the first disclosure of his shadowy activities in the case. He disclaimed participating in any conspiracy. Two days later investigators from the district attorney's office, sent to question him, found his body; he had swallowed poison. The fireplace contained a mass of charred papers. In a wastebasket were two telegrams, the start of a letter to "My dear Judge Hardy," and a rambling note about producing "Miss X." One telegram, dated August 8, read: KINDLY COMMUNICATE WITH US AT EARLIEST CONVENIENCE. HIGHLY IMPORTANT. AIMEE SEMPLE MCPHERSON. The second, dated August 22: PLEASE COMMUNICATE WITH US AT EARLIEST POSSIBLE MOMENT. MRS. KENNEDY.

In Salinas, Judge Bardin and his law partner, Russell Scott, were unable to recognize news photographs of Mrs. Wiseman as the woman who brought "Miss X" to their office, although they did discern a resemblance. Bardin told what had happened that Sunday, August 15. His telephone rang at 7 o'clock that morning; a woman asked to see him at his office right away. Woolley had arrived from Los Angeles the day before to work on the case, and the judge telephoned him at his hotel and asked him to meet him at the office. Bardin arrived there at 8 o'clock and found Woolley in the inner office and Mrs. Wiseman waiting in the reception room. She was a complete stranger to him and Woolley. She said she had important information about the Carmel incident and asked to speak with him alone, but Bardin refused to listen except in Woolley's presence.

Before both attorneys, Mrs. Wiseman unfolded her story: her sister was the "Miss X" of Ormiston's affidavit, she said, and had come back from the East to exonerate Mrs. McPherson in regard to the cottage. As Mrs. Wiseman hung her head in embarrassment, the lawyers suggested her sister could speak for herself; where was she? Right across the street in the Jeffrey House, Mrs. Wiseman replied; but before she would consent to appear, they would have to promise not to question her or demand her name or address. "In view of the shame and humiliation she would suffer if her name became known, she does not care to subject herself to cross-examination or any very careful examination as to who she is, where she lives, or matters of that kind." Anonymity was desirable, also, because of the prominence of their family: one uncle was a justice of the Supreme Court of Idaho. (This was true; Lorraine's mother was attending his funeral in Idaho at the time of her daughter's arrest.)

Mrs. Wiseman assured the lawyers that she was the woman introduced to Benedict, that she signed for the telegram, that she wrote the grocery slips; but she constantly evaded answering questions about Ormiston, about her own place of employment or address, and about the interior arrangements of the Benedict cottage, which were vividly in the attorneys' minds because they had just been there. All these details she would give them later, she declared. She then left and in a few minutes returned with a woman of her own weight and general appearance, whose hair was dark. This person replied to few questions and spoke as little as possible, but signified her readiness to sign an affidavit affirming her presence in May in the Carmel cottage.

Bardin and Woolley were suspicious, but Mrs. Wiseman "gave a good line and stuck to her guns." Two affidavits were drawn, one for each woman, testifying to their separate roles in Carmel. Bardin wrote them in longhand, partly from Mrs. Wiseman's dictation as she read from a notebook she took out of her purse. Woolley then typed the documents, making an original and three copies. It was now noon. Bardin telephoned his partner, Scott, to come over and notarize the signatures, at the same time intimating his suspicions; as a result, Scott took extraordinary precautions in swearing the women and wrote down a description of both. Bardin warned them that false swearing could land them in prison, and he took a handwriting sample from Mrs. Wiseman, which she gave willingly. "Miss X" seemed on the verge of tears, choking with emotion, as she penned her pseudonym.

During the formality, Bardin stepped around the desk and examined the hair of "Miss X" at close range; it seemed to have been dyed; it was streaky, moist-looking, and carelessly combed. "Miss X" murmured that she had applied a tonic; she had just had her hair bobbed. With her permission Bardin felt the hair: it felt oily and greasy. He then asked for a lock from each woman's head, so acute were his forebodings. He rummaged in his secretary's desk but could find no scissors, and Mrs. Wiseman volunteered that the clippings from her sister's hair were in the dresser drawer at the hotel; she would send him over a sample. Shortly afterward the strangers departed, and in a few minutes two locks of hair were brought to the office by a messenger. Bardin filed them. He had alerted a local detective to trail the visitors, and the latter reported they checked out of the hotel in haste, got into a taxi, and drove for seventeen miles at high speed to a point where they caught the bus for Oakland.

Mrs. Wiseman, confessed but not shriven, was released on bail. "What a relief!" she exclaimed. With her lawyer she hurried to a bank where, a few days before, she had rented a safe-deposit box; she had turned over the key to Emma Schaffer after Woolley refused to touch it. The box was opened. Its contents, in nine sealed envelopes, included:

A slip of paper with directions for reaching Ocean Park and the Benedict cottage in Carmel.

A copy of Aimee's crackling radio statement on Cline's arrest.

An August telegram delivered to Mrs. Wiseman at the YWCA in San Francisco: PLEASE COMMUNICATE WITH ME AT ONCE. NEED PARTY'S ASSISTANCE IMMEDIATELY. MOTHER KENNEDY.

A rough draft of the "Miss X" affidavit in longhand, later said by experts to match the handwriting on the grocery slips.

A document indicating an attempt by Mrs. Kennedy to put Mrs. Wiseman in touch with Ormiston. This was a letter, on the stationery of A. W. and Edward H. S. Martin, Attorneys, Chicago, dated July 30, addressed to Mrs. McPherson, and reading "Enclosed herewith is copy of affidavit of K. G. Ormiston which was sent to District Attorney Keyes today. Respectfully yours, Edward H. S. Martin." Across the bottom of the letter, in pen and ink: "This will introduce Lorraine Wiseman. Any information helping us to get a message to Mr. K. G. Ormiston in the interest of justice to Mrs. McPherson will be deeply appreciated. Thank you. Mrs. M. Kennedy 'Mother.' "

Also in the box was a will in Mrs. Wiseman's handwriting: "In case of my death, all the contents of this box number 2A903 is to be delivered to

Facsimiles of the grocery slips (*top, left*) found outside the bungalow at Carmel; a page from the notebook (*top, right*) in which Mrs. Wiseman practiced writing the words that appeared on the slips; and the "Light and Darkness" sermon notes in Mrs. McPherson's handwriting

Aimee Semple McPherson or her children, without restriction, or without being opened." It was dated September 4.

Said Mother, tight-lipped: "She came a stranger and left a stranger."

Said Aimee: "The whole thing is a pack of lies."

"The Walls Came Tumblin' Down"

Bernice Morris lost no time in extricating herself from a dangerous position as soon as Mrs. Wiseman's confession was broadcast. She hurried into the city and met Keyes in a midnight interview. Then she went to the office of the *Times* and made her own confession, which rivaled Mrs. Wiseman's, and in the morning the *Times* was able to preen itself over the discomfited *Examiner*.

Miss Morris recounted that the day McKinley was killed, Mrs. McPherson and her mother picked her up in Woolley's car and during that long drive around Long Beach pleaded with her to carry on her employer's work in negotiating with the kidnapers to tell the whereabouts of the shack. Bernice was excited and unsure. She was twenty-three years old and studying for the bar; she believed that McKinley had no real contacts with the kidnapers; but Sister's personality was persuasive, and the chance to play a role in the biggest legal case of her lifetime was tempting. Pleading youth and inexperience, she hedged.

"Mother Kennedy then spoke up and said she didn't see why we women couldn't take care of this by ourselves and not get anyone else mixed up in it," ran Bernice's account.

Bernice went to the Temple that evening and signed, under protest, a press statement saying that McKinley had been in contact with the abductors, although she believed this statement to be untrue because of the Joe Watts photograph and telephone conversation, which she had helped to engineer. (This was the first time the public enjoyed this laugh.)

The next day the Temple women picked up Bernice in Woolley's car and took her to the Temple, pursued by a car that came to grief in the chase, spilling reporters over the pavement; Mother Kennedy and Aimee received the news of this accident with equanimity. Minnie had another press statement ready for Bernice to sign, asserting that she was carrying on her employer's task. The secretary objected again, but under pressure signed.

A week later, Miss Morris went back to Echo Park and was admitted to the Temple home by Mrs. Wiseman, who was busy advising Roberta to put alum on her chapped lips. Bernice did not know Mrs. Wiseman, and from her familiar manner judged that she was one of the family.

Her statement went on:

Mother Kennedy came in and asked me if I had gotten the map yet. I told her no, that there had been too much talk in the newspapers, that I was afraid to have anything to do with it. Then Mrs. McPherson came in. Mother Kennedy left and Mrs. McPherson began talking about the shack, that if these men produced the real shack, it would have to contain a lot of things she enumerated. . . . She said the furniture might have been removed, but surely the paper was the same; it was a kind of paper you could find anywhere, it could be bought for about five cents a roll, just common paper, kind of smoky-like. She asked me if the shack had a bathroom, and said, "It was a very small bathroom, wasn't it?"

After we talked for some time, Mrs. Kennedy came into the room. Mrs. McPherson said in the presence of her mother that she thought these kidnapers should be able to remember some incident which had happened during the time she was held there. Attempting to test Mrs. McPherson's sincerity, I invented a fictitious incident and related it to her. I said, "One of these men wanted to know whether on one afternoon you did not have a very bad crick in your neck that was so severe that Rose rubbed your neck all afternoon."

Mrs. McPherson at once turned to her mother and said, "Mother dear, I do remember that. I never recalled it before. But you know that I have trouble with my neck." She then started to massage her neck and illustrate to her mother her habit of massaging her neck. [Mother Kennedy agreed that "the crick in the neck is good."] Mrs. McPherson told me she would give everything in the world to vindicate herself, and that all this information would be of no value to her unless I could make the world believe it, and clear her. I kept telling Mrs. McPherson I was afraid of the entire deal. Of course, I knew there were no men and could produce no men. The minute details supplied to me by Mrs. McPherson's indirect suggestions were obviously for the purpose of assisting me to produce testimony corroborating her story.

Just before I left I told Mrs. McPherson that these men couldn't stick around Long Beach all their lives and should be supplied with money for a quick getaway. Mrs. McPherson suggested to her mother to give me some money to give to these men. Mrs. Kennedy said she would give me $100 and wanted me to sign a receipt for it. I refused. Shortly after this I left by the back door. Mrs. McPherson followed me out of the house, put her arm around me and said, "You are a dear little girl and I know you can help me. I am sure those are the right men. Let me hear from you Monday and try to have a map for me." . . . In all our conversations, I gathered the impression that Mrs. Kennedy implicitly believed Mrs. McPherson's kidnaping story and that Mrs. McPherson was fearful of her mother. The one time Mrs. McPherson talked to me alone her demeanor was entirely different than when Mrs. Kennedy was present.

Miss Morris handed to Keyes the water-smeared papers taken off McKinley's body. One was a list of specifications for the kidnap shack to prove it genuine. The other was a letter to the dead attorney, written in a firm hand, dated August 14:

Dear Mr. McKinley: Just starting on my vacation driving north to Canada—expect to be at Palace Hotel, San Francisco, Thursday, Friday and Saturday. If your friends communicate with you and it is necessary for you to reach me, you will know how to do it up to next Saturday inclusive. Thereafter I will not be reachable and you will have to act on your own initiative in co-operation with Mrs. Kennedy who is advised. Best luck. Sincerely yours, Carlos S. Hardy.

August 15 was the day when McKinley went to San Francisco supposedly to keep a rendezvous with Miller or Wilson there.

On the day of Miss Morris's confession, Judge Hardy returned to Los Angeles. He was summoned to Keyes' office and interrogated sharply. Hardy admitted his interest in the case, his friendship for the Temple leaders, and some of the steps he had taken to unravel the mystery. Mrs. Wiseman he had met only once, at his home on August 1, he said. The judge did not show Keyes the reports he had been receiving from detectives, nor volunteer any information regarding their findings. Publicly he said, "I believed that facts that would verify Mrs. McPherson's story would help her. I am of an open mind and await what facts develop with an open mind."

Ryan encountered Mrs. Wiseman by chance one day soon after her release on bail. He was passing the press room in the Hall of Justice, where Mrs. Wiseman was chatting with reporters while waiting for another talk with Keyes. Through the open door a reporter called to the deputy, "You two ought to meet!"

Ryan laughed. "Why didn't you come to see me when I sent word to you last week?" he asked.

"I was afraid you would ask me some questions I couldn't answer," said Lorraine, simpering.

"You found out I wanted to ask you what medicine was left in the cottage by the occupants?"

"Yes."

"What did you do?"

"I told Mrs. McPherson, 'Ryan wants to see me.' She said, 'What about?' I said, 'He wants to see if I know what medicine was left in the cottage.'"

"What did Mrs. McPherson say?"

"She laughed and said, 'Well, that's a good one. Let me see—there was some witch hazel, for one thing.'"

"Did she say that?" Ryan was surprised. "What else did she say?"

"Mrs. Kennedy and some others came in just then and she never got to finish it. She didn't talk so freely when her mother was around. I believe there's a lot Mother Kennedy doesn't know. Aimee's hair is gray, you know that, don't you? She buys hair and colors all of it to do up high on her head and make her hair look like she does."

A reporter inquired, "Was Mrs. McPherson always serious, or did she display a bit of humor over the situation now and then?"

"She was nearly always serious," replied Lorraine merrily, "but she had a sense of humor and she laughed sometimes—when a good one had been put over on the newspapers!"

Three hours of grilling by Keyes failed to sour Mrs. Wiseman's cheerful insouciance. She was sent to a hotel under guard of two police matrons.

Mother Kennedy could not endure the torture of silence; she issued statements and talked with valiant abandon. Regarding Mrs. Wiseman: "She fooled us completely. We have pursued the policy of listening to everybody with the hope that they could bring us a grain of truth concerning the attacks that have been made upon us. When she declared she did not want money for her services, we met her more than halfway."

She paused, then flushed. "It's martyrdom! We've known for weeks that they have planned to drag Sister down from the pulpit of Angelus Temple in a sensational arrest!"

That day (it was the fifth since Mrs. Wiseman's arrest, and the interval had been packed with sensations) Sister preached with her accustomed bounce and fire. She warned her flock to expect the worst. "I have been informed from reliable sources that I may be arrested tonight." A hush fell over the great hall. "I have just telephoned the district attorney's office and asked them if they would arrest me tomorrow before my services are over at five o'clock." She paused. "They told me there would not be anything doing before that time. So stick around and you may see something!"

Hallelujahs, cries, cheers, high-pitched screams broke the tension. Sister smiled. "I only wish," she added, "that I will be given enough time before this action is taken to be prepared and looking right!"

In the evening she spoke of Mrs. Wiseman's betrayal. "I have been a little simpleton. Everyone has said I have talked too much; but I couldn't see why I should not talk when I knew that everything I said was the truth."

Glimpsing her mother standing in a doorway of the second balcony, she called out, "Am I talking too much, Mother?"

Minnie Kennedy shook her head and exclaimed, "I don't blame you!"

"Then I guess I'm all right," resumed Sister, and she told the Wiseman episode:

One day there came to Angelus Temple a woman who tearfully pleaded for a chance to see me, intimating that she could help clear up the Carmel-by-the-Sea incident. We listened to this woman's story and told her to go ahead and do what she could. But we insisted that her story should not become public until it had been thoroughly substantiated. We gave this woman money as we did detectives and others who had come to us with claims that they could help us clear up and substantiate my story. [When Mrs. Wiseman was arrested] we were dumbfounded. We received two notes demanding $3000; if it was not forthcoming, disaster would fall. Then came the bombshell, or the disaster perhaps, to which the writer of the notes referred, with the announcement of the "confession" made by the woman after she had been arrested as a passer of bad checks. Despite the charges against this woman, her story was given credence over mine—I, who for seventeen years in the work of the Lord have borne a stainless reputation—against whom nothing can be found in the whole seventeen years! Sometimes I pinch myself to see whether this is all true and I, a pastor of the Lord, an American citizen and the mother of two children, am being so persistently persecuted—and it is persecution! Never has anyone been so persecuted as I have been!

Thunderous applause drowned out her words.

She brought the service to a close with a dramatic reading of the Beatitudes. (Her daughter, years later, would recall: "Aimee McPherson could read the Twenty-third Psalm the way Judith Anderson could read *Macbeth.*") Leaning on the pulpit, she read, "Blessed are the peacemakers," and interjected, "I only wish there were more peacemakers in Los Angeles!"

"Blessed are they which are persecuted for righteousness' sake," she read on, and referred again to her "persistent persecution"; no one ever was "bombarded by so many forces."

"Blessed are ye, when men shall revile you, and persecute you, and shall say all manner of evil against you falsely, for my sake. Rejoice and be exceeding glad, for great is your reward in Heaven." She drew herself up proudly. "I am not going down in the dirt and answer the accusations of these people! Christ was crucified—but His crucifixion didn't last so long!"

Flipping the Bible shut, she shot out an arm scornfully toward one corner of the Temple and called, "Now, all you newspaper people, jump up and go out and tell that to the world!" Not a person stirred, and, sweeping the congregation with her golden smile, Aimee changed the mood with, "Now is the time to sing and rejoice!" and invited all to join her in a hymn, led by the brass band, the organ, the choir, and the Steinway grand. Cheers and hallelujahs were still echoing when the hymn came to a massive "Amen!"

The melodramatic suggestion that Angelus Temple's pastor might be dragged from her pulpit drew an instant rebuke from the district attorney's camp.

> Mr. Keyes has not the slightest intention of doing what Mrs. McPherson was told would happen. She will be treated with every consideration merited by her sex and her position in life.

During the evening service Aimee had asked her audience and radio listeners "courteously" to protest the "raw deal" she was getting. Within two minutes Keyes' home telephone started to ring and kept ringing until he ordered it disconnected. Guards were posted around the building. Fifty-two telegrams of protest were delivered to his office in the first batch, requesting fair play and denouncing acceptance of Mrs. Wiseman's word over the evangelist's, and this was only an advance trickle.

Asa Keyes could temporize no longer. Mrs. Wiseman and Bernice Morris, two impeaching witnesses, had been dropped on his lap. Their stories of being coached in what they were to say and discover dovetailed too glaringly to be shrugged aside. Maneuvered into an exposed position, the prosecutor acted with rigor. On Thursday, September 16—four months almost to the day after Aimee went for her swim—the district attorney, following the pattern of public announcement that had become standard in the case, dictated a general order to the citizens of Los Angeles and the world:

I have just instructed Mr. Forrest Murray, head of my complaint division, to issue felony complaints against Mrs. Aimee Semple McPherson, Mrs. Minnie Kennedy, Mr. Kenneth G. Ormiston, Mrs. Lorraine Wiseman, and John Doe Martin. Legal action to place before the public of this community all the facts and circumstances of this case and to prosecute before the bar of justice this woman and her associates for tampering with the instrumentalities of the law is imperative.

From the time the story that Mrs. McPherson had been drowned was broadcast throughout the country, there has been the tainted atmosphere of a gigantic hoax surrounding it. As time has progressed this increased with the exposé of the unbelievable story of the kidnaping and the brazen activities of Mrs. McPherson and her friends to build up a false alibi for her.

It is my duty and I can do no less than exert the full power of my office to bring this woman to the bar of justice in order that she may have a fair and public hearing. It is with regret that I take action against a person so high in the religious esteem of many persons, but the community and the upright members of all religions must welcome a fair and open hearing of the situation, which has become a nationwide scandal.

A few hours before Keyes took this decisive step, Aimee, standing in her Temple, in tones that pierced to the heart of every listener, uttered these words: "I expect to meet my God in Heaven as I expect to meet my friends and loyal followers. And I expect to meet my beloved husband, Robert Semple."

Then falling on her knees, with passionate sincerity she cried, "And as I expect to meet my God, my story is as true today as it was the first time I told it!"

THEME IV

The Law's Dismays

"And though they hide themselves
in the top of Carmel, I will search
them and take them out thence; and
though they be hid from my sight
in the bottom of the sea, thence will
I command the serpent, and he shall
bite them."

—Amos 9:3

"Falsely, Wickedly, and Maliciously . . ."

Keyes waited twenty-four hours after announcing his intention to prosecute. All morning Thursday, September 17, he sat in his office, hoping for a response to his last-minute invitation to Aimee and her mother to come talk with him and perhaps work out some accommodation. A messenger brought word from the Temple that Mrs. McPherson was "too sick" to come downtown and Mrs. Kennedy was "too tired." Then came a report that Sister was well enough to be preaching to her followers from her bedroom window, and Keyes grimly ordered prepared the prosecutor's criminal complaint under which he must act, since no new grand jury had been empaneled and he could not proceed by indictment. Instantly extras hit the streets: "Aimee's Arrest Near!"

The complaint (which the newspapers printed verbatim as a historical document) left little to conjecture. It charged Aimee and her asserted confederates with "conspiracy to commit acts injurious to public morals and to prevent and obstruct justice, and to obstruct and pervert the due administration of the laws of California," all of which was "against the peace and dignity of the People of the State of California." It recited that Aimee Semple McPherson "surreptitiously disappeared from Venice, Cal., on or about May 18, 1926, and appeared on or about 2 a.m. on the morning of June 23, 1926, behind a slaughterhouse in Sonora, Mex." That she went before the grand jury and "swore falsely, wickedly, and maliciously, with intent to procure another to be charged, arrested, and indicted of the crime of kidnaping . . . and well knowing at the time that she had not been kidnaped, falsely and fraudulently represented and pretended that she had been kidnaped and kept in an unconscious condition for upwards of thirty (30) days . . . and from the 19th of May up to and including the 29th of May 1926 she resided and remained concealed with goggles and other devices and contrivances at Carmel-by-the-Sea, from which place she departed with Kenneth G. Ormiston, with the full knowledge, acquiescence, and consent of Minnie Kennedy."

225

It recounted Aimee's describing "the alleged kidnapers as 'Rose' and 'Steve' . . . for the purpose of deceiving the grand jury of Los Angeles and inducing them to return an indictment whereby and wherein others would be charged with the said crime." It declared that she hired Mrs. Wiseman to impersonate her, coached her, and paid her to make the false affidavit at Salinas; and that she hired McKinley to produce bogus kidnapers, and attempted to induce Bernice Morris to carry out the criminal hoax.

Against each defendant were invoked two counts, one under Section 182 of the Criminal Code, carrying punishment of up to fourteen years in prison; the other under an 1872 law making the preparation of false evidence a felony, with a penalty of five years' imprisonment. Mother Kennedy was represented as an accomplice from the beginning, acting in concert with her daughter.

The thirteen-page document, the district attorney's staff believed, pinned down the offense securely; but nothing was to come easily for the prosecution. Experts in moot law pounced on the complaint and worried it to ribbons; others were just as assertive that it was watertight. The arguments on both sides were subtle. Mrs. McPherson stood accused of having committed perjury before the grand jury in statements regarding a kidnaping. But, assuming that her statements were false, telling untruths under oath is not perjury, within the meaning of the law, unless it pertains to the "material issue of a crime"—and the crux of this case was that the crime she made her statements about was nonexistent. Can one commit perjury about what does not exist?

Some legal casuists also argued that the nonexistence of Steve and Rose could be proved only negatively, by circumstantial inference; nobody could prove positively that they did not exist. And as for McKinley, what he might have been up to no one would ever know, because he was dead; but whatever it might have been, he certainly had not produced any kidnapers, real or feigned. As for the conspiracy charge, while the statute made the act of having someone "falsely and maliciously indicted" for a crime a felony, nobody had been indicted. And the flaw in the State's contention that acts "injurious to public morals" had been committed lay in the failure of the statute to define what acts might properly come under that provision. It was a legal tantalizer that is still good for debate wherever lawyers gather.

The bemused public sensed, without legal promptings, that the State's position was somehow topsy-turvy. A prosecutor's task obviously is to prove, first, that a crime has been committed, and then to link the accused person with that crime. But here the prosecution was avowedly determined to prove that *no crime* had been committed (no kidnaping), and hence that the defendant's claim of innocent involvement in a non-existent felony was moonshine. But if there really was no kidnaping, and nobody had been indicted, what was the shouting about? Was it a prison offense for a lady to say she was where she wasn't—if she wasn't?

Keyes was not to be deflected by divagations or chop-logic. His advisers assured him the complaint would stand up, and he set to work vigorously to tie together the loose ends of the case. His office became the headquarters of frenzied activity: witnesses streamed in and out; excited deputies, reporters, photographers, detectives, stenographers jostled one another. Statements were taken from new witnesses, fresh statements from old ones—statements on statements stacked up on the deputies' desks. And as fast as the statements accumulated, they were published in the newspapers; nothing, it seemed, was withheld.

Bernice Morris brought in two more letters written by Judge Hardy to McKinley about contacts with the kidnapers. Hardy thereupon gave out that he had told Sister and her mother when the case first broke that as a judge he could not give them legal advice, but as a friend he urged them to get the best detectives and attorneys they could to run down the facts; that was his only role.

Emma Schaffer told of Mrs. Wiseman's giving her the key to the safe-deposit box in Mrs. McPherson's presence; Emma didn't know what was in the box. Lorraine had aroused no sympathy in her. "I didn't believe she was entirely truthful. She had a nervous habit of twitching at her hair; I'm sure it resulted from an overburdened conscience."

Keyes asked Emma's opinion of Mrs. McPherson as a woman.

"She is the most loyal, pure, and honest woman I have ever known," replied Emma stanchly.

Did she still believe the evangelist was kidnaped?

"Absolutely! I am as positive as of anything in the world that Sister McPherson has spoken the truth and nothing but the truth. There has never been anything at all to shake my faith in her."

Mrs. Frame told the prosecutor that she never believed Mrs. Wiseman fully, "but I felt she was helping Sister. She was always mixed-up in her mind." Once, when she observed Lorraine jotting down scraps of conversation as though keeping a record, Mrs. Frame cautioned Mother Kennedy, saying, "Be careful. I don't like the way that woman acts. She has a limpy handshake, for one thing."

"She is sincere, darling," Minnie replied. "She is going to get these witnesses and everything."

Mrs. Frame admitted she had allowed Mrs. Wiseman to use the telephone at her Ocean Park cottage for communicating with the Temple from out of town; they were all convinced the Temple wires were tapped. On Labor Day (September 6) Aimee and her children, with Mrs. Frame and her children and Mrs. Wiseman and her son, had spent the holiday at the beach, swimming and riding the roller coaster; Sister treated everybody to waffles and coffee, and screamed with delight on the rides like the youngest in the party. That night Mrs. McPherson and Mrs. Wiseman shared a bed in the Frame cottage; they rose at 6:30 for a frisk in the sea (both wore *red* bathing suits) and drove back to the Temple for breakfast at 7:30.

Blanche Rice told the district attorney she was on duty at the information window in the Angelus Temple lobby on July 31, when Mrs. Wiseman first appeared and asked if she might see either Mrs. McPherson or Mrs. Kennedy, sighing nervously, "This thing has weighed on me for some time."

"What thing? Are you in trouble?" asked motherly Mrs. Rice.

"It was my sister who was at Carmel."

Blanche bolted into the home next door without knocking, and when Mother appeared on the stair landing, called out, "There is a lady downstairs who says it was her sister who was at Carmel with Ormiston!"

"Bring her up," said Minnie, who was in conference with Veitch.

Mrs. Wiseman filled in her version of the events from then on. Veitch, she said, was unfriendly, but after he left, Mother asked her to talk with Judge Hardy, which she did the next morning, Sunday, at the judge's home. Hardy opened the door himself and brought her into the living room, where Mrs. Hardy was sitting, she said. While the judge asked questions, Mrs. Hardy switched on the radio and got the broadcast from Angelus Temple; Sister McPherson was heard announcing that Mrs. Hardy would speak at the Temple that evening.

The next day, Mrs. Wiseman said, she met Mrs. McPherson for the first time. After some talk Minnie took the visitor across to the Temple and upstairs to the Five Hundred Room, where they would be undisturbed.

"I think," Minnie cautioned, "if you are going to try to bring this little lady forward, it would be better if Mr. Woolley and Mr. Veitch should know nothing about it. We will just keep it among us women."

On their return to the residence, Sister received them with a pensive frown. "You know, while you were gone I just wondered if you were not the lady mistaken for me at the Benedict cottage," she said. "You look so much like me, you even talk like me; your throat is like mine."

Roberta entered the room and Aimee asked her opinion.

"You know, you do look so much like Mama," Mrs. Wiseman quoted Roberta as answering.

During the succeeding days, Mrs. Wiseman said, she shuttled between Los Angeles, Carmel, and San Francisco, negotiating to produce "Miss X," using an assortment of fanciful names—Pauline Mack, Ruth Anderson, Grace McClelland, A. Moore. Expense money was advanced by Minnie, who always took a receipt. Only once did she speak with Aimee alone, she said, and then the evangelist told her it was "all right," to "go right ahead," and gave her three $10 gold pieces. Another time Aimee at the back door slipped $100 into her hand, whispering not to let Mother know.

It became known that disharmony existed between the Temple attorneys and their clients; Woolley had clashed violently with Aimee and her mother over Mrs. Wiseman. "That woman is fire!" he pleaded. "She will blow you into the middle of the ocean!" But Minnie defended Lorraine against the attorney's "prejudice," saying she was doing a fine, sincere action.

The newspapers bulged with revelations. The frantic appeal for bail money which Lorraine sent to Aimee from jail just after her arrest was printed and made reflective reading:

> Oh, what a terrible thing they have done to me. They said they would get me and they think they have. But wait, I have got a card to spring they don't know of yet. Now, dear, if you will send down $3000 for bond in cash by this man, I will get out long enough to get back. Believe me, I only want four hours; I will get them then. They took me unawares, they went through all I had, found nothing much, but Oh, what a terrible thing for my children and for you! But I'll get them, dear, believe me, please, when I tell you this whole thing is framed. Please send me the money within a few minutes, but I will give it back within forty-eight hours, besides having the Times eat dirt. . . . This is just another thing to get you. It is terrible what they say about you. Please dear, put it in an envelope so even this attorney will not know, but please do it. Lorraine.

This approach, and others more threatening, transmitted by the wife of a bail bondsman, had met only silence.

Wallace Moore, the Santa Barbara reporter, informed Keyes that during August he received a telephone call from Mrs. McPherson, urging him to make a statement denying she was the woman in the car he stopped on May 29. "I kept telling her I would be glad to prepare a statement of the event as it occurred, but I would not specify that she was not the woman," he said.

Finally Keyes called in Mrs. Holmes, the woman grand juror suspected of having destroyed the grocery slips, and learned that at one time she and another member of the panel had been carrying on their own unauthorized snooping in the case; they had visited Woolley and invited him to complain about the conduct of the district attorney, but the lawyer bowed them out without giving satisfaction. After this interview with Mrs. Holmes, Keyes prudently ordered every scrap of evidence to be photographed; the negatives he locked in his personal safe.

Keyes announced that his case was complete. He would subpoena thirty-five witnesses, Ryan among them, for the preliminary hearing. This hearing, of course, was not the trial; all Keyes could get from it would be the judge's sanction to have the case tried before a jury. But Keyes promised to lay all his cards on the table, withholding nothing. The hearing, he estimated, might run a week, possibly two weeks. Already on September 17 Municipal Judge Samuel L. Blake had signed warrants for the arrest of Aimee, her mother, Ormiston, the mysterious "Mr. Martin," and two John Does. Mrs. Wiseman was also a defendant; she was living in an apartment at the county's expense, chaperoned by two women deputy sheriffs. But serving the warrant on Aimee was impossible. For in her red-and-blue-floodlighted mansion the evangelist lay dangerously ill, her spirit floundering, at times delirious, crying out hysterically against her martyrdom.

Down—and Up Fighting

While she was preaching, the evening before the complaint was signed, Aimee had felt a stabbing pain in her face. From the platform she went into conference with her attorneys, all the while the pain increasing and her face swelling rapidly. By 2 a.m. the agony became unbearable and a doctor was called. He diagnosed an abscess in the upper nasal passage. The abscess was lanced and the doctor placed two nurses on duty.

All that night (Wednesday, September 15) the Temple grounds remained brilliantly lighted, while guards patrolled the adjacent shadows. Word spread that Sister was ill, and in the Bible School students gathered to sing hymns and pray for their leader. At dawn the faithful clustered below Sister's window, praying in chorus and singing "Stand, Don't Waver!" At 8 o'clock the French window on the little balcony opened and Sister stepped out, pale and trembling. Huskily she said, "After the services last night I was not well, but praise the Lord, I gained the victory at three o'clock this morning."

Amid murmured hallelujahs Mother Kennedy appeared and thanked Sister's well-wishers. Then slowly both women returned inside the house, the window was closed, and the crowd melted away. A bulletin posted at 11 a.m. announced: "Temperature 102, pulse 100, infection not spreading." As the doctor left the house he told reporters the evangelist was suffering from an abscess dangerously close to the brain; if there were complications, it would be very serious.

Thursday (while Keyes was drawing the complaint) Aimee admitted women reporters to her sick room. Her inflamed face was under ice packs and she was in physical and mental anguish, but she insisted that the telephone remain beside the bed and constantly answered calls from prayerful sympathizers. The room was banked with flowers and baskets of fruit; telegrams rustled in from half the world. As 7 o'clock approached she insisted on getting dressed to go to the Temple; the alarmed nurses and her mother telephoned the doctor, and he warned that the effort might kill her. When finally convinced that she could not appear, she sank back, covered her face with her hands, and wept.

"I hope they are satisfied now! They have crucified and reviled me unmercifully! I hope they see their work is nearly completed!" Tears coursed down her puffed, unsightly cheeks. "I am going to prison— I know it! I have been hounded like a wild animal—it's been a hunt— that's what it was—and the hounds and their dripping jaws are closing in!" She shuddered and screamed. "No woman of the streets was ever given less consideration than has been given me!"

The reporters left her moaning convulsively and went across to the Temple, where a full house was singing hymns in an atmosphere of angry tension. In the Prayer Tower, women were beseeching Heaven, not that Sister might be spared her Calvary, but that she might be given strength to pass through it triumphantly. At the moment in the service when Sister customarily made her entrance, striding down the ramp with blue cape billowing behind her, Mother Kennedy appeared. Sister, she told the hushed crowd, was in bed under "the greatest strain ever borne by mortal woman"; her strength had finally given out. However, she sent her love and hoped to be with them again in a few days.

All day Thursday and Friday knots of the curious and of the faithful lingered around the Temple home, while overhead a small plane circled, its passenger waving to the crowds below. The sidewalk loudspeakers were turned off to give the patient quiet. A stream of automobiles passed and repassed incessantly, from which expensively gowned women craned for a glimpse of the bedroom window. Early Friday morning the students congregated again, singing hymns until Sister stepped out on the balcony, weary and wan. Her voice was not strong, but she smiled. "God bless you all! That is beautiful music—like angels singing."

Mother gently led her inside. The doctor reported that his patient was improving but was not out of danger. (That day Judge Blake signed the warrant for Aimee's arrest.) Friday evening she arose from her sick bed and appeared in the Temple to submit to healing prayer, according to the rites of her church.

"I practice what I preach," she told the compassionate crowd. She had brought in a medical doctor, she explained, to satisfy the requirements of the law, but the partial abatement of her illness she ascribed to her followers' prayers. The elders of the church, standing in a semicircle around her, anointed her with oil and imposed hands solemnly. Sister was so invigorated by the ceremony that she spoke with something like her usual fervor, asking for a speedy hearing "at which everything will be cleared up. The sooner it comes now, the better."

Saturday afternoon she again was interviewed, propped in bed; she appealed for fair play. "Tomorrow is a blessed Sabbath day. Let's get back to our calm."

To her callers she seemed much recovered; the facial swelling had gone down, her temperature was almost normal, and she was busy with preparations for Sunday.

Mother Kennedy had need of all her courage in the hour of humiliation Friday when she arrived at the Hall of Justice to surrender to the warrant for her arrest as a conspirator with her daughter. Shepherding her was W. I. Gilbert, a leading criminal lawyer whom she had retained that morning while downtown on a "shopping trip." The courthouse corridors were jammed. Preceded by a smugly complacent bail bondsman, Mother and Gilbert fought their way to the sixth-floor office of the district attorney's detective chief, Ben Cohen. Minnie, wearing a modest black dress with brown bodice, and a soft black hat, held a fixed smile, but her fright and shame were evident.

In Cohen's office the warrant was read and Gilbert accepted it, Mother sitting miserably under the harsh scrutiny of a score of courthouse attachés. When Cohen started to escort her to Judge Blake's chambers on the floor above, she shrank back. Couldn't Judge Blake come downstairs and arraign her there, she pleaded? Blake ordered the defendant be brought to his chambers forthwith, and Cohen whisked her into a waiting elevator. In the judge's office she was arraigned and $2500 bail was posted. Gilbert reported Mrs. McPherson too ill to appear and posted another bond of $2500 for her appearance. The preliminary hearing for both women was set for the 27th.

Hastening to the Temple, Minnie drafted a statement reaffirming her pride and confidence in her daughter and charging that they were the targets of ruthless persecution.

All through sacred history we read of those children of God whose message rang forth in denunciation of sin, who were haled before magistrates and imprisoned and bodily punishment inflicted. Jesus distinctly taught that His church should have persecution. As far as we know, we are the only church in the world today to have this honor.

This broadside goaded Keyes into making his only direct rejoinder during the protracted turmoil:

Mrs. McPherson is not and never has been a victim of persecution in so far as the law-enforcement agencies of this city are concerned. Every act of my office concerning her kidnaping story was weighed carefully and thoughtfully. We went over every shred of evidence before issuing the complaints against Mrs. McPherson and her mother in order that we would not be guilty of hasty or ill-considered conclusions. Mrs. McPherson returned home after a month's absence with a story that she had been kidnaped and held prisoner in a shack by a Steve and Rose whom we now know to be purely mythical. She never brought forward one iota of evidence to back her astounding charges, but went, instead, to the grand jury and attempted to make that body a plaything by asking for indictments against kidnapers that did not exist. This office has its duty to perform and must do it regardless of who is hurt. I am sorry for Mrs. McPherson, but that cannot influence my sworn duty.

Mother marched into the Temple after issuing her manifesto and assured a weeping, shouting, determined throng that "ninety per cent of the people in Los Angeles have been absolutely with us during our troubles. This work will go on! Even the gates of Hell cannot prevail against it!"

"Praise God!" the congregation shouted, and radio listeners heard intermingled cries of "Persecution! Persecution!"

Just before the service, on this day of her great trial, Minnie found time to look in on Roberta's birthday party of young people, held in the Bible School. Her granddaughter was sixteen that day.

By Saturday morning, Mother Kennedy had recovered her spunkiness; she snapped to reporters who demanded where she was going when she stepped out of her home, "I'm going downtown to have my hair fixed. Any objection?" And in Woolley's car she whirled away just as the city was electrified by the offer of attorney Hahn to surrender Ormiston within twenty-four hours, in return for immunity.

Rumors that the radio man was hiding in Southern California had been driving the police frantic. Detectives scurried to the nearby communities of Alhambra, Seal Beach, Redondo Beach, Monterey Park, and even Santa Catalina Island, without finding the man who limped. Keyes brushed aside Hahn's offer with scorn: Ormiston was the key to the whole conspiracy, the prosecutor said, and he wanted him in jail. Ben Cohen was ordered to circularize every police department in the United States and Canada to arrest the fugitive on sight.

Aimee sneered at Hahn's pretensions. "Publicity, a cheap attempt at publicity! He has never been in touch with Ormiston! He has never been in touch with any of his friends for him! We know. . . . We know!"

From Winnipeg, Canada, came a telegram: ORMISTON SICK. WILL SURRENDER IF GRANTED IMMUNITY. THIS IS LAST OFFER. REPLY THROUGH PRESS.

Replied Keyes: "I will not grant immunity. That is final."

In Chicago, the attorney Martin told reporters that Ormiston had offered to meet Keyes in Chicago and discuss the case, but Keyes had not responded.

"Neither I nor my deputies are going to run to Chicago to interview Mr. Ormiston," countered Keyes. "When I talk to Ormiston it is going to be in jail!"

The Los Angeles *Times* received a telegram from Windsor, Ontario, signed "Ormiston," denouncing the stories about his planning to surrender as "bunk."

The public was titivated by the disclosure that Mrs. McPherson was feeling a financial strain. Recording of a deed revealed the sale for $25,-000 of a corner lot in Venice owned by the evangelist and her mother. The hill site in Elysian Park donated to Sister by grateful gypsies already had been sold, and her first home in Los Angeles, the famous "House That God Built," near Culver City, was on the market. And it was learned that on September 10 (a few hours before Lorraine Wiseman was arrested) the deed conveying the Temple to the Echo Park Evangelist Association was at last recorded. The deed had been signed by Aimee and Minnie on November 24, 1925; the conveyance placed the Temple properties beyond the legal reach of possible claims against Mrs. McPherson personally.

That Sunday, ignoring lawyers, hearings, or technicalities, Aimee launched her defense in her own way, and with sure instinct struck straight home to the emotions of her listeners. It was the first Sunday she preached out on bail, and the Temple could not contain the multitudes. Sister appeared briefly at the morning service; she seemed bright and energetic, although the lights had shone in her home until after midnight. Thanking the congregation for their prayers, she said their efficacy was proved that morning when her temperature dropped not only to normal, but below normal. The afternoon service was for children, and Helene Smith, aged thirteen, preaching the sermon, likened Sister to the queen bee of "God's greatest beehive on earth." When Aimee entered she received an ovation; then the children sang a song written for the occasion, "We Are Mrs. McPherson's Boys and Girls." In her talk Sister made only one reference to her troubles: "All these things that people are falsely saying derogatory to my character and our church are absolutely false."

But in the evening she blazed out before a sobbing, moaning, shouting throng cramming every cranny of the Temple. The spectacle was voted by reporters to be as sensational as anything either the city's stage or Angelus Temple itself had ever witnessed. The service was under way when she entered with Rolf and Roberta on either arm, a huge spray of flowers on her shoulder. As she glided down the ramp, the congregation stood and shouted. "Hallelujah!" "Praise the Lord!" "Sweet Jesus!" "Amen!" Her sermon opened with a rapid tracing of the events that had led to her own and her church's plight. The struggle, she said, was the age-old fight between the children of light and the people of darkness, the hordes of evil and the crusaders of Christ. Over and over she repeated that the attack was directed not against her but against Angelus Temple. Dynamically she ridiculed Keyes' accusations, heaped sarcasm on Hahn (whom she compared with Judas Iscariot, to Judas's advantage), indirectly referred to Ormiston as a possible despicable squealer, excoriated the newspapers for "the stuff they are printing" and called for an avalanche of protests to the editors, while disclaiming any intention of exciting public hysteria against the representatives of the press and the state. (Three times during this tirade she halted everything to pose in striking attitudes for the press photographers.) Once when the loudspeaker over her head went out of kilter and squawked raucously, she shouted, "That's the angel Gabriel blowing his horn as a sign of victory!" and brought down the house.

Her mother and herself she described as two gullibles taken in by plotters with mercenary motives. "We're not city folks, we're country folks! I hardly know what it's all about." After her escape from her kidnapers, the county was not spending money to learn the truth, "so we two little women tried in our weak way to find out what we could." They dealt with McKinley in blind hope, and she still did not know whether Mrs. Wiseman was a plant or not.

Tears and stifled groans greeted her recounting of her suffering through the weeks of tension, and how she gained a victory over it, but could gain no victory over the suffering of her mother—"my dear, little, sweet, lovable mother, who has been brought into this diabolical plot! Even the nails in the Cross couldn't hurt worse! I don't care what they do to me—but, oh, my mother! . . ." She burst into uncontrollable sobbing and the thousands sobbed with her. Her voice choking with anguish, she cried, "I wish my mother had died! I wish she would die tomorrow! Isn't it awful to say that? I don't know what is wrong with me to say that!"

In a furious finish, she defied her enemies to do their utmost. "Turn loose your packs, bring on your bloodhounds! Go back over the seventeen years of my life I have devoted to preaching the gospel and see if you can find a flaw anywhere!" Amid cheers she called for the American flag and stood under it; the house lights were dimmed, and while the spotlight played on her, the flag whipping over her head, she led the singing of "The Star-Spangled Banner."

When the lights came up, with brisk confidence she launched a fund to defray her court expenses. She was loath to appeal for money, she explained, but her resources were exhausted. ("Why, we don't even own the roof over our heads!") "You may call it a 'Fight the Devil Fund' if you wish, because that's what it will be used for. Information has come to me that the man who will handle the prosecution said, 'Either she will have to go or we will have to go!' They say, 'It's she or us!' We've got to spend money or we are undone!'"

Calling for a show of hands to vote on the proposal, she received unanimous, yelling approval. Who would contribute $1000? Chilling silence greeted the invitation: none of her followers possessed $1000 to give to even so resplendent a cause; they did not have $500 or $100. No matter: the most humble gifts would be accepted in the name of the Lord. The plates circulated and the coins tinkled, and Aimee gave the benediction with the confident injunction: "Now I don't want to see any long faces! Everything is going to come out all right!"

The next morning attorney Hahn protested in pain against being bracketed with Judas the Sellout. The district attorney's office seethed with indignation at being cast in the role of Hell's henchmen, and Aimee's distracted lawyers implored her to drop that "Fight the Devil" label. Who were her accusers anyway? The People of the State of California! Thereupon the fund became the decorous Aimee Semple McPherson Defense Fund—but "Fight the Devil" as a slogan stuck. Aimee had landed her first thumping counterblow.

During the week Aimee was in exuberant spirits, far from crushed or despondent. Interviewed in the alley between her home and the Bible School (it was known as Newspaper Row or Reporters' Walk) on her way to conduct a Bible class, she laughed at reports of more witnesses being rounded up by Keyes' staff. "Let them get up and perjure themselves," she said, chuckling. "I have several things up my sleeve they would like to know. I was not at Carmel, and that's the story I will carry to my grave." She nodded toward the Bible School where students were singing. "Listen to that. It goes, 'Troubles may come and troubles may go, but we'll believe in Sister, come weal or woe.' That's for me. After seventeen years of effort, you don't think I'd throw all this over, do you?" She challenged the circle. "Do you? Do you?"

Not all her fund-raising was for her own predicament. Hurricanes that week took more than a thousand lives in Florida, and at the Wednesday meeting, before soliciting for her own fund, she read President Coolidge's appeal for relief and collected $682.40 for the Red Cross. "Praise the Lord!" she told the audience. "Everything is going fine and dandy!"

Mother Kennedy issued her own pronunciamento (it took up several columns in the newspapers) in which, regarding Mrs. Wiseman, she contended: "We will have to frankly acknowledge that we were utterly fooled." The conclusion was sturdy: "I am a mother and I will stick by my daughter." Aimee appended the comment: "Of course Mrs. Wiseman fooled us—just as she is fooling the district attorney right now!"

Such thrusts did nothing to help Keyes among a large segment of the public already sharply critical of his official ways. Stories alleging scandalous personal misbehavior by the prosecutor were circulating with a wealth of disparaging detail. Deputy District Attorney E. J. Dennison, who had drawn the coveted assignment to prosecute the case while Ryan watched discontentedly from the sidelines, informed the press that phrases appearing in the "Light and Darkness" notes also appeared in one of the books found in the Carmel bungalow. Aimee countered with a call to her devotees to fast and pray for forty-eight hours; she set aside rooms in the Temple for this purpose, and passed the suggestion along to her radio sympathizers.

In the week just before the preliminary hearing was to start, San Francisco authorities arrested a pair who glibly "confessed" they had schemed with Mrs. McPherson to manufacture evidence to bolster her story. This self-incriminating couple were Harry Melosh, a reform-school alumnus with a long prison record, and Babe Daniels, a pretty, twenty-two-year-old Chicago girl. Melosh said he had been hired by Aimee, her mother, the attorney Veitch, and Nick Harris, while Babe said she was the mysterious woman who signed the "Miss X" affidavit— only she signed it in Veitch's office in Los Angeles, she insisted, and not in Salinas. Melosh volunteered that he was the "Mr. Martin" who brought Lorraine Wiseman into the scheme, and complained that he had never been paid for his services. "Mother Kennedy wanted everybody to work for love, she wouldn't part with a nickel."

Resounding denials were issued by everybody implicated. Keyes had the couple brought to Los Angeles and after a six-hour grilling turned them loose: their story was full of holes, the prosecutor said; Melosh had been confronted by Mrs. Wiseman and did not recognize her, while Russell Scott, the notarizing attorney in Salinas, declared the Daniels girl was not the person who signed as "Miss X."

Aimee ridiculed the farce. "Well, it looks as though we won't need that million dollars after all," she said, beaming before a packed house. "If we keep on getting confessions and Miss X's, the case will fall apart by itself. There have been so many Miss X's a certain party doesn't know whether to drive them tandem or abreast. Why, there are so many they would make a harem! They say I bought these Miss X's. Well, if I did, I bought wholesale! They have three Miss X's on tap right now, and four more have written to me! If all the Miss X's fall to fighting among themselves, the Devil will get his due without any need of help from us!"

The crowd yelled itself hoarse, while Mother smiled from her seat in the balcony as Aimee called for singing "Over the Top with Jesus."

It seemed, that week, as if the name Aimee McPherson cropped up everywhere. Publication of the official returns for a special election held in August disclosed that Aimee had received a sizable write-in vote for governor of the state, Ormiston for lieutenant-governor, and Mother Kennedy for state treasurer. Twice Aimee turned aside to rout minor adversaries. When the City Park Commission cited her because the Temple's sidewalk loudspeakers were drowning out the band concerts in Echo Park, Sister counter-complained that the band concerts were interfering with her religious services, and the action was a stand-off. Then Aimee sailed into court and through her attorneys obtained an injunction against a roadhouse that was doing a thriving business under the name "Aimee's Shack."

On Sunday, September 26, Sister addressed fifteen thousand persons and for the first time turned her vituperation on Keyes. Hitherto she had been tender with the district attorney, calling him "a fair man" who sincerely wanted to get at the truth but was being taken in by liars. Now Keyes was installed at the head of the hosts of darkness. Why, she demanded, did Keyes release Melosh and the Daniels girl after they confessed they had been hired to manufacture evidence? "Why the exception, when they are admittedly guilty of what we are merely charged with? . . . Mr. Keyes means to do aplenty to me! He has already blasted my name with trumpets across the world—settling it before everybody (if his word is the gospel) that I am the worst ever! . . . Some say, 'Why did you believe Mrs. Wiseman?' We did believe her—and when the district attorney is taken in and believes her, then he ought to excuse us. . . . Upon what meat does this Caesar feast himself that he should demand the virtue and blood of a woman evangelist, rather than the blood of self-confessed liars and extortionists with records of penitentiaries and asylums fastened to them? Jesus trod the way before, and we are going through with Him! Pontius Pilate, even Calvary, has no terror for us! Father, forgive them, for they know not what they do!"

She admitted that she might go to prison. "I see now how readily they can plant people and evidence to get the victim they are after, and

I warn my friends not to be surprised at any outcome." Then, in a master stroke of policy, she told all her people to stay away from the courthouse during the hearing. "No one who loves me—no one who cares for me—will go anywhere near the Hall of Justice tomorrow or any day I am there," she commanded earnestly, from the pulpit, through the newspapers, and over the radio. "Only people who want to sate their vulgar curiosity will be there; you would not want to be in such a mob. Mother and I are on trial alone—and Mother and I want to go through with it alone. We are going down there smiling and coming up shining! Hallelujah!"

So loyally was this injunction honored that decades later many of her people could recall with pride, "We never went near the courtroom or read one word of what the newspapers printed."

That evening, in fashionable Wilshire Boulevard Congregational Church, Dr. Frank Dyer preached with heavy heart on the subject the whole city was talking about. He urged all men and women of good will to pray for Mrs. McPherson as a Christian worker; hundreds of heads were bowed.

Events were moving too swiftly for Bob Shuler to keep up. His sermon topic that evening was billed as "Whatever's Latest." Persons coming from his services reported that he was highly critical of Mrs. McPherson.

No Muted Trumpets

Outside Judge Blake's courtroom in the Hall of Justice carpenters had erected a sturdy wooden barrier more than waist high. There were gates in this fence and twenty deputies stood guard on Monday, September 27. They were part of a force that had been on hand since 7 o'clock, prepared to rope off the entire courthouse area, if necessary, to restrain the expected crowd. Inside the courtroom a hundred extra seats had been installed, and an adjoining room was fitted up for the use of the press, with direct telegraph and telephone wires. International interest was typified by the correspondent of the London *Daily Mail,* who was under orders to cable at least a thousand words daily. Boyish-looking Judge Blake had announced that, so far as his powers extended, the hearing would not be turned into a public show. Only persons holding passes signed by himself would be admitted, and the principals, attorneys, witnesses, and press would occupy about all the space. Reporters were immediately offered scalpers' prices for the loan of a pass —as much as $25 for one session; there were no sales.

More than five thousand of the "vulgar curious," most of them women, were pressed around the entrance of the Hall of Justice when Aimee and her mother arrived. Along the corridor to the courtroom several hundred spectators lined the barricade. The evangelist wore a plain tailored street dress of black silk with a round white collar. Her hat was a high-crowned black straw with drooping brim; women reporters noted that it was unbecoming and that the white collar was harsh. The faces of both women were pallid, devoid of make-up. As they left the elevator on the seventh floor they were jostled and pushed by the crowd until the escorting deputies were almost knocked down. Magnesium flashes sent up clouds of acrid smoke. Sister posed obligingly for the cameras as she stepped along the corridor between the staring faces, glancing to neither right nor left, poised and at ease. Mother Kennedy's lips were set rigidly; her face never lost its gray, settled, remote look; she seemed very tired. The two defendants were the first of the principals to arrive; they took seats behind the attorneys' table, inside the railing that shut off the spectators.

At 10 o'clock Mrs. Wiseman appeared, smart in a two-tone outfit with swagger cape, her hat tilted at a stylish angle. She swept to a seat separated by several chairs from Aimee. Reporters decided her poise was half defiance: she looked fashionable but hard-boiled, thrusting out her chin, chatting with her counsel, and looking everywhere except toward the evangelist. Now and then Aimee glanced quietly at her, but Lorraine never turned her head. When Bernice Morris came and sat behind her, Aimee turned and smiled to her sweetly; toward the secretary she seemed to harbor no ill will.

Last to enter were District Attorney Keyes and his two deputies, Dennison and Forrest Murray. While Woolley was greeting Keyes cordially, Aimee and her mother appraised the prosecutor with critical eyes.

Ordinarily a preliminary hearing is disposed of in a quarter of an hour, the lowliest of a prosecutor's aides handling the routine job. The legal battery marshaled here underscored that this preliminary hearing transcended precedent. There were three spokesmen for the People—Keyes, Murray, and Dennison; for the defense there were four—Gilbert, Woolley, Veitch, and Hamner; for Mrs. Wiseman, the shrewd and theatrical Samuel S. Hahn. Mrs. Wiseman had pleaded guilty when she turned State's evidence, but technically she was having her preliminary hearing jointly with the Temple leaders on the separate count of conspiracy.

Judge Blake entered and court was in session. The clerk called the case of a man accused of murder. Aimee glanced pityingly at the handcuffed man standing near her. His case was assigned to another court and he was led away. The clerk read out, "The People versus McPherson." Aimee settled back and scribbled notes as the parade of witnesses began.

Keyes had already outlined his case publicly. He was prepared to prove, he said, that:

(1) The kidnaping story was a fabrication.

(2) To support the kidnaping story, Mrs. McPherson and Mrs. Kennedy conspired to commit acts injurious to public morals and to prevent and obstruct justice.

(3) Mrs. McPherson hid at Carmel with Kenneth Ormiston, with the knowledge and consent of her mother.

(4) Mrs. McPherson tried to have other persons indicted for the fictitious kidnaping.

(5) Mrs. McPherson hired and paid Mrs. Wiseman to produce a false "Miss X."

(6) Mrs. McPherson caused false affidavits to be prepared and signed.

(7) Mrs. McPherson hired and paid McKinley to manufacture false evidence.

The evidence to support this case was divided into five parts: the desert evidence; the Carmel evidence; the evidence indicating a conspiracy to perpetrate a hoax (Mrs. Wiseman, Bernice Morris, McKinley, Waters); the handwriting evidence; and evidence of hotel registrations intended to show that the movements of Ormiston and Mrs. McPherson synchronized before and after her disappearance. People's Exhibit A was a photograph of Kenneth Gladstone Ormiston.

The Carmel witnesses were called first. In rapid succession, five persons positively identified Mrs. McPherson as the woman who occupied the Benedict cottage in May with the man known as George McIntire.

(1) Aimee Semple McPherson in 1923, three years before her disappearance

(2) Angelus Temple, with its own radio station and a seating capacity of 5400, on Echo Park, Los Angeles

(3) The house adjoining the Temple and the Bible Coll (right), in wh Aimee lived w her mother, Minnie Kenned

(4) "I think our little Sister is gone." Mother Kennedy weeping over Aimee's supposed drowning on May 18, 1926

(5) Kenneth G. Ormiston, former Temple radio operator, as he appeared for questioning on May 27

(6) Emma Schaffer, Aimee's faithful secretary (*center*), with the evangelist's children, Rolf McPherson and Roberta Semple

(7) An airplane joins the search at Ocean Park beach. A crowd gathered at the rumor that a body had been found; it was a dead seal

(8) Sister rising from the waves: a composite picture sold by Ocean Park concessionaires while the search went on

(9) Diver R. C. Crawford, about to descend beneath Lick Pier to look for the body; Mother Kennedy followed his progress through earphones

0) A last farewell. Mother Kennedy and Roberta, posed on either side of Aimee's photograph, on the Temple platform, decorated for memorial services held June 20

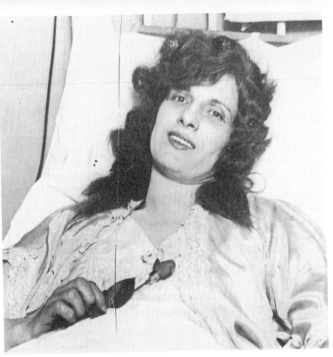

(11) "God has resurrected me from the dead." Aimee in the hospital at Douglas, Arizona, after her reappearance June 23

(12) (*Below*) Triumphal return to Los Angeles, June 26. A crowd of fifty thousand greeted her at the railroad station

13) The evangelist at Ocean Park Beach on the day of her return, with Chief of Detectives Herman Cline and Deputy District Attorney Joseph W. Ryan

14) At the seaside with her son Rolf, Aimee salutes "the kindly sea that did not claim her"

(15) Back in Arizona on July 1, Aimee — defiantly hatless — and searchers comb the sun-baked desert earth for footprints; Mother Kennedy stands disconsolately at right

(16) (*Left*) Dress over her head, Aimee demonstrates how she warded off the sun in her trek across the desert

(17) (*Below*) This wasn't the shack, but it was, Aimee said, the way she had escaped from her kidnapers

(18) Superior Court Judge Carlos S. Hardy, friend and counselor of the Temple leaders

(19) The Reverend Robert P. Shuler, who called Aimee's story "an outrage against Christianity"

(20) Aimee (*extreme left*) with her Temple guard of honor, dressed identically, entering the Hall of Justice on July 8 to testify before the grand jury

(21) Rear view of the Benedict bungalow at Carmel, showing the back door, the garden trampled by sightseers

(22) Books, spice cans, and radio set left in the bungalow

(23) Aimee's first broadcast over her Temple radio station (1924); Ormiston at the controls. The only known picture of the two together, this appeared in Aimee's magazine *The Bridal Call*

(24) Mrs. Lorraine Wiseman-Sielaff, the "hoax woman"

(25) "She had the photographer pose us so I would look as near possible like her," Mrs. Wiseman said of pictures such as this one, found in her possession, showing her (*left, wearing switch*) with Aimee

(26-32) A lesson in coiffure: Aimee shows reporters — as she showed the court — that it's all her own hair, and that she can do it up in three minutes flat, without a mirror

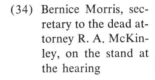

(33) Temple witnesses at the preliminary hearing in October 1926 (*left to right*)
Brother J. W. Arthur, Mrs. Elizabeth
Frame, Emma Schaffer, and Mae Wal-
dron, Temple stenographer

(34) Bernice Morris, sec-
retary to the dead at-
torney R. A. McKin-
ley, on the stand at
the hearing

(35) District Attorney
Asa Keyes

(36) Mrs. Wiseman and her attorney, S. S.
Hahn, in court

(37) The "little blue trunk" that contained so many surprises. Ben Cohen, chief investigator for the district attorney, holds the black satin slippers the State contended were worn by the woman at Carmel

(38) Policewoman wearing the many-buttoned blue serge dress found in the trunk

(39) Aimee as she left for the Holy Land, January 1926, wearing a many-buttoned blue serge dress

(40) Mother Kennedy and Aimee in court during the latter days of the hearing

(41) The evangelist on her thirty-sixth birthday, surrounded by presents from her loyal followers

The lead-off witness was Ralph W. Hersey, a retired engineer and a prominent resident of Santa Barbara. A gentleman of sixty, tall, bespectacled, and composed, he testified with assurance. He said his wife and he drove from San Jose to Carmel on May 25 to visit friends. While turning the corner of Ocean View Avenue and San Antonio Street, he saw a woman standing on the corner. She turned to look at him and he looked at her as the car went by. Keyes asked if he saw Mrs. McPherson in the courtroom.

"I do," was the reply.

"Have you seen her before?"

"I have."

"Where?"

"At Carmel, on the 25th of May, 1926."

Aimee met the witness's gaze steadily, a little smile playing on her lips.

"When did you see her again?"

"At the Temple on the 8th of August."

That day was Sunday, he went on, and Mrs. McPherson was preaching. He stood in a doorway, about a hundred feet from the platform, and observed her for about fifteen minutes. He became positive as he watched her that she was the woman he saw in Carmel; he identified her especially by her "large, open, brilliant, and deep-set" eyes and her "large mouth."

Gilbert peppered the witness with questions. How old was he? How long had he worn glasses? "You have trouble seeing, I presume? I see you are one of those boys who spot the women on the street as they drive past. What is your religion, anyway?"

Judge Blake quickly ruled out that question. Hersey mildly enjoyed the crossfire and remained unruffled and unshaken.

Next came Mrs. Jeannette Parkes, who lived next door to the Benedict cottage in Carmel. She was nervous and tittered as she told of noticing the arrival of a couple next door at 4 a.m. when the light was switched on in the bungalow and it shone into the room where she sat nursing her baby. She noticed the woman's hair, "very beautiful, piled on top of her head." Several days later she saw the woman when she came out of the house and called after the man, who had just driven away in his car; the woman was pleasant-looking; she smiled at Mrs. Parkes but turned and went back into the house immediately.

Deputy prosecutor Dennison asked Mrs. Parkes whether she saw that woman in the courtroom.

"Well," the witness hesitated, "I saw her without a hat on."

Dennison suggested that Aimee remove her hat. Gilbert nodded consent, and without smiling Aimee removed the black straw, revealing a mass of auburn hair bunched tightly in folds high on her head.

Mrs. Parkes gasped. "Oh, dear! . . ."

"What did you say?" asked Dennison.

"Yes, it looks like her," the witness replied and giggled.

Gilbert prodded her about this tentative identification, until suddenly she blurted, "Now I am sure of it!" She had been studying Mrs. McPherson, she explained, and could not be mistaken.

Percy Parkes followed his wife and identified the evangelist as his neighbor for ten days in May. He was cocksure and self-righteous. "That is the woman," he said, pointing. Aimee studied him with her meditative smile, chin cupped in hand.

Ralph Swanson, who delivered groceries and newspapers to the cottage, said that Mrs. McPherson was the woman calling herself Mrs. McIntire.

"Was there anything about her that attracted your attention particularly?" he was asked.

"Her hair."

"Anything else?"

"Her eyes. They were large. They seemed to draw me to her."

Under cross-examination, Swanson protested he had not read the newspaper accounts of the evangelist's disappearance: "I got tired of that case." He confirmed that he told Ryan the woman in the cottage had large ankles.

Ernest Renkert, who brought a truckload of wood to the Benedict cottage on May 25 and saw both the man and the woman while he was stacking the wood in the garage, described the man as "kind of limping."

"Do you see anybody in this courtroom whom you saw out there at the time you delivered that wood?" Dennison asked.

"Yes, sir."

"Referring to Mrs. McPherson, who sits there by her counsel?"

"Yes, sir."

"Notice anything about her hair?"

"Yes, sir. A beautiful head of hair."

"What color?"

The witness studied. "Brown, with a little tint, kind of reddish tint, in it."

"Could you describe how it was on her head?"

"Kind of a knot, kind of fluffed out."

Gilbert asked Renkert to estimate the age of the woman he saw in Carmel.

"Between twenty-five and thirty," replied the truckman.

"How old do you say Mrs. McPherson is now? Take a good look."

"Between twenty-five and thirty."

Aimee beamed.

Mrs. Bostick, who had rented the Carmel bungalow to Ormiston, alias McIntire, related the transaction, by now familiar to millions, and described the client as "tall, slender, walking with a decided lameness; thin nose, sensitive mouth, prominent ears, and baldness on his forehead; dressed in gray tweed."

Under this steady fire, Aimee never appeared ill at ease. Although Mother Kennedy's face was moist with tension, Sister smiled and chatted with reporters during the brief lulls with the grace of a hostess.

"A dreadful ordeal for you," said one woman writer.

"Not as bad as I expected," the evangelist replied. "I am rather enjoying it. I feel I am listening to the unfolding of a story about someone else altogether; they are not really talking about me."

Nevertheless her poise was tested at the noon break when she stepped into the crowded corridor, flanked by Woolley and Gilbert. There was a patter of handclapping and then a burst of hissing. Aimee recoiled; then her head came up and with a courageous smile she walked firmly to the elevator. In the crush Gilbert was knocked off his feet, while deputies fought in sweating futility to clear a path. Later Judge Blake ordered the corridors kept open, but the public pressure was too great; the halls were never emptied.

A few hours after court adjourned for the day, Aimee introduced a diversion in the case that shattered another precedent. Bouncing on the platform at the Temple, vibrant and refreshed, she recounted to the packed house and to an immense radio audience everything that had transpired in the courtroom—with a difference. She derided the witnesses, calling them "a fine little bunch of parrots" who "recited their pieces just as they were schooled to do for months." One man, she rattled on, who was sixty years old and was afflicted with astigmatism, was coming downhill at fifteen miles an hour and saw a woman whom he first thought was one woman, but whom he identified five months later as the pastor of Angelus Temple! Then later the same man stood a hundred and fifteen feet away and identified her by her "large and luscious eyes. Page his optometrist! You folks back there! Can you see my large and luscious eyes?"

Her sermon was on Joseph and Potiphar's wife. Dramatically she described how the lustful woman grabbed Joseph's coat as he ran out of the house. " 'Aha!' she cried. 'Now I've got circumstantial evidence! I've got the coat—and that's better than a grocery slip any day!' " The congregation howled, and the district attorney's staff (half the population of California was listening to the travesty) writhed.

But in the morning courtroom amenity prevailed; opposing counsel, dropping into the spirit of the testimony, frequently addressed each other as "Brother." Judge Blake, looking more boyish than ever, kept the proceedings moving briskly, disposing of objections rapidly and firmly. His unconscious trick of pushing up the tip of his nose while concentrating endeared him to the women present. And comfort was forthcoming for the beleaguered evangelist when three State's witnesses in succession failed to identify her as the woman in the Carmel cottage.

The star witness was Benedict. Well set up, more than six feet tall, erect, with broad shoulders, closely trimmed gray hair, tanned face, and solid features, he was impressive on the stand. He testified crisply, with scrupulous accuracy, yielding occasionally to a smile. He identified a photograph of Ormiston as that of his ten-day tenant, but he would not name Mrs. McPherson as the woman, again using the phrase that he would hesitate to identify his own sister in the get-up the woman wore. She had on black slippers, he said, and as the couple walked back to the house on the random-set flagstones of the garden path he turned to observe them, "mildly curious to see how a New York woman, used to the smooth pavements of that city, would negotiate the rough stepping-stones of our garden. Her skirt was of medium length, halfway between knees and ankles."

"Did you see her ankles?" asked Keyes.

"I did."

"Will you describe the general appearance of the woman?"

Benedict estimated she stood about five feet seven, weighed around a hundred and forty pounds, and was stockily built.

"Have you seen Mrs. McPherson since then?" asked the prosecutor.

"I have."

"How does she compare with the description?"

"Very similar."

"Have you seen her ankles?"

"I have."

"How do her ankles compare with the ankles of the woman you saw at Carmel?"

"Very similar."

At the persistent talk about ankles, women in the room grew self-conscious and tucked theirs under their chair. But not Mrs. Wiseman; hers, slender, gleamingly hosed, remained impudently exposed.

With Benedict's testimony the State started to lay the foundation for its contention that Mrs. McPherson concocted a hoax with Mrs. Wiseman. The transcript of Benedict's interview with Lorraine at the Glendale Sanatorium in August was introduced and read; this contained his firm conclusion that Mrs. Wiseman was not the woman at Carmel "and she knew I knew it."

Sitting in a hot closed automobile outside the hospital that afternoon, he had told Keyes why he was in the sanatorium: the rubberneck invasion of Carmel was ruining his health. Seventy-five thousand sightseers had clobbered his cottage and more were coming.

> We might as well be living in a jail. People peeping through the windows at all hours of the day and night, hundreds standing on the sidewalk, staring. They think nothing of going up on the roof, trampling the flowers, sitting on the front porch. We had a fence built on the beach side; people climb over the fence. They gouge pieces out of the stucco. The flower garden on the Scenic Drive side is trampled to bare earth. Our shades are pulled down all day long. We have to hire a guard. I'm sorry it had to be my place and not somebody else's, if it had to be!

With this outburst off his chest, the transcript showed, Benedict expressed readiness to listen to Mrs. Wiseman, whom Keyes had brought along. "If she can convince me, I'd like to be convinced." She was called from the porch where she was sitting and opened the interview by saying she recognized Benedict at once.

"What makes you think you have seen me?" he responded.

"You were in the garden when you met me. I can tell you things I don't think anybody else knows. I can tell you how your house was furnished in every room, pretty near."

What was the picture that hung over the mantel? Benedict asked. She recollected the subject ("It was not what I would call very artistic") but was uncertain about the details. She was unable to name the color of skirt she was wearing when Ormiston introduced them. Some facts about the furniture she was sure of; others, she said, escaped her memory.

"Does your sister look like you?" the landlord asked.

"She is shorter than I."

"Heavier built?"

"I was twenty pounds heavier then; I weighed a hundred and forty-six pounds."

"That shows what worry will do," he replied cheerfully. "Here is the situation. You are attempting to hang yourself."

"Oh, no!" she cried. "I know you feel you recognize me in some way, don't you now?"

"I can't say that I do. I don't see that we are getting anywhere, sitting here and chewing this over. There is no use frying in this car any longer."

After the interview, the transcript read, Benedict gave Keyes his considered opinion: Mrs. Wiseman had told him incidents and described things that could be known only to the woman who was in the bungalow, but he did not believe Mrs. Wiseman was that woman; in fact, he was positive she was not.

Several times during the reading of this transcript Mrs. Wiseman laughed and exchanged smiles with the witness. In cross-examination, Gilbert adverted to this opinion clearly expressed by Benedict in August: "You concluded that Mrs. Wiseman was a monumental falsifier, and the only thing you were interested in was what her object was, is that true?"

"That is true," Benedict replied.

Gilbert handed to the witness a photograph of Mrs. McPherson on which Benedict had written, on August 8: "There is nothing about this photo that suggests to me Mrs. McIntire who occupied my cottage at Carmel-by-the-Sea the latter part of May 1926." And a second photograph; on which was noted, in Benedict's handwriting, over his signature: "This photo does not in any way suggest to me Mrs. McIntire." Benedict acknowledged the notations.

On redirect, Keyes brought out that the photographs were studio portraits of the evangelist taken in Rochester, New York, five years previously.

Hahn, over Gilbert's objection, drew from Benedict the opinion that Mrs. Wiseman's ankles were nothing like those of the woman at Carmel. "They were very dissimilar," the witness said, after studying the pair that

Mrs. Wiseman pushed forward. "Mrs. Wiseman's ankles are slender. The ankles of the woman at Carmel were considerably heavier."

When Benedict left the stand, Aimee reached out and shook his hand pleasantly.

Jesse Lynch Williams, a Western Union messenger, was called and testified that he delivered the "Lease expires tonight" telegram to the Benedict cottage on May 28. (This cryptic message, the public finally learned, was signed "Walter.") The messenger saw the woman sign the receipt, standing in the doorway. Asked by Dennison whether he saw the same woman in the courtroom, Williams gazed at the ceiling, glanced toward the back of the room, and mumbled, "No." Dennison urged him to look around a bit more. He looked out the window, up at the ceiling, ran his eye swiftly around the room.

"Do you see her?"

"Naw."

The prosecution was nettled, and their annoyance increased when William H. McMichael, carpenter and stonemason, also failed to identify Aimee. In broad Scots he said he was working on the boundary line adjoining the Benedict property all but two of the days the McIntires were there, and he saw both the man and the woman several times. He noticed the man was lame. He saw a bathing suit on the clothesline, "green with some other color." He stood as close as eight or ten feet to the woman, and he estimated she was about thirty years old, five feet three or four inches in height. Murray, the assistant district attorney, asked whether he could identify Mrs. McPherson. The stonemason said that he had seen the Carmel woman without a hat; at Gilbert's nod Aimee again removed her hat and faced the witness steadily.

"Ever see her before?" pressed Murray.

"Never saw her before in my life," came the reply.

Fireworks flashed frequently; at one point Gilbert proposed that the hearing be moved to Carmel, since the State seemed to believe some offense had been committed there.

"The offense has been committed all over the world!" Keyes snorted, and the judge warned counsel to moderate their courtesies. But when Gilbert interrupted the State's presentation to request permission to put a defense witness (August C. England, town marshal of Carmel) on the stand out of turn, so that he might return to his job, Dennison was indignant.

"I know what his proof in this matter will be," he objected to the court, "and she has a magnificent opportunity to herald garbled statements in relation to this witness over the radio, and tonight we would have her chanting over the radio—"

"Don't let us bring in this radio business!" warily interposed the judge. He ruled that England might testify. The witness thereupon was sworn and, while the prosecution grimaced, related that Benedict had requested him to keep an eye on the cottage while the tenants were there, and in consequence he had ridden past the house on horseback every day; he had seen both the man and the woman several times, the woman both with and without a hat and with and without sun-glasses or goggles, at a distance of not more than eight feet. What was the color of her hair? The marshal described it as "light."

"You recognized Mrs. McPherson here now?" Gilbert asked.

"Yes, sir."

"I will ask you to tell the court whether or not Mrs. McPherson was the woman who was there at that place."

"Positively not the woman," came the reply.

During the cross-examination altercations were frequent, Dennison again putting it to the court that this trick of breaking into the prosecution's case was an adroit move to provide ammunition for the defendant to use over the radio.

"If your honor takes the occasion to be on the radio tonight, you will hear all about it!" he advised bitterly.

"I assure you, I will not!" snapped Blake.

Gilbert flew into a pat fury. "I have been here at the bar twenty-five years, and I've heard something today enough to turn anybody's hair gray!" he shouted, sweeping a contemptuous hand toward the transcript of Aimee's testimony before the grand jury, which the prosecution had insisted on reading in full earlier in the session. "The district attorney with Mrs. McPherson before the grand jury and clubbing her while she was there!"

Keyes flung up his head. Murray started out of his chair. Dennison gaped.

"You mean—"

"I mean just what I say!" shouted the wily Gilbert.

"You mean we clubbed her? We certainly were criticized for our leniency to her!"

"Gentlemen, gentlemen," the judge said. "Let us try this law suit."

So fair an opportunity was seized by Sister that evening in a way that enthralled a million radio fans as well as her eager Temple audience. "It was one hundred per cent for us in court today!" she shouted jubilantly from the platform, and then proceeded to give a burlesque performance of how, she said, the prosecution was overcome by confusion and chagrin when the testimony started to go in her favor. She mimicked Keyes, seated listening to the witnesses with calm, dignified approval. Then came the unexpected testimony, the refusals to identify her; whereupon, with consternation in her face, she bounced up and down on her pulpit chair in a frenzy of frustration. The audience screamed with laughter.

"It was amazing to see," exclaimed Sister, "how they hurry to get their heads together—how they quickly confer and say, 'How are we going to overcome this? How are we going to get around it?' Oh, brothers and sisters, why wouldn't they leap to their feet and cry, 'Hold on there, boys! This farce has gone far enough! Let's get down on our knees and beg pardon for the wrong we have done!'"

Far from discontinuing her Bulletin Hour containing the daily résumé of courtroom news, she announced that it would be made a regular program feature, every evening at the same time. Exhorting her followers to "keep on believing," she added that they might pray for "the ministers who have been running up and down the steps of the Hall of Justice" in a campaign to spur on her persecutors. And just as she closed, she deftly spitted her prosecutor, Keyes, with a question lifted, in her own way, from the afternoon's courtroom altercation: "What did Mr. Dennison mean, and whom was he talking about, when he said you were accused of 'not clubbing Mrs. McPherson enough'?"

A Lesson in Coiffure

The testimony continued to favor embattled Aimee. Wallace Moore, the Santa Barbara reporter, proved a total disappointment to the State. Again and again Keyes tried to pin him down on his impression of the couple in the car he stopped on the night of May 29, but either Moore could not make up his mind, or he was afraid to; to reporters present he gave every appearance of being a terrified witness. The man in the car he finally did identify from a photograph as Ormiston (or rather, he identified a photograph of Ormiston as that of the man in the car, stipulating that he did not know whether the photograph was of Ormiston or not), but he refused to make any commitment about the woman. When Gilbert demanded categorically whether it was not a fact that, after interviewing the pair in the car, Moore had returned to his office and reported that the woman was *not* Mrs. McPherson, it took seven minutes of prodding to get an answer. It was "Yes." Gilbert in disgust moved to strike Moore's entire testimony, and Keyes almost agreed.

The tension in the courtroom was exacerbated by the clatter of riveters working on the steel skeleton of the new City Hall being erected across the street. The weather had turned warm and all the windows were open; the rat-tat was distracting and drowned out the witnesses' words repeatedly; but Emma Schaffer proved impervious to noise when she took the stand. Emma was a good witness: she volunteered nothing, answered questions curtly and directly, and could not be shaken. Dennison led the secretary through the events of May 18, just as she had told them before. At no time, she stated firmly, did she telephone Mother Kennedy saying Sister was "drowned"; although she feared Aimee indeed was drowned, she never uttered the word, saying only, over and over, that Sister had "disappeared in the water."

While Emma testified, Aimee worked on the sermon she was to preach that evening. At the top of the page she wrote: "Baptismal Sermon, Thursday Night," then the Bible text underneath and the title, "Christ on Trial." Under that, in parallel columns, "Jesus" and "Barabbas."

Emma said she was the one who received the "Avengers" ransom letter at the Temple and there was no special-delivery stamp on it. She handed it to Mrs. Kennedy without reading it all the way through.

Dennison shifted to Aimee's accouterments on the visit to Ocean Park. "Did you get her jewelry?" he asked.

"She had no jewelry."

"Was her watch in her purse?"

"No."

"Did she wear a hair net on that ride to the ocean?"

"Yes."

"Had it on?"

"Yes."

"Was it a silk hair net?"

"Just ordinary hair net."

Dennison showed the secretary a photograph of the evangelist and asked suavely, "Do you know whether a great deal of that hair is false?"

"Her hair is not false," came the decisive response.

"Just comes down to her shoulders?"

"It is short and very thick."

"Then she packs it up on her head?"

"Yes."

"And places this net on top?"

"Yes."

Aimee glanced up from her scribbling and Gilbert spoke. "You want her to do her hair up? I'll have her do it up in the courtroom. I'll have her take her hair down and do it up as it is in the picture if you think it can't be done."

At this point the judge called a five-minute recess, and when court reconvened the prosecutor started in on the hair net again. Upon a nod from Gilbert, Aimee suddenly removed her hat, deftly pulled out a few hairpins, and shook her tumbling tresses into fluffiness around her head. Spectators gasped, women exclaiming in amazement, while the startled judge and delighted reporters stared. The evangelist's hair was all her own, and the surprise was that it barely reached her shoulders. The mass "piled on top of her head," identified by so many witnesses—the "great masses of hair" viewed by thousands, any one of whom probably would undertake to identify it after one glimpse—was short and bushy, just as Emma had said.

Gilbert motioned Aimee to stand up. Tossing her finely proportioned head and showing her strong teeth in a grin, she arose.

"If you want to see this hair, Mr. Dennison, you can look, or you can look the other way," Gilbert drawled. "I am showing you all about it. You have been talking about short hair and switches."

Dennison stammered, "Oh, I admire short hair!" and blushed. With the rest of the fascinated audience he watched Aimee pile the hair up again with swift, sure movements of her hands, her plain platinum wedding band flashing; then she pinned it and hid it under what one woman shuddered at as "that mean black hat." Sitting down composedly, she resumed her sermon writing. Reporters trampled each other scrambling for the telephones.

Dennison turned to the issue of the wrist watch. On this detail Emma blandly and stubbornly contradicted her adored employer: the watch, she insisted, was at a jeweler's being repaired all the time Sister was missing. Emma herself gave it to her after the return from Douglas.

Emma said she knew both McKinley and Waters, but she did not know their business at the Temple. She also knew Kenneth Ormiston, but she never mailed any letter to him for either Mother Kennedy or Sister. Hadn't Mrs. Kennedy communicated with persons by code telegrams signed "Rehtom" ("Mother" spelled backward)? The secretary did not know.

When the State finished with the witness, Hahn undertook a cross-examination that aroused the buzz-saw qualities in Emma's nature. His hostility was met at first with a superior little smile.

"You saw Mrs. Wiseman in the home of Mrs. McPherson?"

"I did."

"And you know that she slept in the home of Mrs. McPherson?"

"Two nights."

"Before Mrs. Wiseman occupied any of these bedrooms, who occupied that bedroom?"

"Mrs. McPherson."

The attorney moved to show the intimacy existing between his client and her Temple hostess, but all he obtained was a picture of Emma's loving care for Sister during a time when she understood that her employer was in some deep, inexplicable trouble.

"Mrs. McPherson moved out of that room and gave it to Mrs. Wiseman and went into another room?" Hahn asked.

"No, she went and slept in the swing."

Hahn affected astonishment. "Mrs. McPherson slept in the swing and let Mrs. Wiseman sleep in her bedroom?"

"She certainly did."

"How do you know she slept there in the swing all night?"

"Because I know she did."

"You watched her all night?"

"About every hour."

"You got out of your bed every hour to see if Mrs. McPherson was asleep?" Hahn exuded incredulity.

"My bedroom was right above where she was sleeping." Emma closed her lips tightly.

When the secretary left the stand, Aimee drew her to her chair and kissed her; tears of love and pride glistened in the eyes of the grim-visaged, elderly woman.

But the atmosphere changed when Walter B. Lambert, proprietor of a haberdashery shop at 458 South Hill Street, in the same block as the Clark Hotel, was called. He testified that just after 10 o'clock on the morning of May 18, as he was returning from the bank, he saw Mrs. McPherson walking ahead of him. He recognized her, and out of curiosity quickened his steps. He said she was carrying a briefcase stamped "Aimee Semple McPherson" in gilt letters. She turned into the Clark lobby, and a man standing in the entrance tipped his hat, although Lambert could not be sure whether to her or to someone else. A minute later the man also went inside; he walked with a limp.

The shopkeeper was taken over the jumps by Gilbert. Lambert would not divulge his home address, giving as his reason that he dreaded getting mixed up in the distasteful case; he was married with four small children, and he didn't want his family "annoyed by cranks and fanatics. My wife is a nervous woman, she doesn't even know I am giving this testimony."

Keyes sympathized. "I have gone through much of the trouble he refers to," he told the judge, and the court ruled that the witness might give the defense counsel his home address privately.

Gilbert challenged Lambert's memory and his eyesight. The haberdasher could not recall any detail of the dress of the woman he saw, or any personal peculiarity, such as, perhaps, ankles. Gilbert got him to specify how far away he was when he read the lettering on the briefcase. Whereupon Gilbert held up a briefcase at the same distance and asked the haberdasher to read the initials on it. Lambert read "A.E.W." Aimee smiled; the bag belonged to Veitch and the initials were "A.L.V." Turning to Nick Harris, who was lounging in a chair beside her, chewing gum, she whispered audibly, "I never had a briefcase with my name on it in my life."

While Lambert was on the stand, Mrs. Wiseman was handed a letter, which she opened and with a smile passed to reporters—a longhand note from Judge Carlos Hardy, posted in Seattle August 25, addressed to her at the YWCA in San Francisco. It had been wandering since then, and was finally routed to the Los Angeles County Jail and thence to the district attorney's office. The letter expressed the judge's hope that her activities were fructifying, and gave instructions as to just when and where he could be reached on his return to San Francisco from the Canadian Northwest.

"Our day again," said Aimee as she left court, holding her head high, greeting acquaintances pleasantly.

As soon as she reached home, for the benefit of the importunate news-reel cameramen Aimee re-enacted the hair-do incident. "Don't laugh," she told the sniggering males. "You'd be surprised how many women—thousands of them over a period of years—have asked me how I do my hair. Many have said I spend two hours a day with a hairdresser, which is absurd."

The whole job, without a mirror, took her exactly three minutes.

The faithful at the Temple got a frequently uproarious report on the day. Sister portrayed Moore's perspiring agitation; she ridiculed the observant haberdasher, with side references to his wife and four children afraid of "fanatics." With the help of Brother Argue and Evangelist Billy Black, she demonstrated the fallibility of his eyesight, holding up briefcases in the pulpit while the brothers misread the initials on them from the back of the auditorium. The shopkeeper's testimony, Aimee concluded, was "bought by my perse— pardon me, my prosecutors."

Keyes next called to the stand a newcomer to the case, Agnes Callahan, a chambermaid at the Ambassador Hotel. Gilbert roared objections until the judge required the district attorney to make clear his purpose in calling the witness; Keyes replied that he intended to prove that an intimate relationship existed between Mrs. McPherson and Kenneth Ormiston long before the evangelist disappeared.

This statement brought a rush of angry color to Aimee's cheeks, and throughout the testimony she glared.

Agnes Callahan recounted that she was assigned to the third floor of the hotel during the summer of 1925, and during that time Mrs. McPherson occupied room 330, at the end of a corridor, several times. On six occasions, or thereabouts, the maid saw a man who limped in the corridor near room 330, and once she saw him go into the room. When the man encountered her in the hall, she said, he stepped to a window and looked out until she had passed.

Spectators strained forward when Gilbert arose to cross-examine. Had the chambermaid ever found Mrs. McPherson's room door locked? Gilbert asked sarcastically. She had never found it locked. Aimee leaned over and whispered questions to her counsel, which he repeated to the witness, until the cross-examination became largely the evangelist's own.

"Did you know Mrs. Armstrong, who lived in the room right across the hall from Mrs. McPherson?"

"I did not."

"You knew she was there?"

"I did."

"You knew she was a crippled member of Mrs. McPherson's church, didn't you?"

"She wasn't crippled, by any means—"

"What's your religion?" cut in Gilbert, but the judge overruled the answer before it could be given. Snatching up a paper Gilbert snapped, "Well, I am prepared to prove this witness is a Catholic!" and sat down.

Colonel Albert L. Denman, the assistant manager of the Ambassador Hotel, was sworn next. Denman gallantly disclaimed that he was appearing as an adverse witness against Mrs. McPherson, but he supported the chambermaid's story to some extent. He also had seen a man in the corridor near room 330, during Christmas week of 1925, and he identified a photograph of Ormiston as the man. "The gentleman had a very decided limp; my impression is it was with the left leg he limped."

Everybody who knew Ormiston recognized that he limped with the left leg.

"Who was in that room across the hall from Mrs. McPherson?" asked Gilbert.

"There was a lady, a crippled lady, who had been there for months."

"And her nurse?"

"Yes, sir."

"You have seen Mrs. McPherson there many times?"

"I have seen Mrs. McPherson there a good many times." His answer was friendly.

"She just came in the front end of the Ambassador Hotel like she was a clean American woman and signed her name on the register, 'Aimee Semple McPherson,' did she not?"

"Absolutely," the manager assented. "At about one o'clock in the morning, Mrs. McPherson used to come in."

Gilbert also brought out that there had been no report made or suspicion of any impropriety at the time.

When Denman stepped down, noon recess was called and reporters swarmed around Aimee. Her face was taut with anger. Never, never had Ormiston visited her room at the Ambassador, she repeated passionately; the only time she ever saw him in the hotel was during a radio show at which she spoke, when there were hundreds of people present.

"How long do you expect this trial to last?" a reporter asked.

"Forever! Forever!" she answered miserably. "They have tasted blood! They'll never give up!"

Thomas Scott Melville, doorman at the Clark Hotel, was the next witness. He was not a member of the Angelus Temple, he said, but he had been baptized there by Sister only a week previously. (All through his testimony he called the evangelist "Sister.") His story—told with earnestness and obvious heart-searching—was that he saw Mrs. McPherson ("Sister, that is") enter the Clark lobby at about 10 o'clock on the morning of May 18: he knew her well, had often been to the Temple, recognized her, and was confirmed in his recognition by the name on the leather portfolio she was carrying, "Aimee Semple McPherson" in gilt letters. He said she got into an elevator and rode to an upper floor, then emerged from the hotel about half an hour later. He was certain of the time, because he was checking taxis, and also because his wife always came by at 10:30 bringing his lunch.

Under a scorching cross-examination the doorman said he went to the Temple with his story on the evening of May 18, just after the newspapers first announced Sister's disappearance. Recently he had been requested by "one of the ladies from Angelus Temple" to see Roland Rich Woolley, which he did, giving the attorney a full statement. The transcript of that conversation was read. At one point Woolley was quoted as saying, "You would not swear it was her that day? I mean, from the dress and everything you thought it was her, but you would not swear it was her?"

"If I said it was not her," the doorman replied, "I would be lying to my conscience. I hope you can prove I am mistaken. . . . I think it is conclusive proof to you that I know, when I came and was baptized since she returned."

When, on the heels of Melville's testimony, Keyes moved to introduce the grand-jury testimony of Mrs. Kennedy, Gilbert exploded. This district attorney, he charged, had deliberately contrived a trap in the grand-jury room to bring about the prosecution of the Temple women on trumped-up complaints. Aimee and her mother, Gilbert said, were haled before the grand jury not for the purpose of obtaining information in order to capture the kidnapers, but to lay a foundation for their indictment. "You"—he shook a denunciatory finger at Keyes—"were not looking for any kidnapers! You were trying to get testimony before the grand jury to base this complaint on!"

The outburst shattered Aimee's composure. In a moment of shocked silence after Gilbert's rampage, she cried emotionally, "Absolutely!" The judge sternly ordered that the transcript be read.

Aimee left the courtroom unsmiling. "It will never end, never until I die!" she murmured again, waving reporters aside.

But the fight was not out of her. At the Temple that evening (it was Friday) she told her flock she had emerged from "the most exquisite cruelty and suffering that finite mind can conjure up." She had been warned on the way to court that this was to be the prosecution's "big day," and that if she could weather this crisis the worst would be past. Then she read her nightly bulletin. Her target was Asa Keyes. "The vile insinuations which fell from the lips of Mr. Keyes during this examination could not, in my opinion, exist in the mind of any pure man!" she exclaimed. She often stayed overnight at the Ambassador and other hotels during 1925, she said, in order to get some respite from the dust and noise caused by the construction work on the Bible School building, almost outside her window, and to write and study. "I entered the Ambassador Hotel like any other guest, after my night meetings, and registered my full name, a fact known to my family, many of my friends, and announced from my pulpit. Everybody knows I am not charged with being in the Ambassador Hotel!" Blazing with anger, she departed from her written text and spat into the microphone: "Asa Keyes—if you are listening in—you are a dirty, lecherous libertine!" Every listener who was a taxpayer she urged to inquire at the district attorney's office "what the bill for the McPherson case has been to date. Ask what it cost for the district attorney's men—and their wives—for the Carmel, Arizona, and other trips!"

Her voice was hoarse from overmuch preaching, but she boldly announced her schedule for the coming Sunday: three services, three sermons. In the morning, Holy Communion would be celebrated, with the "largest Communion service in the world," serving five thousand persons at one sitting. In the afternoon, an elaborate stage production entitled "March of the Martyrs" would depict in dramatic terms "the history of religious persecution." (The newspapers printed a detailed scenario in advance.) The spectacle would be repeated in the evening, with, as an added attraction, an illustrated sermon on "The Great Coronation Day," for which two huge crowns would be built on the platform—one a crown of thorns, "such as sinners make for Christ," the other a crown of jewels, "the offering of a Christian, a crown of gold."

On Sunday more than 40,000 persons turned out, during the course of the day, in a scramble to witness these super-productions. Thousands of them were disappointed, the capacity of the Angelus Temple being inadequate to handle the crush. The lucky thousands inside "oh-ed" and "ah-ed" and applauded through two hours of sacred horrors. Seven times the blue curtains on the rostrum parted and seven times the audience beheld martyrs being butchered by diverse devices. Sister, in the role of narrator, explained that the Devil was stronger today than in olden times, but since physical torture had been outlawed he thought up mental and spiritual tortures to inflict on the objects of his hatred. Among such unholy means she listed false witnesses, manufactured evidence, and "the besmirching of a little, all-alone woman's good name." Describing the sensations of one martyr being sawed in half, she asked the congregation, "Now, how would you like that?" None of the spectators seemed to relish the prospect, but at testimonial time later many assured their pastor that should martyrdom become their privilege they would embrace it with a song.

The lead-off tableau was "The Crucifixion." The Cross stood out, large and rough-hewn, constructed of massive timbers. A pile of rocks at its base indicated that it stood on a hilltop, and, though the figure of Christ was not presented, red paint showed where He had bled. While the band played a dirge, Aimee posed in the spotlight, arms extended, yearning face uplifted, in crucificial attitude, her elongated shadow falling athwart the arms of the stage prop behind her.

The curtains closed to reopen on the scene of Stephen's violent dispatch to a heavenly reward. His actual slaughter was not shown, but a circle of white-robed men stood around him, holding up tremendous boulders. As one newspaper critic put it (the newspapers covered the event like a theatrical first night), "It was easy to see what Steve was up against."

The scenes continued bloodily. Paul knelt with his head on the chopping block; above him towered a centurion in armor, sword upraised, realistically indicating the fate about to befall the Apostle to the Gentiles. Then Nero, richly caparisoned, lolled on a couch, his fawning courtiers around him, while on crosses and poles in the imperial gardens Christians dipped in tar blazed fiercely. Whatever their pangs, with placid gaze they looked upward unmoved, portraying, Sister explained, the joy of martyrdom.

In the next scene, back to back, Ridley and Latimer burned sedately, while a little way off (thus providing a double feature) Joan of Arc in silver armor was about to be incinerated.

Moving to modern times, the last tableau displayed an enormous Bible and beside it a pair of monstrous shears and a platter of mud.

These, Sister explained, symbolized jealous rivals among the churches and clergy who "cut the heart out of the Bible," and who flung mud at preachers who insisted on expounding "the entire word of God." One figure in this scene strongly resembled the recently demised William Jennings Bryan (who more than once had spoken in the Temple as Sister's guest), and there was audible debate whether the figure—fat and bald, looking at times real, at times like wax—was an actor or a dummy.

The show was repeated brilliantly Sunday evening, with twelve thousand shut-outs listening to Sister's narration over the outdoor loudspeakers. She drove home the moral: "The cradle of every great religious movement has been rocked by persecution, but it brings forth a healthy baby every time! If we sink, we sink together—but praise God, I think we will rise!"

During that evening Judge Blake testily called in the district attorney and Aimee's lawyers, to consult about a man who was posing in bars as "Judge Blake," talking loudly about the case and promising to hand down a decision "that will surprise everybody." Judge Blake ordered the impostor arrested. He was never found.

"*A Liar and a Hypocrite*"

The besmirching of a "little, all-alone woman's" reputation for veracity was pressed further in court the next week when Oliver Allstrom, a free-lance writer, produced testimony intended to show that when Aimee professed before the grand jury to have no knowledge of the death of Captain Ed Harrison, the diver, she prevaricated. Allstrom, who styled himself "The Kipling of Texas" and testified in a large, brassy voice, said that early in July he had written to Mrs. McPherson about a book he was writing about her adventures; he had suggested that she might like to check its accuracy, or alternatively might wish to buy the manuscript and destroy it, which she might do for $500. Subsequently he met the evangelist, he continued, in the presence of Mrs. Kennedy and their attorney, and it was verbally agreed that he should write the book from material supplied by Aimee, and it would be published over her signature. Aimee thought *Kidnaped* would be a good title. Allstrom pointed out that Robert Louis Stevenson had used that title, but Aimee answered that she knew nothing about that, the book would be entitled *"Kidnaped,* by Aimee Semple McPherson." Eventually she lost interest, the witness said, but he produced a sheaf of notes which he said he had gathered from her before the time of the grand-jury hearing, touching on the search for her body and the death of Harrison.

The sagebrush Kipling bragged that he had shown a draft of the book to Bob Shuler.

Gilbert became curious. "What did that bird have to say about it?" he inquired.

"Strike that," said the court, but Allstrom answered anyway.

"That it was a magnificent production, that it would do Mrs. McPherson a great deal of good."

Shuler wanted to buy the book, he added, but it had been committed to the Kansas publisher Haldeman Julius. Almost before the witness stepped down, stinging denials emanated from both Haldeman Julius and Shuler that they ever wanted to buy the book, which they had inspected with loathing.

Outside the courtroom, disclosures tumbled from the district attorney's office into the receptive columns of the newspapers. The opinions of handwriting experts were released, stating that the penciled rough draft of the "Miss X" affidavit which was found in Mrs. Wiseman's safe-deposit box was in Aimee's handwriting. Mrs. Wiseman told reporters that the document was dictated by Mother Kennedy and written down by Mrs. McPherson while the three were in close conference in Sister's bedroom, before Lorraine went to Salinas, where the final affidavit was signed.

Also disclosed was the interesting fact that Ormiston had been a guest at the Alexandria Hotel, in downtown Los Angeles, shortly before Mrs. McPherson's disappearance, and that the evangelist had stayed in the same hotel on the same dates. On May 9, at 11:22 p.m., the hotel register showed, Aimee checked into the Alexandria and was assigned to room 657. At 11:58 that same evening Ormiston checked in as "Frank Gibson" and was given room 824. The evangelist checked out the next morning and returned that night; she finally departed at 1:20 p.m. on May 11. Ormiston checked out the evening of May 11. Sunday, May 9, was the day on which, according to the statements of Aimee and the radio man, Ormiston had appeared briefly at Angelus

Temple and hailed the pastor casually at the close of her evening sermon.

Tying in with Ormiston's renting the Benedict bungalow in Carmel on May 14, testimony by a procession of witnesses from the Clark Hotel showed that Ormiston had stayed there from May 15 to May 18. He arrived, in the blue Chrysler, at 6:15 a.m. on May 15, registered as "George McIntire," and was taken to room 938; his car was stored in the Clark garage. He remained in his room most of the time during the next four days, eating his meals there. On May 17 he ventured out at dusk, calling for his car at 6 p.m. and returning it to the garage at 10:30 p.m. On May 18, at five minutes before 1 p.m., he checked out of the hotel, ordered his car brought from the garage, and drove away, leaving no forwarding address. This was a couple of hours before Mrs. Oberman said she saw a man dressed in gray, who walked with a peculiar gait, talking with Mrs. McPherson on the beach at Ocean Park. The chambermaid in charge of the ninth floor at the Clark recalled the man in 938 because he limped, and because she saw a radio set in his room, the first she ever saw in a guest's room. A bellboy proved remarkably vague on the stand, provoking Dennison to wonder sharply why his recollection had become blank in two days. The hotel porter and the garage attendant identified records which confirmed the time of "McIntire's" checking in and out and the movements of the Chrysler car. The night clerk and the cashier also testified regarding the guest's ordering his meals sent to his room.

This skirmishing was only a curtain-raiser to the introduction of the State's star witness, black-haired, aggressive Joseph Ryan. He took the stand and gave his name, address, and occupation briskly and gravely. Then his serious expression lifted and he smiled. Aimee, sitting a few feet away, smiled back. As Forrest Murray directed the questioning, she rested her chin on her hand and her fingers toyed around her lips; occasionally she bit her nails while she listened intently, her intelligent, vivacious, expressive eyes seldom leaving the witness's face.

Ryan's testimony covered well-traversed ground, but his telling of the trip to Douglas and the fabled events that flowed thereafter thrilled the auditors. The clothing worn by Sister when she was admitted to Calumet Hospital was introduced in evidence, and Ryan identified each garment separately. While the clothing was being ticketed, Aimee shifted uneasily in her chair and whispered to her mother. Minnie watched with steady, shrewd eyes, motionless in her chair.

Ryan described the evangelist's appearance in the hospital as normal.

"Her eyes had the same light, the same vivacity and reaction they have now," he said, looking at Aimee. "The coloring of her skin was the same as it is now. Her hair showed well-defined waves in it. She sat up unassisted. Her lips were normal."

Murray asked if she was able to talk. "She talked thirty-five pages," Ryan retorted.

When he swore he saw cosmetic traces under her eyes on the train ride back to Los Angeles, Aimee leaned forward and whispered with animation to Gilbert, who listened apparently sleepily. Ryan told of finding imprints of a woman's shoes in the desert quite close to Agua Prieta, and said the prints fitted Aimee's shoes. The slippers were held up for identification; they looked quite new, and the trademark "New Era" on the rubber heels was easily legible. On a blackboard Ryan drew a map showing the location of the footprints, the place where the automobile turned around in the road, and the position of the numerous shacks he had inspected alone or in the company of the evangelist.

Gilbert moved into cross-examination roughly, his questioning at times bringing all three prosecutors to their feet; but Ryan matched the older man barb for barb. Gilbert pounded to prove that the deputy was prejudiced against Mrs. McPherson from the start. He shouted, "I am not asking this witness a single question for any living purpose except to show the unholy interest he has taken in this prosecution, and the venom he displayed in it!"

Ryan leaned forward with a pugnacious glint. "I took no unholy interest in this case. This has been the most atrocious thing that ever transpired!"

"You batted a woman's name around because your curiosity was aroused?"

"No, sir," replied the deputy, playing with a piece of chalk. "I didn't bat her name around. She batted her name around."

"I want you to tell the court when you made up your mind that Aimee Semple McPherson's story of her kidnaping was false."

Objections swirled around the bench. Aimee leaned tensely, her eyes darting and dancing. Finally the judge ruled that Ryan might answer.

"I made up my mind," came the clear response, "when I saw that Kenneth G. Ormiston was up there at Carmel, and when I examined those grocery slips, and when I compared the handwriting with the 'Light and Darkness' sermon written by Mrs. McPherson, and when I had an opportunity to trace down Ormiston's movements step by step."

He went to Douglas, Ryan said, with an open mind, solely to find out the truth, and "it stood up like a monument." Frequently during his testimony he paused, leaned forward, elbow resting on the railing of the witness box, head on hand, and concentrated, then fired back his answer.

Gilbert grilled him on how he came into the case, bringing out that he was the son-in-law of Herman Cline, who "was a police officer."

"And still is!" snapped Ryan. He countered that he had been assigned to the investigation in the regular way as a trial deputy in the district attorney's office; his father-in-law did not request his assignment, and they never discussed the case until their trip to Douglas.

The "Daughter O.K." telegram, illegibly signed "Dr. Merton" or perhaps "Ormiston," was produced, and Ryan told of his futile efforts to trace the sender, although the handwriting seemed to be that of Ormiston. A barrage of objections failed to block introduction of the telegram as an exhibit. Once, when Ryan told about a letter which he said Mrs. McPherson had given to the press attacking his motives, Aimee exclaimed, "Oh, that's a lie!"

The disappearance of the grocery slips was minutely described; spectators strained to catch every word above the din of the riveters outside, piercing the hot, stuffy courtroom. On the blackboard Ryan showed where, in relation to the back steps of the bungalow, they were found.

"What did you do with those grocery slips?" asked Murray on direct examination.

"I retained them in my possession until the time when I gave them to the grand jury in session."

"Do you know where the grocery slips are at the present time?"

"They are gone."

"Where were they the last time you saw them?"

"The last time I saw them they were going around the grand jury. Mrs. Holmes received them, and Mrs. Holmes got up and went out and came back again."

Gilbert, in cross-examination, continued with the subject. "Mr. Ryan, the slips the last time you saw them were in the grand-jury room, is that right?"

"That is the room I saw them in, yes, sir."

"What other search did you make that afternoon besides just concluding that Mrs. Holmes did it?"

"I looked through her pocketbook—she had a small trunk that she carried. I looked everywhere."

"Is that the only place you looked?"

Dennison broke in, scandalized. "He couldn't look where she put them! He couldn't go there!"

Ryan shrugged. "I never went to El Segundo."

"I think that is sufficient," interposed the court and hastily called an adjournment.

The next morning Ryan underwent another verbal mauling by Gilbert that exceeded in relentlessness anything known in Los Angeles courts. Ryan could not be shaken. Aimee, wearing a different costume (black satin with wing cape lined with flesh-colored silk, a flesh-colored collar, and a black satin hat with drooping brim that concealed her features from reporters) sat with bowed head while the witness and Gilbert sparred; now and then she prompted her attorney in a rapid whisper. Mother Kennedy sat, as usual, motionless and expressionless.

Ryan stuck to his assertion that he traveled to Douglas with an open mind, and heard the evangelist in the hospital without preconceived opinion. What did he think of her story?

"I considered it a good narrative."

By the time he left Douglas, he believed some parts of it and disbelieved others. "I believed the part about the jaunt on the desert, the objects, the houses and the people she described, and I was still giving her the benefit of the doubt," he said.

"What parts of her story didn't you believe?"

"What didn't I believe? You want everything?"

"You heard my question."

Ryan set his jaw. "All right, I'll give it all to you. I didn't believe in the existence of the shack. I didn't believe in Rose and Steve. I don't believe she was bound. I don't believe she was ever incarcerated. I don't believe she walked that distance. And that's that."

"Didn't you say you were going to Douglas to break Mrs. McPherson?"

"Absolutely not!"

Gilbert wanted to know about the behavior of the evangelist's children. "The little children were not involved in this gigantic conspiracy, were they? They hadn't seen her while she was away, had they?"

"I am not so sure," came Ryan's reply. On the journey to Douglas they displayed a "total lack of emotion," he said, and they were just as stolid and unmoved when they first met their mother in the hospital. Aimee called them to her, one on either side of the bed, he said; she kissed them and asked, "Aren't you glad your mother is alive?" And then, right away, "Let's have our pictures taken!"

Weren't the children embarrassed by all those cameramen? Gilbert inquired.

"No," Ryan shot back, "they had had too many rehearsals!"

"And when did you first make up your mind that Mrs. McPherson's story was a fake?"

Blurted Ryan, "When I returned from Carmel, then I knew she was a fake and a hypocrite!"

Aimee stiffened. Mother Kennedy glared.

Sergeant Alonzo B. Murchison of the Douglas police followed Ryan on the stand and testified that no evidence whatever to substantiate Mrs. McPherson's kidnaping story had been found in his researches around Agua Prieta. Every trace, he said, pointed to one conclusion, namely, that the evangelist had walked around the garita, about three miles from Agua Prieta, and a little around the slaughterhouse, a mile out of town, and that was all. The broad-shouldered, six-foot desert veteran spoke so softly that his answers were inaudible; Gilbert repeated them loudly for the benefit of the press. Murchison drew a map of the territory he had explored in the hunt for an adobe shack with a wooden floor, then peppered the drawing with crosses indicating the location of every shack, hut, or windbreak within a twenty-mile circuit, both inside and outside the critical triangle. He was shown the dress Aimee wore on her desert hike, and pointed to the lack of sweat stains, the skirt not torn.

During this exchange Keyes jumped up excitedly and demanded that the judge order Gilbert to stop "smudging the evidence." Gilbert had the dress on the counsel table, wet with spillings from several pitchers of ice water, and Keyes complained that Gilbert was dipping the dress in the water and letting it fall on the floor. Gilbert protested he was doing nothing of the kind, but the judge ordered the clerk to impound the clothing.

When Judge Blake announced that there would be no court session the following day, Aimee sprang up, exclaiming heartily, "Now for a good swim!" She spent the holiday at the beach.

The Whole Town Talking

In this hearing without precedent, rules seemed knocked about like tenpins, and a growing jumpiness among the prosecutors was not without sound basis. Nightly they heard themselves chanted over the radio in ignominious guises. Daily courtroom correctness was shattered by the unpredictability of Aimee's Puckish counsel, Gilbert. When Keyes suddenly found himself being sworn as a witness for the defense, his bewilderment was obvious; gingerly he assumed the witness chair and sat crossing and uncrossing his legs and clasping his hands nervously while Murray and Dennison laid down salvos of objections. The court finally excused him before a question could be put.

Then it was Murray's turn: Gilbert planted him on the hot seat of inquiry and jabbed questions at him about how much the State was paying its witnesses by way of expenses; the vociferations of Keyes and Dennison, uttered in solo and in duet, rescued their colleague from this frustrating dilemma.

Soon after that, Gilbert said, "Call Samuel S. Hahn," and Mrs. Wiseman's waspish counsel raised his hand to swear that he would tell the whole truth. Wistfully he appealed to the court: "Since I have no counsel, will I be permitted to make my own objections?" The court allowed that that might be reasonable, and Gilbert proceeded to force his witness to admit that he had not been in Cuba on a certain date (as he was telling the newspapers) but actually was interviewing a client in the county jail. Before Hahn could exercise his dual role of witness-objicient, Gilbert dismissed him with an indifferent "That's all." Hahn stepped down, groggy.

The strangest backlash on Keyes came during torrid October, when he found himself a defendant answering criminal charges in a courtroom only a few yards from where he was prosecuting the West's leading evangelist. The cause was a political dispute; the issues were tangled. While Ryan was testifying, Keyes, in the course of carrying on the other duties of his office, had signed criminal complaints against Los Angeles County's Board of Supervisors and other officials, alleging conspiracy to defraud the county and to manufacture false evidence. In essence, he charged that the supervisors had taken land acquired by the county for a children's summer camp, and were maintaining it at the taxpayers' expense as a sort of private country club for their personal recreation. The supervisors, amiably surrendering to the sheriff, retaliated by swearing out a complaint against Keyes, asserting that he had improperly diverted money from his secret fund, voted annually by the board for the purpose of "putting thieves, murderers, and other criminals in prison." Whether significant or not, a request by Keyes for an additional $5000, presumably for use in the McPherson prosecution, was pending before the supervisors.

Keyes stepped from Judge Blake's courtroom into the nearby court of Municipal Judge Baird to be arraigned. Tersely he requested that his preliminary hearing be set over for ten days because he was "otherwise occupied." The court granted the request, and Keyes announced that he would continue to prosecute Mrs. McPherson and her mother in spite of the embarrassing contretemps. He also started a backfire by declaring that one of his accusers, Chairman McClellan of the board of supervisors, had attempted to get possession of the State's prime evidence against Mrs. McPherson—the clothing she wore in the desert. McClellan admitted that he had prompted a more or less official inquiry to that end, but insisted he had acted at a time when the district attorney was saying the investigation was closed; under the circumstances, Mrs. McPherson did not care to have her intimate garments kicking around a public office, and "it seemed to me that she was entitled to them."

From the Temple, on the day of Keyes' arraignment, came a brief comment by Aimee: "I am sorry for anyone who is in trouble, no matter who they may be." Later, from her pulpit, she noted that "Mr. Keyes now faces a felony charge equally as grave if not more serious than that with which I stand charged. I trust that every fair-thinking, God-fearing, straightforward member of this and every other church will withhold judgment until he has been fairly and honestly tried in court. In other words, I hope the people will do unto Mr. Keyes as I would that they should do unto me."

Bob Shuler, preparing to preach on "Hiding in the Deep or the Desert," quickly added a subtopic: "Is McClellan Also in the Flypaper?" In his magazine (sold at his church and on all newsstands) he promised a new treatise shortly, to be entitled "Miss X and the 2 K's"—"Affectionately dedicated to Judge Carlos S. Hardy, who ought to be off the Superior bench if ever in the history of the world a man ought to be removed from that important position." The "2 K's," of course, were Keetch and Keyes.

Shuler also reported that an evangelist had written to the county clerk expressing a desire to establish a temple in Los Angeles for preaching "the Six Square Gospel." Shuler advised the applicant to consult Judges Keetch and Hardy, and perhaps also Asa Keyes, Woolley, and the Nick Harris detective agency. But he warned frankly, "Of course, we cannot expect a gentleman, even with a Six Square Gospel, to receive the co-operation from Superior judges and county officials that a lady 'evangelist' may secure, though with fewer squares to her credit."

Shuler's magazine was a forum for the hundreds of letters with which the Trinity Church mailbag was bulging. Among them were such as these:

> Bob: You are a dirty dog and ought to be killed piece by piece. If she wants a friend Mr. Ormiston, that's her affair. Can't a Christian have a friend? More than that, if there wasn't a cabin in the desert, couldn't God build one and then take it away? Answer me that one, you dirty dog. [Signed] A WHITE MAN.

Another, redolent of femininity:

> Well, Robert, you make me sick. Mrs. McPherson had an operation once and did not even know she was in a bathing suit. I have easily walked 10 miles in June in Arizona without food or water. Safely past men too. [Signed] A COW GIRL OF ORE.

On the opposite side of the altercation:

> Reverend Sir: Go to it! Keetch says Ryan talked too much after Carmel—yes, made the case harder for them to get rid of! [Signed] TRULY JAMES.

On a post card without salutation:

> Your attack upon Aimee is on a par with what the Protestants have done for years, tear down those with whom they do not agree. If Aimee has done what the pack of hyenas attempt to make the public believe, it will develop without your help. Bah on such a Christian. [Signed] A CATHOLIC WHO IS WATCHING YOU.

From another branch of the faith:

> Rev. B. Shuler: You haven't the brains to do the miracles this precious woman is doing. I hope you will get your eyes open and

quit fighting the Temple, for they are praying every minute, day and night, for you. [Signed] A MEMBER OF THE M.E. CHURCH.

Many of Sister's epistolary sympathizers waived the question of the truth of her story as immaterial. One wrote:

It seems to me that the thing for all Christians to do is to get down on their knees and pray the good God in heaven that her story is true as she tells it. If it isn't, and I confess the facts seem against her, the thing to do is pity rather than condemn.

And another:

I am not defending Mrs. McPherson's story. I have doubted it from the beginning, but I have never doubted her. She may have had a mental lapse, as brilliant people often do, but that she is genuine is proved every day by her works.

A third was bluntly frank:

Call me a fool if you want to, but if Mrs. McPherson should confess every word of the Carmel story, it would not shake my faith in her. I would simply say that she had the same weaknesses that God's saints have always had.

And from San Francisco came a proudly partisan testimonial:

Dear Sir: I will not call you brother any more than a skunk is a brother. You are a disgrace to the animal family. You raise old Ned because a woman becomes so tired with the religious cranks and crippled nuts that surround her that she once and a while wants to get away from them to where she can be natural. Shame on you! Mrs. McPherson is a human being, isn't she? Perhaps she has repented of any little things she may have done wrong. Mrs. McPherson has healed me of seventeen diseases already and I am going back to the Temple to be healed again next month.

One woman reduced the entire desert enigma to a problem in perspiration: "Had Aimee sweated more then, she might be sweating less now."

Chatter about the case that was not committed to paper was similarly divided. Wherever one went in the city, Aimee and her troubles were discussed, acidly, with tolerance, with salacious guffaws. A reporter who set out one day to transcribe this gossip garnered columns, among them these bits:

HEARD ON A STREET CAR

Conductor: The crowd down there gets bigger by the trip. It beats me.

Woman with Shopping Bag: Maybe she was in a trance. I got a spiritualist friend says she saw her stretched out like a corpse and she was dreamin' about bein' kidnaped.

Man with a Cigar: I say, let the poor woman alone. I ain't got nothin' against her but the way she gasses about it. If she wanted to take a little vacation she didn't have to make all this fuss about it.

Nice Old Lady: It's dirty politics. She's a saint. They framed it up on her. I never did see a nicer bunch of boys and girls than she has got down to her Temple.

HEARD AT A THEATER FIRST NIGHT

Dame in Diamonds: I think she is perfectly marvelous. Such poise! Is it true that she took drama under Bernhardt?

Giggling Flapper: All the men are crazy about her, the lawyers on both sides and all the reporters.

Banker: Utter foolishness. It will cost the county $150,000 before they're through. Why can't they drop the case?

Gray-Haired Matron: I'd love to see her vindicated. It's persecution of the female by the male!

Blonde: I couldn't believe it was that creature Ormiston! She nearly converted me, you know!

HEARD IN A DOCTOR'S WAITING ROOM

Lady in Corner: But if she is innocent, why does she bribe all the officials and judges?

Small Boy: Ma, we got a teacher they call "Aimee" at my school because she's got red hair and she went to Mexico on her vacation. Why are they talkin' about Aimee?

Receptionist: I won't hear another word against her! I'm a member of her Temple, and I love her! I'd die for her! (Bursts into tears.)

Fat Woman: It's men's minds holding the wrong thought on her. Dirty gossips!

Lady in Corner: I got my thoughts. . . .

The whole town talked. The hearing was two weeks old, with no ending in sight. Saturday, October 9, was Aimee's thirty-sixth birthday. (The newspapers misstated her age as thirty-five; she did not correct them.) A surprise party started the festivities at the Temple at one minute after midnight Friday, when Bible students ushered their leader to the roof garden of the Bible School building and entertained her with songs and a huge birthday cake. Sister sliced generous chunks for everybody while the Temple Silver Band serenaded her. Sunday morning the children of the Temple brought their presents in a special party. Aimee was photographed in her living room with stacks of gifts around her—baskets of fruit, flowers, candy, lingerie, a canary bird. Telegrams from well-wishers came from all parts of the world.

"One bright spot in the midst of a sordid time," she said happily. "But for the fact that I am borne up by the arms of God, incidents of the last few weeks would have been impossible for me to bear." Never, she added, had she been "so absolutely sure of complete vindication."

But millions laughed. The show was better than those "Follies" and "Scandals" and "Vanities" that mirrored the fleshy cynicisms of the gaudy age; this was "The Great Kidnap Caper of 1926." Friends meeting on the street would wink and exchange ribaldries on "that famous ninth chapter of Amos":

> And though they hide themselves in the top of Carmel, I will search and take them out thence; and though they be hid from my sight in the bottom of the sea, thence will I command the serpent, and he shall bite them.

A Week of Wiseman

While the evangelist was celebrating her birthday, Judge Blake was placed under armed guard—at his home, the Hall of Justice, his courtroom—because of threatening letters.

The witness on the Monday morning opening the third week of the hearing was Mrs. Wiseman. The State admitted she was their prize package; in fact, the conspiracy case pivoted on her testimony.

Mrs. Wiseman took the stand with poise and assurance. She was attired modishly in a dress of old rose and a black picture hat on which two crossed skewers glinted; open-mouthed flappers in court frankly admired her elegance. From Monday through Friday she gave her testimony, facing Sister Aimee without embarrasssment, meeting the sarcasm of the defense and the asperity of the prosecution with matching sarcasm and tartness.

Gilbert opened by challenging her competence to testify, on the ground that she was a lunatic. "I desire, if your honor please," he submitted, "to offer as an exhibit in this case the certified copy of the lunatic asylum in Utah, disclosing that this woman was declared to be insane, and that her form of insanity took the very form it has taken in this case, incorrigible unveracity. The presumption is that she is still under the judgment of insanity and therefore incompetent to testify until a court has ruled her sane. No court has so ruled."

A legal Donnybrook broke out. Mrs. Wiseman tossed her head nonchalantly, while Hahn stuck in his oar, objecting to Gilbert's "making any reflections on my client."

The judge calmed the storm and ruled that Mrs. Wiseman could testify.

Several times during her glib chatter Mother Kennedy blushed hotly, and Aimee shook her head in sorrowful denial, her eyes fixed in pity on the witness; but the accused women made no other demonstration of hostility or concern.

Within five minutes Lorraine testified that Aimee herself told her she was the woman with Ormiston at Carmel. She said they cooked up the "Miss X" hoax together, and Mother was in on it. She also asserted that the first time she met Judge Hardy, the judge without ado coached her on the subject of Ormiston, telling her intimate details about the radio operator's married life, his wife's inordinate jealousy, Mrs. McPherson's having carried on what Mother Kennedy believed was a flirtation with him, what the radio man looked like, his temperament, and his getting into money scrapes (over the sale of radio sets) from which he let Mrs. Kennedy and her daughter extricate him. She said Hardy offered to hire a detective to assist her.

"Assist you in what?" she was asked.

"Oh, I don't know," came the airy reply, "but I have my idea."

Mother Kennedy and she, the witness went on, arranged a code so they might communicate secretly: "east" stood for "south," "daughter" meant "Mrs. Wiseman," and so forth. She identified telegrams sent to her in San Francisco by Mrs. Kennedy and wires she sent in reply. The Salinas affidavit signed "Miss X" was prepared from the rough draft found in her safe-deposit box, she declared, after she had been sent to Carmel to spy out the terrain. She prowled the town in disguise, once in her son's clothing, another time wearing a gray wig. On her return she reported to Mrs. McPherson the names of the witnesses who were claiming to recognize her photograph and what they were saying. She told of receiving doles of money from Mother Kennedy, usually in $5 bills, and Mrs. Kennedy's insisting that she sign a receipt every time, because Mother had to account for every cent of Temple outgo. Receipts for sums up to $50 were introduced, marked for "expenses," "loans," and other purposes.

Mrs. Wiseman recounted how Sister suggested she buy special hats, clothing, and dark glasses, also false hair, so they could have their picture taken together. There was a stir among the film coterie and girls in the courtroom when the witness removed her hat and demonstrated how she ordinarily wore her hair, and how she rearranged it under the evangelist's tutoring. Sister inquired, she said, whether Lorraine had worn a red hat while she was with "Miss X" and McIntire at Carmel, and when Lorraine said she had never worn a red hat Aimee suggested she buy one. She also bought a white felt that could be pulled well down on the neck, and was photographed wearing it.

Her story of meeting the mysterious "Mr. Martin" in San Francisco, and being engaged on the spot for the delicate mission on behalf of Mrs. McPherson, drew Gilbert's sharpest attention. She gave the date of their conversation as July 7, and said she asked "Mr. Martin" frankly, "Is Mrs. McPherson the lady that was at Carmel, or was she kidnaped?"

"Well, of course," she quoted her interlocutor as replying, "I would not be asking you to work on this if it was not Mrs. McPherson who was at the Benedict cottage."

She remembered they talked about the matter from 11 o'clock until 12:45. Gilbert objected that the witness was talking idiotically, since by her account she knew all about the Carmel episode "twenty days before Carmel was ever heard of!" Reporters judged this remark unduly harsh on the Carmel Chamber of Commerce, but the fact was that the Carmel disclosures had not broken until three weeks after July 7.

Amusement swept the room when Lorraine testified that "Mr. Martin" selected her "because I was of an individual type, and also for the reason that I could keep things to myself." And the courtroom shook with laughter when Keyes, reading one of the innumerable statements she made to newspapers and investigators, tripped over the phrase, "I wish to do all that within me lies." Lorraine joined in the merriment.

On dates she proved remarkably quick, but the dates she assigned were all askew. Times, places rattled off her tongue, until Gilbert again arose wrathfully: the dates she was giving were more than a month out of line with her previous testimony! The State fought furiously against admitting the objection, but was embarrassed when Aimee, skimming through the transcript, pointed out for Gilbert specific instances to cite, while Mother Kennedy scribbled rapidly in her cramped handwriting. Mrs. Wiseman listened to the argument with a smirk; her self-confidence never left her. Constantly she prefaced her answers with "I certainly did," "I certainly can," "I certainly will," "I certainly have." When finally the judge ruled that she might rectify her errors and she was asked formally, "Do you wish to correct your testimony?" the answer came firmly and loudly, "I certainly do."

Much of the testimony revolved around affidavits given under oath, which Lorraine light-heartedly admitted were false from beginning to end. And she was voluble even against the cautioning of the judge. Once when she attempted to answer a question over Gilbert's objection before the court could rule, Gilbert snapped, "Just a minute! Don't answer that one!"

"Now, don't get excited, Brother Gilbert," admonished Keyes.

"I'm not getting excited," retorted Gilbert. "I'm just trying to keep one jump ahead of this witness, and believe me, it takes a kangaroo to do it!"

The scene in Judge Bardin's office, when Mrs. Wiseman appeared there to arrange the signing of the "Miss X" affidavit, was graphically recounted. Bardin, said the witness, was suspicious. "How do I know that you are the party that was in the cottage?" the lawyer asked her. "I don't know anything about it. I'll have nothing to do with it until I know more about this."

Woolley, who was present, Lorraine testified, "said he knew me, had known of me through Mrs. Kennedy and Mrs. McPherson, and he had been given to understand I was there with 'Miss X' and would give an affidavit or something of the kind that we were the parties at the Benedict cottage. Then Judge Bardin spoke up. He said, 'I won't have anything to do with it. You must prove to me—how do I know who you are?' "

"Where was 'Miss X' at that time?" asked Keyes.

"She was over to the hotel, just across the street from Judge Bardin's office."

"Where did she come from?"

"From San Francisco—" The witness bit her lip. "She came from Philadelphia."

Although she asserted that Woolley said he had been told about her mission in Salinas (the lawyer, on his part, had stated most positively that she was a complete stranger to him when they met in Bardin's office), she cleared the attorney of complicity in the plot concocted without his knowledge by his clients.

"I am just as positive as I am sitting in this chair," she said, "that that man did not know it was a frame-up positively."

The witness swore stubbornly that the woman who signed as "Miss X" was "Rachel Wells," of Philadelphia. After signing the affidavit, she said, "Miss Wells" accompanied her back to Los Angeles, where Lorraine checked into the Clark Hotel under the name "A. Moore," while "Miss Wells" stayed in Redondo.

"Let's get that address in Redondo," interjected Gilbert.

"Where in Redondo?" asked Keyes.

"I do not best remember now," came the snippish reply.

All week the name "Ormiston" sounded like a thorough-bass through the testimony. Mrs. Wiseman asserted that Sister had dictated a letter to him on September 2, asking him to write or telephone her directly; she added a postscript in longhand which Lorraine did not see; the letter was mailed to the lawyer Martin in Chicago to be forwarded. On September 9, the witness related, Mrs. McPherson spoke with Ormiston by long-distance telephone, saying the next time he called she would introduce Lorraine to him on the phone so they could "get acquainted."

"Mrs. McPherson seemed very happy over the affair," the witness recalled. "She told me Mother Kennedy forbade her to tell anyone what had occurred, but she considered it such good news she had to tell me."

This occurred just a few hours before Lorraine was arrested.

Before this, she went on, Mother and she had discussed the advisability of her going to Chicago to meet Ormiston. Finally—on August 23, she first said—Mother gave her the letter of introduction written on the foot of lawyer Martin's letter. This date proved to be another slip.

"On what date did Mrs. Kennedy write the postscript on that letter?" she was asked again.

"On September second, between ten and eleven o'clock in the morning," came the slick correction.

Gilbert grinned. Mother Kennedy glared and slowly her ears became scarlet.

The supposed coaching by Aimee on details of the Carmel bungalow, as well as her interviews with Benedict, Lorraine went into circumstantially. After their first meeting, she said, when she came back to the Temple and reported that Benedict was not convinced, Aimee and her mother were disgusted. Mrs. Wiseman reassured them that although she and Benedict did not hit it off very well, he was "too much of a gentleman" to deny her story if she gave it to the newspapers. Later, when she consulted with Woolley and Mrs. Kennedy about approaching the papers, Mother used the same phrase—that Benedict would not publicly dispute her story, because he was too much of a gentleman, and also because he had visited the Temple and had seen "the splendid work being done there." At this point the witness got a laugh by saying, "Mr. Woolley looked at me and winked."

Mrs. Wiseman related that Emma Schaffer was on hand when Sister suggested that Lorraine should impersonate her in photographs. But she paid the secretary the tribute of remarking, "If that woman was killed, she would go to the grave with her mouth shut. She hated me."

Aimee turned toward Emma, sitting beside her, and squeezed her hand. The secretary blushed and squeezed back happily.

Keyes absented himself from Judge Blake's court on Wednesday long enough to appear as defendant in his own case and win a further postponement of his preliminary hearing. Thursday morning the district attorney did not arrive in court at all, and Dennison announced, after some confusion, that Keyes was suffering from ptomaine poisoning.

Mrs. Wiseman opened her testimony that day with the statement that Aimee told her, on September 3, in her home adjoining Angelus Temple, that she once demonstrated to four persons how she could cut a rope off her wrists without injuring herself.

(This demonstration had in fact been given. One evening at the close of her service, the evangelist called to Joe Henderson, a Bible student who served as usher, "Joe, come over to the house with me; there is something I want you to do." With Gladwyn Nichols and two other Temple leaders, Joe went across to the McPherson home; none of them had any notion what Sister wanted them for. In the entrance hall, the rugs had been taken up and a couch was placed in the center. Sister handed Henderson a stout rope, the kind cowboys use for lariats, and told him to tie her wrists tightly behind her back. Henderson made a firm knot, then Sister lay down on the couch and had Henderson tie her ankles. After ordering her audience to stand back, she rolled off the couch and worked herself, tightly trussed, toward a five-gallon oil tin that stood on the waxed floor, its top cut off roughly. The tin slithered crazily around the polished surface, but Aimee at last succeeded in jamming it against the wall behind her. After a long struggle, sawing the rope gingerly on the jagged edge of the can, she cut her bonds, freed her wrists, untied her ankles, and stood up unaided. Her wrists were not even scratched. One of the witnesses of this acrobatic feat years afterward confessed that he would never have believed it possible, had he not seen it with his own eyes. At about the same time, Sister re-enacted for her church elders the circumstances of her abduction. Standing with one foot on the running board of her car, stretching out a hand as if toward someone in the back seat, she ordered an elder to give her a shove, and "her body slid right slick into that car," in the words of one spectator.)

When Gilbert arose to cross-examine Mrs. Wiseman, he went back into her memory of dates, wanting to know where she was, what she was doing, on every day in June, the month before she became involved in the McPherson business. She was unable to recall, and Gilbert directed the attention of the court to the fact that she could remember every date and event the prosecution wanted to know about, but two hours later was completely at sea about other dates and events. Under Gilbert's persistence, Lorraine constantly corrected dates she had given erroneously in her earlier testimony. The date on which she sent $150 to "Rachel Wells" to pay her railroad fare west from Philadelphia she corrected to August 4, with the offhand explanation, "I looked it up in my book last night."

Gilbert proposed that she bring this invaluable memorandum book to court.

"I don't know that I can," was her reply. "I probably destroyed it."

The attorney was incredulous. "You looked at it last night and tore it up?"

"Yes, the girls saw me tear it."

"The deputy sheriffs who are guarding you? They saw you look in that book and destroy it? Did they say anything about destroying a memorandum connected with this case?"

"Certainly not. They didn't ask me no questions whatever. I do as I please."

When Gilbert asked whether she had been confined in a Utah asylum, she replied nonchalantly. Yes, she said, for two months in 1915 "for a crime committed by another person"; when the mistake was proved, she was "turned out entirely." She professed to know nothing about the statement made by her sister, Mrs. Virla Kimball, that she had been released in the custody of her mother.

Gilbert flourished before her the San Francisco *Examiner* containing her son's death notice; she denied having inserted the ad. Questioned about "Rachel Wells," she was stubbornly insistent that there was such a person, saying they had been friends for two and a half years, having met when "Miss Wells" was working in a cafeteria in San Francisco. She did not recall where "Miss Wells" was living at that time ("it was somewhere on Steiner Street, with some people"), although she had preserved her telephone number in her address book; unfortunately she had torn out that page in jail the night she was arrested, because she did not want her friend's name "thrashed around." She always corresponded with "Rachel" through General Delivery at Philadelphia, even sending special-delivery letters to that address. The replies she received she had destroyed. ("I destroyed four at one time.") She recalled having given Judge Bardin a lock of her hair and one from the head of "Miss X," who was "Rachel Wells," but she could offer no adequate description of the appearance of "Miss Wells" except that her hair was rather dark and she was about Mrs. Wiseman's own height and weight.

"I want to know if you can tell this court of a single, solitary scrap of paper, letter, telegram, anything that is written, that we can look at, that will furnish this court the slightest information as to the existence of this 'Miss Wells,'" Gilbert pressed.

"Not at this instant, no," was the calm reply.

Gilbert then charged that the woman who signed the "Miss X" affidavit in Judge Bardin's office was Lorraine's twin sister, Mrs. Kimball. Had they not arrived in Salinas at night and left at night in order to prevent anybody from recognizing her sister? he demanded. Mrs. Wiseman angrily snapped that such was not the purpose of the night travel, and her companion in Salinas was not her sister.

"How did you know this 'Rachel Wells' would go into this hoax with you?" prodded Gilbert.

"I knew she would."

"How did you know it?"

"My own intuition."

"You have not been involved in any other schemes like this before?"

The prosecution arose in bitter objection. "I submit, your honor," cried Dennison, "I do not believe there was another such hoax as this since the dawn of civilization!"

"Certainly not!" sneered Mrs. Wiseman.

Aimee's mouth rounded in a long-drawn "O-o-oh!"

"I would like to know," taunted Gilbert, "whether counsel means the hoax about 'Miss X' or the hoax about the district attorney trying to persecute this—"

He was drowned out by Dennison's impassioned, "I mean this blasphemy perpetrated here!' '

"Gentlemen, gentlemen, gentlemen, gentlemen!" pleaded the judge. "Let us try this law suit."

Gilbert subsided into a scrutiny of the itemized "expense account" found in Mrs. Wiseman's purse; she was unable to remember what most of the entries stood for. About a few she was positive, such as, "Glasses $7.50."

"Do you remember all about that?" Gilbert prodded.

"I sure do!"

A second item, "Glasses $7.50," she also was clear about; that was when Mrs. McPherson sent her back to buy another kind to be photographed in.

She was asked about the hotels where she stayed. "Were you registered under your own name?"

"Certainly not!" She appeared affronted.

Reporters checked the cast of characters and concluded that the only person in the drama who showed no reluctance to sign a hotel register with her right name was Aimee Semple McPherson.

The final clash came when Mrs. Wiseman recounted her arrest and her subsequent all-night confessional session in the *Examiner* office. Hahn, she related, told her he would not represent her unless she told the truth—"that I was working for fakers and hypocrites, people who should be in the penitentiary for manslaughter—"

Gilbert encouraged her slyly: "Yes?"

"And they were robbers and thieves, taking other people's money," she went on spitefully, "and unless I did tell the truth he would expose the most of it, as he knew it, and I told him rather than lose him I would do it."

"Did you notice," said Gilbert silkily, "when Mr. Hahn had worked himself up to this spasm of righteous indignation, did you notice whether he was frothing at the mouth?"

Hahn was on his feet righteously objecting and the question was withdrawn. Lorraine laughed, amused by the set-to.

Friday afternoon Gilbert at last said, "That's all," and Mrs. Wiseman stepped down, still jaunty and at ease.

The State Rests

Sister hastened to the Temple and paid her respects rather mildly to "the dear little lady on the stand," toward whom, she said, she felt no ill will. "Oh, what a silly I was!" she said. "I guess I was just a gullible goose to believe her story!"

Sunday evening Mrs. Virla Kimball arrived in Los Angeles under subpoena as a defense witness, but immediately placed herself in the hands of the prosecution and her sister's attorney, threatening the evangelist (who had paid her fare south) with an action for slander and expressing indignation at being drawn into the affair. She denied that she had signed the "Miss X" affidavit, contending she was at home with her five children and her brother-in-law, Sielaff, when the affidavit was signed. Hahn backed this with an announcement that Mrs. Kimball admitted she visited Salinas on August 15, "at the request of her sister, but, learning what was wanted of her, refused to sign any affidavit and returned home after cautioning her sister to stay out of trouble."

Keyes spent the week end at home, his assistants said, still in the toils of ptomaine. In her sermon Aimee quipped that an enemy of hers had a fine stock of "Kentucky rye" cached behind several barrels of crockery in his cellar. The congregation whooped.

Aimee preached three times Sunday with a temperature of 101. She was suffering intense pain from a recurrence of the infection that had struck her in September; this time it broke out in an abscess below the left knee. Not until the close of the evening service did she inform her followers of her condition; then she asked for their prayers. Monday morning she limped into court and took a seat beside Mrs. Wiseman. Her knee, she told reporters, apparently had been infected by a scratch she received from a courtroom chair.

The witness of the day was Bernice Morris. In a long direct examination, and under hours of hammering by Gilbert, McKinley's secretary told of her dealings with the Temple women in connection with a fictitious shack, and as much as she knew about her employer's role. Her testimony contained no surprises, but opened more windows on the intimate words and manner of Sister Aimee during those feverish days after McKinley's death.

Twice Miss Morris's composure broke and she brushed tears from her eyes; both times it was when she identified the crumpled, stained papers taken from McKinley's body. She had confided once to Mother Kennedy that she felt the dead lawyer's spirit was beside her all the time.

Bernice's account of the famous automobile ride through Long Beach with Aimee and her mother the day after McKinley's death brought ripples of amusement; Aimee watched with a whimsical, rueful smile.

"The first thing I remember Mrs. McPherson saying," Bernice testified, "was in connection with Rose. She said, 'I wonder what has happened to Rose? I wonder if they were mean to her after she let me get away?'"

"What did you say to that?" Dennison led.

"I told her I didn't know anything about that. Mrs. Kennedy was looking at some pamphlets she had in her lap, and she handed me one and I looked at it and laughed and made some comment; it was a poem dedicated to Captain Cline. We laughed about it."

Dennison went into the party's arrival at the Temple. There was talk with Mother Kennedy about the kidnapers with whom McKinley was supposed to be negotiating, Bernice said. "Mrs. McPherson asked me if I had ever been to one of their meetings. She had just come downstairs dressed in her uniform. I commented on her hair being so pretty. She said they were having a wedding that night, and she wished I could stay. I told her I would like to, but I had to go back. She told me I was a dear little girl, she knew I would be able to help her. Then Mrs. McPherson went on into the Temple and Mrs. Kennedy came in and handed me a bill folded up and said, 'We will try to have something nice for you, dear, the next time you are here, and here is twenty dollars.'"

"Was it twenty dollars?"

"Yes, sir!"

This money, Bernice said, was the only money she took at any time.

The "crick in the neck" fabrication was described amid laughter, Mother Kennedy joining in when Bernice quoted her as saying "the crick in the neck is good."

"At this time," the witness continued, "Mrs. Wiseman turned to me and said, 'When do you think you are going to have these kidnapers here?' I said, 'Pardon me, who is this? Is this Miss Schaffer?' Mrs. Kennedy said, 'No, this is Mrs. Wiseman. This is the little lady who is "Miss X's" sister, who had been helping us.' And I turned to Mrs. Wiseman and said, 'I am sure I don't know.' Then Mother Kennedy said, 'It is strange, it seems that nearly everyone who has been trying to help us has something happen to them. This little lady,' she said, pointing to Mrs. Wiseman, 'was almost run over in San Francisco.' I said, 'Is that so?' and Mrs. Wiseman said, 'Yes.' "

For her cross-examination, Bernice changed from the abbreviated black dress she had worn in the morning to a hunter's green frock with a skirt considerably more demure. She met Gilbert's slashing questions with determination, delineating clearly her attitude in the entire matter and emphasizing that the Temple leaders approached her with suggestions and appeals that she procure a shack and a road map; never did she make any advances or give them a pledge. Gilbert opened by establishing that her age was twenty-three, that she was a graduate of both high school and normal school, and that she had been married twice and divorced twice; her second decree was not yet final. Dennison had constantly referred to the witness as a girl, a child, overawed by a "brilliant and powerful woman"; and when Dennison obstructed Gilbert by incessant objections, the defense attorney cut back with his laziest sarcasm: "Of course, your honor, we do not want to be put in the attitude of having perpetrated a fraud upon a child with two divorced husbands. But she is here as a witness, twenty-three years old!"

The court squelched the acrimony and Gilbert so far reversed himself as to call the witness "baby doll." But he drew no signifiant admissions from Bernice.

The final prosecution witness was Milton Carlson, a handwriting expert, who testified that the writing on the grocery slips matched that on the "Light and Darkness" sermon notes, on the rough draft of the "Miss X" affidavit, and on the Carmel telegram receipt. Specimens of Ormiston's handwriting, under his own name and under many aliases, Carlson also identified as emanating from the same hand.

While Carlson was characterizing the evangelist's half-written, half-printed script as slovenly and immature, but strong and practical—like Ormiston's, it showed no unnecessary strokes—Sister leaned to a woman reporter and whispered, laughing, "See how childish my handwriting is? Anybody could copy it. I've never grown up."

The defense strove valiantly to exclude the grocery slips because the originals had been destroyed and only photographs existed, but the court overruled. During Gilbert's hour-long cross-examination of the expert, with the aid of photographs of single letters and curves and pencil strokes blown up to monstrous size, Dennison jumped up and called the court's attention to the defense's handwriting expert sitting among the spectators. The judge expelled him.

That day, Tuesday, October 19, the State rested, in the fourth week of the hearing, and the defense opened its case. Aimee was far from well. By the noon recess the pain in her leg had become intolerable. A surgeon diagnosed an old-fashioned carbuncle complicated by the onset of gangrene. He lanced the abscess twice. Against his advice, Sister returned to the courtroom, although the doctor forbade her to place any weight on the affected limb. When the elevator stopped at the seventh floor, she was carried along the corridor in a low chair on the shoulders of three deputies; the crowd surged around her and there were cheers of encouragement. Lifting the chair over the wooden barrier, the deputies brought it carefully into the courtroom; it was so low that Aimee sat almost hidden from view. Often resting her head on her hand, she appeared to fight off recurrent spasms of pain, but she remained attentive to the proceedings.

As lead-off witness, the defense called Cross, the desert tracker, from Douglas. The gist of his testimony was that after Mrs. McPherson's reappearance he found a woman's footprints at least nine miles outside Agua Prieta. Also, he upheld the possibility of Aimee's having made the desert journey she described, basing his belief on his own experience: once, while working as a ranch hand, he fell and his horse fell on him, and he walked twenty-two miles without food or water, and was back at work the next day.

The prosecution scored when Cross was unable to identify a photograph of Niggerhead mountain, a landmark he saw every day. The ex-cowboy got a laugh when he hoisted his feet up on the railing of the witness box to display his stout desert boots—the same, he swore, he wore shack hunting, and he had worn them every day since June 23 except for two days. They did not appear to be scratched or scuffed unduly.

After Cross's testimony, he joined half a score of other visitors from Arizona as guests of Mrs. McPherson at Angelus Temple. Cook, the truant officer; O. E. Patterson; Sims, the deputy United States marshal; Henry, the Douglas newspaperman; Leslie Gatliff of the Douglas police —they were all on hand, as were also Ramon Gonzales, the Agua Prieta tavern keeper, and his pretty wife, Teresa. Although running a temperature of 100 degrees, Aimee, with her lawyers present to make fitting conversation, performed the honors graciously. There was no limit to the ice cream and everybody had a pleasant, instructive time. The prosecutors were not invited—an omission they did not fail to bring up in court the next day.

The defense called Douglas police officer Patterson, who testified that Mrs. McPherson seemed exhausted when he first saw her in the taxi outside the Douglas police station, and later when he accompanied her to Calumet Hospital. He told of backtracking and finding a woman's footprints eight miles from Agua Prieta, although he could not be positive about these all the way. He denied categorically that he ever told any newspaper reporter that in his opinion no woman could have made the walk Aimee said she made and be in her condition.

Cook, the merchant patrolman, testified that Mrs. McPherson was "all in" when she reached Douglas. She told him her name while she was sitting in the taxi.

"Did you realize you were beholding the great Bernhardt of the pulpit?" inquired Dennison. Gilbert objected.

The truant officer said he, his wife, and their four-year-old daughter had hiked four miles across the desert in June, and the little girl's open-toed sandals were not scuffed or scratched, nor did the wind and sun blister or injure her legs, although she wore short socks.

Gonzales through an interpreter testified how he found Mrs. McPherson slumped at his front gate at 1 a.m. on June 23, and how relieved he was when he established that she was not a corpse. She drank two glasses of water at his house, he said. She seemed highly nervous. Teresa Gonzales confirmed her husband's testimony, and volunteered that Mrs. McPherson did not ask for water until an hour after her appearance at their home, when she was given two glasses.

Three more Douglas witnesses gave support to Sister's desert-flight story. Lieutenant Gatliff, Deputy Marshal Sims, and Harold Henry, the reporter, all swore they saw tracks made by a woman's shoes more than fifteen miles east of Agua Prieta. These were the tracks reported along the Gallardo fence, which ran from Niggerhead mountain south to Cenesas—the footprints that showed in the sandy washes or gullies over a distance of several hundred yards. The witnesses also said they saw a gap in the Gallardo fence that had been cut with pliers recently—such a gap as a person might conceivably pass through without noticing the fence. On the point of damage to shoes, the witnesses were unanimous: all three lofted their shoes, which they said were the same they had worn through days of shack hunting. The substantial brogans were not noticeably cut up. All the witnesses were asked whether they had attended the ice-cream party at the Temple the evening before. They were there. When asked how much they expected to be paid for testifying, most of them reckoned that about $10 a day and expenses would be fair, to compensate for loss of wages and for their trouble.

That evening, overruling the doctor, Sister spoke at the midweek prayer meeting. In high spirits, although still suffering intense pain, she confided that her doctors had about washed their hands of her because she persisted in putting her faith in prayer for healing; in fact, they had warned her she might lose a leg. She alluded a little bitterly to the way the prosecution was playing up her "simple act of hospitality" in serving ice cream and cake to the defense witnesses. Paying the expenses of witnesses was customary and necessary for both the State and the defense, she pointed out impatiently. Then, with a smile replacing the lines of pain on her face, she made the ringing assertion, "I feel certain I am on the eve of a complete vindication and victory! If the children of Israel could walk forty years in the wilderness without wearing out shoes or clothing, why couldn't Mrs. McPherson walk twenty miles without coming in barefoot?"

Two Judges on the Pan

When Mrs. Kimball was called to the stand, the courtroom was tense. Mrs. Kimball testified that the first time she had ever been in Salinas was on August 15, when she visited her sister at the hotel where "Rachel Wells" also was staying. She arrived by bus from Oakland at 3 a.m. and left at 7:30 the same morning, she said. (The "Miss X" affidavit was signed after noon that day.)

"Did you go to Judge Bardin's home that morning?" Gilbert asked her.

"I did not," came the tight-lipped response.

Gilbert at this point requested that Judge Bardin and Russell Scott be brought into the courtroom. The partners entered and stood watching Mrs. Kimball on the witness stand, her hat off; after a moment they left. Cross-examined by Hahn, Mrs. Kimball decisively denied that she had signed the "Miss X" affidavit or that she had given Judge Bardin or anybody else a lock of her hair.

Judge Bardin then was sworn.

"Did you see the woman who was on the witness stand before you?" Gilbert asked him.

"I did."

"Tell me whether or not she is the woman who signed the 'Miss X' affidavit in your office."

The reply was measured and confident. "The woman I saw on the witness stand signed the 'Miss X' affidavit in my office."

There was a clatter as reporters pushed back their chairs and started for the door.

"That was the lady who was on the stand?" Gilbert insisted meticulously.

"That is the woman who was on the stand preceding me here—Mrs. Kimball. Mrs. Kimball entered my office, took a seat across from my desk, as close as Mr. Dennison is from me now. She was very reticent, had little to say, volunteered nothing, and answered few questions."

Keyes, in cross-examination, wanted to know why Bardin kept a sample of Mrs. Wiseman's handwriting.

"I didn't know who the woman was," Bardin explained. "It was done as a matter of precaution, like any other attorney would do. I wanted some tangible clue to their identity. We had discussed the grocery slips and she said she had written them. I asked her if she had seen the photostatic copies of the slips, and she said she had, and they proved she had written them."

He said Mrs. Wiseman appeared at ease during the interview, but "Miss X" was constrained. At Keyes' request, Bardin produced two locks of hair which he said Mrs. Wiseman gave him as samples from the women's heads. The locks were introduced as exhibits.

After Judge Bardin, Scott testified. He was not so emphatic in his identification of Mrs. Kimball, saying only that she looked "very much like" the woman who signed the affidavit in his presence.

The third of the Salinas witnesses was Joseph Levinson, a taxi driver, who swore that Mrs. Wiseman and Mrs. Kimball were the two women he drove to the Jeffrey House in Salinas on August 15, and later to Bardin's office. The prosecution did not cross-examine him; they told reporters they were not concerned with the identity of "Miss X"—let the defense worry about that; the State was concerned only with Mrs. Wiseman's duplicity and scheming.

Judge Bardin's testimony amused Mrs. Wiseman. "Bunk!" she said. "That's another one of those Temple things! I snipped one lock of hair from my switch and the other from Rachel Wells' switch. I suggest Mr. Woolley send them to an expert—he'll probably find they came from a horse's tail!"

The appearance of Superior Judge Carlos S. Hardy as a defense witness brought a packed courtroom with a crowd pushing for admission. At this point Aimee reversed her policy of censorship for Temple members; instead of forbidding them to go near the hearing, she invited everybody to attend. Mother Kennedy and Sister beamed as the dignified jurist seated himself in the witness chair and gave his name and position in a clear, firm voice. He first met the Temple leaders in January 1923, he stated, and had remained "more or less friendly" with them ever since. In detail he recounted his dealings with McKinley and "Dr." Waters. McKinley approached him first with the story about Miller and Wilson. He produced a letter from McKinley listing expenses totaling $27.50 incurred in his activities on the case; it stressed that the attorney had no intention of capitalizing on the incident and had included no charge for his time, because he wished to cooperate in the effort to clear Mrs. McPherson. Hardy said he told McKinley that he would be paid, but he never advanced him any money and knew nothing about his being given $1000 at the Temple.

Waters, the judge testified, "told me he was a member of my church, the Baptist Church, and that he had some information about the McPherson case." Hardy had Waters write out what he said he knew and kept the statement; it was produced in court.

Hardy denied that he had told Burns detectives to find Ormiston. He said Ormiston's name was often mentioned in discussions at the Temple, and once Mother Kennedy had said she wished Ormiston would come forward and tell the truth. But he denied that while the evangelist was missing Mother Kennedy had confided to him her private belief that her daughter was alive. Mother repeatedly told him, he said, that she believed Aimee was drowned.

On the subject of Mrs. Wiseman he was emphatic. He admitted that he had talked with her in his home just after she came to Los Angeles. He listened to her story, he said—it involved "Belle Owens" and the latter's supposed sister as the woman at Carmel—but he did not discuss Ormiston or the radio man's domestic or financial troubles, or offer to engage a detective to work with her, or do other things Mrs. Wiseman had sworn to.

Lorraine listened to this testimony intently, leaning forward on her elbows, smiling cynically. Aimee sketched caricatures of the attorneys around the counsel table. One of Dennison (printed in the *Examiner* the next day) made him look discouraged.

Dennison opened the cross-examination. "Judge Hardy, did you believe the story of McKinley?"

"Yes, I believed it," was the candid reply.

"Do you believe Mrs. McPherson was kidnaped?"

A hush fell. Judge Blake meditatively pushed up the tip of his nose.

"I have no reason to believe otherwise," replied Hardy evenly.

"I didn't ask you that," Dennison purred. "I asked you whether you still believed Mrs. McPherson was kidnaped?"

The witness hesitated. Then he spoke quietly. "Yes, I do."

"Did you believe Mrs. Wiseman's story?"

"I believed a portion of it but not all of it, and I told Mrs. Kennedy."

"You knew it had been publicly reported that Ormiston and Mrs. McPherson fled from the Carmel cottage and that they had been seen about the cottage?"

"Yes."

"Did Mrs. Wiseman's exoneration of Mrs. McPherson impress you?"

"It did."

"How?"

"I assumed she had found additional evidence, but I did not pass on it as an exoneration of Mrs. McPherson."

Later, while on his vacation trip, he read the statement Mrs. Wiseman gave to the newspapers and was struck unpleasantly because it contradicted the statement she had given to him. Nevertheless, he had written to her suggesting that they meet in San Francisco on his return southward.

Mother Kennedy and Aimee were jubilant when Hardy finished, and at the Temple paeans of victory resounded. Mother rushed out a statement triumphantly declaring: "Now you can see there was no conspiracy on our part and that the only conspiracy there was existed in the minds of the district attorney's office."

Sister predicted full victory. Hardy's testimony, she said, showed that McKinley was making an honest effort to find the kidnapers, and the Douglas witnesses proved her footprints were found far out on the desert, and that there were shacks in that area.

"It's marvelous how the mist of insinuation and falsehood lifted yesterday!" she shouted. "It was a wonderful day for the defense—a glorious unfolding of fact—a victory!"

The subject of her sermon was "Shoes." On the platform were lined all sorts of footgear from wooden pattens to high Cossack boots.

"People who think I can't walk twenty miles," said the preacher, "make me sick."

The Court Rules

The wonderful days continued as the defense witnesses trooped through the box. Two more desert figures told of finding a woman's footprints beside the Gallardo fence, far from Agua Prieta—Constable Ash and M. E. Irwin, a free-lance photographer. Ash volunteered that he was wearing the same coat and shoes he had on while combing the desert, and he too elevated his footgear for inspection. Irwin conceded that he had tried unsuccessfully to sell one of his shack photographs to a newspaper as a picture of the veritable captivity hut. Several Temple witnesses described Mother Kennedy's grief after her daughter's disappearance. The daughter of Mrs. Elizabeth Frame, Mother Kennedy's close friend, testified that she overheard a telephone conversation in Mrs. Frame's home in which Sister spoke with a man supposed to be one of the kidnapers; she quoted Sister as saying, "It sounds like his voice, but I am not sure"—not, she said, "My God, it's him!" The defense's handwriting expert, Douglas L. Swan, disputed the validity of the photographs of the grocery slips for purposes of evidence, because the originals had been "altered, patched, erased, rewritten, overwritten, traced, and otherwise strengthened" before the photographs were taken. Judge Blake pressed him sharply to express an opinion as to the probable author, but Swan refused to commit himself. Then Mrs. Wiseman's attorney, Hahn, suffered a setback in his attempt to establish the origin of the strawberry-pink corset worn by Aimee in the desert. Brandishing the garment, Hahn cried that he was prepared to prove it was a make sold in only two stores in Southern California, and that it was purchased by Mrs. McPherson in Los Angeles shortly before May 18. The judge ruled the corset was immaterial, and its origin was never officially traced.

Blanche Rice brought the story full circle when she told how she re-

292 THE VANISHING EVANGELIST

ceived the first telephone call from the beach saying Sister was missing. "Oh, Mr. Gilbert, do I have to tell all this? It is so hard to relate!" She wept; it was the second time tears had flowed during the hearing. But she collected herself sufficiently to certify that Mother's grief-stricken attitude did not alter during the weeks Sister was away.

With her tears the defense rested, on Thursday, October 28, in the fifth week of the hearing. Adjournment was taken until Wednesday of the next week, to permit the judge to review the mountain of evidence in preparation for his decision. The transcript bulked to 3600 pages filling forty-five volumes. The hearing already was the longest in California legal history.

From the time the defense rested, Aimee discontinued her nightly radio bulletins; no explanation was given. Never did she appear more confident. At the Thursday baptismal service, her carbuncled knee almost healed, she stood waist-deep in water and baptized sixty converts, men and women, in batches of four and five. The altar and pulpit were smothered in flowers.

On Monday, November 1, the defense and prosecution filed their briefs. The defense asked for dismissal of the case on legal grounds, based on the prosecution's theory that no kidnaping had occurred; hence, if there was no kidnaping, it was no crime for Mrs. McPherson or her mother to say there was. As for perjury, they relied on "no material issue."

The State bore down heavily on the charge of corrupting public morals:

> From the fact of her presence at Carmel with Ormiston, coupled with acts and declarations and telegrams and subterfuges given out to the press by both Mrs. McPherson and her mother, and by the testimony of Bardin and Hardy, the conclusion is irresistible that she went there by agreement to foist upon the public this gigantic hoax and to support it by the manufacture of false evidence, by perjury and by subornation of perjury. When the defense called to the stand Judge Bardin and Judge Hardy, and it was shown by their testimony that they had aided and abetted this woman, however innocently, one in the manufacture of the "Miss X" affidavit, the other in going down to Long Beach to induce a blind attorney to advertise for phantom kidnapers, this conspiracy stood forth in all its hideousness, and to say that they were dupes is to be charitable toward them. The infamy of the act that made a judge of the Superior Court of this county the dupe of this conspirator is an assault upon the integrity of our judiciary that will last as long as the waves wash the shores of California.

Aimee Semple McPherson, Minnie Kennedy and the others combined together with the object of perpetrating a gigantic hoax in the name of that which the people hold sacred, namely, religion. That such a thing is corruption of public morals is without contradiction. That a judge of the bench of California should be the victim of this monstrous hoax is a reason why the press, the pulpit and the legal machinery of the State should see that the laws are upheld and this combination of unholy conspirators placed beyond the possibility of doing further damage or injury.

Judge Bardin resented the prosecutor's tongue-lashing: "Anything I have done in this case was done in good faith and with honorable intentions. It is unfortunate if I have been imposed upon."

Judge Hardy's rebuttal was sophisticate: "That's just his argument."

On Tuesday, the day before Judge Blake was to render his decision, Keyes received a letter mailed in Oakland and signed by a Miss Alice A. Ammerer. The writer said that in May she had spent two weeks in Carmel. One day while walking she slipped and fell. A woman came out of the house in front of which she fell and helped her pick up the spilled contents of her vanity case. While she rested a little, the woman asked her if she belonged to a church. When Miss Ammerer said no, the woman said she should be a Christian. The letter continued:

She spoke admiringly of the blue silk dress I wore and said it was her favorite color. She asked me to wait a moment and brought out a book, saying it would be helpful to me. I took the book and opened it to look at the first page. There was some writing, but before I could see what it was, she quickly took the book from my hands and tore out that page, saying I did not need that. I thought no more of the matter until a few days ago, when I was again in Carmel before leaving for my home in Portland. I spoke about a lady giving me a religious book, when my aunt said she believed the place where I fell was in front of the Benedict cottage. After supper we walked over there and sure enough, that was the place.

I would not be a witness in this affair for the world, and don't want the book. I don't see that it is of any use to you except to show that the woman in the cottage on that Sunday last May was a religious woman. Anyway, at my aunt's suggestion I am sending the book to you.

The book arrived. The first page was missing. Entitled *The Divine Plan of the Ages, for Bible Students,* it was a textbook used by students at the Angelus Temple Bible School. Before Miss Ammerer could be interviewed by Oakland police, she had left the state.

Court convened at 10 a.m., Wednesday, November 3. Aimee, dressed in white, arrived smiling, jaunty, and unworried. She chatted and laughed while the courtroom filled, and even Mother Kennedy, on whom the strain of the tense weeks had told visibly, appeared relaxed.

Gilbert addressed the court in closing argument, summarizing the legal points set forth in his written brief and attacking the propriety of the prosecution. Hahn presented a short argument confessing Mrs. Wiseman to be as guilty as the Temple leaders, and asking that all three be held for trial. Then Keyes spoke at length. No crime, he agreed, was involved in Mrs. McPherson's disappearing, or in her going to Carmel, which he said the evidence proved. "She may or may not have been guilty of violating a rooming-house ordinance of Carmel or Monterey, but we are not concerned with that."

Aimee and her mother listened gravely, the smile fading from Aimee's lips and her face tightening into a little frown. Minnie's lips moved silently and steadily.

Keyes digressed from the record and described the scene in the grand-jury room when Mrs. McPherson appeared there to testify. "I cannot forget," he exclaimed, "the impressive manner in which Mrs. McPherson swore to tell the truth with the oath, 'So help me God'—and the impressive way she uttered those words—'So help me God!'" Ormiston he excoriated as "a coward, hiding and slinking, afraid to come before this court, his co-defendants, and the world." Pointing to Aimee he called her "perjurer." "It outrages human intelligence to believe that Mrs. McPherson was kidnaped! Mrs. McPherson and Mrs. Kennedy committed perjury, and then coached Mrs. Wiseman, and now we have subornation of perjury!"

The judge called a ten-minute recess when the district attorney finished. When Blake emerged again from his chambers, stillness settled over the room and Aimee's eyes riveted on the judge's impassive, youthful face as he read his terse decision. It startled everybody by its brevity.

> The issue presented to the court is not the guilt or innocence of these defendants of the crime charged in the deposition and the court is not passing upon such an issue. That is the province of a jury. However, this court is called upon to determine whether or not the offense or offenses have been committed, and whether or not there is sufficient cause to believe the defendants committed such offense

or offenses. "Sufficient cause" is and has been construed as "reasonable or probable cause," which means such a state of facts as would lead a man of ordinary caution and prudence to believe and conscientiously entertain a strong suspicion that the persons accused are guilty. After a full examination of the entire evidence, there is sufficient cause to believe the defendants guilty.

He ordered the three women held for trial on three counts, each count carrying a penalty of one to fourteen years in prison. Present bail was continued.

Aimee sat as if stunned. Mother Kennedy smiled. Mrs. Wiseman appeared unconcerned, chatting with her neighbors while the judge closed the hearing. As reporters tumbled toward the door, both Mother and Lorraine turned to observe the commotion, but Aimee sat staring. At last she stood up, and turning to friends said in a loud voice, "As God is my judge, I am innocent of these charges!"

Then she pushed her way toward the crowded doorway, flushing with annoyance when people blocked her path. "This is enough to make one shiver," she muttered; she hastened to a waiting elevator and left the building.

As the last spectator was leaving the courtroom, a woman walked in; she had come all the way from New York, she said, to be on hand the final day, and then had been unable to get past the guard at the door. Looking around, she inquired, "Where did Aimee sit?"

A bailiff pointed.

"Well," she said, "at least I can see the chair she sat in."

THEME V:

The Answer
to Nobody's Prayer

"The enemy gave out that I was
crazy and wholly unmanned, but my
vitals held sound, nor was I any
more delirious than I had been from
my youth up."

—ETHAN ALLEN

The News Is Blue

Outside the courtroom, sensations had been exploding with a din like that of an old-fashioned Fourth of July. On Thursday, the day the defense rested, the *Examiner* screamed the news that a trunk had been seized in New York, crammed with feminine apparel linked to Mrs. McPherson. The trunk was said to be Kenneth Ormiston's. Already it was on its way to Los Angeles. Page after page displayed photographs of creased and rumpled finery. All the clothing, the paper said, was purchased in Los Angeles. Every garment had been sprinkled with perfume except one silk evangelist's robe—red with grayish lavender collar and lining. The gowns were size 38. (Aimee's desert corset was size 37.) There was a dress bearing a Los Angeles laundry mark and a white flannel sports blouse with the mark of a Carmel dry cleaner. There were several pairs of custom shoes from a Los Angeles shop where Sister maintained a charge account. And there was a pair of black satin slippers believed to be those worn by the woman in Carmel.

Keyes confirmed that the trunk had been seized at the Cumberland Hotel, Broadway at 54th Street, by New York District Attorney Blanton on September 27, the day the preliminary hearing opened in Los Angeles, but at Keyes' request the seizure had been kept secret. "The solution of this case is at hand," said the prosecutor gaily.

New York authorities had listed the trunk's contents, and it was then sealed, photographed from all sides, nailed in a wooden shipping crate which also was sealed and photographed, and forwarded under $5000 bond, in charge of two express guards; these extraordinary precautions were designed to prevent tampering along the way. Most important, a strand of reddish hair found on a boudoir cap had been forwarded separately by airmail. Keyes and others had compared it with samples of Mrs. McPherson's hair; their verdict was that "anyone could see that they came from the same head." Nevertheless, Keyes was sending it to the University of California crime-detection laboratory in Berkeley for irrefragable tests.

Seizure of the trunk had resulted from the relentless search for Ormiston carried on by the newspapers. The radio man, reporters in New York learned, in the course of moving from city to city through the East had checked into the Cumberland Hotel in New York on August 29, under the name "Ralph Stringer." He arrived with two suitcases and a handbag. The trunk reached the Cumberland on September 12, coming from Jacksonville, Florida; it was addressed to "Ralph Stringer" and was kept in the hotel storeroom until September 17, when "Stringer" asked that it be brought up to his room, 1217. The porter was instructed through the closed door to leave the trunk in the hall; as he was moving away he glanced back and saw "Stringer" pull the trunk into the room and shut the door. The incident stuck in the porter's mind because he got no tip, and he groused to the chambermaid about "stingy Stringer." Two hours later the porter was called to take the trunk back to the storeroom; he found it in the hall outside the closed door, and again there was no tip. "Stringer" checked out of the hotel that evening, saying he would send for the trunk. A radio set in his room he left as a present for the housemaid. Reporters and detectives arrived to question him forty-eight hours after he checked out.

From the express company's records it was established that the trunk had been shipped from Pasadena on May 6 to Jacksonville, addressed to "Ralph Stringer," with instructions to hold until called for. The trunk reached Jacksonville on May 11 and remained there until September 9, when it was forwarded to the Cumberland Hotel on instructions contained in a letter signed "Ralph Stringer," mailed in New York on September 7. Now it was on its way to Los Angeles.

Keyes capped the trunk seizure with a second sensational disclosure —his possession of a letter, written in code on stationery such as women commonly use, enclosed in a small pink envelope, and mailed to "Ralph Stringer" on September 27 from the Arcade post office in Los Angeles. This was just when Los Angeles newspapers were carrying stories that Ormiston planned to surrender. Composed partly in script and partly in printed capital letters, the cipher had been unscrambled to their satisfaction by the prosecutor's staff. The facsimile of the document and its translation were published, again in the *Examiner,* to the chagrin of the rival *Times.* The public glanced, looked again, gawked, and gloated.

Couched in sweetheart terms and baby talk, the letter plainly was written by a person undergoing some kind of ordeal. The salutation "D D M" the decoders translated as "Dear Darling Man." "T I F A G W L Y W A H H! W U F F!" became "This is from a girl

who loves you with all her heart! Wuff!" The cryptic "O I L Y D D M
I L Y W A M H!" was resolved into "Oh, I love you, dear, darling man!
I love you with all my heart!" The complete letter read:

> Dear Darling Man: This is from a girl who loves you with all her
> heart! Wuff! Putting up noble fight here. Now, for any sakes, keep
> cool. That person did not get your letter so you are all right on that
> score! I don't want you to think that your B. W. [Beloved Woman]
> did those sijjy sings. Those people were plants who forced way in.
> Think everything will ultimately be all right! Don't worry self sick,
> dear. If I were sure you would get this I would send you thou [thou-
> sand dollars]. How can I tell? Have you all you need? Are you tak-
> ing care of yourself? Oh, I love you, dear, darling man! I love you
> with all my heart! Why did you let me come back? A O W E T H
> [indecipherable]. Forever—some day all will come out right! Come,
> cheer up, and I'll be K O I think unless 'E' breaks—and God forbid
> that happening! Hold that end down whatever you do and leave the
> rest to me. God bless you and comfort you, my dear—this is hard
> enough for me, but poor you—you must be nearly insane. My heart
> aches for you—I feel your arms and comfort all the time. Poor little
> Ba Ba Be wants U! But gotta do down there today and growl at the
> whole world to beat the band. Head up now—and whatever happens,
> don't come. Your Own Darling Woman That's Always Yours!
> J A C K I E.

"This letter," said Keyes expansively, "absolutely clinches the case.
The identity of the writer is so plain an expert's opinion is hardly necessary. The letter was positively written by Aimee Semple McPherson."

Two other letters to Ormiston, written by the evangelist, partly hand-
printed and in the same code, were in his possession, the district attorney
volunteered. He withheld their contents, but said they contained the
same endearing terms, were signed "Jackie," and had been mailed by
a woman whom he described obliquely as "close to Mrs. McPherson and
whose name has already entered the case." The women meeting that
definition, whose names began with "E," the newspapers surmised, were
Mrs. Elizabeth Frame and Emma Schaffer. Neither, however, was questioned on the subject by the prosecutor's office.

To the hullabaloo raised by these revelations Aimee retorted with
derision. Quizzed by reporters about the trunk, she joked that in a mystery story every trunk is expected to have a body in it—preferably
mangled. "As a matter of fact, I understand Mr. Ormiston's own body is
in that trunk." As for the strand of reddish hair: "That hair didn't come
from my head and I know nothing about it and care less."

"Ridiculous!" said Mother Kennedy.

At the Temple Sister told cheering thousands that while it was all too foolish to answer, she did want to make clear that she did not say "Wuff!" "Around the house, when playing with my children, I sometimes use the expression 'Woof!' Those folks who are trying to put over this gigantic frame-up ought to learn the correct spelling before they write letters!"

The district attorney seemed to think "D D M" stood for "Dear Darling Man." Well, it could just as well stand for "Dirty Desert Man" or "Dirty Disreputable Monkey!" "Nobody could translate such hieroglyphics without having written them themselves or having known who wrote them!"

The trunk was part of the frame-up. "I would receive the greatest shock of my life if something of mine had not been planted in that trunk! This is a newspaper war, feeding on the rivalry of great syndicates. Newspaper men have been allowed the freedom of my house throughout, with access to everything therein. And nothing is stopped at to make a 'big scandal story'!" This frame-up, she said, was the last straw on her followers' patience, and the newspapers were behind the whole plot. "The newspaper that broke the trunk story and the 'Wuff-Jackie' letter," she declared, had offered two of her intimate friends a million dollars to betray her. Well, a week from then she would preach a special sermon on "The Biggest Liar in Los Angeles."

The newspaper accused, of course, was the Los Angeles *Examiner.* That day the representative of the *Examiner* observing the scene at the Temple reported with a tinge of awe: "She was cheered as no football hero ever was cheered. The enthusiasm was never more frenzied. She radiated confidence, courage, defiance, and stood before her people like a triumphant empress." These were the words of the newspaper that had just fired its heaviest broadside against her, and found her indestructible.

That evening, in the photographic room of the Los Angeles *Times,* a sudden fire destroyed a large quantity of negatives having to do with the McPherson case. Nothing else was burned.

The trunk reached the district attorney and was opened ceremoniously before a gallery of witnesses. Keyes, Murray, Dennison, Chief Deputy Prosecutor Davis, and Ben Cohen grouped around the sealed crate for an official (and newspaper) photograph. Then the hammer was swung by Davis and the trunk was uncovered. It was blue, a small, stout steamer trunk of no distinction.

Piece by piece, it yielded an amazing quantity of feminine apparel—costly lingerie, evening gowns, hair ornaments, and custom shoes. The amount of material spilling out astonished beholders; apart from a few trinkets, the contents were inventoried as sixty-odd separate articles of wearing apparel and personal possessions. The official list was published in newspapers from coast to coast; even the New York *Times* printed it accurately and in full, as follows:

1 green dress (dark cloth).
1 blue evening gown with pink and red roses around belt, with gold lace.
1 bright cerise gown lined with gray iridescent silk.
1 white silk dressing gown with blue silk flowers.
1 gold beaded evening gown with tag "Imported by Bullock's" [a Los Angeles department store] at bottom.
1 black beaded evening gown.
1 black scarf with silver beads.
1 blue dressing robe with gold thread embroidery.
1 silver sash.
1 gold head band.
1 embroidered Arabic table cover.
1 bath towel with blue crocheted lace.
1 pair pajamas, two-piece, chemise and bloomers, pink.
1 morning gown, peach color, with green crepe de Chine.
1 blue and gray ribbed silk dress.
1 purple dressing gown with embroidered gold thread.
2 rhinestone hair ornaments.
1 pink crepe de Chine dress with rhinestones and pearls.
1 pair brown kid shoes with pair brown silk stockings.
1 pink nightgown, crepe de Chine, with lace.
1 pink silk slip.
1 purple sash with embroidery (Chinese).
1 small linen lace handkerchief.
1 gray coat with cape effect.
1 black silk cape lined with white.
1 purple Chinese or Japanese kimono embroidered.
1 dark blue serge dress with cape.
1 black velvet hoop-skirt dress with flowers.
1 pair black satin slippers with steel buckles.
1 pair brown patent slippers with snakeskin, trademarked "Laird Schober."
1 pink evening dress beaded with gold and silver lace and thread embroidery with rose on shoulder.

1 pair pink satin slippers with gold braided strap.
1 white crepe de Chine dress.
1 pale green dress with lace overslip (filet lace).
1 pink nightgown.
1 burnt orange scarf, shaded.
1 light tan slip.
1 sport coat with fur collar.
1 dark blue silk umbrella with black tassel.
1 black velvet sleeveless gown with red inserts and red and white
steel beads.
1 peach morning gown with lace trimming.
1 blue case containing two perfume bottles.
1 pair peach silk hose.
1 two-piece blue sport dress.
1 embroidered white slip.
1 flesh silk brassière.
1 pair pink silk bloomers.
1 peach-colored nightgown.
1 pink nightgown.
1 pink boudoir cap.
1 pink panne velvet dress with salmon rose.
1 lace morning gown.
1 black silk slip and black overdress.
12 water-wave combs.
1 orchid slip.
1 small black lace shawl.
1 dress slip, flesh colored, plaited.
1 lace boudoir cap, trimmed with little flowers and ribbon.
1 lavender embroidered nightgown.
1 lace hair band with pink ostrich feathers.
1 pair silver slippers with buckles.
1 pair green hose.
1 salmon chemise.
1 fur jabot trimmed with black crepe de Chine.
1 pair white shoe covers, cotton.

The trunk seemed as inexhaustible as a magician's hat; the onlookers were bewildered. When everything had been catalogued, the lot was bundled up again and carted to a bank vault for safekeeping.

Four articles on the original list from New York engaged the special attention of the prosecutor's researchers: the dark blue serge traveling dress, the blue and gray corded silk dress, a sports blouse marked by a Carmel dry cleaner, and the black satin slippers, well worn, from which all markings had been removed. Confusion arose when the Carmel cleaner arrived in town to identify the sports blouse; he was taken to the bank vault by Detective Cohen, but the blouse could not be found. On second thought, nobody could recall having seen it when the trunk was unpacked, and it did not appear in the Los Angeles official list made when the garments were examined in Keyes' office. The baffled district attorney wired to New York inquiring what had happened to the vitally needed garment. New York authorities insisted that everything in the trunk had been sent along, absolutely nothing abstracted except the strand of auburn hair, which had been forwarded by mail. Yet the blouse had been specifically described in newspaper dispatches from New York. Thus was added a new mystery.

The blue and gray ribbed silk dress, however, was in hand, and the cleaner's tag inside the right shoulder was traced to the Fanchet Dye Works at 2995 Glendale Boulevard. (Angelus Temple is at 1100 Glendale Boulevard.) Records showed the dress had been brought in by Dorothy Ayres, a Temple stenographer, on November 13, 1925, and was billed to Emma Schaffer. The dress had four tassels, two hanging down at the collar, two at the waistline. During the cleaning one of the tassels came off. It was found after the dress had been delivered, but it had never been called for. The dress in the trunk had three tassels attached and one plainly missing. The cleaner brought in the retrieved tassel: it matched the three on the frock exactly.

The blue serge traveling dress interested investigators because of two fashion peculiarities: the tight-fitting, wrist-length sleeves decorated with close-set black buttons, ten in a row under each forearm; and the short cape with braided collar and scalloped edge. Photographs of Sister McPherson waving good-by from the train when she departed for the Holy Land in January showed her wearing a dark blue serge traveling dress of the same design, on each underarm a row of ten close-set ornamental buttons, and a short cape with braided collar and scalloped edge.

Ben Cohen added his own discovery. A wash cloth found in the Benedict cottage after the McIntyres left had a blue crocheted border. In the trunk was a bath towel with a blue crocheted border, and the crochet stitch, Cohen pointed out, as well as the thread and the pattern in both borders were the same; the two pieces formed a set.

The district attorney was abundantly content with this first Monday in November when, on the motion of the state attorney general, the felony charges against him were quashed. And Alameda County District Attorney Earl Warren showed friendly cooperation when he wired from

Oakland that a woman had come to him with the information that just before her disappearance Mrs. McPherson bought $2500 worth of expensive lingerie; the informant named shops in Los Angeles where the purchases were supposed to have been made. But Keyes' detectives were unable to find any trace of this reported trousseau.

Aimee's retort to all this was to assail the district attorney for "vicious and untruthful statements." Her case, she said, must not be shuffled off under a cloud.

"Absolute vindication—that is our goal—and nothing short of it! For the cause of Christ, for my hundreds of thousands of friends, for my two beautiful children, for my precious, faithful mother, for right and decency, for the honor of womanhood!"

The Biggest Liar

Judge Blake received more death threats immediately after handing down his decision. Keyes, to clarify the public's mind after weeks of obfuscation, summarized the ten points on which he said the testimony proved Mrs. McPherson's kidnaping story was a fabrication:

(1) Before May 6, Mrs. McPherson conceived the idea of running away with Kenneth Ormiston.

(2) On the night of May 9 she met Ormiston at the Alexandria Hotel and they plotted their flight.

(3) She provided the money for Ormiston to go to Oakland on May 11, and thence to Carmel, where he rented the cottage on May 14.

(4) He returned to Los Angeles on May 14 and went into hiding at the Clark Hotel, where he met Mrs. McPherson on the morning of May 18.

(5) Ormiston checked out of the Clark at 1 p.m. on May 18. Mrs. McPherson disappeared between 3 and 4 p.m. They met and drove in Ormiston's Chrysler to Carmel, where they arrived at 4 a.m. the next day.

(6) They stayed in Carmel until May 29; then, fearing exposure, they traveled south, were intercepted in Santa Barbara, and learned that Mrs. McPherson could not return easily because the pursuit was too hot.

(7) Mother Kennedy, knowing her daughter was alive, caused hundreds of Temple workers to carry out the search for her daughter's drowned body and hired divers and airplanes to carry on the pretense; at least two men died as a result of these activities.

(8) Ormiston instigated a scheme to make it appear that Mrs. McPherson had been kidnaped by engineering an approach to McKinley, offering to produce her in return for heavy ransom.

(9) Pursuant to this plan, Mrs. McPherson traveled to Agua Prieta, walked into the village, and announced that she had been kidnaped but had escaped from her abductors, named Steve and Rose, and had walked seventeen miles across the desert with the thermometer at 120 degrees Fahrenheit.

(10) In an effort to influence the public mind and make the public believe her story, Mrs. McPherson conspired with Mrs. Wiseman to stage the Carmel hoax and caused her to sign false affidavits stating that Ormiston's Carmel companion was "Miss X."

The theory that the mysterious Miller and Wilson existed and were emissaries sent by Ormiston and Mrs. McPherson to enlist McKinley's help in the kidnaping hoax (with presumably a plan to split the ransom money several ways) the prosecution said was borne out by Ormiston's presence in Long Beach from May 6 to May 9, where he was registered at the Virginia Hotel as "Frank Gibson." On May 8, Mrs. McPherson parked her car in the Virginia Hotel garage and went into the hotel through a directly connecting door, after telling the garage attendant that she was going to lunch there and would pick up her car immediately afterward. Proof of this hotel visit, with identification by the garage and hotel employees, was produced.

To bolster its contention that the evangelist deliberately planned to disappear, the State produced a cablegram sent from Angelus Temple on May 6 to a minister in England, offering him the pulpit for two months, and agreeing to cable him transportation money if he would start at once. This cable was filed just before midnight on May 6, about the time when Ormiston was registering at the Virginia Hotel in Long Beach.

At the same time the prosecution stated its theory that when Aimee and Ormiston were halted by Wallace Moore outside Santa Barbara on May 29 (the State holding that their identity was proved), they were hurrying south to carry out a prearranged plan for the evangelist to be discovered bound in a shack in lonely Topanga Canyon, a desolate, wild tract near Malibu, northwest of Los Angeles; but the encounter with Moore convinced them they could not enter the Los Angeles area unobserved, and they turned and fled north again. The prosecution believed they separated temporarily, but met again in Oakland and traveled by train from there to Seattle; then they separated again and made their way separately to Chicago. The State theorized that Ormiston carried the satin slippers and other clothing worn by Aimee in Carmel eastward in a handbag, and transferred whatever he had not destroyed to the blue trunk in New York. Aimee was believed to have turned southward from Chicago, traveling by bus to New Mexico and Arizona, where for several days just before her reappearance she was hidden on Hallenbeck's ranch; her description of her captivity hut was believed to have been inspired by roughly similar shacks on that ranch. This theory in full was never buttressed by testimony in court, and its tenuousness was implied by the fact that it was modified several times during the course of the preliminary hearing. Against the theory was the indisputable fact that no one ever, at any time during the case or in the years thereafter, came forward claiming to know where the evangelist had been for the twenty-four days between May 29 and June 23.

Rumors that she was in need of a rest and planned to take a vacation were bumptiously denied by Aimee, while the controversy over the trunk raged. The Sunday after she was held for trial, she preached her scheduled sermon on "The Biggest Liar in Los Angeles." For an hour she held the audience in suspense while she enumerated the lies circulated in the city, mainly about herself.

"In Los Angeles," she summarized, "there is a tremendous liar. There are a lot, but there is one man who is at the fountainhead of this thing. He has been trying to put the skids under Angelus Temple—has circulated rumors—written letters to destroy the Temple—and I'm going to name that man if it's the last thing I do before I die."

The audience shouted for blood.

"There have been so many lies circulated about Angelus Temple and Sister McPherson! One says, 'She charges money for people who come up here to get healed.' It's a lie. Another is that Sister McPherson made up her mind to run away. It's a lie. Then they said I wrote letters. When I start, I'll do better than that 'D D M' which wise heads interpreted to mean 'Dear Darling Man'! And then they found some clothes in a trunk in New York. These dresses were cut low in front and low in back; they had spangles on them, red, blue, purple, green—as a matter of fact, I think it's a circus performer's costume!"

She ticked off the lies told about her and denied each one:

She didn't have any electrical gadgets in her baptismal tank to make her converts jump and shout when they were immersed.

She didn't pay fake cripples to enact fake cures.

She didn't give back money to persons cured after they testified over her radio.

Angelus Temple had no "padded room" for fanatics—unless people meant the radio broadcasting studio.

She didn't run away to hoax the public and raise a huge memorial fund.

There wasn't any memorial fund; all the money raised was for the Bible School "and went there and is there. If I wanted to raise money, I wouldn't run away to do it; I'd stay right here and raise any amount I asked for!"

She wasn't at Carmel, and if she did try to hide she wouldn't put on dark glasses and a veil and sneak around mysteriously so as to attract attention.

Why didn't Ormiston come back? Probably because the woman who was with him wouldn't let him, and if the woman didn't come back with him, what good would it do? "I certainly wouldn't come back if I was that woman!"

She didn't pay anybody to manufacture evidence.

Her income tax wasn't the largest filed in Los Angeles except for one film star.

She didn't own a stable of horses that she raced at Tijuana.

She didn't make her money by gambling.

And finally—while it doubtless was going to disappoint a lot of people who had been told differently (she glanced archly toward the reporters under the balcony)—her hair was *not* red!

Then, in her concluding words, she identified the biggest liar in the city—"the Devil, father of lies."

Reporters said a handful of soreheads stamped out in disgust after this letdown, but most of the crowd enjoyed the joke, and Sister enjoyed it with them.

But Aimee sensed that outside the Temple the public was weary of the case. The Sunday after this effort she had announced she would preach on "The Little Blue Trunk"; a real baggage smasher would throw out of a baggage car "the district attorney's trunk," "the reporter's trunk," "the evangelist's trunk," and their secret contents would be displayed. But instead she abruptly informed her congregation that "people in Los Angeles are tired of 'little blue trunks' and want to hear the word of God," and comment on the affair from her platform ceased.

Bob Shuler belatedly followed suit, turning his inquiring mind to the Hall-Mills murder with the debatable question: "Is Murder a Solution for Marital Infidelity?"

A somber note crept into the news with word that Ben Cohen, jogging to Carmel with the black satin slippers taken from the blue trunk in an effort to have Benedict identify them, found the owner of the Scenic Drive cottage close to death, a victim of the furor that had beat around him since May. His doctor held no hope; Cohen returned without an interview. On November 20 Benedict died. His son publicly blamed the McPherson case. Aimee and Mother Kennedy telegraphed condolences to the widow: MR. BENEDICT HAS LEFT WITH US THE MEMORY OF A SINCERE, ABLE AND SPLENDID GENTLEMAN. Both Gilbert and Keyes lamented the loss of one of their strongest witnesses.

Benedict's death was the eighth involving a figure in the case. Four of the dead were linked directly—the diver Ed Harrison, Waters, Mc-Kinley, and Benedict. Two men died with McKinley in the overturned car; a man thought to be demented perished when he leaped into the sea during the search for the evangelist's body; and a youth swimming far out to check on a dark patch on the water was drowned.

Keyes at this juncture received a welcome call to Washington, D.C., to testify there as a character witness in the Fall-Doheny oil-lease trials, the Teapot Dome case. The date for his filing an information in the Mc-Pherson case—the legal formality that would institute the trial—was moved up by consent of the defense to January 10.

Before he headed east, Keyes received another letter from Ormiston, forwarded through his Chicago attorney, in which the radio man derided the value of the trunk, the "Jackie" letter, and the clothing. "I have no means of knowing whether the trunk reported delivered in Los Angeles is or is not my property. As for its contents, I know no more than any other gullible reader of the scandal sheets."

Ormiston, Keyes commented grimly, might "write letters until the cows come home"; he was interested in nothing that fugitive had to say unless it was said in front of him. With that, Keyes left town.

Then, on December 6, Ormiston's blue Chrysler coupe was found in Oakland.

Two days later Ormiston himself was tracked down in Harrisburg, Pennsylvania, and the tangled fugue played out its final theme.

"The Answer to Nobody's Prayer"

In Los Angeles a newsboy, crying the extra on Ormiston's arrest, was shot in the back by a sniper. He suffered only a flesh wound, but the incident was indicative of the excited upsurge of interest when the so-long-sought radio operator was dramatically brought to bay.

Behind the headlines lay a race against time of which the public knew nothing. For months those rivals, the Los Angeles *Examiner* and the Los Angeles *Times,* had been picking up Ormiston's zigzag trail. The *Times* moved methodically, and by early December was close to its quarry. Twice its reporters met in a night-long session with Mrs. McPherson and canvassed their findings, to her apparent unconcern. The *Times* had established, and published, that on April 25, the day after the evangelist returned from Europe, Ormiston was driving along Glendale Boulevard, from the general direction of Angelus Temple, in his blue coupe, with a woman companion, when his car broke down. He had the car towed to the Maryland Garage, 125 Maryland Street, Glendale, and there called a taxi. The taxi driver reported that he took Ormiston and the woman to Pasadena and let them out a block from the Maryland Hotel there, where the radio man had registered the day before as "H. C. Cornell." On April 26 Ormiston reclaimed his car, paying $12 for the repairs. Prosecutor's detectives obtained the repair tag as proof.

On May 1, Ormiston bought the blue steamer trunk at the Herbold Luggage Shop in Pasadena, a few blocks from the Maryland Hotel, and ordered it to be sent to "Cornell" at the hotel. The trunk arrived on May 3, empty, and was carried to Ormiston's room. On May 6, Ormiston checked out of the Maryland, leaving the trunk to be picked up by American Express and shipped to "Ralph Stringer, Jacksonville, Florida." The expressman weighed the trunk at seventy-two pounds. The trunk when received by Keyes weighed roughly seventy-two pounds.

The *Times* was closing in. At this juncture Hearst editors reportedly made a deal with friends of Ormiston in Los Angeles who were in no way associated with Angelus Temple, persuading them that Kenneth's discovery was a matter of days, and that he would be well advised to surrender under favorable conditions.

Just then investigators in Oakland stumbled on the missing blue Chrysler coupe. It had been in the Beverly Garage there since June 24, the day after Mrs. McPherson reappeared; the man leaving it gave the name "Duffy" and said he would pick up the car in a few days. After several weeks the garage owners put the car on blocks, but did nothing further until a stranger, unshaven and poorly dressed, appeared and claimed the machine. He looked nothing like "Duffy," but he had the pink registration slip with the name "Kenneth G. Ormiston." The garage notified police. Two days later Ormiston Senior admitted he had tried to get possession of his son's car.

Detectives hurried up from Los Angeles and broke open the rear compartment of the auto in the presence of thirty-five reporters; they found a typewriter, the missing half of the radio receiving set left in Benedict's bungalow, articles of men's clothing, a woman's handkerchief with a laundry mark, a piece of a broken earring or necklace, a pair of dark glasses and (they said) two strands of hair with a copperish glint on the seat cushion.

Ormiston Senior exploded. "Yesterday, when they opened the rear compartment of Kenneth's car, I was watching them. But afterward, when I wasn't watching, they said they found some hair and a pendant from a necklace. While I was looking they didn't find anything like that!"

Asked to comment on the find, Mrs. McPherson was cool. "I hardly understand why I should be called upon to comment on the things in Mr. Ormiston's car. The discovery is as much news to me as it is to the general public."

Then came the bombshell: "Ormiston Arrested in Harrisburg!" After a month of comparative quiescence, the Aimee story was on the front pages again.

Ormiston was found living in an apartment at 25 Front Street in Harrisburg. He had been there since October 6, under the name "Fred Linninger." His neighbors were respectable: directly below him lived the Pennsylvania director of the committee on publications of the Christian Science Church, while overhead resided the Reverend Silas S. Swallow, an octogenarian Methodist minister who twice had run for President of the United States on the Prohibition ticket. The owner of the building, Mrs. Gustav Koster, said "Linninger" was a quiet, unassuming tenant who never attracted suspicion. "He told me he was an engineer. He seemed a very nice man. He paid the rent in advance, always paying cash." The charwoman reported he had worked at night, apparently in a machine shop, because he came in regularly at 4 a.m. and his clothes were greasy.

The circumstances of his "arrest" started a hullabaloo. Ormiston, it developed, was taken into custody by a Chicago detective, Sergeant Harry Donnelly, who was acting without orders from Chicago. With Donnelly were a Harrisburg detective, Oscar (Kit) Carson, and a Hearst newspaper reporter-detective. None of them had a warrant. At the moment of Ormiston's arrest, a few blocks away Chicago Police Chief Morgan Collins was addressing a police convention of which Harrisburg Police Chief Joseph Thompson was chairman; both chiefs were as startled by the news as the public, and much more embarrassed.

Ormiston's apprehenders whisked him to a hotel overnight, then boarded a train for Chicago in secrecy. The radio man was reported to be almost broke; his possessions comprised clothing, one traveling bag, a typewriter, a radio set, and detective and radio magazines—in a couple of which were technical articles he had sold under his own name during his concealment. Harrisburg Detective Carson admitted that he had smelled something fishy when they found Ormiston waiting with his bag packed; he even seemed put out because they were late. The fugitive, said Carson, had grown a mustache and was wearing heavy horn-rimmed spectacles and was unrecognizable from the photographs circulated by the Los Angeles police. None of the circulars, said Carson, mentioned that the man limped.

In Chicago, Ormiston met his lawyer, Martin, then moved into a South Side apartment and passed the time pleasantly riffling through the offers for his story that rained from newspapers, syndicates, and book publishers. In Los Angeles, Dennison clamored for his proper arrest. Chief Collins retorted that Chicago held no warrant, and besides, "he never hurt anybody or committed perjury in Chicago." Sergeant Donnelly was threatened with disciplinary dismissal from the force, until the explanation was accepted that he had not "arrested" the radio man but had merely "escorted" him to Chicago.

Dennison wired to Collins and to Cook County State's Attorney Pat Crowe demanding an arrest, airmailing the warrant. Then he hustled before the grand jury and obtained an indictment that was twenty-four pages and ten thousand words long. Still Chicago did not oblige; Ormiston roamed the city at will, shielded from prying rival reporters by representatives of the Hearst press. Keyes, departing Washington for a week or so of show-going in New York, assured reporters that every effort would be put forth to return Ormiston to Los Angeles immediately. On arriving in Philadelphia a few hours later, he seemed barely interested. "I haven't had time to give this matter consideration," he said negligently. "If I get an opportunity to stop off in Chicago on my return to the West Coast, I may run in and have a look at Ormiston. He is only a sidelight in the McPherson case right now."

"Well, that's pretty good!" exploded Crowe in Illinois. "When they couldn't find this man and thought he was securely planted for the duration of the McPherson trial, they yelled to high heaven for his apprehension! Now he is here and within reach—if officially wanted—the Los Angeles district attorney gets buck fever and describes the fugitive as merely a 'sidelight'!"

However, when the warrant arrived from Los Angeles, Crowe carried it to Chief Collins' office and demanded that Ormiston be arrested. It couldn't be done, replied Collins; he didn't know where the man was. Besides, Ormiston had made an appointment to drop in at the chief's office the next day and surrender peaceably. "All we can do is sit and wait," he said.

The day Ormiston was scheduled to surrender was Wednesday. The setting was impressive. Before a battery of news cameras and reporters that overflowed into the corridor, Chief Collins sat at his desk, warrant in hand. Two o'clock was the hour. At two o'clock the telephone rang. It was lawyer Martin. His client, the attorney informed the chief, would be unable to keep the appointment. "He has a little cold and is indisposed. Anyway, he has gone out of the city for a couple of days and I guess we had better set the time up to Friday at eleven a.m. Maybe he'll come in then."

Collins flushed. It made no difference to him whether Ormiston came in on Friday or a year from Friday, he muttered, and vented a tirade against Los Angeles and its law-enforcement agents. "Keyes doesn't want this man and I'm not going to fool with him! He stands off and howls for the Chicago police to pull his chestnuts out of the fire, and that's not going to be done by this office! I don't know whether I'd arrest this man if I ran into him on the street!"

But Collins tried again Friday—news cameras on hand, warrant in fist, a scowl on his face. Eleven o'clock and no Ormiston. The telephone tinkled; Martin reported his client would be around at 3 o'clock that afternoon, so sorry for the delay. Collins repeated the whole business at 3 o'clock. At 3:48 he gave up. "Somebody is making a monkey out of this office!" he barked, chased out the reporters, locked the door, and went home.

At about that hour, Ormiston, in a limousine described as long and sleek, surrounded by an escort of newspaper men, rolled into Los Angeles. His journey westward was recounted exclusively in the *Examiner* the next morning; Ormiston, said that paper, "tired of waiting to be arrested in Chicago, came back to find out what it's all about."

The disgusted *Times* headlined its acidulous report, "Mr. Ormiston Is Here to See Us," and sneered at its hijacked quarry as "the answer to nobody's prayer."

"Our Heavenly Father
Is with Her"

Ormiston's advent brought from Mrs. McPherson only the comment, tart and terse: "I have no statement to make on the predicament of Mr. Ormiston. I am not concerned with his travels, and whether he is in Chicago, California, or Timbuctoo means nothing to me."

At 10:30 a.m., the day after his arrival, by arrangement Ormiston strolled into Keyes' office. The entire staff was lined up to welcome him. A throng of women filled the corridor outside, and half a hundred reporters and photographers struggled to record the scene. Affable and smiling, Ormiston shook hands with Murray and Chief Deputy Prosecutor Davis (whom he knew from grammar-school days) and was introduced to Dennison. Cohen served the warrant, and amid the booming of flashlights the genial party crossed to the courtroom of Judge Elliott Craig, where they posed for more photographs, the judge included. The court was then advised of the significance of the visit. Ormiston, who had sunk into a chair, arose.

"Your Honor," he said, "I came to California voluntarily and of my own free will. By doing this I saved the County of Los Angeles a great expense. In view of this fact, I will ask the court to reduce my bond from $10,000 to $2500."

Said Dennison, "The State joins in the motion."

Said the judge, "Bail reduced."

That, courtroom veterans remarked, for a litigant without counsel was remarkably effective talking. A bail bondsman was at hand and bond was posted. The entire proceedings (photographs included) took ten minutes.

Reporters swarmed around, but Ormiston cut them them off with friendly firmness. "I cannot talk about the McPherson case," he said.

"What about the evidence found in your car?" Silence. "What about 'Miss X'?" Silence. "What about Carmel?" Silence. "Will Mrs. McPherson's attorneys represent you?"

"I think not," he replied with a grin.

"Are you going to see Mrs. McPherson?"

Not deigning to reply, Ormiston stepped back into Keyes' office, and using the district attorney's typewriter tapped out a statement which, he informed the press crew, contained all he intended to say:

> I am very happy to be here in Los Angeles and face the charges brought against me in a square and dignified manner. Intrigue and hokum are as thick as a San Francisco fog, and it most certainly is not my intention further to complicate the situation; nor is it in my mind to enter the spotlight as a figure of public interest. I was located in the East by a newspaper reporter, and I have been accompanied by reporters to Los Angeles. My movements were entirely voluntary throughout.

With a friendly nod all around, he departed the Hall of Justice, registered at the Rosslyn Hotel not far away, and left immediately to spend the evening with his brother, Thomas, and meet his brand-new niece.

The date was Saturday, December 18. The district attorney's office settled back to normalcy and around town the California weather resumed its place of priority among topics of conversation.

"I am sorry Mr. Ormiston came all the way back from Chicago to find it raining here," contributed Aimee Semple McPherson.

The holiday season was approaching, and with it Keyes approached by deliberate stages the city of his responsibilities. He got back just before Christmas, and to critics of his dilatoriness in the Ormiston imbroglio he replied that he had gone east on personal business and did not have the time to go to Chicago; his itinerary had been plotted down to the "split second." He warmly commended the Hearst newspapers for their handling of the situation.

The feeling in the city was sampled at the time by no less sagacious a reporter than H. L. Mencken, who was on a tour of the West. As a connoisseur of revivalists, he hustled to Angelus Temple to witness Sister in action. Her hair was not red, he wired the Baltimore *Sunpapers,* it was mahogany-colored, and "the more civilized Angelenos all sympathize with her and wish her well." With Maryland gallantry he pointed out that she simply had been asked whether she was guilty of immorality, and when she answered "No" was prosecuted. No judge of the Free State, drunk or sober, he opined, would entertain such a charge against a woman, nor would any Maryland grand jury indict her. While District Attorney Keyes obviously had the newspapers on his side, Sister had the radio, and in the long haul, Mencken guessed, the radio would win. "Unless I err grievously, our Heavenly Father is with her."

The betting popularly was that Aimee would never come to trial. The city seethed with rumors, and so did Angelus Temple. Strange faces were appearing there—outsiders, worldly people, and especially two newspapermen, one until recently with the *Examiner* and the other from the *Times.* This pair moved in during December and assumed almost dictatorial control of the defense tactics, with Sister's eager cooperation. Gilbert later admitted that he never knew from day to day where he stood, and Woolley found the interference intolerable; he withdrew as counsel. Mrs. McPherson promptly engaged the rising Jerry Giesler to assist Gilbert, but made clear that the latter had not been supplanted. All over the city spies were on watch to see whether the evangelist and Ormiston would communicate, but the snoopers had nothing to report except rumors.

Two days after Christmas Ormiston was granted a further continuance of his arraignment. "What's all the excitement about?" he quipped to photographers. "I'm just a big trunk man from Harrisburg, P.A." He also got back his car, on the promise to produce it when wanted.

The last day on which the district attorney could file an information against Mrs. McPherson, Mrs. Kennedy, and the other defendants, was January 10. Should the information not be filed, the case would expire automatically. On December 29, amid increasing rumors that a sensational turn of events was imminent, Keyes announced that because of the collapse of Mrs. Wiseman's testimony, the charges probably would be dropped.

"The McPherson case is now in such a muddled state that a conviction is almost impossible," he said sourly. "The principal witness is a turncoat and a perjurer and has told a different story every day. In view of this fact, it would be impossible to obtain a conviction."

What had happened was that in a new version of her introduction to the plot, Mrs. Wiseman accused Roland Rich Woolley of being the principal instigator. She said Woolley drew her into the hoax through his brother, Jack Woolley, who was the mysterious "Mr. Martin" she met in San Francisco. When she first arrived in Los Angeles, she added, she went directly to Woolley's office, where she got instructions on how to frame the "Miss X" evidence.

Keyes brought Woolley before almost the entire staff of his deputies and questioned him all day under conditions of virtual arrest. Not only was the attorney's reputation at stake, his professional career was threatened. Mrs. Wiseman stormed through the room, accusing Woolley of having improper relations with her when they attended the same high school in Salt Lake City. In this assertion she was supported by her sister, Mrs. Kimball, and by their mother, Mrs. Clara McDonald.

Woolley made an outraged denial. The first time he had ever laid eyes on Mrs. Wiseman, he repeated, was on August 15 in Judge Bardin's office in Salinas. He had warned Mrs. Kennedy and Mrs. McPherson against her. Mrs. Wiseman had specifically cleared him of complicity in the "Miss X" hoax in her testimony during the preliminary hearing. Hamner, the associate Temple attorney, confirmed Woolley's statement.

Woolley then prepared a formal statement, distributed on December 29 to all the newspapers and carried identically by them, in which he recorded "a blanket denial of each and all the charges" Mrs. Wiseman had made against him. He repeated his specific denial of each point in her accusation and said, "My position in the McPherson case has been strictly professional, open and aboveboard, and if any underhanded methods or framing of hoaxes have been carried on, I have not been a party to them."

Keyes ordered both Mrs. Wiseman and Woolley before the grand jury. The jurors heard the conflicting stories and completely cleared Woolley of any suspicion of complicity. Keyes gave the lawyer a public testimonial of clearance, in the form of a letter in which he said that from the investigation he was "convinced that any statements reflecting upon you . . . are entirely unjustified and without foundation in fact." Woolley, then, at considerable expense and annoyance to himself, obtained from Utah records and affidavits proving the impossibility of Mrs. Wiseman's accusations: he had never attended school with her and their paths could not have crossed.

Many people were convinced that the attack was no vagary on Mrs. Wiseman's part, but was a stratagem (now that Woolley had withdrawn as the Temple counsel) to throw the blame on him for the "Miss X" hoax, thus opening a way for Mrs. McPherson and Mrs. Kennedy to plead that they had merely acted on the instructions of their attorney.

Sister's only comment on the blow-up was: "As far as Mrs. Wiseman is concerned, the least said the better. I feel confident that Mr. Keyes will do the just thing when all the true facts are presented to him."

On second thought, Keyes concluded that this brainstorm on the part of the State's key witness did not vitiate the prosecution's case after all: from the first, the State had rested their case not on Mrs. Wiseman's word, but on the corroborating evidence and testimony of others. He then reversed himself again and on December 31 declared the trial would go on.

Still rumors of a dismissal persisted. Around Angelus Temple reporters caught whispers that Sister was placing her reliance in three "deliverers" —believed to be her two newspaper consultants and a press agent who had been hired before the preliminary hearing—and there were frightened allusions to "payoffs."

On New Year's Day, Aimee announced that she was planning a tour of eastern cities—"as soon as my case is disposed of." The same day Ormiston started the serial story of his Odyssey, exclusively in the *Examiner*. He identified "Miss X" as a nurse from Seattle. At the Temple Aimee said, "Ormiston can talk until he is blue in the face—but why should it interest me? I was not at Carmel, and that settles that."

All New Year's week, Keyes wavered. "This is a very important matter and cannot be decided in a minute," he grumbled. "I intend to take all the time necessary to make up my mind."

On Sunday, January 9, Aimee, attired in the hoop skirt of an antebellum belle, preached her "farewell sermon" on the topic "Slavery Days"; around her sprouted a field of cotton, dusky toilers bending along its rows and a villainous Simon Legree cracking a blacksnake whip intermittently. A Negro choir sang spirituals, with special lyrics by Aimee. The allegory was the slavery of sin, with Satan the taskmaster. At the close the Temple was emptied and immediately filled up again, and Sister repeated the performance.

On Monday, January 10, Aimee and her mother did not appear in Judge Stephens' courtroom. Ormiston was on hand because he was due to be arraigned, and Mrs. Wiseman, the fourth defendant, was there with Hahn. Keyes entered, flanked by Murray and Dennison, and proceeded without preamble to ask the court to dismiss the charges against all the defendants. For the record, he read a statement (in which Dennison and Murray concurred) setting forth the reasons for his request. This statement (like most other utterances in the case) was addressed less to the court than to the public:

> Evidence was laid before me which tended to show that after Mrs. McPherson had gone to Carmel, and had returned with an unbelievable story of a kidnaping, she and others had induced Mrs. Lorraine Wiseman-Sielaff to produce false testimony or evidence in the nature of an alibi for the Carmel episode. This evidence was the testimony of Mrs. Wiseman. Without her testimony, proof of the alleged conspiracy is impossible. Since the preliminary hearing, Mrs. Wiseman has changed her story almost daily, until it now contains so many contradictions and inconsistencies to the one given in court that she has become a witness for whose truth and credibility no prosecutor could vouch.

Mrs. McPherson was not spared in the valedictory.

> The fact that this defendant fabricated a kidnaping story, or that she spent a time at Carmel, are not, in themselves, offenses of which this court can entertain jurisdiction. Reputable witnesses have testified sufficiently concerning both the Carmel incident and the return of Mrs. McPherson from her so-called kidnaping adventure to enable her to be judged in the only court of her jurisdiction—the court of public opinion.

Stating that the case as it stood "cannot be prosecuted with honor or with any reasonable hope of success," Keyes asked dismissal. The court granted the request.

The *Examiner* flashed the decision to its reporter, waiting with Sister at the Temple.

"It's over," said the reporter at the telephone.

"O-o-o-oh!" A long, nervous, quavering scream, and Aimee swayed and fainted into the arms of Emma Schaffer. She was carried to a couch, trembling violently, but quickly revived. A batch of telegrams was brought in—invitations to speak in eastern cities. She tried to read them but was too dazed.

"The world is going round and round," she whispered with a wan smile, "but I'll be all right in a minute. Read me the telegrams."

The telephone jangled. Messages of joy. Hallelujahs. Outside the house newsboys started screeching the headlines: "Aimee case dismissed!" "Aimee wins!" Across the alley in the Temple a crowd sang, "Jesus Brought the Sunshine In."

Lying on the couch in her long white gown, Sister apologized for creating the scene. "I couldn't help it. I'm sorry," she said. "It's been so hard, all these months, for two defenseless women to fight against this tower of lies. But all through the trouble the Lord prepared a table before me in the presence of mine enemies. His work will go on now bigger than ever."

Mother Kennedy was asked to make a statement. Her eyes dripping tears, her sturdy figure shaken by quiverings of emotion, Minnie whispered, "Sister has told it all!"

In a few minutes Aimee was up and dictating a formal statement for the newspapers, extending forgiveness to her enemies, and arranging with Mother for a jubilee that evening in the Temple. Then she sat down to check through the congratulatory messages.

"Remind me," she tossed back to Emma Schaffer. "The front door of the Bible School must be fixed."

Coda

The celebration at Angelus Temple the evening of Monday, January 10, 1927, exceeded in noise and jubilation all previous rejoicings there. For more than a quarter of an hour Sister was not permitted to speak; there were cheers, whistling, confetti throwing, hallelujahs. Students and workers thronged around her, bedewing her with kisses and tears of thankfulness. At last able to deliver her farewell, she preached on "Victory," the Lord's conquest of His enemies, and the ascendancy of love over hate, as exemplified in her own triumph.

"The whole structure of this case against me was built like the Tower of Babel," she expounded, "rotten from the bottom. Each block, built one upon another, reached just so high, and then, like the Tower of Babel, God looked down and confused the tongues of the builders. Each told a different story. One confused the other, and thus it has ended, leaving standing only the true facts as told by me."

The next day she departed on a "Vindication Tour" that was to carry her as far as New York. The Temple band and five hundred followers (with jaded press contingent) crowded the station yard to bid her Godspeed. Sister joked to friends: "I didn't wear my goggles today, so the reporters found me!" She shook hands with everybody and tossed out roses and candy as the train pulled away at one minute past noon. "Take good care of Mother!" she called, while the band droned "God Be with You Till We Meet Again." Mother Kennedy wept copiously. Eight months of turmoil were ended, but the echoes reverberated.

Hardly was Aimee aboard the train when a resolution was offered in the Senate at Sacramento to demand an accounting, item by item, of public money squandered by District Attorney Keyes on the inglorious fiasco. "It is common knowledge that a great deal of money of the State of California has been expended in the prosecution of Aimee Semple McPherson," the resolution set forth. A parliamentary dilemma arose over the proper committee to which to refer the resolution, one senator favoring the Committee on Public Morals, another holding for

Judiciary, while a third advocated that it be "laid away in the little blue trunk."

Keyes replied through normal channels (i.e., the press) that the case had cost the taxpayers nothing like $150,000, as rumor had it; "the official records of my office show the amount expended by the district attorney was actually between $4000 and $5000." Newspapers and private investigators who bore the financial brunt had made this cut rate possible.

The cost to the defense was gossiped to run as high as a quarter of a million dollars. No figure was ever authoritatively revealed, although in 1928 Mrs. Kennedy put the cost at $100,000. A single page of a Temple ledger headed "Legal and Defense" (studied years later by the Legislature) listed expenditures totaling more than $33,000, mostly fees to attorneys, but the account was only a fragment. (Woolley sued and collected his fee of $19,500—reduced from the $26,500 he originally demanded.) In 1931 the federal government sued Mrs. McPherson for unpaid taxes on $169,000 collected during 1926 and 1927, which she listed as church income but which the revenue bureau declared was personal income spent in defending herself against criminal charges having nothing to do with the church. How the case was settled was not disclosed.

When Mrs. Wiseman was freed of the bad-check charges standing against her during the conspiracy hearing, she was immediately rearrested on a new complaint—the fictitious check for $50 which she had cashed in a store in San Jose. She was remanded to jail, loudly protesting against the "discrimination," until her sister frantically wired the money from Oakland. Then she, too, was turned loose; her valedictory to the press was, "I am indeed happy to be a free woman again—*without anything on my conscience.*"

Hahn, her lawyer, announced that she planned vaudeville appearances in every city where Mrs. McPherson would preach. She opened on The Pike, a Long Beach amusement concession zone, in a booth under the billing "Hear the Hoax Woman Tell the Truth About the McPherson Case." A barker, a mandolin, and a guitar player supported her and police were on hand to cope with possible disorder. The attraction provoked a wave of public apathy and in a few days the barker, the mandolinist, and the guitar player were at liberty. The "Hoax Woman" thereafter relapsed into incorrigible obscurity.

When Ormiston stepped from the courtroom he immediately retrieved his radio, typewriter, and other impounded possessions. The blue trunk and its contents, still under bond, were shipped back to New York to be claimed by "Ralph Stringer" or anyone else who could establish ownership. There is no record of its final disposition.

Early in February, Mrs. Ruth Ormiston landed at San Francisco with trumpet blasts of publicity. Declining to discuss Mrs. McPherson, she did allude to an "impertinent letter" she had received from the evangelist, mailed in Los Angeles on May 18, 1926, with a note from Mother Kennedy enclosed; she would not divulge the contents. On February 14 she received a decree of divorce, alleging desertion and naming no corespondent. Her husband did not contest the action, and Mrs. Ormiston sailed back to Australia at once.

Ormiston served notice on the newspapers that for him the episode was ended. "Henceforth I want it to be known that I am shaking off all identification with the 'phantom radio man,' " his ultimatum read. "I expect to be actively engaged in the radio business here in Los Angeles." Carrying out his purpose, he slipped easily into his profession, and at his death in 1937 at forty-one, after an appendectomy, was chief engineer for a Los Angeles radio station, widely respected and popular. Newspaper obituaries recalled his role in the kidnaping extravaganza, which the public had almost forgotten, and approvingly recorded that he had defended Mrs. McPherson silently and stubbornly to the end. The judgment of press, police, and public was unanimous: "He behaved like a gentleman."

Bernice Morris, the secretary whose feet remained firmly on the ground in the hurly-burly, continued her law studies and was graduated with highest honors, at the top of her class.

Mrs. Ed Harrison, widow of the Santa Catalina constable who died supposedly from exposure and exhaustion after diving for Mrs. McPherson's body, pressed a claim against the county for compensation for his death in line of duty. The county contested the claim, the sheriff's office denying that Harrison had been "ordered" to dive, although the chief of the sheriff's homicide squad testified that he "told" the constable to do so. Angelus Temple disclaimed responsibility, Mother Kennedy testifying that the first time she heard about Harrison was when somebody asked her whether she was going to his funeral. She felt shocked, she said, and the Temple did vote $500 to the widow as a token of sympathy. The check was returned uncashed. Mrs. Harrison testified that two Temple workers had come to her home with a check for $500, and when she referred them to her lawyer they became "impudent" and left, calling her a "bitter woman." She collected nothing.

Captain Herman Cline retired from the police force as soon as he became eligible for a pension. The Azusa misadventure he always treated philosophically. He was not drunk, he said, and he held no rancor. "The Azusa police did what they thought was their duty. They were perfectly right. I received the same treatment as any other citizen." After his retirement he bought a ranch in the San Fernando valley and lived in seclusion, rarely returning to the scenes of his police exploits. Twice his name appeared in the news during those years, both times as a result of smashing his car into obstacles—a railroad sign and a café. In 1937 he succumbed to a heart attack at the age of sixty.

When Joseph Ryan resigned as deputy district attorney in 1927, he precipitated an uproar by charging grave irregularities in the prosecutor's office. "I was not cognizant of the condition prevailing in your office until your dismissal of the Aimee McPherson case," he wrote District Attorney Keyes. Characteristically, Keyes was out of the city on a hunting trip when the storm broke; by the time he returned it had simmered down, apparently, to a contest of words between Ryan and Chief Deputy District Attorney Davis. But the McPherson affair, which had already been the source of so many infelicities, ironically led to Keyes' destruction.

After the break, Ryan confided to friends that during the McPherson hearing his chief never drew a sober breath. This, while never proved, was believable, for during those furious weeks the prosecutor was buffeted by contradictory currents of partisanship, prejudice, and passion until he became as helpless to control his course as a man going over a falls. When the charges were dismissed, motives of the most dishonest nature were ascribed to Keyes by factions balked of a clean-cut decision, and the rumor gained currency that $30,000 had passed from the Temple to certain public officials. Ryan's explosive letter of resignation brought this rumor into the open, and investigation of Keyes' tenure of office tardily ensued. Both that investigation and a later one, conducted by a legislative committee, established beyond question the uprightness of the badgered prosecutor in the McPherson affair, and Keyes was publicly exonerated of all suspicion of venality in that case. Unhappily, the investigation did uncover improprieties in entirely different actions, and as a result Keyes was indicted for accepting bribes in the Julian oil scandals. After a stormy trial he was convicted and served nineteen months in San Quentin prison. In 1931 he was paroled and two years later received a full pardon and restoration of rights from Governor Rolph. He retained a multitude of friends, but the shock had affected his health and in 1934, at the age of fifty-two, he succumbed to a stroke in his Beverly Hills home.

Ryan practiced law successfully but never participated actively in the exciting political life of his county. In 1951 he was stricken by a heart attack in a downtown parking lot and died on his way to the hospital, aged fifty-three.

Judge Carlos Hardy paid abundantly for his indiscretions. In 1928 the $2500 "love offering" he accepted from the Temple came to light (the check had lain buried in Keyes' private files) and after a tumultuous legislative inquiry he was impeached on four counts: practicing law while serving on the bench, unethical conduct, obstructing justice, and intimidating a witness (Wallace Moore). His trial before the State Senate (the first impeachment trial in California in sixty-seven years) was a virtual rerun of the McPherson hearing; many of the original witnesses repeated their testimony, some much more enlighteningly.

Wallace Moore, for example, who in 1926 dodged and squirmed, refusing to make any identification of the woman in the car he stopped outside Santa Barbara, as an impeachment-trial witness in 1929 identified that woman as Aimee Semple McPherson. Lieutenant Governor Carnaham, presiding, put the question on behalf of a senator: "Can you identify the woman as Mrs. McPherson?"

Moore's answer boomed through the loudspeaker confidently. "Yes, sir, I think she was."

A hush fell over the chamber. Judge Hardy sat stiffly, his face a blank. The testimony had come three years too late.

In his exculpation Hardy denied under oath having coerced Moore or committed acts of malfeasance. His behind-the-scenes activities in the McPherson case were perhaps a mistake, he admitted, but they were within proper bounds and were motivated by friendship and self-preservation; having been associated closely with Angelus Temple, he feared that if its leader were discredited he would be made to look very silly. "I believed that if Angelus Temple went down and was destroyed, I would go down with it," he told the State Bar. "My offense is the offense of friendship." At the trial, when asked directly, "Did you believe Mrs. McPherson had been kidnaped?" he paraphrased his 1926 equivocation: "There was no evidence to the contrary."

"Do you still believe it?" his questioner jabbed.

Objections by counsel forestalled a reply, but it was remarked that in his testimony Hardy used the phrase "the alleged kidnaping."

Hardy was acquitted, by split votes, on all four counts. Off the record, senators conceded that he had certainly been indiscreet and unethical, but they felt he had not been wilfully corrupt. Hardy had already been expelled by the American Bar Association for violation of its judicial and ethical canons. A few months after his acquittal, the verdict of the public was made clear when the voters of Los Angeles County decisively rejected his bid for a second term on the bench. (Judge Keetch also ran for re-election that year and was returned handily.) Hardy practiced law in Los Angeles and lived to the patriarchal age of eighty-one; he died in 1948.

In 1929 the McPherson case became outlawed under the statute of limitations. In 1931 the Benedict cottage at Carmel was still of sufficient notoriety for two Los Angeles promoters to lease it for a tourist peepshow.

On the 18th of May, 1927, the faithful of Angeles Temple congregated at Ocean Park beach to celebrate the first anniversary of Sister's swim with a marshmallow roast and taffy pull. (Mother Kennedy had said that the date would be kept as a holy day.) Sister did not join the frolic on the sands; she was busy at the Temple conducting a healing service. Nor did Fighting Bob Shuler comment on the jolly occasion. Long before, he had delivered his last sermon on the subject, his topic the question, "Is GOD a liar?"

Chronology

January 1, 1926 (about). Kenneth G. Ormiston ceases to be employed as operator of station KFSG at Angelus Temple.

January 11. Aimee leaves Los Angeles on trip to Holy Land.

January 22. Mrs. Ruth Ormiston reports her husband missing and shortly thereafter sails home to Australia.

March 15. $1500 is telegraphed to Ormiston in Seattle from Venice, California, in the name of James Wallace, Mrs. McPherson's long dead half-brother. Ormiston buys blue Chrysler coupe same day.

April 24. Sister Aimee returns to Los Angeles from Europe.

April 25. Ormiston's Chrysler breaks down in Glendale; he and a woman companion take a taxi to the Maryland Hotel in Pasadena, where Ormiston registers as "H. C. Cornell."

May 1. Ormiston purchases a blue steamer trunk in Pasadena.

May 3. Trunk is delivered to "H. C. Cornell" at Maryland Hotel, Pasadena.

May 6. Ormiston checks out of Maryland Hotel, Pasadena, leaving trunk to be shipped to "Ralph Stringer," Jacksonville, Florida, to be held until called for. Same day he checks into the Virginia Hotel in Long Beach as "Frank Gibson."

May 8. Aimee visits the Virginia Hotel, Long Beach, parking her car in the hotel garage.

May 9. Ormiston checks out of Virginia Hotel. Same day registers at the Alexandria Hotel, in downtown Los Angeles, as "Frank Gibson." Also on this day is seen at Angelus Temple.

May 9 and 10. Aimee registers at Alexandria Hotel, checks out each time the next morning.

May 11. Ormiston checks out of Alexandria Hotel.

May 12. Ormiston visits his parents in San Francisco.

May 14. Ormiston, using the name "George McIntire," rents the Benedict cottage in Carmel.

May 15. Ormiston registers as "George McIntire" at the Clark Hotel in downtown Los Angeles.

May 18. Forenoon: A doorman and a haberdasher believe they see Aimee entering the lobby of the Clark Hotel. Noon: Aimee drives to Ocean Park. 1 p.m.: Ormiston checks out of Clark Hotel and drives away in his Chrysler. 3 to 4 p.m.: Aimee disappears at Ocean Park.

May 19. Ormiston and a woman companion arrive at the Benedict cottage in Carmel at 4 a.m.

May 20. Temple followers organize beach patrol to watch for Sister's body.

May 21. Mother Kennedy receives "Dr. Merton" ("Daughter O.K.") telegram sent same day from Oakland.

May 25. Ormiston in San Francisco changes car's Washington license plates for California plates. Reporters get number. Same day Mrs. Kennedy receives "Revengers" letter demanding $500,000, mailed in San Francisco.

May 26. Ormiston's name is publicly brought into the case for first time. Announcement is broadcast that Keyes wants to question him.

May 27. Ormiston appears at Ocean Park beach and is questioned by detectives and press; takes a train north that evening. Same day Mother Kennedy posts $25,000 reward for the safe return of her daughter.

May 28. Ormiston registers at St. Mark Hotel in Oakland as "K. Gladstone." A telegram sent from Oakland ("Lease expires tonight"), addressed to "Mrs. McIntire," is signed for by the woman in the Benedict bungalow. Late that evening, Ormiston picks up his car left at the Highway Garage in Salinas.

May 29. 1 a.m.: Ormiston reappears at Highway Garage with a woman in his car; buys gas and drives southward. 6 a.m.: Ormiston and woman companion register at Andrews Hotel in San Luis Obispo as "Mr. and Mrs. Frank Gibson." 5 p.m.: They check out. 11 p.m.: Ormiston and woman companion, in Ormiston's Chrysler, are stopped just north of Santa Barbara by Wallace Moore. Meanwhile Benedict in Carmel has received a letter mailed in Salinas saying his tenants have been called east.

June 1. Blind attorney McKinley tells District Attorney Keyes and police about the visit of Miller and Wilson, who say they are holding Mrs. McPherson for $25,000 ransom.

June 2. Ormiston checks out of St. Mark Hotel, Oakland. McKinley gets the test questions from Mrs. Kennedy to submit to kidnapers.

June 3. Rolf McPherson and Minnie Kennedy in final tribute strew flowers at Ocean Park where Aimee disappeared.

June 18. "Avengers" ransom letter demanding $500,000 is mailed on a train between El Paso and Tucson.

June 19. "Avengers" letter is delivered to Angelus Temple by special delivery.

June 20. All-day memorial services held for Aimee at Temple, with collection.

June 23. 1 a.m.: Aimee walks in from the desert at Agua Prieta. Afternoon: Mother Kennedy, Ryan, and Cline board train in Los Angeles for Douglas. Posses hunt kidnap shack.

June 24. Mother Kennedy and party reach Douglas. Aimee repeats story to Ryan and Cline: later joins hunt for shack. In Oakland, Ormiston's blue Chrysler coupe is left at a garage by a man giving the name "Duffy."

June 25. Continuing search for shack is unsuccessful. Aimee departs for Los Angeles.

June 26. Aimee receives triumphal welcome in Los Angeles. Later she retraces the kidnaping events at the beach for Ryan and Cline.

June 28–29. Aimee and Mother Kennedy assail doubters of the evangelist's story.

June 30. Aimee and Minnie secretly start back to Douglas to make another effort to find shack.

July 1. Aimee spends all day on desert, is unable to identify shack.

July 2. Aimee and Minnie return to Los Angeles. Federal authorities look into mystery of "Avengers" ransom letter, charging use of the mails to defraud.

July 6. Aimee and her mother subpoenaed to appear before the grand jury.

July 8. Aimee testifies before the grand jury.

July 13. Mrs. Kennedy testifies before the grand jury.

July 15. Aimee is positively identified in grand-jury room by automobile dealer Pape as the woman he saw in Agua Prieta just before June 23.

July 17. Aimee secretly visits McKinley's office in Long Beach.

July 20. Grand jury refuses to indict kidnapers. Ryan departs hurriedly for Carmel.

July 21–23. Benedict cottage disclosures made by Ryan and Cline in Carmel. Aimee refuses to give fingerprints and handwriting or face witnesses.

July 25. McKinley in consultation with Aimee and Mrs. Kennedy.

July 28. Aimee attacks Ryan and Cline as "persecutors"; calls for "showdown."

July 30. "Belle Owens" telegram is received at Keyes' office; a mystery to the district attorney and to the press.

July 31. Mrs. Lorraine Wiseman arrives in Los Angeles, goes to Temple, meets Mrs. Kennedy.

August 1. Ormiston's "Miss X" affidavit arrives from Chicago. Judge Hardy confers with Mrs. Wiseman in his home.

August 3. Keyes and Ryan go before the grand jury and present the Carmel evidence. The grocery-order slips disappear.

August 5. Ryan is sent back to his routine trial duties, dismissed from case.

August 8. Grand-jury scandal becomes public.

August 12. Grand jurors vote confidence in the accused woman juror and recess for two-week vacation.

August 15. "Miss X" affidavit is signed in Judge Bardin's office in Salinas by an unknown woman appearing with Mrs. Wiseman, represented to be Mrs. Wiseman's sister.

August 16. Judge Hardy interviews Wallace Moore in Santa Barbara.

August 19. Mrs. Wiseman is questioned by Keyes, who doubts her story.

August 20. Mrs. Wiseman meets Benedict; he refuses to identify her as the woman in the cottage.

August 22. Mrs. Wiseman tells her story to the press. Captain Cline is arrested in Azusa.

August 23. Captain Cline is suspended from duty.

August 25. Morning: Joe Watts speaks to Aimee over telephone; she identifies his voice. Evening: McKinley is killed in automobile accident.

August 26. Aimee and Mother Kennedy beg Bernice Morris to continue McKinley's dickering with the kidnapers. Judge Hardy's letter is taken off McKinley's body. Mother releases a press statement revealing that McKinley had been in touch with the kidnapers and that Sister had spoken to them on the telephone.

August 29. Ormiston checks into Cumberland Hotel, New York City, as "Ralph Stringer."

September 2. Judge Keetch dismisses the grand jury.

September 10. Mrs. Wiseman is arrested on bad-check charges. She appeals to the Temple for bail unsuccessfully.

September 12. Mrs. Wiseman confesses, charges that Aimee and Mother Kennedy hired her to perpetrate a hoax. In New York, a blue steamer trunk arrives at the Cumberland Hotel for "Ralph Stringer," shipped from Jacksonville, Florida.

September 15. Bernice Morris confesses that Aimee and her mother attempted to have her produce faked evidence of shack and kidnapers. Same day "Dr." Waters, go-between, commits suicide, leaving papers implicating Aimee and Minnie Kennedy.

September 16. Keyes issues complaints against Mrs. McPherson, Mrs. Kennedy, Mrs. Wiseman, and Ormiston, charging corruption of public morals, obstruction of justice, and conspiracy to manufacture evidence. Aimee is desperately ill.

September 17. Mother Kennedy surrenders, is released on bail. Aimee still ill. Hardy returns to Los Angeles from his vacation, is questioned by Keyes. In New York, Ormiston, as "Ralph Stringer," checks out of the Cumberland Hotel, leaving the blue steamer trunk behind.

September 19. Aimee preaches three times, launches "Fight the Devil" fund.

September 22. Aimee asks forty-eight hours of prayer and fasting.

September 27. Preliminary hearing opens in Judge Blake's court. In New York, the blue trunk is seized by District Attorney Blanton.

September 30. Wallace Moore on stand, a hesitant witness, fails to identify Aimee as the woman in the car he stopped on May 29.

October 3. Aimee presents "March on the Martyrs" at the Temple.

October 4–5. Ryan on stand terms Aimee "a fake and a hypocrite."

October 6. Ormiston rents an apartment in Harrisburg, Pennsylvania, under the name "Fred Linninger."

October 9. Aimee celebrates her thirty-sixth birthday during a three-day series of parties at the Temple.

October 11–15. Mrs. Wiseman on stand, sticks to her story.

October 18. Bernice Morris on stand tells of McKinley's activities.

October 19. Aimee's defense opens. Aimee, ill, is carried into court in a chair.

October 21. Judge Bardin on stand positively identifies Mrs. Virla Kimball, Mrs. Wiseman's twin sister, as the woman who signed the "Miss X" affidavit.

October 25. Judge Hardy on stand swears he still believes Aimee was kidnaped.

October 28. Seizure of Ormiston's trunk in New York revealed; it is on its way to Los Angeles.

October 29. "Jackie" ("Wuff") letter decoded and published.

November 1. Ormiston's trunk arrives from New York under seal; its contents are listed and photographed.

November 3. Judge Blake holds Aimee, her mother, Mrs. Wiseman, and Ormiston for trial. Aimee demands speedy trial and "absolute vindication."

November 7. Aimee preaches on "The Greatest Liar in Los Angeles."

November 20. Benedict, owner of the Carmel cottage, dies in Carmel.

November 29. Keyes and Aimee's counsel agree to extend the date for opening of the trial until January 10.

December 6. Ormiston's Chrysler is found stored in an Oakland garage.

December 8. Ormiston surrenders to reporters in Harrisburg, Pennsylvania, and is escorted to Chicago.

December 10. Los Angeles authorities wire, then airmail, a warrant for Ormiston's arrest by Chicago police.

December 15. Ormiston fails to appear in Chicago to be arrested. In Los Angeles, the grand jury indicts him.

December 17. Ormiston arrives in Los Angeles.

December 18. Ormiston surrenders in the district attorney's office, is quickly arraigned and released in nominal bail.

December 29. Mrs. Wiseman changes her story of how she was brought into the plot, implicates Aimee's counsel, Roland Rich Woolley. Keyes says the case may be dropped, since he can no longer vouch for his chief witness.

December 30. Grand jury clears Woolley of any complicity.

December 31. Keyes pledges trial will go on.

January 1, 1927. Aimee reveals plans for a nationwide tour.

January 3. Keyes uncertain about disposition of the case.

January 10. Keyes asks court to dismiss the charges against everybody, on the ground that it would be impossible to get a conviction. Court accedes. Aimee faints on receiving news.

January 11. Aimee leaves Los Angeles on "Vindication Tour" of the nation.

February 5. Mrs. Ruth Ormiston arrives in Los Angeles from Australia.

February 14. She is granted an uncontested divorce on the ground of desertion; names no other woman.